The
PROMISE
of
SUNRISE

*Finding Solace
in a
Broken World*

TED LEVIN

The
PROMISE
of
SUNRISE

❧

Finding Solace
in a
Broken World

Illustrations by Jeanette Fournier

GREEN WRITERS PRESS | *Brattleboro, Vermont*

Printed in the United States

10 9 8 7 6 5 4 3 2 1

Green Writers Press is a Vermont-based publisher whose mission is to spread a message of hope and renewal through the words and images we publish. Throughout we will adhere to our commitment to preserving and protecting the natural resources of the earth. To that end, a percentage of our proceeds will be donated to environmental and social-activist groups. Green Writers Press gratefully acknowledges support from individual donors, friends, and readers to help support the environment and our publishing initiative.

Giving Voice to Writers & Artists Who Will Make the World a Better Place
Green Writers Press | Brattleboro, Vermont
www.greenwriterspress.com

ISBN: 979-8-9891784-2-1

COVER ART & INTERIOR ILLUSTRATIONS:
JEANETTE FOURNIER

PRINTED AT KASE PRINTERS, ON FSC-CERTIFIED PAPER AND PRINTED WITH SOY-BASED INK, DEDICATED TO SOUND ENVIRONMENTAL PRACTICES AND MAKING ONGOING EFFORTS TO REDUCE OUR CARBON FOOTPRINT. WITH PAPER AS A CORE PART OF OUR BUSINESS, KASE IS COMMITTED TO IMPLEMENTING POLICIES THAT FACILITATE CONSERVATION AND SUSTAINABLE PRACTICES. KASE SOURCES PRINTING PAPERS FROM RESPONSIBLE MILLS AND DISTRIBUTORS THAT ARE CERTIFIED WITH AT LEAST ONE CERTIFICATION FROM AN INDEPENDENT THIRD PARTY VERIFICATION, SOURCED DIRECTLY FROM RESPONSIBLY MANAGED FORESTS. WE ALSO MAKE ONGOING EFFORTS TO REDUCE OUR CARBON FOOTPRINT, REUSE ENERGY AND RESOURCES, MINIMIZE WASTE DURING THE MANUFACTURING PROCESS, AND RECYCLE 100% OF SCRAPS, TRASH, CARTRIDGES, EQUIPMENT, AND SOLVENTS WHENEVER POSSIBLE. WE ARE A FAMILY-RUN BUSINESS, LOCATED IN HUDSON, NEW HAMPSHIRE.

For Isabelle and Aiden
onward and upward

Contents

Summer 2020

Autumn 2020

Winter 2020-2021

Spring 2021

Summer 2021

Prologue

The pursuit of truth and beauty is a sphere
of activity in which we are permitted
to remain children all our lives.
ALBERT EINSTEIN

I boarded a crowded plane in the wee hours of 14 March 2020. Having spent twelve days in Costa Rica ignoring the media, in the company of fourteen naturalists, hummingbirds, macaws, and rainbow-colored frogs, I wasn't disquieted by mention of Covid-19. The coronavirus was an Asian problem, a European problem, remote from the remoteness of jungle twilight and its enhancement of bright green moths.

I had just finished guiding a nature tour with my Costa Rican friend Gilbert Calvo Morera. Gil has piloted six tours with me in the past twenty years. He's an ample, affable, highly energetic ambassador for everything Costa Rican, a natural historian par excellence. Like a godwit migrating over open ocean, Gil imbues unshakable confidence and self-acceptance. He laughs easily, leads tours with lighthearted dignity, molds strangers into friends, friends into family, family into a nucleus of one. Our family ate together; hiked together; debated the identity of unknown birds and butterflies; watched a resplendent quetzal stir the dawn with long, green, pendant plumes, each thin as a swizzle stick. After twelve days, we had become acculturated, assimilated, associated—a tender, mobile unit verging on dispersal. Then, our sad goodbyes. My god . . . we had *no* idea what was behind the curtain.

As we taxied down the runway, a woman directly across the aisle from me adjusted a surgical facemask. A facemask? Next, she disinfected her tray table. I leaned in, asked why she thought the mask and disinfectant was necessary. *I promised my daughter,* she said, her voice laced more with resignation than conviction. Skeptical, I settled in for a day of travel. When the flight disembarked at Miami International Airport, I stepped through the looking-glass onto the threshold of a bizarre new world soon to be bogged down by its own monotonously repetitious wordbook: *sanitizing; social distancing; contact-tracing; self-quarantining; self-isolation; shelter-in-place; super-spreader; droplet transmission; community spread; flattening the curve; herd immunity; personal protective equipment.* And my favorite, *covidiot:* the unvaccinated, unmasked, public sneezer. In time, I would learn the definition of *fomite;* the difference between *outbreak, epidemic,* and *pandemic;* the nuances of *contagious* and *infectious.* I would understand where Covid-19 was *endemic*—and why.

That morning in Miami, skepticism waned. After idling in line at Customs, anxious for the flight home, I joined the partially masked herd, pulled my shirt over my nose, opened the bathroom door with a paper towel, and washed my hands twenty times during the five-hour layover.

Travel-weary and virus-conscious, I reached east-central Vermont late that afternoon. In the interests of a ventilator-free existence, my personal geography shrank: I was a self-employed, free-ranging naturalist home in an empty house. I sheltered in place until 15 April 2021, thirteen months—394 days, 9,456 hours, 567,360 minutes—drifting between rooms, discovering the joy and frustrations of Zoom. I taught myself to make graham cracker piecrust, seared scallops, shrimp rolls, garlic-encrusted cod, ginger salmon, and chicken in cider. To stay mentally and emotionally afloat, to create order through repetition and output, I tried to be a homebound Joe DiMaggio, dependable, productive, generating a seemingly unstoppable string of hits, but with a much better eye for wildlife.

In time, notwithstanding, urgencies mounted. I began to hate my furniture (notably, the living-room sofa and the dining-room table), and I craved physical contact, especially after the Colorado birth of my granddaughter, Isabelle Linny. Nonetheless, the landscape of Covid-19's new normal offered a comforting prospect, directly in my sightline. To stave off boredom and favor creativity, I immersed myself in the arc of time. I walked at sunrise, daily, tapping notes into my cellphone that I recast into journal posts for two birding listservs, one regional, the other statewide. Unconsciously, I had re-engaged the Zen of stillness, the spin of Earth as sensed from the corner of a single valley. Feasting on the vagaries of dawn and the delicacy of the seasons, German shepherds on leashes (tails in compliance), I'd walk downhill along a curving dirt road, past rocky streams and fallen trees, and gaze across an unblemished marsh and a man-made pond, looking deeply into a landscape I thought I knew. I fed off sunrise like a dog at dawn for nearly four hundred consecutive days. Then, I left for Colorado to meet my granddaughter, and when I returned home (like DiMaggio), I began another streak. Encouraged by friends, the journal evolved into a blog (I hate the word) called *Homeboy at Home During the Coronavirus*, published in a Substack newsletter. One hour walking, looking, considering, and then four or five hours writing. My morning activities had centered me, had given me purpose, order, and beauty, an outlet for my emotions. Something I looked forward to during a time clouded with uncertainty.

Homeboy grew a small, loyal following. Once a week, a regional online newsletter called *Daybreak* posted the link. Friends of friends began to forward *Homeboy*, which eventually appeared in the inboxes of home-bound readers in more than twenty states and foreign countries. I chronicled the vagaries of dawn—the writer writing, interpreting the wind. I gained a sense of purpose in a time of purposelessness. Process yielded outcome, and I craved both—both were inextricably linked. Walking begot writing, and writing begot an audience that nourished me with correspondence. I read what readers suggested: Faulkner, Oliver, Berry, Whitman, Borland, Sachs, and Max Boyce, a lockdowned Irish poet who lamented the restrictions imposed by Covid in "When Just the Tide Went Out."

Bewitched by sunlight and clouds, my quarantining at home had become more heartfelt than heartache, more joyous than tragic, more centering than scattering. To reacquaint with little things long ignored and bigger things long taken for granted, the entire and ongoing saga of my valley—ceiling to floor—had become a collateral gift of staying put. I began to engage my home ground with childlike awareness, the open-eyed observer awed by the ordinary, stunned by the exotic. Cedar waxwings eating blackberries became provisional art. A bobcat in the alders became sacred.

Every walk had been substantially different, each an endless manuscript multiauthored by clouds, trees, flowers, streams, mammals, amphibians, turtles, and birds. Edited by the seasons and earthly trends, some surreptitious, some blatant, some mysterious. Snakes made cameo appearances, solemn as prophets, unspooling on the fringe of the narrative. Insects hijacked some of the many plotlines. Narrative threads, like cloudscapes, unstable and ever evolving. Things too small to describe may have composed the ending. Although I saw a *very* small part of my valley's improbable and dependable details, what tethered me to these walks was the predictability of change, a fathomless, reassuring commodity; and, when I returned home, the joy and struggle of expressing what I saw and felt, what it all evoked. I tried to channel the vitality of the morning, to paint with words, to freely associate, to hack through the underbrush of my own history.

Chickadees—companionable and busy—cinched the seasons; when one sang on a frigid January morning, thin breaths rising like smoke, I glimpsed spring, a gray-feathered promise. Snapping turtles, goshawks, and loons took stage in the wings, sometimes commandeering my attention in absentia. I roamed the valley for more than a year, happily engaged in a second childhood of my own making, witnessing and participating in the profound and gorgeous forces of life. Thriving on the consistency of ritual.

A Brief History of Place

In October 1997, Linny and I and our boys, Casey (ten) and Jordan (two), moved to a geographic bump on the eastern flank of Robinson Hill, within the village of Thetford Center, in the town of Thetford, in a county called Orange. Surrounded by overproductive oaks and underproductive lawn, our house looked down on sixty-five acres of marsh, a fusion of unkempt reeds and isles of sweetgale, a drainage basin for both water and cold air. Channels laced the marsh, peppered with pools, paved with boot-sucking mud. Several dead pines, barkless and branchless, enticed raptors to pause, to gather thoughts and ignite the valley with primeval cries. Not a house marred our view. Yet, Thetford Elementary School was only four miles away, the interstate a mile farther. Linny loved the landscape, had eyed the property for nearly twenty years. When it was rumored that Wes Kelley planned to sell, she pounced. And so, for twenty-four years, I've lived in the company of bitterns.

Five miles to the east, the Connecticut River separates Vermont from New Hampshire, a four-hundred-mile long, south-flowing umbilicus that drains four states and feeds Long Island Sound scraps from our valley. Less than a mile to the north, Lake Fairlee hosts five historic summer camps. I'm close enough to the village of Post Mills to hear church bells and the combustible sigh of hot air balloons that launch from the tiny airport between the cemetery and the Little League field. On a clear day, forty miles southwest, Mount Ascutney teases the horizon, more afterthought than keynote, far beyond the domination of Gove Hill, which lords over Thetford. The slightest haze screens Ascutney. The sun and the morning star set over Gile Mountain.

Although labeled *Gillette Swamp* on the United States Geologic Survey Lyme Quadrangle, Casey and Jordan renamed our valley *Coyote Hollow* because wild dogs sang the night we moved in. Hemming the marsh, technically an *intermittent fen*—peaty, alkaline, nutrient poor—are alders along the east and north, evergreens along the west and south.

Two brooks flow off the western face of Robinson Hill, another off the steeper, rockier eastern face, and unload their freight in the marsh. All three braid together into the main channel, which bisects the marsh before pouring out of the wreckage of an old beaver dam and coalescing into an unnamed brook that feeds the East Branch of the Ompompanoosuc River, two miles away.

When we moved to Coyote Hollow in 1997, the water level was much higher. Beaver—a keystone species, as important to the Northeast as bison were to the Great Plains—had incised a dozen shallow passages into the peat and maintained the outlet dam, which backed water up to the edge of our lower pasture. Casey and I snorkeled the main channel, four feet deep and decorated with water lilies. Jordan directed traffic from a kayak.

Back then, marsh wrens and snipe nested in the cattails. Seven muskrat houses rose out of the reeds. Mink birthed in a derelict beaver lodge. On spring nights, windows open, I'd fall asleep serenaded by snipe and bittern. Windows didn't need to be open to hear frogs, six different species. Wandering moose grazed the lilies. Wandering eagles and osprey studied the water, anticipating fish, which were scarce—and tiny. Migrating kestrels hawked dragonflies, and then fed on the wing or hovered above the reeds, laser eyes searching. Flying ants lured southbound nighthawks. And one cold December morning, an orbiting golden eagle took the measure of Coyote Hollow. When their food supply dwindled, the beavers left. Water levels fell, which ended kayaking and snorkeling. Wrens, snipe, and muskrats moved on. I haven't seen a moose in years. Bitterns, frogs, and red-shouldered hawks stayed. Itinerant otter and mink still follow the brooks. Deer still roam the interior of the marsh, still fawn on the sweetgale isles. And barred owls and coyotes continue to underscore the night, giving weight to the stars.

My boys grew up in Coyote Hollow. Played baseball. Made music. Helped in the garden. Mowed the lawn. Stacked wood. Fed horses and chickens and dogs. Caught frogs and snakes and smiling salamanders with cosmetic spots. Netted hatchling turtles. Threaded worms on fishhooks. Watched fledgling grosbeaks beg for sunflower seeds. The boys hid beer in the woodpile, weed in the closet. Behaved appropriately and inappropriately. Their boyhood triumphs and disappointments unfolded here, bloomed and faded like orchids. Coyote Hollow was their home ground, as the beaches, greenbelts, and windowwells of Long Island had been mine.

Casey and Jordan have moved on to pursue their own dreams, to build their own lives. Linny died. On 14 March 2020, just home from Costa Rica, I faced an empty house with a view, prepared to shelter in place, unaccompanied. A nature writer whose last day job had been during the Nixon Administration, who had freely roamed the hemisphere, a confidant of polar bears and eyelash vipers. Who among us, hunkered down at home alone in the shadow of Covid, hollowed out and exhausted, hadn't longed for a hug after dark?

I have a girlfriend with hazel eyes and a broad, fetching smile, an excellent fit for our similarities and differences. Covid tempered our relationship. When the pandemic landed, we had already been dating for three years. As a social worker, Nancy's work was deemed essential. When I returned home from Costa Rica, our relationship was mostly limited to incinerating the phone lines. When we got together, we were outside, socially distanced (until vaccines arrived), sitting around our front yards or wandering the backroads. Inside, we wore masks and barely touched . . . no exceptions.

To compensate, I embraced the hills and the valley, the corrugated world I hadn't fully embraced in many years. To be clear, based on a pair of books I had written while living in the Hollow, I knew more about the Florida Everglades than I did about my own wetlands, had associated more with timber rattlesnakes than with my own dooryard birds. But stuck at home for more than a year, I began to take solace from the rising sun, became a student (again) of a landscape so personal that sometimes it hurt to recall my own history. But chickadees (bless 'em) taught me to pivot. I became the beneficiary of chance and hope . . . saw myself, again, flawed but striving, at play in a gorgeous and brittle world underwritten by joy and sadness, dependency and change.

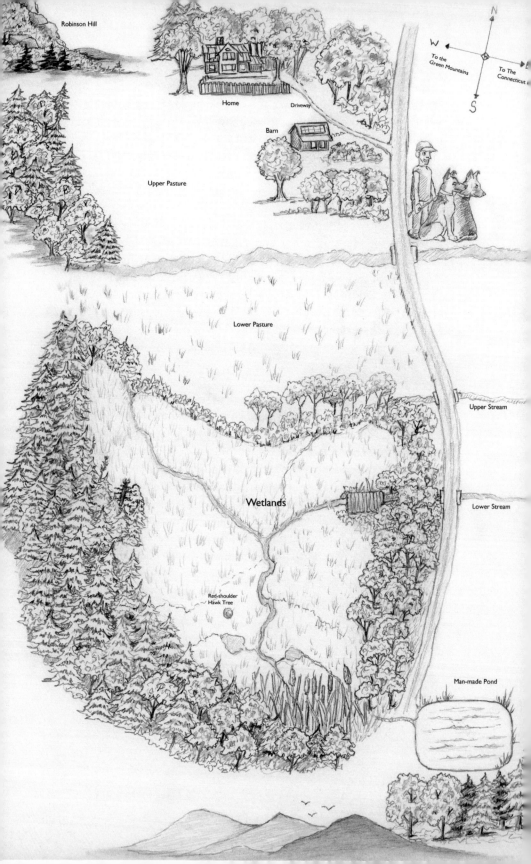

AN INTRODUCTION
Day 161
25 August 2020

Linny's 69th birthday

*In three words I can sum up
everything I've learned about life:
It goes on.*
Robert Frost

6:05 A.M. (sunrise one minute later than yester). 63 degrees, wind SSE 3 mph. Sky: dispersing ground-fog lifts, unveiling a lightly rubbled heaven, a mix of overexposed blue and wool-white, hints of peach across the west. Permanent streams: upper, jittery flow, flickering light, running out of water; lower, a single worried puddle, emblem of the parched summer. Wetlands: mist-softened colors; across the marsh, a tree falls, fracturing the lullaby of the breeze. Pond: sans mist, sans most everything—no otter, no hooded merganser, no bittern—except for errant methane bubbles and a lone turtle, a black, shiny disc with little webbed feet, rising and sinking, a reptilian marionette. Frogs press against the shoreline like S&H Green Stamps to their pages. Crickets, early morning's metronome.

AOR (alive on road): two hermit thrushes wandering the edge.

Two little brown bats (*Myotis lucifugus*), constricted figure eights above the front yard, trolling for flying ants and mosquitoes, survivors of their own pandemic. A solitary tricolored bat (*Perimyotis subflavus*), a tiny (very tiny) bat, busily erratic, courses above treetops; looks like a hummingbird moth, a flesh-winged spark combing insects out of fertile airways. Tricolored bat, once known as the eastern pipistrelle, and little brown bat, both victims of white-nose syndrome, ignored social distancing at their own peril. (Sound familiar?)

Chickadee rips breakfast out of a dewy spider web, then sings;

reminds me of midwinter when spring was a dream. Why sing when the Hollow braces for autumn? Three pewees join in, slurred whistles, a dampened version of plaintive summer song, equally longing, equally sad, simple to mimic. First winter wren I've heard in more than two months; a truncated version of the effervescent piccolo, which, when blended with the drumming of a far-off pileated, ushers me back to early May, when the mornings were colder and birdsongs hotter. Winter wren and pileated: the fife and drum corps, an unexpected engagement. Catbird meows. Another pulse of red-breasted nuthatches passes south through Coyote Hollow, nasal calls roll off tree trunks like a flock of tricycle horns. Ovenbird, first I've heard in a month, sings a clipped version of *teacher, teacher, teacher* . . . more like *teach, teach, teach,* an encouraging note on the threshold of the weirdest school year I remember.

⤳

Today's Linny's birth. She would have been sixty-nine. When she died, I mourned what the boys had lost and lamented her absence from our lives, a litany of inconsolable everyday losses, my sorrow often masked by immersion in family survival. I skated around the death of hope, staggeringly fragile, avoiding (as best I could) dwelling on personal loss—the closest of friends; companion, confidant; a fellow explorer of the recesses of the world. Oh, how I missed her burnt toast and her infectious laugh, so buoyant and contagious—but I had a ship to right, boys to grow.

Casey and Jordan loved to travel. And, for the most part, they were easy to travel with. Few complaints or outlandish requests. From the time they were infants, we took them everywhere—they nursed themselves to sleep in tents from Alaska to Newfoundland to the desert Southwest. A hint of campfire smoke lingered on their outdoor clothes. When Casey was five, on a boardwalk in Florida, he lured a barred owl to within five feet, hooting softly from the seat of his bicycle. Jordan had never met a snake or a frog he didn't like, and he broadcast enthusiasm whenever he discovered a strange-looking insect.

Although the boys loved the wonders of nature and appreciated life's grand diversity, for quite a while after their mother died, I hardly took them anywhere. Whenever we traveled as a family, Linny had been the organizer, the program director. I had been the consultant, the mule, the cheerleader. She would remember the toys, the books, the snacks, the toenail clippers. After Linny died, life without a compass seemed best lived closer to home.

Travel did return to our lives (often with a vengeance), but the sense of loss still lingers. Yester, Casey and daughter-in-law Becky texted me the sonogram of a fetal heartbeat. I longed to see Linny's irrepressible smile—one more time—rising like the tide at news she'd be a grandmother.

Three phoebe chicks in the front-yard apple tree, wings drooped and quivering, mouths cranked open, sunrise colors . . . begging, begging, begging. I stop and watch phoebe destiny: mostly moths, a steady procession, a seasonal harvest. No matter how much I ache, I can't suppress smiling. Time has a way of passing, of blunting loss, casting light across dark shadows, uncoiling the future.

SPRING

2020

ABBREVIATION KEY:

AOR - Alive on Road
DOR - Dead on Road
SOR - Scat on Road
BT - Before Present Time
FOY - First of the Year

Day 1

18 March 2020

. . . our minds are the outcome of things as they are,
and all of our ideas of value are based upon the
lessons we learn in this world.

JOHN BURROUGHS

6:56 A.M. (sunrise two minutes earlier than yesterday). 28 degrees, wind
NNW 7 mph, across the Eastern Seaboard headwinds stymie the northward progress of migratory songbirds, which shelter in place (much like
me). Sky: in the east, waning crescent moon appears and disappears
behind a flotilla of small clouds, aerial scree. Permanent streams: full,
loud, gin-clear. Wetlands: reeds, collapsed under the weight of winter, a
beige welcome mat for a wandering bear, main channel dark and snow
trimmed. Pond: rotting ice withdraws from shoreline.

Two golden-crowned kinglets, tiny birds, high in pines. Hovering.
Wings flick, nervous appendages. Hearts pound a thousand beats a minute. Kinglets harvest insect eggs and larvae and spiders buried in needle
tufts and scaly bark. Nonstop: searching and feeding. A restless focused
appetite. Kinglets flash their crowns; specks of color in colorless March,
yellow and orange, black-bordered . . . dwarf war bonnets. Kinglets whisper: *tsee, tsee, tsee.* I struggle to hear them. I work to see them, high in
the green sweep, keeping each other company. At night, to conserve heat,
kinglets roost together, packed like sardines, up to ten, lulled by the lullaby of their heartbeats.

Kinglet weighs about as much as a nickel; in winter, to stay warm,
needs at least eight calories a day. At my weight (165 pounds), I would
require more than 110,000 calories a day, the equivalent of 205 Big Macs.
(If I eschewed processed food, to meet my winter caloric needs, I'd need
to eat an acre of wheat or a half-acre of corn a day.)

Chickadee and titmouse join kinglets, probing among the evergreens.
Everyone pauses to sing to the west wind, a late winter ensemble full of
verve. Nearby, a brown creeper lands on the side of a maple, tail pressed
to bark, joins chorus. Sibilant whispering . . . barely audible. Jays and
crows mutter in the distance.

Then, high on the shoulder of Robinson Hill, pileated laughs, loudly, lustily, hijacking sunrise, a crazed voice that overflows the valley, spilling down the hill like cold air. A year-round resident, lifelong needs fulfilled right here in Coyote Hollow. Unlike me, pileated has a complete absence of wanderlust. Marooned with the woodpecker, I walk a dirt road that once hosted cars, under a sky that once hosted aircraft. In these hills, mask off, I breathe deeply in the secrecy and pretense of quarantining, remain astonished by the language of the seasons, garlanded by kinglets and chickadees and the horns of the fading moon.

Day 9

26 March 2020

Pay attention.
Be astonished.
Tell about it.
MARY OLIVER

6:41 A.M. (sunrise two minutes earlier than yesterday). 21 degrees, wind NNW 4 mph. Sky: clear and delicate, hint of rose across the west grading to yellow, then to pale, daylight blue; sunshine like honey oozes down Robinson Hill, trees and outcrops glow. Sap rising, sugar maple buds red-brown and swollen.

In late March 1978, my first spring in Vermont, a South Strafford neighbor, draft horses hitched to a sleigh, emptied sap buckets into wooden barrels across a woodland smothered by snow. He had set his maple taps by town meeting day, first Tuesday in March, as dependable a sign of spring as the lengthening of the day and the caroling of robins.

No longer.

Over the past four decades, sugaring season has started earlier—and gotten shorter. Sap starts running eight days earlier and ends eleven days earlier on average, according to the Vermont Maple Sugar Makers' Association. In 2019, taps were set in late December, and sap ran by early February 2020. (In 2017, sap ran in late January.) Upwardly mobile temperatures move, on average, thirty feet north per day, twenty miles per decade, leaving some biologists to wonder whether, in a century or two, Vermont will remain hospitable to sugar maples (or beech or red spruce).

In the forty-three years since I moved to Vermont, I have kept an on-again-off-again journal noting (among other things) phenology, the science of seasonal natural phenomena, which for more than three decades I mined for either a weekly syndicated newspaper column or commentaries broadcast on Vermont Public Radio.

In her epic 1951 book, *The Sea Around Us*, Rachel Carson devoted four pages to climate change. *The frigid top of the world is very clearly warming up*, she wrote. *The long trend is toward a warmer earth; the pendulum is swinging.*

Has swung—will continue to swing.

But no longer do I need to look to the Arctic to confirm that swing. It's right here in Coyote Hollow—in backyards, in gardens, in parks.

◦◦◦

Back on April 7, 1980, I wrote, "Sunny, sixty degrees. Sap running. At night, twenty-two degrees and six more inches of snow." When I settled in east-central Vermont, robins, phoebes, and woodcock arrived by late March or early April. Peepers and wood frogs chorused after the first warm, rainy night of spring, usually the second or third week in April; American toads joined in during the first week in May, when apple blossoms lit the dooryard. If a gray tree frog called before the third week in May, I considered it early. In 2020, the warmth of late February ushered worm-probing woodcock back the fourth week of the month, and then sardonically turned the ground to iron. As if scripted by Poe, a vanguard of amorous amphibians lured by late February's cordial weather reached the spawning pools in time to brace themselves against a prolonged, deep, macabre (and occasionally fatal) March freeze.

In the late seventies, Linny planted frost-sensitive vegetables—basil, tomatoes, peppers, squash, and so forth—over Memorial Day weekend, although an early June frost was *not* uncommon. Now, they're in the ground by mid-May. Blackflies plagued us from Mother's Day to Father's Day. Now, they appear in my garden on warm, late-April afternoons, when I fuss over lettuce and peas. Mosquitos appeared in late May (instead of year round in my basement, as they do now), deerflies and horseflies in late June, no-see-ums in high summer. Throughout the eighties, ticks were rare; I'd pluck (on average) one or two per summer from my dog. Lyme Disease was little known and coastal.

Some years, frost visited our garden before Labor Day, and we'd have to scramble to insulate the zucchini and basil with sheets of protective newspaper (or make pesto all night), and we'd harvest every reasonably ripe tomato and pepper. Color began earlier then, igniting the outer branches of wetland maples in late August, flashing across the hills by mid-September, and more or less extinguishing itself around Columbus Day. Now, killing frost may not visit my garden until mid-October; color lingers into November.

Traditionally a two- or three-day respite, the January Thaw lasted three weeks in 2017, extending well into February, which the National Oceanic and Atmospheric Administration called the warmest February on record. January 11, 2020, the temperature crested at fifty-nine degrees and never dropped below forty-eight degrees. Thirty years ago, Linny skated the Connecticut River eight miles to Hanover. Collectively, during two recent winters, the Connecticut opened and closed seven times. In February 2017, there was *no* ice at all, not even along the river's rim, and then, during the first week of March, the river froze shut . . . again.

By midday, several hours after my walk, temperatures rise into the mid-fifties. More than a hundred robins descend on the upper pasture, everywhere and hungry. They dash about the sorry-looking grass, stooping, pecking, swallowing worms, and then leave, abruptly . . . a small part of the feathered world in flux. Throughout this past winter, small bands of robins, once the harbinger of spring, roamed east-central Vermont, dooryard to dooryard, storefront to storefront, gorging on withered crabapples and highbush cranberries, a rare occurrence in the seventies.

Climate change has rewritten—and continues to rewrite—the timing of bird migration.

Arctic-breeding waterfowl and shorebirds are among the groups that lose out. As the tundra defrosts earlier, a hatching bonanza of midge and mosquito larvae—stimulated by the rising temperatures—become less available to chicks, whose parents arrive on the tundra according to species-specific photoperiods, the so-called *phenological mismatch*, which jeopardizes long-distance migrants far more than short-distance migrants like dooryard robins.

Mismatches in phenology are also less of a concern for black-throated blue warblers and scarlet tanagers. Around Coyote Hollow, the abundance and diversity of insects in the northern hardwood forest buffer the effects of climate change. We have no summer insect peak;

thus, our local migrants have a sweeping smorgasbord of soft-bodied insects to feed their chicks, a menu that includes hundreds of species of protein-rich caterpillars.

Robins . . . may you always pause in my pasture before heading north into uncertain skies.

Day 21

7 April 2020

A bird doesn't sing because it has an answer,
It sings because it has a song.
MAYA ANGELOU

6:18 A.M. (sunrise two minutes earlier than yesterday). 34 degrees, wind N 5 mph. Sky: nearly clear, a few high clouds, lemony pink, gilded by sunlight; sinking moon full, a shiny coin in the barren west. Permanent streams: clear and loud, pour through spongy woods. Wetlands: three dark, undulating ribbons coalesce across a bed of disorganized reeds, broken by the weight of winter. Waterlogged basin half full. From the far side of the marsh, where spruce and fir comb the sky, a jazzed-up grouse drums. No ducks. No frogs. Pond: ice gives way to frigid water.

By the time I reach the pond, hollow-voice owl falls silent, absorbed into the benevolence of evergreens, safe from violation. Ravens, magnanimous minstrels, fill a momentary void, salute sunrise with wild emotion, the world made new by guttural conversation.

Walking downhill, the road absent of traffic, two winter wrens bolster their claim to the turf on either side of the road Surround sound. Rich notes of great projection. Stopping to listen, an auditory voyeur in the demilitarized zone, I witness a war of music. Long, sweet, effervescent. Background vocals (*Twenty Feet From Stardom*): robins, juncos, white-breasted nuthatch, goldfinch, mourning dove, titmouse, and chickadee. Always a chickadee. Every house hosts a phoebe, every hedgerow a song sparrow. Blue jays, raucous and ubiquitous. Turkeys and red-shouldered hawks keeping to themselves, silent as stone.

Inside, during the oddness of the pandemic, as the memory of Costa Rica fades into the distance, shopping carts have become symbols of selfishness, radios and televisions virtuosos of contradiction and misinformation. But outside, back roads have become welcoming footpaths, the sky a population of stars and planets, unmarred by planes. All the while, April advances—fickle, indiscriminate, inexorable—and me along for the ride, trying to live seriously in a seriously disturbed world. As Covid reshuffles the deck, chickadee becomes my totem, a minor god, common yet comforting, purveyor of goodwill—overlooked at my own peril.

Day 27

13 April 2020

Nowadays, people are so jeezled up.
If they took some chamomile tea
and spent more time rocking on the porch in the evening
listening to the liquid song of the hermit thrush,
they might enjoy life more.
TASHA TUDOR

6:10 A.M. (sunrise one minute earlier than yesterday). 46 degrees, wind S 14 mph. Sky: gray as the Gulf of Maine, top-to-bottom saturation, sideways drizzle; amplifying sound, the garage roof converts shower to downpour, a meteorological buffing by galvanized steel. Venus and the vestigial moon doused by fog. Permanent streams: clear and high, bobbing and weaving around the rounded bones of Robinson Hill. Wetlands: dark braids escape their respective lanes—rising, sloshing, spreading—surrounding umber-colored islands. Pond: surface OCD; peppered by rain, driven by wind, a repetitive agitation. Several feet from the water on the eastern shore, an otter toilet, black as the River Styx, a damp clot of scales, fragile bones, and pieces of crayfish. I'm a cartoon character on a stroll, wind wreaking havoc with my umbrella, large dogs in tow.

Last night, a woodcock twittered in the lower pasture—first of the year (FOY). I went to bed, windows open, lulled by the urgency of frogs, and by the rain and wind, especially the wind. From a nearby shadow, a barred owl awoke to the possibilities of night. On the morning side of midnight, a bear took down the bird feeders; plundered the pail of sunflower seeds in the garage.

At sunrise, inside the garage, the smell of bear drives the dogs crazy, reminding me that I live amid an invisible olfactory landscape. The contours of scent, overlapping and reeking, trace pathways, mark time, and can be loosely assigned to one of five Fs: *fear, fighting, fornication, family,* and *food.*

Scenting is a silent note written in urine, scat, and glandular secretions—from cheeks, butt, *violet* gland (on the upper surface of a coyote or fox's tail), and from the bottom of a bear's feet and between its shoulder blades. For us, scent is a forgotten language, but it's the *lingua franca* of mammals, which read each other's discourses with their nose. Bears know who's healthy—who's not. Sebaceous glands at the base of hair follicles and anal scent glands on either side of the sphincter secrete an oily, waxy discharge. Coyotes spread the joy with their cheeks, depositing and accumulating scents. Among their preferred emanations are dead rodents, scat and urine, putrid venison, Chanel No. 5, and Avon After Shave.

A urine message may last two days, and face rubbing twenty minutes. A good face rub shortens the life expectancy of urine, exhausting the message. In the case of foxes, they weaken coyotes, the more dominant of the two—simultaneously adding a note of their own. If I homogenized and incorporated the senses of the tens of millions of species that have ever lived on Earth, I might better understand how our planet presents itself. Take the red fox or coyote: reads the world with his nose; writes with his butt and cheeks. My dogs read oily fox and coyote scribble. Apparently, they also read foot secretions of black bear—and react accordingly.

Attempting to leave, I lean thirty degrees from vertical, against 250 pounds of shepherds, as though water skiing. Umbrella blows inside out . . . puddled frustration. Burdened neither by weather nor self-regard, tom turkeys perform in the canes, tails spread like poker hands, wings down, quivering and dripping. Unimpressed (or oblivious), hens play hard to get.

Overhead, ravens speak in tongues. Down the road, in a blackberry jumble, two white-throated sparrows whisper, tentatively, tenuously.

Nearby, louder and more vibrant, a fox sparrow warbles. Both FOY. Brown creeper wanders up a maple; thin voice hijacked by wind, tail pressed to trunk . . . woodpecker wannabe.

From the maples below an outcropped ledge, the angelic voice of a hermit thrush, third morning in a row. Same place. Same time. Same bird? Who knows? A disciple of Darwin (and Wallace), I admire natural selection's interpretation of the environment as organism design. Like a sculptor molding shapeless clay into form and function. No two species are quite the same. The sweet-voiced thrush, forged in the furnaces of maple prehistory, sings a song shaped by the proximity of its neighbors and by the density of trees; notes coded in DNA, the endless draft of possibilities, tweaked by the wooded hills, arranged by the yellow light of sunrise, performed by a brown bird with a russet tail.

For an enchanted moment, the wet woods belong to hermit thrushes, four of them. One whispers across the marsh; two others down the road, and the fourth moored to the outcrop. If there's a finer song, I've yet to hear it. Companion notes, paired and sung simultaneously. Nothing is static about the music of a hermit thrush, pliable and ethereal, the canonization of a cold, wet April morning. I appreciate wood thrushes, too . . . but a wood thrush is a restricted musician: same melody, same pace, same notes. To compare the song of a wood thrush to the song of a hermit thrush would be like comparing the music of the Monkees to that of the Byrds. With the Byrds you never knew what you were going to hear, and it was always beautifully inventive.

Anticipating a nap by the wood stove, dogs skip home. A goose over-head trails his voice behind him. Out of the crosswise mizzle, pileated laughs, infectiously.

How fortunate to be home on the threshold of spring, to be able to walk through paradise beyond the front door, alone on a road without cars, under a heaven without contrails, in the audio crossfire of hermit thrushes, tethered to a pulse of triumphant ascendancy.

Day 32

18 April 2020

There is in us a deeply seated
response to the natural universe,
which is part of our humanity.
RACHEL CARSON

6:03 A.M. (sunrise one minute early than yesterday). 28 degrees, wind WNW 8 mph. Canoe moon, bright and overturned in a pale sky; horns pointing south to the land where all the birds are . . . biding their time until the winds shift. I went to bed reading an essay in *The New Yorker* about avalanches and awake to snow, microflakes (maybe itsy-bitsy hail), each flake no bigger than a grain of sugar.. Everything is dusted white. A confectioner's snowfall. Panes of ice seal puddles, last night's cellophane; crystals crusting mud. Intermittent streams: dark ribbons amid the leaves, degenerate pools connected to drying braids. Along the edge of one, robin probes a patch of unfrozen, saturated earth. Permanent streams: upper and lower, ice-rimmed rocks. Wetlands: frogs (salamanders, too) chill beneath a patina of ice, under blankets of mud and drowned leaves, waiting for the world to unlock (again), their early-evening jam a faded memory. Pond: ice blooms along the edge; wood ducks embrace the middle, a drake and a hen bolt when they see me.

Yesterday evening, a hermit thrush stalked under the clothesline, below the memory of damp clothes. Grabbed an earthworm, a snake-sized nightcrawler. Wings flicking. Red tail pumping, slowly. Pale bill working overtime. *Snap, snap, snap.* Up and down the worm's chilled length. Sufficiently softened, the worm vanished in a slow slurp. Thrush fluffed out as though trying to stay warm, worm bulging from its throat like a goiter. The bird retreated, satisfied, into the oaks and I into the kitchen.

Turkeys gobble. Crows protest. At the mouth of the driveway, a red-bellied woodpecker screams. A band of rowdy chickadees chases one another back and forth between two broken pines, expressing unmitigated displeasure: *Dee, dee, dee, dee, dee.* Breeding season: the disintegration of a flock. Males are full of beans. Nearby, hidden, the object of all the jousting; eventually, she crowns the winner based on a constellation of signals beyond my understanding. Every chickadee looks the same, sounds the same, behaves the same. So common a bird . . .

but *familiar* and *understood* are not synonymous. A quarantine project: turn prose into poetry. Turn domestic into exotic . . . unravel the secrets of the chickadee, a trusting front yard sprite. There's so much I don't understand.

Two male yellow-bellied sapsuckers, chattering, fly past me. Chaser and chased, eye-level across the road. Both birds pitch into hemlock, green as the British Isles. One sapsucker peels off. He lands on a blackberry cane, which bends under his weight like a shepherd's hook—the other bird flies directly into him, a full body shot. Woodpeckers bounce apart and then leave.

A big brown bat (*Eptesicus fuscus*) flutters just above tree level, following the road's undulations, flexibly, vertically downhill toward the marsh as though out for a stroll—a mammalian drone. The bat confirms a suspicion: I'm a cast member of an unscripted zombie film, ad-libbing my lines.

A barred owl, somewhere in the northern end (my end) of the valley, hits a single hollow note and holds it. Another day turns over.

Day 35

21 April 2020

How we spend our days, of course,
is how we spend our lives.
ANNIE DILLARD

5:44 A.M. (sunrise two minutes earlier than yesterday). 28 degrees, wind N less than 1 mph. Sky: clear, bright, hopeful. Permanent streams: ice coats overhanging branches, glazes stream stones. Wetlands: reeds sparkle. Pond: mist, an aimless wander.

Owls in the oaks. Chickadees in the lilacs. Male sapsucker broadcasts intentions: dashes, dots, pauses, tempo changes. Starts and stops, switches gear, sputters and then stalls (again), much like my lawnmower. Male wanders up a barkless trunk, pausing to tap. Dulcet notes, a disruptive serenade, woodland Morse code. Female can't resist, follows behind. Today's instrument of choice: big-toothed aspen, porous and soft. Both sapsuckers glow in fresh yellow light. Farther down the road, pileated works a sugar maple, nothing subtle here. Dense wood requires masculine drumming. Jackhammer blows. If pileated visits aspen, the tree falls apart. If sapsucker visits maple, he leaves with a broken bill and BTSD (Beak Traumatic Stress Syndrome).

Song sparrow on uppermost alder branch leans back and sings, bill at forty-five degrees; trill accompanied by a subtle, full-body quiver. Second sparrow answers from deeper in the alders. First sparrow turns toward him, sings, a hint of body English. Dueling trills: a bloodless battle of notes. Keeping their distance, sparrows face each other and sing—a Margaret Morse Nice moment.

During the 1920s and '30s, Margaret Nice, a self-made field ornithologist, watched song sparrows in the floodplain of the Olentangy River, north of Columbus, Ohio, while raising five daughters and catering to her husband's academic career. Outside the gravitational pull of a male-dominated field, Nice transformed the studies of animal behavior and ethology. She fixed colored leg bands on individual birds, then watched and watched and watched, calling her technique the *phenomenological method*. Nice studied the day-to-day activities of generations of song sparrows and discovered that birdsong provided a balm against overcrowding. Her subjects were characters in an unscripted play.

On March 26 I . . . banded a very important individual—my first Song Sparrow—later called Uno. He owned the territory next to our house and on May 22 I found his nest with three eggs, two of which hatched on May 28 and 29. For five days I spent a total of 18 hours watching the family. Uno's mate was evidently an experienced bird for she fed more than he did during four hours on the 29th, but after that he outdid her record . . . the two babies were carried off by some enemy the night of June 2 and so ended my observations on Song Sparrows in the spring of 1928 except for my becoming acquainted with Uno's spirited neighbor, later dubbed 4M, and my recording in words and symbols of his four distinctive songs.

When I first studied the Song Sparrow . . . I had looked upon Song Sparrow 4M as a truculent, meddlesome neighbor; but . . . I discovered him to be a delightful bird, spirited, an accomplished songster and a devoted father.

More than eighty years later, Nice's two-volume *Studies in the Life History of the Song Sparrow* (1937, 1943) revolutionized ornithology and remains the template for single-species ornithological research, also known as longitudinal studies, which follow individual birds over time. The life of any animal (or plant) is the wondrous sum of collisions and collusions with climate, geography, travels, seasonal needs, and simple twists of fate.

Flicker (FOY) on the front lawn; grass stiff, enameled in frost. Searches for ants. Sees me and retreats to aspen, laughing all the way. Nice wrote,

> I decided it would be better to be a bird. Birds are very busy at one period each year caring for babies, but this lasts only a few weeks with many of them, and then their babies are grown and gone. Best of all, they leave their houses forever and take to camping for the rest of the year. No wonder they are happy.

Having kept the company of timber rattlesnakes for eight years, I learned a lesson from Margaret Morse Nice: to truly see, my mind must be quiet. Now, a Covid hostage in my own home, stuck in a time warp, I latch on to the passage of time, to seasonal change, life's most felicitous feature. Tune out the media, stay away from crowds . . . the blueprint for contentment.

Day 36

22 April 2020

50th EARTH DAY

*The ultimate test of man's conscience may
be his willingness to sacrifice something
today for future generations whose
words of thanks will not be heard.*

GAYLORD NELSON

5:55 A.M. (sunrise one minute earlier than yesterday). 21 degrees, wind WNW 12 mph, trees sway and moan. Sky: thickly overcast, spitting snow, already a quarter-inch. Permanent streams: purl with slightly less authority than yesterday, icy edges and water-bound stones. Wetlands: mottled beige and white, cut by threads of dark water. Pond: pair of hooded mergansers swim in tight circles, bulbous-headed male crest up; ducks touch bills. Male sees me, then quick exit. Dash and launch—over the berm, the road, and the alders, flinging into the pool on the marsh side of the old beaver dam.

Inclement weather lures ground feeders out of the woods. Hermit thrushes, robins, and juncos assemble along both sides of the road, hopping, pecking; zigzag tracks: an interwoven, species-specific calligraphy. Forage for food too small for me to see (even with 10 x 42 Swarovski binoculars).

Just above my head, winter wren sings his heart out. A delicately puffed ball, feathers flare. Earth-colored back, solid. Barred flanks, a blend of cinnamon and brown. Short tail held vertical, a semaphore of sorts. Out of a bill barely opened pours a piercing falsetto—long, loud, effervescent warbles and trills. Jeff Buckley with feathers. Wren profile: adorable. Head on: a pop-eyed vocalist, sufferer of *exophthalmia* in need of thyroid medicine.

Chickadees, titmice, nuthatches, and jays call in the woods. Out of streaked shadows, a grouse drums, low and rapid, felt as much as heard; heartbeat of the valley. Owl pair in the pines, far side of the pastures. Hollow voices roll up the valley, accompany an invisible sunrise. Overhead, three crows, black birds amid white streaks, engage in Talmudic discussions. Under the feeders, chipping sparrow, (FOY), joins juncos to clean up sunflower seeds. Inadvertent dispensation, jays' largesse.

Fifty years ago today, a senior at Ball State University, I held a placard at the Scramble Light on the corner of McKinley and Riverside that announced something inflammatory about the mistreatment of the planet; among 10 percent of the U.S. population that participated in Earth Day #1. In 1970, John Muir was a footnote in environmental science, plate tectonics a footnote in geology, Alfred Russell Wallace a footnote in evolution, bison a footnote on the Great Plains, bald eagles a footnote in the American sky. Fifty years ago, the Cuyahoga River caught fire, Agent Orange defoliated Vietnam, and the Beatles broke up. 22 April 1970: the first Earth Day, the brainchild of Wisconsin Senator Gaylord Nelson, led to the passage of the Clean Air Act, the Clean Water Act, the Endangered Species Act, the banning of DDT, and the creation of the EPA, all during the reign of Richard Nixon. Without Rachel Carson's epic *Silent Spring* (1962), Gaylord Nelson might not have progressed environmentally beyond fishing for walleyes in Lake Winnebago.

Fifty years later, after Covid's sudden and poignant reshuffling of social norms, I'm free to examine my home ground inside and out, an unforeseen gift of the coronavirus: a valley scrubbed and carved by glaciers that hosted potatoes and stills in the 1930s. Hauntings: stonewalls assembled before the Civil War; overgrown cellar holes; a disassembled tractor. Home alone indulged by indulgent seasons and irrepressible thoughts . . . *Silent Spring*—a woodland without birds would be like a playground without children.

Day 40

26 April 2020

*The time you enjoy wasting
is not wasted time.*
BERTRAND RUSSELL

5:49 A.M. (sunrise one minute earlier than yesterday). 34 degrees, wind S 1 mph. Sky: thinly clouded, more sheet than cluster, more gray than white. Raven flyby, black-on-gray embossed, a linguistic belcher, ferrying an expressive mind across the valley. Intermittent streams: receding . . . reduced to pools strung together by muddy threads. Permanent streams: less roiling, less frothing, less water. Wetlands: sinuous ribbons weave through flattened reeds; marsh in need of a transfusion. Two mallards idle in a dark knot, green heads luminous. Six snipe (FOY) arrow by, winnowing. Pond: hapless frogs, silent; pair of hooded mergansers trace the far shoreline, female nearly camouflaged by gray water.

An American bittern (FOY) called last night from the juncture of the reeds and alders; a striped, tapered heron, beige as a cattail, bill to the stars. Single resounding gulps. A ventriloquist, flanked by a legion of reeds, hurling his voice like a boomerang. Edgar Bergen of the marsh, gulps rising from everywhere and nowhere. A starlit serenade to drive the season forward.

Turkey and grouse, gobbling and drumming. Grouse, the morning metronome, takes over from bittern, a deep, rapid pulse. Fans the air with short, stiff wings, feathers vibrating below the hearing threshold of great horned owls. To eat grouse, owl has to catch the performance. Blue-headed vireo (FOY) from the roadside pines close to the wetlands. Repetitive phrases. Leaves the listener space to contemplate. Not the worn, endless dawn- to-dusk monotony of the red-eyed vireo, which I appreciate in late August when every other singer except cuckoos and pewees keep mum. Phoebe sings from a limb over the snowmobile bridge. No virtuoso, guttural and tedious, like a sweet chickadee needing a voice coach, gray as a dull cloud. Perching with purpose, a reminder of good posture, bolt upright. Pumping tail, a nervous tic. Darts from limb to limb. Catches a moth on the wing and returns to the same branch, tail stirring the air. Phoebes nest inside my barn, on a beam above the barn porch, and a third on the solar hot-water pipes. Nest of mud and moss, a disheveled affair, guano everywhere. By summer's end, a major cleanup.

Quietly tapping, female hairy woodpecker in black cherry. Sees me. Calls: *peek, peek, peek,* then moves to the other side of the cherry trunk, resumes tapping. She's larger and two-F-stops lighter than the hairy woodpeckers that I recently watched on the side of a dormant Costa Rican volcano.

∾

In 1947, Marjory Stoneman Douglas wrote *The Everglades: River of Grass,* a paean to a marsh the size of New Jersey, one of the most influential (and gorgeous) conservation books of the 20th century. Douglas, who lived to 108 and devoted more than sixty years to the conservation of the

Florida Everglades, told *National Geographic* that she and the Everglades had a relationship that did not require close physical contact (she disliked insects).

Douglas notwithstanding, my relationship with the Hollow is not platonic. I wave the Covid flag, fashioning virtue out of a virus, and renew an affinity with my home ground once ignored at my own peril. My morning walks have become a portal into the fluctuating world of inconsistency, each day a variation within a routine of self-imposed seclusion. Here, I pause beneath dawn's spare, yellow light, my day framed by inordinate possibilities; interests ubiquitous, attachments unembroidered. Here, memory unfurls beneath the freedom of the stars and the thumb of cancer. Linny died on the 9th of November, twenty years ago, the day before Jordan's fifth birthday. Casey was thirteen. Her ashes now lie beneath the frogs, her brass buttons beneath the tomatoes. I still sense her in the ineffable beauty of drifting clouds and the delicacy of wildflowers.

Note to self: Be a small, thoughtful force, covalently bound to the valley. Rejoice in memory, a lover in a loving and loveable landscape . . . an avatar of *topophilia*.

Sunlight puddles in the marsh. A robin walks across cold grass. Every day is a gift.

Day 41

27 April 2020

To be a Flower, is profound
Responsibility—
EMILY DICKINSON

5:47 A.M. (sunrise two minutes earlier than yesterday). 34 degrees, wind N 6 mph. Sky: thickly overcast and leaking. Mist grades to snow, shapeless flakes. In between drizzle and rain, sometimes hail—the size and color of Polyfil beanbag stuffing—that bounces off the road and sticks to the dogs. Then, rain, rain, rain, and the disappearance of polished clouds.

Depressions in the woods morph into puddles. Permanent streams: turbulent and dirty, rushing headlong into the marsh. Wetlands: female hooded merganser rises from a tongue of dark water and circles the marsh, wings stirring rain. Bittern calls, a hollow sound like popping the inside of your cheek with your finger (a captivating activity for toddlers and grandfathers). Pitch the only difference. Bittern call carries a mile; cheek-popping?—inaudible in the next room. Pond: schools of fat, cold-stunned tadpoles along the shoreline; frogs underneath quilts of leaves and mud . . . torpid.

Patches of red maple flowers (males) pepper the road, anthers empty. Beech buds slowly unwrap. Aspen flowers swollen. Yesterday, in Pomfret, twenty miles southwest, trout lily bloomed, and ramps (wild leeks) paved rich, leafless slopes. At nine hundred feet above sea level, Coyote Hollow, sandy and nutrient-poor, the residue of the last glacier, hosts less diversity, less abundance. A few days (if not a week) behind Nancy's Pomfret neighborhood, every April I lose a bet with her about who'll hear the first peeper, the first woodcock, the first snipe; who'll find the first morel, conical, honeycombed, and delicious.

Carnal stirrings: pushy turkey in the lower pasture, dancing and gobbling. Everybody else . . . laconic. Robins and thrushes hushed by weather. Lone winter wren, a halfhearted song, barely audible above the rain. Cohorts in default mode, silent as stone. Few woodpeckers drum or scold.

Neither snow nor rain nor heat nor gloom. Nothing slows a chickadee, the postal service poster bird. Only chickadees broadcast exuberance. A small gray bird with a black bib and cap sings with gusto: *Hey sweetie,* the first note higher than the second.

An odd morning, chilly and wet. And stunning in a late-April sort of way. I remind myself I'm standing in the rain.

Day 42

28 April 2020

For the mind disturbed,
the still beauty of dawn is nature's finest balm.
Edwin Way Teale

5:46 A.M. (sunrise one minute earlier than yesterday). 35 degrees, wind NW 3 mph. Sky: tarnished silver, horizon to horizon. Treetop mist. An inverted watershed spreads, shrinks, frays; matches the outlines and the dimensions of marsh and pond, ribbons, streams and rivers; two miles south, over the East Branch of the Ompompanoosuc, a thick, wooly highway—like the river itself—curls toward Union Village Dam. Permanent streams: clear (again) and loud, headlong rush into a rain-swollen marsh. Wetlands: bittern in patch of flattened reeds, calling. A fairy-tale character: bill to the sky, the wind teasing white shoulder plumes, yellow eyes downward focus. A polygamist? (Many marsh birds are.) Besotted. Coy female (or two) stays hidden, lured from the starry sky. Pond: stylized reflections, tree trunks shimmy upside down and mesmerizing. Male hooded merganser, tail cocked and hammerhead crest erect. Nattily attired: black and white, hints of tan, flies across the pond to join hen, which, disconcerted, bolts, wings singing like a cricket.

AOR: red eft, stunned by cold. Warmed in my hands and released. Wooly bear balled up. Deer wandered around the road last night, curlicues of prints, back and forth.

Road litter: more maple flowers and a few red-green aspen catkins, fuzzy as a wooly bear.

Standing on the border of sapsucker territories. Birds are visible, tapping on opposite sides of the road, first one, then the other. A mysterious, low-key battle of telegraph keys, not the wild jackhammering of pileateds. Robins quiet . . . well, quiet for robins. Dogs, whose interest in the wild aligns more with deer than with thrushes, tighten leashes when a whitetail bounds, immaculate tail erect. Hermit thrushes pick up the slack. One sings overhead, bill delicately opening and closing, an ethereal song for the ages, the icing on a morning walk.

A few warblers dropped down last night, a bundle of motion high in the hemlocks. More spill out, then fall out. They're coming. They're coming.

Chickadee

Three chickadees chase each other around front-yard trees. Lots of *dee, dee, dee, dee, dee*. A measure of their aggravation, of which there's plenty. As common as they are, black-capped chickadees usually keep their personal affairs offstage like many of my taciturn neighbors. Not today. Two consummate nuptials in a maple. Bliss on a branch. A delicate encounter that lasts seconds. Third chickadee? An unmitigated pest. Another tick on the life list of bird sex that includes, among other species: belted kingfisher (he pulled her crest), pileated woodpecker (he also pulled her crest), bald eagle, snail kite, barred owl (he gave her a pig frog), eastern bluebird, tree swallow, dark-eyed junco, and red-shouldered hawk (on a horizontal oak branch, just off the driveway, while I idled the Prius, windows open).

Shameless chickadees fuse again, tails to the side. Voyeur bird pauses just below the trysting twig. Chickadees endure winter for nanoseconds of springtime pleasure. The end product: four white eggs speckled reddish brown, the size of my fingernails, deposited in a tree cavity excavated in soft, punky wood (birch or aspen), or appropriated from a small woodpecker . . . the hatching of possibility.

Stuck at home, watching, waiting. The rebirth of a season. Boredom held at bay by frolicking chickadees.

Tarnished sky fades, fractures. Fingers of sunlight caress the valley.

Day 45

1 May 2020

Whoever you are, no matter how lonely,
the world offers itself to your imagination,
calls to you like the wild geese, harsh and exciting—
over and over announcing your place
in the family of things.
Mary Oliver

5:40 A.M. (sunrise two minutes earlier than yesterday). 48 degrees, wind S 1 mph. Sky: overcast with light rain. Poured all night; water, the valley's early-morning theme, an extension of April (perhaps April 31).

Permanent streams: swollen, earthy solutions fill floodplains and run brownish toward the marsh. The birth of streams, every crease in the landscape holds water; tributaries of tributaries murmur. Wetlands: monster sponge, collecting, straining, cleansing, seeping, draining; small channels devoured by large channels. Yesterday's dendritic flow metastasizes into an expansive pool. Two mallards, green heads above brown water, float the ballooning main branch. Along the far side of the marsh, northern water thrush (FOY) sings loudly. Pond: pockmarked surface.

Red maple flowers, mere stains on the road. Aspen catkins hang down and shed pollen. Beech buds stretch out, leaves deferred. Beads of rainwater everywhere. Each one is an inverted reflection of Coyote Hollow, Vermont, in a raindrop.

Downy, hairy, and pileated woodpeckers are silent. Red-bellied woodpecker picks up the slack, calls, and drums in the pines below the driveway. Likely to no avail. Visited the feeder all winter, the only prolonged visit by a red-bellied in twenty-three years. Never a female. Sooner or later, like the first female Florida panther that crossed the Caloosahatchee River after more than twenty years, a lady red-bellied woodpecker will disperse into The Hollow and be drawn to the male as he drums from Dylan's *Desolation Row*.

Hermit thrush song hangs in the damp air.

Four chickadees chase each other through a hemlock crown, loosening suspended raindrops. Agitated chickadees sound as though they're trilling, an intertwining cascade of *dee-dee-dee-dee-dee*. Someone's not happy. A frenetic courtship that has perpetuated the species for more than a million years, past grazing mammoths and browsing mastodons, past Woodland Indians and hillside farmers, past modern dilemmas. It's incomprehensible to me how the female ultimately selects a suitor, a behavior best understood by chickadees, which will carry them far beyond the confines of Covid.

Back home, I slide the barn door open to welcome little brown bats (*Myotis lucifugus*), which have clung to the wall behind the open door for years, albeit lately in much-reduced numbers. Then, under a drizzle, I brush the shepherds. Immediately, the chickadee leaves the feeder, gathers a tuft that sticks haphazardly out of its beak, and flies away. A utilitarian songbird.

A red-shouldered hawk screams, piercing sunrise with its harpoon cry. Under the birdfeeder, lone turkey scavenges spilled sunflower seeds. Pauses to dance. Strutting, tail spread like a card trick. Auditioning for next spring.

Day 49

5 May 2020

Cinco de Mayo

The world's favorite season is spring.
All things seem possible in May.
EDWIN WAY TEALE

5:35 A.M. (sunrise one minute earlier than yesterday). 34 degrees, wind NW 13 mph (red pines swaying, stirring, and creaking; hardwood twigs in perpetual motion). Sky: mottled. Mount Ascutney in vague relief against the southwestern horizon, a dark thumbprint against striated clouds gilded along the edges. Intermittent streams: puddles reconnected; slow, gurgling flow. Permanent streams: clear and loud. Wetlands: first hint of new-growth green amid fawn-colored mats; male mallard still in the main channel; bittern in the reeds, calling. Pond: surface whitecaps.

Beech buds unfurling. Red maple keys extend beyond faded flowers; a million tiny, red *V*s salute the season. Aspen heavy with catkins, a blizzard of seeds in the making. Red trillium in flower; coltsfoot gone to seed.

Scarlet tanager (FOY) singing in the pines. No Pavarotti, a robin needing a voice coach. I recall in April 2029, Pacific pitch of Costa Rica—more specifically, a tropical woodland. Uphill from where I stood, three male scarlet tanagers, amicable as pigeons, perched side by side in a cecropia, their black and red feathers effervescing in the dim light. Back home in east-central Vermont, they arrive with attitude, chasing each other through the oaks.

Six white-throated sparrows took the red-eye into the front yard. Several sing. Thrushes still. Winter wrens in auditory high gear. Juncos and chipping sparrows trilling; sparrows longer and more mechanical. Three black and white warblers singing. Can't find them.

☙

Two male rose-breasted grosbeaks visit sunflower feeders, black and white and red. Casey and Jordan call them *Rosy*, a name coined by their mom and employed with the same familiarity as if an old friend had stopped by for coffee. We raised the roof whenever Rosy came . . . every Rosy from May through September was a treat. Like fingerprints, each male's rose-colored chevron varies in length, width, and shape, an indelible ID . . . framed by ivory white, capped by jet black. The collo-quial name *cut-throat* pales by comparison to *Rosy*. We coveted subtle differences as though trading in baseball cards: skinny Rosy, long Rosy, wide Rosy, faded Rosy. Eye-popping, electric-red Rosy, the dooryard equivalent of a Derek Jeter rookie card.

When toddlers, chins barely above the windowsill, Casey and Jordan broadcast fervor whenever a Rosy appeared. He was their bird. The fam-ily bird, the totem that arrived suddenly on a sweet May morning . . . a bird from far beyond the doorstep. And, now and forever more, Rosy reminds them of Linny's legacy.

Owl voices tail off. Bittern resumes calling: *Gloonk, gloonk* . . . like a giant rock dropped a short distance into the water, a deep, hollow sound that fills the valley. Called all night, secreted in muck and mire. Prefers the northwest corner of the marsh, beyond my prying eyes. Over the years, I've seen him on the pond's rim. On the road, yellow bill skyward, rocking back and forth (fooling no one). Looking lost on a neighbor's front lawn. After listening to the baritone serenade for decades, I sought bittern out as one would an old, reclusive friend. I sloshed into the wetlands, dressed in hip waders, an expensive Vermont Public Radio tape recorder hanging from my neck. Eventually, after several hours of slow pursuit, knee-deep in organic crud, I stood twenty feet from the lovestruck bird. Bittern, preoccupied, ignored me, chest heaving with each *gloonk*. Yellow eyes, inscrutable and resolute, bright as the sun, burned a hole through the dawn. I lost interest long before he did.

Pair of phoebes in the apple tree, fluffed against the wind. Like her-mit thrush, the male sings, beak barely open, face expressionless. No one would mistake him for a thrush, which is likely why Walt Whitman did not write sonnets to the phoebe and why the hermit thrush, not the eastern phoebe, is the state bird of Vermont.

Chickadee zips around the sturdy, ornamental cherry tree full of unvarnished candor, the tree the children of Thetford Elementary School gave Casey and Jordan when their mother died. On a lonesome morning in late November 2000, E. C. Brown delivered and planted the tree. He advised me to remarry ASAP—I did, in the summer of 2002, prema-turely . . . but bottomless loss was hard to replace. Annie and I tried to make the relationship work. We flourished at first, decorating the night sky like fireworks, great arcs of phosphorescent love. Unfortunately, our high-octane fuel petered out, and our relationship dimmed. We grew apart (several times). Eleven years—on-again, off-again. What's left? A mother figure for Jordan; a two-stall horse barn with Dutch doors and phoebes in the rafters, two pastures, a fenced riding ring, a fondness for youth hockey, and poignant vignettes of joyful moments and fruitless effort. And an unquenchable thirst, the oldest of adolescent adversaries.

Annie's son, William, a year-and-a-half older than Jordan and six years younger than Casey, three electrons that still orbit each other's lives. The boys bonded and shared friendship and friends, baseball, hockey, storytelling, sundry animals, hard lemonade, soft pornography, and rose-breasted grosbeaks. They're Rosy to William and Annie, too, and seven years after she left The Hollow, Annie thinks of Jordan whenever she sees one.

Full of personality and purpose, chickadee flies onto the porch, gathering bits of dog fur, dust bunnies, and spiderwebs . . . putting to use the flotsam and jetsam of my life.

Day 52

8 May 2020

How sad would be November
if we had no knowledge of spring.
EDWIN WAY TEALE

5:31 A.M. (sunrise one minute earlier than yesterday). 34 degrees, wind SSW 11 mph. Sky: marbled. Moon full, luminous, and low in the west, bright as a lightbulb; behind the moon, hints of rose. Rising and dispersing mist above the East Branch of the Ompompanoosuc. All night downpours, road puddled, the edge of the woods traced in snow. Permanent streams: earth-stained and loud. Wetlands: reeds greening, alders flowering, tiny maroon cones; willow catkins pollen heavy, yellow dust in the air. Tissue-thin ground fog. Pond: rolling surface, wind-driven mist.

Although leaves are opening along the Connecticut River, the floodplain a pastel wash (autumn without the density of color), at nine hundred feet above sea level, Coyote Hollow lags behind. Up here, it's a vernal creep: black cherry and red oak dormant; flower buds of white ash swollen, dark knobs on the end of twigs; road carmine spotted, littered with a fresh crop of red maple flowers; sugar maple, a faint suggestion of green.

Loon overhead passing between Post Pond and Lake Fairlee, laughing all the way. Blue-headed vireos balkanize the valley; set territories, marking boundaries with slow, methodical songs (given at intervals of nearly three seconds) and slow, methodical movements, branch to branch, tree to tree. They're easy to see in the naked woods. Spectacles, wing bars, white belly, yellowish flanks, blue-gray heads. In a week, only their song will seep through the leaves. Whenever I see a blue-headed vireo, I think of her as an old friend who changed her name, preferring the name first learned when we were introduced ... *solitary vireo*, part of a soothing, boyhood lexicon. Like physical intimacy and comfort foods (bagels and lox, spare ribs on the bone, eggplant Parmesan, mac and cheese), I'm drawn to bird names first learned along the outer beaches of Long Island: marsh hawk, duck hawk, pigeon hawk, sparrow hawk, oldsquaw, yellow-shafted flicker, slate-colored junco, myrtle warbler.

Yellow-rumped warbler (FOY) in big-toothed aspen. Sixty years ago, in the damp swales of the primary dunes, the yellow-rumped was called *myrtle warbler*, warbler of my youth. They wintered along the barrier beaches, subsisted on bayberry's hard, waxy fruit (hence, the name). Digesting the wax, defecating the seed. The Johnny Appleseed of bayberry. In 1973, the American Ornithological Union—now the American Ornithological Society—which sets the laws of nomenclature, lumped *myrtle warbler* of the east and north and *Audubon's warbler* of the west into a single species, the *yellow-rumped warbler*. Based on more sophisticated DNA sequencing, the warblers may again be split into separate species. I hope so.

The name *myrtle* tethered the bird to a unique ecological function and to a winter landscape, to sand dunes, salt air, and the gray, compulsive break of waves. And ... to my boyhood, when I roamed the beaches in joyous delirium, free from the asphyxiating burdens of suburbia. *Yellow-rumped* is just the color of its *tuchus*.

Day 54

10 May 2020
Mother's Day

I have walked this south stream
when to believe in spring was an act of faith.

ANN ZWINGER

5:28 A.M. (sunrise two minutes earlier than yesterday). 34 degrees, wind WNW 11 mph. Pines gossip. Hardwoods complain. Wind roars with traffic intensity. Sky: partially overcast; three-quarter moon halfway between the eastern and western horizon, tarnished. Along the edge of the road, moldered leaves snow dusted. Permanent streams: rocks iceless. Wetlands: new reeds, emerald green, collectively an herbal compass, a million sedges pointing southeast; old growth collapsed pale brown. Pond: wavelets on autopilot, one after the other; no mergansers.

Last night, an owl called from a snag in the marsh, the one the redshoulder uses during the day, and a jetliner awakened the sky. Unable to fall back to sleep, I considered the plane and who flew the red-eye during a pandemic. Semester-abroad students escaping the geographically flourishing virus? Businessmen as usual in an unusual world? Doctors with borders? Out-of-order diplomats escaping quarantine? An empty plane returning to port? This was only the second jet I've been aware of in the past two months—heaven for landscape photographers. A sky empty of contrails.

Toggling from one bird to another. Thrushes and vireos sing. Ovenbirds holler. Grouse drums, woodland tachycardia. Chickadees meet, forum in a hemlock. Background vocals (birds close to stardom): robins, white-breasted and red-breasted nuthatches, titmouse, junco, phoebe, black and white warbler, myrtle warbler, magnolia warbler (FOY), mourning dove, blue jay, bittern, clipped calls from a veil of reeds.

Broad-winged hawk (FOY) soars through a weft of branches. Lands on a maple limb. Stares down, looking for chipmunk, garter snake, or a plump toad en route to spawn. A stout bird by hawk standards. Short, wide tail and long, broad wings. An ideal design for riding a thermal, bubbles of heated air rising off ledges and boulders and highways . . . up, up, and away all the way from Amazonia. Not a good design for spirited chases, which are best left to goshawks. Two months ago, I watched a lone broadwing headed north above La Selva Biological Station on the Caribbean slope of Costa Rica. Bereft of its own migratory flock, which sometimes numbers in the tens of thousands, the broadwing trailed a crowd of thirty turkey vultures. This morning's hawk switches limbs and trees and stares at the forest floor, then lingers on a suitable perch with the patience of Job.

Yesterday, after my old friend Richie from Apollo Beach told me that clouds of migrants were passing up the Florida peninsula, I imagined a light wave of Neotropical birds stretched from the Gulf of Mexico to Coyote Hollow, fifteen hundred miles of ambitious feathers. The vanguards already here doing the heavy lifting: frozen ground, NW winds, insects too cold to move, iced-over puddles, icicles hanging down from the hummingbird feeder, and now snow. If the birds survive, tough-guy genes pass on to the next generation. If the birds perish, the genes are out of circulation. When I moved to the Upper Valley in 1977, the Montshire Museum's bird collection had ten or twelve freeze-dried scarlet tanagers and a dozen warblers, vireos, swallows, and orioles with the same collection date on their specimen labels: 7 May 1976. The day before, six inches of snow had blanketed the Connecticut Valley. Many migrants, forced to forage along the rim of Route 10, starved to death and were collected and donated to the museum by Hanover commuters.

White-throated sparrows sing an unalloyed five-note whistle, arguably Vermont's most idiosyncratic bird song, certainly one of the easiest to mimic. My sweet spot of the morning. *Ol' Sam Peabody, Peabody, Peabody, Peabody* out of the front yard raspberries, the bramble-filled clear cut, the edge of the road, the bushes along the far side of the pond, the spruce and hemlock-hemmed marsh, and from beyond my sightline. I whistle back, bilingual in a world of deliciously chaotic sound, moved by a sparrow for reasons I cannot fathom.

Jordan graduated from Kenyon College last year. He moved home to work in the cardiology department at Dartmouth Hitchcock Medical Center to rack up patient-contact hours to qualify for admission into a Physician's Associate program. Because Jordan occasionally hooks Covid patients to heart monitors, life at home indoors sometimes morphs into Russian roulette. Sunrise walks resemble carefree days along the ocean when hours roll by like waves. Every iteration of birdsong, every gilded cloud a thrill . . . homeboy at home watching the passage of time. No plans. Few worries or intervening thoughts.

Indoors, I hold my breath; outdoors, the bewitching timelessness of the moment. Too bad the remainder of the day's broadcast news and social media tilts toward rash assumptions and calumnies.

Day 57

13 May 2020

All things by immortal power,
Near or far,
Hiddenly
to each other linked are,
That thou canst not stir a flower
without troubling a star . . .
Francis Thompson

5:24 A.M. (sunrise two minutes earlier than yesterday). 27 degrees. Wind SE 4 mph. Sky: cloudless, sunlight cascading down the valley's western flank. Half-moon east of center. Three geese honking, head north. One loon lit by the sun, heads east, yodels echoing across The Hollow. Is there a more haunting call? Permanent streams: gurgling. Ice coats rocks and low, overhanging branches. Wetlands: frosted. Pond: ice on the rim, tissue thin.

ᕤ

Entering the digital age: Yesterday, after much gnashing of teeth and much assistance from friends, I posted my first entry on Substack, the online newsletter. For someone who struggles using Google Maps and Venmo, for me the digital equivalent of breaking the three-minute mile.

ᕤ

Last night, I read an article on an obscure aspect of bird migration in *Ecology*. Every year, more than two billion birds cross the Gulf of Mexico, hemisphere to hemisphere. No surprise. En route, thousands, maybe tens of thousands, perhaps millions, die. Flocks starve. Exhausted and disoriented, birds land on the water and can't take off. Others fly too low and get engulfed by waves, consumed by an unforgiving sea. Birds hit bell buoys and oil rigs and boats. Still, no surprise. The magic of the article: newborn tiger sharks gather off the coasts of Alabama and Mississippi, waiting for hapless migrants, a predictable source of protein for pups learning to hunt. The article listed eleven species identified in baby tiger sharks' bellies: yellow-bellied sapsucker, swamp sparrow, eastern kingbird, and common yellowthroat among them. All birds that live in Coyote Hollow. Notorious for dietary breadth, tiger sharks eat almost anything: big, small, alive, dead, inorganic. Dining with a proprietary air. Who knew that tiger sharks depend on the sky to deliver protein during a brief stage in their lives? How much we don't know about where we live.

White-throated sparrows pair up; both sexes sing. Blue-headed vireos pair up; both sexes don't sing. Nashville warbler (FOY) in yellow birch. Wood thrush (FOY) hops from pine branch to pine branch. Carols, an enchanting song. But as avian troubadours go . . . I'm all in on hermit thrush.

Red-eyed vireo (FOY), fresh from the Amazon basin, doggedly sings in the maples. The most abundant bird in the northern hardwood forest, red-eyed vireo maintains and defends a small territory. Sings constantly to refresh audio-boundary markers. In the early fifties, a biologist more mathematically inclined than I determined that a male red-eyed vireo sings more than twenty thousand songs daily. Eat. Sing. Sing. Sing. Eat. Woodland elevator music with a persistence that borders on the pathological (for both bird and biologist). Red-eyed vireo sings throughout the summer, dawn to dusk . . . let the monotony begin.

Ovenbirds everywhere; twelve along the road, all singing. Screaming. *Teacher, teacher, teacher, teacher.* Look and behave more like thrushes than warblers. Six mingle on the front lawn, stand erect . . . an ovenbird congress far away from tropics mixing with the hoi polloi. One picks up a numb earthworm. Another flips oak leaves. Butterscotch light spills down the western ledges.

Day 59

15 May 2020

The truth is . . . there is nothing very 'normal' about nature.
Once upon a time there were no flowers.
LOREN EISELEY

5:22 A.M. (sunrise one minute earlier than yesterday). 50 degrees, wind N 2 mph. An absence of the down jacket, ski cap, and winter gloves. Sky: waning moon eclipsed by a blanket of high clouds, corner to corner, blue-gray, ready to release. Permanent streams: swollen and loud. Wetland: viridescent. Leafless shadbush, white petaled, lights up the eastern rim of the marsh. Three swamp sparrows chase each other around the alders. Pond: green tadpoles along the edge. The world, my world, Coyote Hollow, a valley within a valley within a valley within the corrugated Northeast, finds equilibrium.

Beech leaves unwrapped, tiny, delicate, vibrant. Sugar maple leaves open, flowers extending.

Last night, not quite the Wonderful World of Warblers. Not yet. I see one Nashville, one black and white, three yellowthroats, and one black-throated green (FOY). Four ovenbirds sing from shadows. Male myrtle visits sapsucker holes around the trunk of a sugar maple. Sips sap; punctuates meal with a burst of song. A pissed-off woodpecker flies in and screams, the sound a cat might make if you stepped on its tail. Routed warbler vanishes into spring. Sapsucker, a more-or-less beaked dowser, goes back to excavating a necklace of tiny cavities around the tree; muted taps barely audible from twenty feet. Before long (I hope), a hummingbird will visit the holes, drink the sap, and cull the insects that also came for sap; eventually select a personal sapsucker (this one?), which he'll defend against interloping hummingbirds. (Red flowers are in minimal supply in mid-May.) Hummingbirds and sapsuckers engage in a one-sided relationship called *commensalism* that benefits one species while neither helping nor harming the other—like a coyote catching ground squirrels that exit the back door as an oblivious badger, head in a hole, bores through the front.

A male rose-breasted grosbeak, eating maple buds, a study in contrast and simplicity. Like the old joke, *What's black and white and re(a)d all over?* For a birder, the answer would be grosbeak, not newspaper. Ivory-colored bill set in a black face; blood-red breast smears white chest and belly (like a fingerprint, the unique extent of red identifies individual males); black back; white rump. Inner tail feathers: black. Outer tail feathers: white. Black wings with white blotches and bars and red pits. Sings sweetly and loudly, long fluent warbles, an avian prodigy.

On the pond's south end, a pair of house wrens inspect a cavity in busted red pine. Male sings loudly, pace varying between typewriter and machine gun, an uninterrupted explosion. An unhinged serenade.

Phoebes nest building in the barn. Behind the nearby west-facing door, a little brown bat. It might be the same one I watched troll for insects above the upper pasture last evening. Twenty years ago, ten or twelve roosted behind the door. Now, thanks to white-nose syndrome, one becomes a cause for celebration.

What makes spring so fascinating? I grew tired of winter; I yearned for pulsing life, rich color, warm weather, and voices in the night. Though trending earlier and earlier during my lifetime, spring's arrival is still a prolonged, unpredictable, uncompromising event. I thrive on variety and surprise. Spring in Vermont delivers in spades. And I'm stuck at home watching.

Two months ago, I voluntarily accepted an invitation offered me by the coronavirus, what thus far has been the gilded edge of a dark cloud . . . reacquaint with Coyote Hollow, the prosaic and mundane. Face the seasons (at least at sunrise) instead of the disharmonies and uncertainties of life. I took my home ground for granted for nearly two decades, only sporadically listened to the music of The Hollow, and had forgotten how fantastic my wild surroundings were. Now, day by day, marooned by a pandemic, I rediscover my home ground and its idiosyncrasies, upgrading a vestigial geographic relationship.

Day 61

17 May 2020

The Earth laughs in flowers.
RALPH WALDO EMERSON

5:20 A.M. (sunrise one minute earlier than yesterday). 45 degrees, wind NE 2 mph. Sky: clouded over, a rumpled blanket with holes and tears in the east, radiant along the edges; lit by a hidden sun (again). What's left of the moon hides behind the eastern hills. Pillars of fog rising from the saturated ground, awnings of moisture like a jungle sunrise without parrots. Wetlands: greener and greener. Bittern calls from the northwest corner of the marsh. A pair of Canada geese fly in from the northeast, join mallard in the reeds, then exit southwest, their voices fading in the distance. Pond: surface still, legions of overwintered tadpoles, greens and bulls, the size of small fish. House wrens off the east shoreline; least flycatcher (FOY) off the west.

Coltsfoot in seed. Purple trillium, sessile bellwort, and round-leafed hepatica in flower. Big-toothed aspen catkins litter the road. Yellow birch, a riot of mustard-colored catkins, a thousand two-inch bottle-brushes, pollen sacs awaiting their appointment with the wind. Woods a quilt of pastel, a dozen shades of green, like the names of Benjamin Moore paint chips: Kelly green, avocado green, lime green, more yellow than green, emerald green. Red maple leaves (for the moment) are more red than green. Aspen is more gray than green. Pine needles dull, tired green. Mallard's head is a blend of malachite and olive, a bright, glowing shade of green.

AOR: red eft and earthworm coated in tiny pebbles, annelid chain mail. Moved both.

DOR: American toad, female, loaded with strings of black eggs, headed to the marsh; spotted salamander, breeding over, left marsh, headed home. Both are in decent shape.

Last night, not ideal migration conditions. Warblers, like paper air-planes, do better in a tailwind, stay aloft longer, cover more ground, and expend less energy. Thus far, migration across Coyote Hollow is more spill-out than fallout, more dribble than spate, more whisper than shout. Today's roster: black-throated green, black and white, northern parula (FOY), yellowthroat, ovenbird (three), yellow, blackburnian (FOY); Nashville. My last real warbler fallout, 16 May 2016, Magee Marsh, south shore of Lake Erie, northwestern Ohio. En route to western Colorado from Kenyon College, Jordan and I were overwhelmed by nineteen spe-cies. Many at eye level and arm's length, idled on railings and benches, flitted through shrubs. Exhausted warblers. Hungry warblers. Gorgeous warblers. Some so close we took portraits with cell phones. Waves of bay-breasted and Cape May warblers, birds I don't often see in Vermont. Dozens of hooded and prothonotary and cerulean warblers, birds I never see in Vermont. Birds beyond counting, as though the sky gave birth to birds. Joyous and bewildered, we just looked. The fallout also included rock-star birders Victor Emanuel and Kenn Kaufman, who we also looked at.

A migratory event not repeated here in Coyote Hollow. Four Nashville warblers and one Tennessee warbler, neither of which nest in the Volunteer State. Tennessee passing through, but Nashvilles fol-low the game plan pioneered last week by ovenbirds—divvy the valley; sing with alacrity and verve above the edges of footpaths, driveways, and woodland openings, pausing to feed now and again amid clusters of infant leaves. One Nashville in a black cherry probes old webworm webs, which hang like frayed socks. Pauses to sing a two-part song. Blackburnian sings within a veil of hemlock needles. More whisper than croon. (Who needs AARP's invitation to check my hearing? I hear blackburnian high notes, like the tinkling of distant chimes.) Female myrtle warbler visits a fresh ring of sapsucker holes, while the sapsucker, preoccupied, practices Morse code elsewhere.

Barred owl in the patch cut, hooting above the turkeys, which still ramp it up. Yard robins noisy, quiet everywhere else. Wood thrush and winter wrens (two), subdued songs. Titmice whistle loudly. Juncos and chickadees, trills and whistles. Silence from the corvids.

Three male yellowthroats bolt upright in alders, singing. Squeaky whistles. *Wich-e-ty, wich-e-ty, wich-e-ty, wich-e-ty* . . . four or five phrases, given at intervals of five or six seconds. Wear masks and practice social distancing. Poster birds for Covid-19.

Day 64

20 May 2020

When the thumb of fear lifts,
we are so alive.
MARY OLIVER

5:18 A.M. (sunrise one minute earlier than yesterday). Wind NNW less than 1 mph. Sky: immaculate, rose petal in the south, pale blue in the north. Intermittent streams: shallowest reduced to thumbprints, long and narrow; deepest, more dark slashes than ribbons of water, whispering current barely visible. Permanent streams: churning along, still polishing rock. Wetlands: peepers calling; from the cattails, guttural song of red-winged black birds; male mallards in main channel; two veeries (FOY), songs spiraling out of the willows, fluty and descending, the voice of avatars. Alder twigs, bands of tiny purple flowers, female flowers. Pond: rising mist dissipates in the cool air; flows into the marsh, morning's breath, a weak planetary exhalation. Again and again and again, the embodiment of Zen stillness.

Along the road, coltsfoot, vertical fluff, radiates around seed-like petals; superficially, seed heads look like dwarf oxeye daisies. White ash buds, knobs like knuckles dark on the end of twigs. All other trees in leaf. Baby beech leaves, which drooped yesterday, rise today. Close to horizontal. Small patches of tender sugar maple leaves on the road, some with petioles, some without. (Spring is in its infancy, already dropping leaves.) There is no sign of foul play, neither holes in the leaves nor chew marks.

Warblers: nine species. Vireos: two species: Flycatchers: three species. Thrushes: three species. Northern parulas arrived last night, singing from the crowns of white pine—toneless buzzes rising with the sun. My neck cramps watching them. Two black-throated green warblers perch close to each other in neighboring hemlocks and sing, phrases rising, falling, rising again. Birds of cool, shady woods and damp ravines, black-throated greens are as much at home in the rhododendrons and Fraser fir in the Great Smoky Mountains as in the eastern hemlocks of the Green Mountains, their devotion to place as much as to the trees. They sing their hearts out . . . hemlocks come to life. In fact, black-throated green warblers are to hemlocks what lox is to bagels: a holy alliance, each made infinitely better by the presence of the other.

Female sapsucker quietly works maple for the fifth day in a row. A pair of wood thrushes chase each other through streamside shrubs. One pauses to sing. Theodore Roosevelt declared from his North Shore home on Sagamore Hill that *our most beautiful singers are the wood thrushes*. He should have traipsed to the South Shore with Walt Whitman, across the Long Island Pine Barrens, where the poet and hermit had intimate dealings. At the moment, Coyote Hollow is all wood thrush; hermits secret themselves in cups of elaborate ground nests with warm pale blue eggs or perhaps feed helpless, grotesque chicks.

A million years before Tuvan throat-singers learned to mimic the sounds of the Russian steppe, a prototype thrush began to harmonize with himself; produced paired notes, independently and simultaneously, deep within his voice box (syrinx). Poignant and evocative, the songs of wood thrush and veery echo across Coyote Hollow and, for the moment, render every other sound less significant.

Chestnut-sided warbler croons in aspen, bird and canopy touched by the first rays of sunlight, everything below in the shade. Picks inch worms off delicate leaves, then announces: *Pleased, pleased, pleased to meet-ya.* Charismatic microfauna—white cheeks, yellow crown, chestnut sides infringe on an otherwise pure white belly and breast. Warbler bathed in butterscotch light, amid tiny, viridescent leaves . . . sweet spot of the morning.

To counterpoint the veeries and chestnut-side warblers, white-breasted nuthatch calls from the pines, short, nasal *yanks*, a tricycle horn, or a Harpo Marx impersonation.

On the pond's south end, two house wrens chase each other. Type-A personalities, house wrens could be clinically diagnosed with ADHD. Everything about them is perpetual motion, physically and acoustically. Male sings a disjointed mix: warbles, trills, hisses, bubbly notes, rising and falling. Sounds much too loud for such a small bird. Never a dull moment in the beautiful world of house wrens, the perfect antidote for Covid hysteria, my concentration refocused in a nanosecond. Wrens are devilishly chaotic, demand attention, and command attention. I forgive them for every swallow nest they've trashed, for every hole they've poked in a bluebird egg, both bittersweet infractions in the scheme of interspecies coexistence.

Feeling blue and unfocused? Covid-19 got you down? Find a house wren and come along for the ride.

On the edge of this dirt road, one of tens of thousands in the northern Appalachians, I am fortunate to wander out my front door into a beckoning landscape. How can I separate light from bird when each enhances the other?

~

11:27 A.M. 64 degrees. Wind SSE 4 mph. Sky: pristine blue. In the middle of the marsh, sinking. Blind channels and drying pockets. The shallowest is already dry or clogging with gem-green algae, closing in from the edges. To the northwest, a pyramid of stone, the ledges, where a tide of green rises toward the summit, still reddish-brown with mouse-ear oak leaves.

Yellowthroat obeys pandemic rules, follows the directive of Governor Scott, wears a mask in public, and self-isolates on the island of sweetgale. I walk sunk up to my knees in unconsolidated muck. Warbler's way of enforcing social distancing. Safe and sound, yellowthroat keeps singing. Bittern watches me watch him. Birding on an organic trampoline.

Pair of solitary sandpipers (FOY), headed north, probe the rim of the main channel. Trusting and silent. Busy foraging for aquatic insect larvae and wood frog tadpoles that hatch in the heat. I'm within twenty feet of the sandpipers. Dark back, speckled. White eye-ring and pale gray legs, the color of aspen catkins. Birds I rarely see, probing and picking along the edge of a drying pool, just across from an antediluvian turtle the size of a kitchen sink.

Green frog hops on folded reeds. Painted turtle slides off a log. Swamp sparrow trills. Hen wood duck flushes; then, a male mallard. Drinking in the afternoon, my solitude catalyzed by a pandemic . . . I'm far from my suburban roots, which I progressively outgrew by seventeen and discarded like ill-fitting shoes. I couldn't leave Long Island fast enough.

❧

Day 66

22 May 2020

*A short scuffle, and then out into the gloom, her grey
crest raised and her barred chest feathers puffed up into a
meringue of aggression and fear, came a huge old female
goshawk. Old because her feet were gnarled and dusty,
her eyes a deep, fiery orange, and she was beautiful.
Beautiful like a granite cliff or a thunder-cloud.*
HELEN MACDONALD

5:16 A.M. (sunrise same time as yesterday). 41 degrees, wind less than 1 mph. Sky: blue and thin, wispy yellow-gilded clouds; at thirty thousand feet, a pair of contrails, conspicuous because of their absence the past two months. I follow one with binoculars, heads SSW, spewing backlit emissions across the vault of heaven, a flight from Europe to JFK or Dulles. When will I board a commercial flight? Intermittent streams: ribbons of water run quietly, some barely so. Gullies dry along the road. Depressions in the woods drain into mud bowls, some attended by robins. Wetlands: anorexic mist. Two male mallards, one much lighter than the other, graze the bank of the main channel. Hen wood duck bolts from the reeds. Have the solitary sandpipers headed north, leaving the marsh to the snapping turtle, whose investment here is for life? Pond: mist rises straight up.

Warblers by descending volume of songs: ovenbird (screams); redstart; yellowthroat; chestnut-sided; black-throated green; parula; Nashville; black and white (whispers). The whisperer sings high (both voice and perch), nests low, often at the base of a tree. Fussy junco picks grit along the road, inspecting each pebble as though panning for gold. Chickadee in needle cluster of red pine, just as picky as junco. None of us is in a big hurry.

Late yesterday afternoon, a neighbor, Mike, Thetford's deputy police chief, led me along a forested crease on the northeastern slope of Coyote Hollow, not too far from his home. Halfway up an unimposing white pine, a pair of goshawks had wedged a nest, a burden of sticks decorated with a few evergreen sprigs, substantial for substantial birds. The female (much the larger of the pair) tore through a weft of branches . . . shouting, shouting, shouting, wild like a banshee. Perched. Flew. Perched. Always yelling. The male, also screaming, appeared and disappeared. Never perched. Magisterial birds, pale as moonlight. Red eyes burn holes in squirrels and hares and large songbirds. The grouses' grim reaper. For me, they're unalloyed magic, giving weight to a landscape without being seen. In fact, until yesterday, I had no idea goshawks lived here.

Aerial gymnast scorches nearly forty mph through the woods. Quick acceleration. Rapid maneuvers. Short, powerful wings; long rudder tail. Aggressive. Twisting and turning between limbs, around trees, diving into bushes and brambles, running into water after ducklings. While gravity assists a diving peregrine, a goshawk assists itself. An epitome of hyperactivity, acutely and deadly focused, a gray-feathered, heat-seeking missile. Type-A personality, maybe triple-A. A weasel with wings, a hummingbird with an appetite, goshawk burns calories. Needs plenty of food. Birds and mammals, primarily. Hunts a dozen valleys, perhaps an entire watershed, which is why goshawks are uncommon and as hard to find as truth.

Immediately, goshawks loan the Hollow their unimpeachable gravitas. Bitterns beware. Turkeys take cover.

Pine warbler pair chase each other from spruce to cherry. Chestnut-sided warbler visits the cherry, then sings. Not impressed, a female American goldfinch shoos him away. Sapsucker, a Powerbar for a goshawk, taps the same maple the fifth morning in a row.

Heading home, I think of goshawks; my view of the neighborhood has undergone a seismic shift.

Day 68

24 May 2020

History is not the prerogative of the human species.
In the living world there are millions of histories.

E. O. WILSON

5:14 A.M. (sunrise one minute earlier than yesterday). Wind SSW 1 mph, barely noticeable. Sky: blue with filigrees of white and hints of magenta; long rents between shaped and shapeless moisture, all the way to Valhalla. Permanent streams: no longer in a hurry; slowing down. Day by day, exposed sandbars widen and lengthen. Wetlands: vividly green and mistless. Pond: still surface; tailed froglets line up along the shore; rolling mist.

The valley is green from ridge to marsh. The intermittent streams stagnate, and the permanent ones run quietly. Trees, conduits between ground and sky, living science. Rain soaks into the ground. Roots siphon water. Leaves exhale moisture. Millions and millions of gallons of groundwater become clouds. One big aqueous family. A majestic cycle . . . nothing left out. My mind drifts to goshawks, somewhere in the woods, rogue birds on a broken limb . . . watching.

Ash buds opening slowly (finally). Oak leaves are more significant and greener. Black cherry flower buds ready to pop. Pin cherry already has. I imagine the spinning Earth, a landscape leavened by sunshine. A tide of chlorophyll rises impeccably and (almost) imperceptibly by the day, hour, moment. Out of Carolina and eventually reaching Coyote Hollow . . . bringing gifts of a ripening season. And me, stuck home attending the harvest.

Veery's cascading song. Behind a curtain of trees, grouse drums on a log, heedless and lonely. A seductive dance, but he can't be sure who's watching. Nearly a century ago, a winter influx of goshawks on Martha's Vineyard eliminated the last heath hens on Earth. For a preforming grouse, attracting a mate and not a predator . . . life is brittle and on the cusp of paralytic fear.

High in big-toothed aspen, framed by a cluster of bright green leaves, red-eyed vireo sings a tedious song. On and on and on, ad infinitum. Above the vireo, sapsucker rings a limb. But the morning belongs to black-throated green warblers and ovenbirds, vigorously singing, jockeying for territory, however temporary, allocating resources within every dip and outcrop of the Hollow . . . the Great Land Grab of 2020, repeated each year, endlessly until time stops. To me, a roadside attraction holding a pair of leashed German shepherds, the birds are oblivious. Sing and sing and sing some more.

Farther down the valley, a fluffed-out chestnut-sided warbler perches on a cherry twig, trimmed in warm light, a voice like Nina Simone, husky and sweet. Veeries sing morsels of song, picking up the choral slack left by hermit thrushes who are now handicapped by domestic chores. Robin wanders up a dry streambed, flipping matted leaves, finds a worm, and then another. Pileated laughs, loudly and infectiously. Blue jay cobbles together a song, part honk, part hawk.

❧

11:46 A.M. 64 degrees. Wind SSE 10 mph, precisely what the warblers and I waited for two weeks ago. Large bird sails over the trees, in and out of view; across a bay of sedge and cattail, wings tucked, long tail pinched. I'm not sure what it is . . . though I'm sure what it isn't. Not a broad-winged hawk nor a red-shouldered hawk. Not a red-tailed hawk nor a raven. Definitely not a bald eagle. I'm left with two choices: crow and goshawk (wishful thinking).

Black and white warbler on a maple limb, striped like a cartoon jailbird, sings a song barely audible. An hors d'oeuvre for a goshawk. Red-eyed vireo, a between-meal snack, sings tediously and tenuously, not up to his usual standards. A more substantial morsel, the robin picks through the leaf litter, more to its breast than brick-colored feathers. Goshawk knows that.

And the day continues . . .

Goshawk

The Promise of Sunrise

Day 71

27 May 2020

The best remedy for those who are afraid, lonely or unhappy
is to go outside, somewhere where they can be quite alone
with the heavens, nature and God . . .
And I firmly believe that nature brings solace to all.

ANNE FRANK

5:12 A.M. (sunrise same time as yesterday). 61 degrees, wind N less than 1 mph, a morning without breath; mosquito weather. Sky: clear, moonless. Mount Ascutney is eclipsed by haze. Intermittent streams: puddling. Some already dry. Permanent streams: the marsh's umbilical connection from the east moves far less water and freight than last month, substantially quieting down (veeries pick up the slack). Wetlands: mist-filled, far shoreline obscured. Pond: male mallard on the bank, veiled by mist; nearby, chestnut-sided warbler in small black cherry, eye-level and arm's length away. Sings, head back, beak to the sky, guttural and predictable. Not likely headed for a 2021 Grammy nomination. Even the dogs notice.

Windrow of yellow birch catkins gathers along the road. Ash buds open; leaves emerald green and lacy. Embedded in fog, one sapling reminds me of a Japanese rice painting; every twig of every angled branch supports a bouquet of delicate compound leaves. As if to highlight the sense of the Far East, two chickadees, black-throated blue warbler (FOY), and Tennessee warbler measure several clusters and tweeze inchworms (*Geometrid* moth larva). Mammal-like, ash has separate sexes. As a boy playing on the sandlots of Long Island, I was under the spell of white ash, the only wood that ever spoke to me. Its pitch, its resonance. I lived for that sound. Sitting in the bleachers at Yankee Stadium, light years from home plate, I held my breath whenever Mickey Mantle launched a baseball. Oh, such a distinctive chill-producing *crack* of the bat. White ash and white ash only. Who had ever heard of an aluminum baseball bat?

DOR: pre-shed milk snake, skin dulled by winter; large enough to swallow a chipmunk; slow enough to be run over on her way to the marsh, to a smorgasbord of rodents.

AOR: robin and junco grit-gathering. And a slug that appears lost.

Chickadee preens under a wing, held at a crooked angle. I stop to watch. Mosquitos stop to feed.

Last night, I heard gray tree frogs (*Dryophytes versicolor*; FOY) on their way to wetlands' nether regions. An uvular trill or three spilling out of the aspens. Vermont's version of a chameleon. Inside thighs bright, eye-popping yellow, everything else variable: green, gray, black, brown, and almost white. Unlike a true chameleon, the frog transitions its outfit slowly, too slowly to notice. Gray tree frog once showed me the only ruby-throated hummingbird nest I've ever seen. Some years ago, looking through the viewfinder of my camera, framing a tree frog on a branch, an out-of-focus hummingbird passed into my field of view, then settled onto her nest just behind the frog: tiny, lichen-decorated, and scarcely as big as a thimble.

∼

10:32 A.M. 78 degrees (starting to cook). Wind SSE 3 mph. In a dip on the valley's eastern rim, just above a rock outcrop, the female goshawk spots me looking for her. Flies just above the canopy, screaming. Lands in full view, then flies, lands, flies . . . again. Stout and maneuverable, a Jim Brown among birds. If I had to draft a football team composed solely of diurnal birds of prey, the goshawk's my fullback, no question . . . maybe the entire backfield rolled into one robust, energetic bundle of life. (Peregrine's my wide receiver, also no question.)

Goshawk leads me around. Hermit thrush and blackburnian warbler sing in hemlock shade, unfazed that they live within the shadow of a Grim Reaper. Neighborhood songbirds, background vocals for drowsy hawklets. Snack-packs for the adults.

Rose-breasted grosbeak sings high in maple, a heartfelt song that reminds me of my boys, when every Rosy initiated bursts of unbridled enthusiasm, short celebrations of black and white and red that lasted as long as the bird stayed in view. Our world always more vibrant for it. Thoughts of boys entwine with grosbeak lyrics, unspooling primal memories, a salve for loneliness and disorientation Covid brings.

Casey and Jordan named *Coyote Hollow* as homage to wild canids that sang them to sleep the night we moved in nearly a quarter-century ago. This was their valley, a synthesis of wet and dry, the seat of their childhood. They grew up on a landscape gorged with detail, often roaming with abandon, unfettered from time and, momentarily, from responsibility. Encouraged by their mother (and later Annie), they gathered tadpoles, cocoons, and little snakes with red bellies; incubated snapping turtle eggs and milk snake eggs; discovered where vultures nested and otters played. Cared for a weasel and a kestrel. Merged

Annie and William into their lives. Coyote Hollow forever colors Casey and Jordan's memory, beauty tinged with sadness. The seat of life's earliest and most complex lessons . . . and their mother's ashes are here to remind them.

Day 73

29 May 2020

Her feathers, their quiet and their modest hue
No remit from all that spring requires
While his give honest signal of desire
Blood-red, his heart worn upon his breast

Apart, they journeyed north, and together
Found this welcome span of trees
From their crowns, he sang, hoarse and sweet
Concealed, she heard, and then revealed.

PEPPER TRAIL

5:11 A.M. (sunrise same time as yesterday). 68 degrees, wind SSE 10 mph, mosquitos held at bay (mostly). Sky: hoary and bright; very humid. (I marinate inside a denim jacket.) Not a morning to hang laundry. I'm not sure the atmosphere can hold any more moisture without springing a leak. An encapsulation of May 2020: snow to mosquitos, quickly; a smattering of migrants, some still on the move. Intermittent streams: on life support. Permanent streams: creep and whisper; channels narrow to a heartbeat of puddles. Wetlands: red-shouldered hawk, fixed to the last snag standing, watches the marsh wake up, an unconfined perspective. Flushes. Doe, swollen with fawn, idles in the road, staring at me. Bounds into the marsh, tail up, vanishing into the reeds like a magician's trick. Dogs lollygag, unaware, tongues extended, moisture condensing and dripping. By now, wolves would have organized a hunt and drawn a strategy in the sand. Wolves to dogs, five thousand years of selective breeding; the equivalent of genetic root canal. Pond: agitated surface.

Red oak catkins: clustered strings hang like confetti from leaf axils; compared to *zaftig* catkins of aspen and birch, oaks are anemic. Oak leaves not fully grown are already developing oak galls. Oak itself is a popular restaurant, either sit-down or take-out. Acorns keep all winter (unlike white oak, which sprouts in the fall) and feed the masses: crow, blue jay, and squirrels bury them for the future. Turkey, grouse, bear, deer, gray fox, raccoon, and small rodents beyond naming eat them on site. While working on a master's degree, I unzipped dozens of fishers caught during the New Hampshire trapping season, their stomachs jammed with acorns and apples (not porcupine or house cat or chickens).

Yellow birch drops more catkins. Crabapple and cherry petals sweep across the lawn. Miterwort and starflower blooming.

Warblers: black-throated blue; black-throated green; chestnut-sided, yellowthroat, Nashville, black and white, ovenbird. Although perhaps not the most numerous warbler, ovenbird by far the most conspicuous; calls attention to himself . . . like Hermione Granger impatiently waving her hand in class. Olive-sided flycatcher (FOY) in alders, singing, a brief respite before moving on. Around the time the Vietnam War heated up, Dr. Wise, my ornithology prof, told me the olive-sided says, *quick three beers, quick three beers.* (A mnemonic device suitable for an undergraduate.) Seems too early to drink, but what do I know? I didn't arrive here on the far side of midnight. A more decorous chestnut-sided warbler in black cherry (again) sings without a reference to alcohol. Favorite tree, though moored to a different twig.

Ruby-throated hummingbird and evening grosbeak at the feeders. Scarlet tanager high in ash, screened by leaves closer to yellow than blue. Standing under the trees looking straight up, I see red, a most brilliant red. Tanager red, a shade suitable for Crayola. Transparently gorgeous, a jungle bird, straight out of a Costa Rican rainforest. Hemorrhages song: five rapid notes, raspy and unabated, a song more powerful than despair. If rose-breasted grosbeaks sound like robins that have taken voice lessons, tanagers sound like robins with pack-a-day habits.

⁓

12:16 P.M. 80 degrees, wind S 9 mph. Sky: a mountain of clouds, one leaking. Three goshawk chicks, white as snowballs, hug the rim of the nest, seventy-five feet above the ground, fifteen feet below the canopy. Untamable stares. Crèche: shaped like a squat ice cream cone, a platform of sticks. A world on the half shell. Glimpsed through tangled limbs, mother goshawk flies from tree to tree, hollering. Dad hunts twenty-square miles of east-central Vermont and west-central New Hampshire, a hypothetical line that extends two-and-a-half miles in every direction from the nest. This implies, among other vital statistics, that a maple creemee could be picked up at King Cone on his way home.

For a magical moment, I stand in the glow of goshawks, unleashed from the coronavirus. A black and yellow butterfly floats by.

Day 75

31 May 2020

Some things happen only once, twice in a lifetime.
The world is full of signs and wonders that come, and go,
and if you are lucky you might be alive to see them.
HELEN MACDONALD

5:09 A.M. (sunrise one minute earlier than yesterday). 45 degrees, at 11 mph, the north wind speaks in tongues, hijacking warbler songs, dispersing pollen, and holding down mosquitos. Ravens at play, four black birds barrel-rolling on a cool stream of air. Tree crowns in perpetual motion, rough ride for a bit of bird. Sky: clouds on the move, trimmed in rose-colored sunlight. Intermittent streams: damp gutters in green woods. Permanent streams: infused by showers, a little fuller, a little louder. Wetlands: pileated exits a wall of spruce, undulates over the marsh, flashing black and white wings. The erect red crest reminds me of a pterodactyl. Sunlight turns the woodpecker into unabridged wonder and the marsh into a luminous sea of green motion. Pond: wind-driven current; frogs on the shore; tadpoles in the shallows. The morning beckons.

Oak galls on the road, soft, round, green, packed with tiny wasp eggs. Above the galls, raspy-voiced tanager, screened by leaves, sings. Pondside chestnut-sided warbler clings to pin cherry twig, up and down, back and forth, sings amid white flowers.

DOR: spotted salamander, charismatic megafauna of nearby vernal pool. Chipmunk is attended by a botfly and a pair of scarab beetles.

AOR: two earthworms, weighed down by grit, struggle west. The crossing guard: I help them. Slug, antennae up and far less gritty than the worm, also heads west with no help from me. Hermaphrodites embody the full complement of pronouns.

Catbird in the alders, adjacent to the marsh, sings—long, rambling, harsh, inventive, rarely repetitive. No thrush. An off-key jumble of discord. A mimic mimicking no one . . . except for a cat. When Jordan and William were young, Annie and I introduced them to simple bird songs and calls. One afternoon, I called their attention to a gentle *meow, meow*, the buzz of a catbird, which I said sounded just like a hungry kitty. Jordan, his Yankee cap askew, stepped off the road and into the shrubs for a closer look. *Pop*, he announced, loud enough to stir leaves. *It's not a catbird. It's a real kitty* . . . and that's how a cat entered our lives.

Chestnut-sided warbler sings in pin cherry, framed by white flowers. Pauses to eat a green caterpillar. Resumes song until displaced by a hungry, noticeably bigger chickadee. Flies to the next tree, black cherry still in bud, the tree I usually find him in. More singing, more eating. Alder flycatcher (FOY) in alders (where else?). Wood thrush moved on. Hermit thrush incubating or rearing chicks. Veeries take over the airwaves, voices spiraling down the musical scale. Then fade . . . like May itself.

Back home: great crested flycatcher joins tanager in oaks; phoebes nest in the barn, the garage, and the solar hot-water pipes. A small colony; everybody calls at once. Three male rose-breasted grosbeaks and two evening grosbeaks, a convocation, jockey for position on the bird-feeders. Female grosbeaks join doves on the ground, demurely eating what males spill. Blue jays everywhere—compost pile, raspberry patch, the lawn, the feeders, the barn—and quiet.

Last night, at 7:54 P.M., snapping turtle, heavy with eggs, visited the front lawn. An epic trek, more than half a mile from the wetlands. Probably took days; life in the slow, prehistoric lane. Route (best guess): north out of the marsh via the permanent upper stream, disembarked in lower pasture, crossed through both, and entered the commodious front yard. Dug a series of nest scrapes between the blue patio stone; none to her liking. I gathered her, holding a handful of the tail and the back of her spiky carapace, placed her in a garbage pail, and ferried her to the pond's outlet stream, the deep one that flows into the south end of the marsh. She wasn't happy. Splash. Sink. Freedom . . . try again for a suitable nest site.

Snapping turtle left her essence in the car and patio stone. This morning, dogs visit the front yard, noses to the ground, vigorously inhaling the turtle.

I recall reading an interview with Edward Abbey, in which he said he was willing to rail about our abuses of nature half of the time if he could be lost in the desert, alone, the other half. Mary Oliver, the poet laureate of wrens and owls, also rejoiced in the great family of things. *If you pay attention, you see more*, she wrote. Unlike Abbey, Oliver never scolded humanity about environmental missteps. Instead, she wrote of the beauty and mystery of nature trimmed in language so gorgeous her poems ushered me outside. A pandemic confined me to my home ground, but a curmudgeon and a poet reaffirmed that Coyote Hollow, a valley within progressively bigger valleys, like landscaped Russian dolls, has all the drama of Earth.

Oliver and Abbey understood that to help Earth, you need to love Earth. To love Earth, you must be within her circle of intimates; you need to speak the language of wind and be open to scenes that move you for reasons you cannot understand.

I admire a bird I took for granted. Robin, schmutz on his beak, scolds me; an *ordinary* bird in marvelous light bestows blessings.

Day 77

02 June 2020

The hawk's cry is as sharp as its beak.
EDWARD ABBEY

5:08 A.M. (sunrise one minute earlier than yesterday). 36 degrees, wind ESE less than 1 mph. (More April than June; dressed in down and gloved up.) Sky: Coyote Hollow lies pale under a mattress of fog, a homogeneous topography. A devoured landscape, swaddled, constricted, planed. Gone: Mount Ascutney, Gove Hill, Gile Mountain, and the imposing ledges to the west. I can barely make out the barn and pasture fence. Useless binoculars turn fog to chowder. Permanent streams: shed heat, contributing to ground fog. Wetlands: shed fog and mallard, which flies directly overhead (otherwise, I wouldn't have seen him). Pond: sheds heat, a cylinder of mist, rising and sprawling, mixing with everything else. Frogs and tadpoles bedded down.

Mosquitos stunned by cold, flying a suicide mission. And for the moment, I happily disregard ticks.

Maidenhair ferns brighten somber woods, lacy parasols. Willow seed heads have swollen, ready to open. Big-toothed aspen, seventy feet tall and near the end of life, slants toward the road. More than two-feet thick at breast height, lower branches dead, punky and leafless, upper branches barely in leaf. A fast-growing, short-lived tree, losing out to maples in the struggle for sunlight. Aspen wood is soft, easy to excavate, and perfect for small-beaked woodpeckers, whose cavities provide excellent apartment hunting opportunities for titmice, chickadees, house wrens, and nuthatches ... but foreclosure imminent.

Red-shouldered hawk impales the morning with razor cries. Flycatchers outnumber warblers, five to four: pewee in maples; least in red pines; phoebe in the barn; great crested in hardwoods; alder in alders, wrapped in fog, prepares for a give-away, repeats the harsh mantra *free-BEE, free-BEE, free-BEE*. He gives away affirmation and assurance that the morning's fruits, low and mutable, are mine to harvest at no cost, a spiritual food bank ... and all I have to do is go outside.

Tanager in oak and blue-headed vireo in ash, both solo, heedless of fog and temperature, four degrees from ice. Nothing keeps the red-eyed vireo from singing its wearisome rounds ad nauseam. Pileated laughs. Hermit thrush, revived by cold; voice of Joan Baez. Owl in hemlocks, barking; between the density of the evergreens and density of the fog, might as well be midnight.

Goshawks hide in unbroken woods, waiting to make an appearance, to impinge on other lives. Responsible parents of three. Yesterday, a neighbor emailed me a photo of the female hawk, standing on a heap of wild turkey six times her size, wings spread, mantling. Stiletto talons impaled in flesh. Feathers scattered across the lawn like an eviscerated pillow. Goshawk the broncobuster, a life-and-death rodeo in the front yard. Life ebbed away. Food-chain decorum: crystalline and profound.

But how do goshawks hunt when the lights are out?

Chestnut-sided Warbler

Day 80

05 June 2020

If you think you are too small to make a
difference, try sleeping with a mosquito.
Dalai Lama

5:07 A.M. (sunrise one minute earlier than yesterday). 60 degrees, wind breathless out of the north (mosquitos everywhere and hungry; the late George Craig, a biology professor at Notre Dame University, predicted that it would take 1,120,000 mosquito bites to exsanguinate an average-size human). Sky: made for the Hudson River School; subtly overcast, blue-gray to white, some clouds edged in pale rose; some ruffled, others skin tight; a portal into the ionosphere, an excellent glimpse of infinity. Intermittent streams: despair beneath archways of ferns. Permanent streams: languish, shrink, and almost inaudible, channel bottoms drying, mudflats extending. Wetlands: main channel in the marsh, a crease in green reeds that push up everywhere. Bittern in the north end *ga-lunking*. Pond: not a ripple.

Merganser and seven ducklings cruise in and out of a mesh of mist. See me and retreat to the far shoreline, flanked by emerging cattails. Huddled and alert, ducklings' dark and light slashes like sunlight on water. Frozen in place, hen's expressive crest slicked back or pompadoured; in between, a composite of Little Richard and a Spartan helmet. The ducklings hatched on the side of a hemlock in a nest box Annie had given me one birthday. Standing in the rounded doorway, looking north, the soft, bouncy mergansers could gaze across the cattails and sedges, the distant pastures to my front yard . . . where they may have caught a glimpse of me filling the bird feeders in my underwear.

To reach the pond, ducklings crossed the marsh, in and out of a phalanx of cattails and congestion of alders, climbed the west road bank, crossed the dirt road, and climbed the east bank. The pond offers aquatic insects, crayfish, and jumbo tadpoles, some the size of small fish already sprouting legs and gulping air . . . *Bon appetit*.

Red-shouldered hawks above the marsh, circling and calling, longer, louder, sharper than blue jay's knockoff, which tumbles out of the treetops, an avian version of a tribute band. Red-shoulder's original falls from the sky, a thousand feet or more. Second hawk appears. The two fly in tandem, rising and falling on a whim; voices like lances pierce the sky.

Chestnut-sided warbler, ovenbird, and, of course, red-eyed vireo rule the airwaves. Singing, singing, singing. Lone redstart chimes in. Two robins, unbraided, chase each other along a stonewall; wings akimbo slap ferns. Seems serious. Hermit thrush broadcasts from the eastern rim of the Hollow, rendering everything else pedestrian. Sapsucker, a month tapping a sugar maple, prospects for sap and harvests bugs drawn to it. Pileated wallops a trunk, a message of intent . . . excellent echoes. Pack-a-day scarlet tanager in oaks, harsh song, gorgeous color; screened by green. Tom Waits of songbirds. Sartorial elegance unburdened by self-regard.

I visited the goshawk nest yesterday—a thick, cupless platform pressed into the splayed pine trunk; framed by a whorl of four limbs that grow upward at forty-five-degree angles. Chicks watched me. White faces streaked with brown, darkening. The female escorted me through the woods, screaming; her laser eyes bored holes in the morning. In the duff below the nest, a chipmunk head, red lungs attached, a snack, more concept than substance. And an oval pellet, tightly packed with gray squirrel fur. No bones. Chicks, growing by the moment, need a lunch wagon.

Predation: a by-product of population. Life beneath the canopy is dynamic, dramatic, spellbinding . . . but seldom understood. Every species has a carrying capacity; the population size that a wild neighborhood supports. And that number fluctuates. The *availability* and *vulnerability* of prey determine the goshawk's hunting success. Squirrels and chipmunks become vulnerable and available when overcrowded and food insecure, when lovestruck, or when young and reckless . . . and goshawks are there to dampen their enthusiasm.

Pellets: a woodland vignette, secrets revealed. With more corrosive stomach acids than owls, hawks spit up feathers and hair but not many bones. I've picked apart merlin pellets packed with taxicab-yellow feathers; red-tailed hawk with rabbit fur; snowy owl with vole skulls, sardonically grinning back; barn owl with shrews and mice bones; horned owl with everything from black racer to woodcock to mink. One goshawk pellet I gathered last week, a cylinder of gray squirrel fur and a framework of ribs, held a pair of broken, hollow femurs from a midsize bird, perhaps a robin or jay . . . the prize at the bottom of the Cracker Jack box.

The best pellet I ever collected was donated by a short-eared owl. Summer 1978, a salt marsh in Oak Beach, Long Island. In front of a derelict dory, Richie (from Apollo Beach) and I filled a grocery bag with several hundred pellets regurgitated by a family of eight: two adults and six chicks, the last known short-eared owl nest on Long Island. One pellet, opened years later, held an aluminum bird band, which I mailed to the United States Fish and Wildlife Service in Patuxent, Maryland. An acknowledgment letter from USFW said the band belonged to a common tern chick, ringed by Michael Gochfeld from Rutgers University Medical School. Thirty-eight years later, eighty miles off the coast of Nantucket, on a boat in the Gulf Stream searching for white-faced storm petrel, Richie and I met Gochfeld. He remembered the band, the only one ever retrieved from an owl pellet and returned years later.

Under the spell of goshawks, Coyote Hollow shapeshifts into an even wilder, more remote valley, a resplendent illusion of isolation, primordial North America reimagined . . . four miles from the elementary school, five miles from the interstate. Beguiled by emergent beauty, I pause in the audience of young hawks, something vital swirling inside me, a precoital level of desire and suspense.

Day 83

08 June 2020

We get into trouble these days
because we think the only magic is what we do.
JOHN HAY

5:06 A.M. (sunrise one minute earlier than yesterday). 41 degrees, wind ESE less than 1 mph. Sky: three-quarter moon midway above the valley, lit by an unseen sun. Primarily clear; rose-tinted, pastel clouds to the south; small groups of fine lines and serpentine tufts. Tendrils of mist rise from the marsh and pond, muting colors (mostly green). River water above the Ompompanoosuc, fog hangs at canopy level and traces the river into the hinterlands, joining Connecticut River fog, a vaporous watershed. Permanent streams: barely invigorated by yesterday's thunderstorms. Wetlands: north-end bittern, calling, a volley of four or five *ga-lunks*; a pause of fifteen or twenty seconds, and then another volley. Pause. Volley. Pause. Volley. The pattern began at 3:45 in the morning, when the moon cast pale across the lawn. Pond: south end, perched on a broken red pine, hairy woodpecker chick, still fluffy, patiently and quietly watches its father flick pieces of bark off the trunk. Each scrap floats earthward, spinning and drifting. A slow-motion descent. Eventually, the woodpecker finds a grub and feeds the chick, his long, thick tongue-depressor bill deep in the chick's throat.

The long-suffering chick swallows and blinks . . . not quite the mayhem I recall after Little League games when boys rolled into the kitchen hell-bent on dinner.

Black cherry in bloom, but chestnut-sided warbler sings elsewhere. Deer bolts across the road. Dogs alert in a way they seldom are for Nashville warblers. Blue jays out of the nest follow parents to the feeders, begging. Spot-breast robin chick trails parents, also begging. Crow family assembles on the railing of the compost pile. Chicks mechanically cluck, longer, faster, sharper than a tree frog—rapid, hollow call I don't often hear, except in the front yard . . . *tattoo, tattoo, tattoo.*

Red-winged blackbird perched on an island of sweet gale screeches; a flash of red epaulets emphatically disabusing other blackbirds of any claim to the title. One afternoon, many years ago, when we were college roommates, Stephan, an observant sort, reported that a noisy and nameless flock of birds had just passed through our backyard. They were black birds, he said, with a red patch on each wing. *Oh, red-winged blackbirds.* Duh. Stephan thought my suggestion apocryphal and began to laugh sincerely. Now, more than fifty years later, we're still laughing.

Of course, the origin of many bird names is not so obvious. Take the name *goose*. With the domestication of the horse, people moved east and west across the steppes of Eurasia, and the names of birds moved with them. Goose—the oldest, most tenacious of all bird names still in use—dates back more than five thousand years to an ancient Paleo-Indo European language. A concept euphemistically known as *caveman taxonomy* implies that anything fat and edible, abundant and highly migratory, like geese, would be quickly named. That one stuck.

Black-throated blue warbler, black-throated green warbler, and alder flycatcher, the origin of their names as evident as their songs. The etymology of the name *bittern*, still booming in the northeast corner of the marsh, however, is not so obvious. The name goes back two thousand years to Pliny the Elder, the Roman naturalist who thought the bird sounded like a bellowing bull. *Bittern* first appeared in English in 1530, from the Middle English *bitoure*, from Anglo-French *butor*, from Vulgar Latin *butitarus*, a combination of Latin for hawk (*buteo*) and bull (*taurus*).

◠◡

The old maple snag along the edge of the road, barkless, crownless, and woodpecker riddled, collapsed, chips on the ground like prayer beads. I had stuck my fist in the oval craters, many beyond my wrist. Rotten wood, a gift for northern red-backed salamanders and ring-necked snakes (the root of both names as obvious as that of the Red Sox), which convene beneath disassembled trees. At five hundred to a pound, red-backed salamanders are the most abundant vertebrates in the northern hardwood forest by both weight and number. According to Al Breisch, a retired New York State herpetologist, in deciduous woods, like Coyote Hollow, red-backed salamanders weigh twice as much as songbirds and about the same as small mammals. Calculations based on statewide surveys suggest possibly fourteen billion live in New York leaf litter, about fourteen thousand tons of salamanders, a primary source of energy flow throughout the woodlands.

Along the side of the garage, red-backed salamanders convene under the woodpile, rocks, and bark slabs, and slither toward dark quarters—snakelike—when exposed to daylight, more swim than walk. Less than four inches long and thin as a pencil, backs the color of a robin's breast, bellies and sides the color of lead. A less-common color morph lacks the red back, though I've never found one in The Hollow. Once in a blue moon, I'd find an egg sac under a log, suspended like a lantern. No spawning run. Disconnected from standing water, redback tadpoles metamorphose inside the egg and hatch as miniature replicas of the adults. Lungless, redbacks breathe through their skin, called *cutaneous respiration*, advancement on the more massive, more primitive spotted salamanders, which gather by the dozens to spawn in the marsh and pond, throats gently pulsing with air.

Along the sandy outwash plains of the South Shore of Long Island, I knew but one species of salamander, the red-backed. A resident of maritime woods. A prisoner of basement window wells and forgotten cemeteries. For me, redbacks were a diversion from the *long*, stagnant Yom Kippur service, when children under thirteen were ushered out of the synagogue during *Yizkor*, public mourning, to avoid witnessing mascara and rouge smeared like war paint down the faces of bereaved mothers. Behind the Wantagh Jewish Center, hard on the southeast corner of

Woodbine Avenue, was a mile-long greenbelt, framed by Seamans Neck Road on the east and fenced-off suburbia on the west; the woods extend to Park Avenue, close to the Long Island Railroad. I caught salamanders and green frogs during Yizkor, my dress shoes and pants cuffs caked with mud, my tie askew, dirt under my fingernails. Having fasted for twenty-four hours, my sad, hungry parents never complained . . . unless I tore my pants.

～

The north-end bittern, foraged in the furnace of intense competition, is more concerned with maintaining property rights and raising a family than with derivation of his name. Erect and motionless, he salutes the sun, repeatedly calling, an otherworldly sound, hollow and resonant, setting the morning on end.

At home, the morning morphs into a cacophonous blend of flutes, twangs, quacks, croaks, belches, tweets, slurs, hoots, *ga-lunks*, whistles, caws, barks, peeps, buzzes, chides, honks, screams, trills, warbles. Two notes. Three notes. Long chains of notes. Piccolo melodies and pack-a-day phrases.

A lifeline of voices moors me to The Hollow.

Day 84

09 June 2020

*Why do the world's shadows come
so close as its wonders beckon?*
HENRI COLE

5:06 A.M. (sunrise same time as yesterday). 51 degrees, wind E 2 mph. Sky: overcast, pallid highlights, lightly drizzling. My morning transformed, I'm on a goshawk mission. Skipping the marsh and pond. On the eastern rim of Coyote Hollow, I walk into cool, green shade, directly to the nest.

The female screams, the goshawk playbook (no surprise). But a distant, deadened repertoire without commitment. Then, she hears me shuffle leaves; her calls ratchet up. Goshawk appears and escorts me through the woods at a respectful distance, just below the canopy, more casual than cautious, a gray ghost offhandedly calling. Through binoculars, I see the nest, which appears empty. No twitchy wings. No dark eyes staring. A platform of sticks vacant of curiosity. Mother goshawk remains nearby, subdued (for a goshawk). I doubt the chicks fledged. I never saw them exercising their flight muscles, fanning the air with preparatory wingbeats. Were they something else's lunch, a dietary reversal of fortune? Goshawk settles on a crooked limb a hundred feet from the nest and continues soft, admonishing cries; red eyes hollow out the morning. The hawk, the nest, and I form an equilateral triangle.

Mother goshawk is exquisite: fine gray barring, scrimshaw on bone-white undersides, back dark as dusk. White undertail coverts, wet and splayed, hang down like a miniskirt, setting off the black-and-gray-striped tail, the rudder, the instrument of hairpin turns. Goshawk never takes her red eyes off me. Stares me down. Big head capped in black. Face striped: dark mask, white above and below. Throat white, finely barred. Bulky body tapered at both ends, thick in the middle, a well-muscled football of a bird that flies like a fighter jet, pivots on a dime . . . forty miles an hour among trunks and limbs. Raises hell in the woods.

Nervy blue jay, the epitome of *chutzpah*, calls and then torments hawk, passing back and forth in front of her sober stare. Goshawk tucks her head, weaves back and forth as though avoiding punches, then retreats farther into the woods . . . and I home.

10:32 A.M. 70 degrees, wind SSE 8 mph. Canopy in motion, gently rocks an empty nest. I'm in the company of five biologists, two licensed bird banders and one eight-year-old playing hooky from third-grade online. Adult hawks, conspicuous by their absence, hunt in silence somewhere else. The chicks' fate becomes the subject of Talmudic debate. In the spirit of Holmes and Watson, we comb the vicinity of the nest, unraveling the abduction, a grimly fascinating tale of a food-chain blasphemy. Several feathers in the duff, one blooming in its sheath like a rose on a vine. Breast down stuck on branch stubs; two broken lines run down the tree trunk, lint from the fabric of life, from below the nest to the ground, a path of consequence. Scratches on pine bark. In some fluted corner of the valley, bobcat kittens, also fashioned of hunger and bile, build muscle out of hawk.

My plan vanquished, I head home under summer's sun ascending. Somewhere beyond the eastern rim, a goshawk calls—*kree, kree, kree, kree, kree*—a forlorn cry not meant for me.

I remember the night you died. The rattling of your last breath. And the immeasurable sadness I felt without you. To know I would continue the trek alone, in the house on the hill, the sole curator of childhood dreams. You loved hawks, their clean and deadly precision, their sleek beauty. You adored rose-breasted grosbeaks and every flower that ever bloomed above treeline. You laughed and grieved easily. You would have cried to know the chicks' fate. Your eyes twinkled with sympathy even as the light went out.

A luna moth wing, pink and green on the road, like heaven and earth, a covenant with darkness. Even galaxies die.

Day 89

14 June 2020

*Genius is nothing more nor less
than childhood recovered at will.*

CHARLES PIERRE BAUDELAIRE

5:06 A.M. (sunrise same time seventh day in a row). 37 degrees, wind S 1 mph. Sky: lines of dark clouds in the southwest, pink blushed; clean blue in the north. Kaleidoscopic metamorphosis; clouds elongate, disassemble, disappear. Sun a flickering spotlight. Permanent streams: slowing down, pooling; water striders skate the surface without being swept away. Mudbank expanding. Wetlands: thin mist (beyond subtle) softening the far shore like dawn through a screen door. Worn cloud stalls at treetop height, above the marsh, unsubstantiated moisture. The East Branch of the Ompompanoosuc is substantiated by mist. Chestnut-sided warbler flies out of alders, a green caterpillar crosswise in his bill. Pond: sheds heat, thin tendrils of mist roll southeast, emaciated moisture, and then gone, recalled by the sky. Mother merganser, crest tight and face honed to a point, and eight chicks move as one, bunched and vigilant, close to the security of cattails. Along the southwestern shoreline, wild iris blooms, blue laced with gold, medallions of the saturated earth. Twanging green frog needs tuning. Over Lake Fairlee, a northbound loon wails, one long transformative cry.

Aspen leaves flutter; oak and maple oblivious. Sapsucker drills maple, a self-assignment that's lasted more than a month, a line of fresh, oozing holes inside the heartwood, stripes and rings, sylvan Braille read by thirsty insects and birds.

Audio waterboarding: red-eyed vireos and ovenbirds. More subdued: least flycatcher, Nashville warbler, black-throated blue warbler, swamp sparrow, white-throated sparrow, song sparrow, winter wren. Chestnut-sided warbler sings in front of me. I can almost touch him; a beautiful bird—yellow crown; black eyeliner and mustache; white throat, chest, and belly; chestnut sides; wings and back streaked black and white. Veery, the volume turned down, spins a muted version of his song, soft and distant but still grand. Robin searches the road; finds another smashed June bug. Swallows and blinks. A little late to the dance, turkey calling and strutting, preparing for the 2021 draft.

Motormouthed blue jays in and out of the hardwoods. Chicks begging and gesturing. Parents braced for days of provisioning, screaming what amounts to avian profanity, their emancipation a week or more away.

❧

Six years after Linny died, Casey left for college. I braced myself for an emotional goodbye. Relinquishing influence and changing roles (any role)—never easy for me—I fully expected to melt down. Jordan and I helped lug Casey's things up the zigzaggy dormitory stairs. Casey organized his room (not exactly how I would have) and settled on his bed for a moment of leisure. When it was time say goodbye, the three of us walked downstairs, emotions airborne on a congested August afternoon. As Casey bent to hug his little brother, Jordan leaped into his arms, legs scissoring his waist, and began to cry uncontrollably. Ten years old . . . facing an absence of permanency beyond the impact of his own mother's death.

❧

Blue jays are the single most important distributor of oak trees, the Johnny Appleseed of acorns. Twelve thousand years ago, the range of Eastern and Midwestern oak trees—northern red, southern red, swamp red, scarlet, white (my favorite), swamp white, black, post, pin, chinquapin, chestnut, willow, overcup, basket, bur, shingle, blackjack, scrub—expanded northward out of refuges in the deep and ice-free south because jays ferried acorns in their bills and crops . . . hungry and impartial foresters who reshuffled the continent's vegetation. Disseminators of oaks. Jays plant acorns here and there, one per site, just under the duff, often miles from the parent tree. Gray squirrels, who receive too much credit as foresters, they bury their harvest in piles deeper in the ground close to the parent tree.

Many years ago, Les Line, then the editor of *Audubon Magazine*, published a series of photographs of a blue jay standing on the rim of a Baltimore oriole nest. Leaning far into the stocking nest, the jay pulled out a hapless chick, which I assumed was fed to its own fledglings. Some people don't like blue jays; they think them rude and aggressive. Blue jays are, of course, much more: intelligent, resourceful, gregarious, loquacious, supercilious, adaptable, bellicose . . . more or less just like us.

Day 90

15 June 2020

Spend the afternoon.
You can't take it with you.
Annie Dillard

5:06 A.M. (sunrise same time eighth day in a row). 49 degrees, wind WSW less than 1 mph. Sky: delightfully overcast. Suitable for a Winslow Homer or Thomas Moran painting, detail-rich and colorful; textured and windowed; cracks and bumps and holes trimmed in lambent runs of sunlight, shiny like polished silver. Lavender accents. Just above the hilltops to the south, a line of blush. Permanent streams: no mist and almost no running water. Wetlands: greener and drier than yesterday. Pond: still surface broken by striders and whirligigs. Woods: shadowed and cool.

The barn: bat has left after four days of roosting behind the door, a free spirit. Above the three light fixtures inside and on the porch are phoebe nests, six of them, all well preserved, a history of our symbiosis. Something for an avian archeologist to contemplate. The nest on the west end—the end closest to the absent bat—is active (and messy). Beyond the door, parents perch on oak limbs quietly chipping, tails marking time. Brief forays for breakfast . . . little white moths.

Both sides of the road, stereophonic red-eyed vireos, urgent and tiresome. Bashful blue-headed vireo in a nearby maple was far less enthusiastic. My neck aches searching for it. Parula warbler in maple, a buzzy rising song that jumps a notch at the end; a pole-vaulting song with a final kick over the bar. House wren on Prozac prunes his song; sounds drugged.

Robin, street-stalking, picks at items smaller than June bugs. Unfortunately, familiarity has bred disregard. The loss is mine. Robin was the first bird I met on my parents' suburban lawn. Since then, I've seen them everywhere, from Central Park to Hudson Bay. On Kodiak Island, robins hopped through the leaf litter in the shadow of brown bears. In the 1970s, they were rare winter birds that occasionally visited dairy farms; now, in January, they strip my winterberries. In the mid-eighties, clouds of tens of thousands (maybe more) descended on the Florida Everglades; they survived on the red fruit of an invasive shrub called Brazilian pepper. Defecating robins spread pepper seeds. Today, a portion of the multibillion-dollar Everglades restoration includes control of ubiquitous Brazilian pepper, whose stranglehold on the mangrove jungles is due partly to the discharge of robins.

In front of me, a robin works the roadside, hopping and pecking, flicking leaves. If Gil Morera, my Costa Rican friend and tour partner, saw an American robin, he'd notice a resemblance to the Costa Rica national bird, the clay-colored thrush. Erect and plump, carries a tune; an inveterate leaf flipper. Gil would also notice how handsome a robin is: an Ansel-Adams, middle-tone gray back, darker head and face; black eyes hemmed by white; bright yellow bill; burnt orange chest and belly; white undertail coverts; dark tail with white spots on the corners that flash when it flies.

Removing the blinkers and describing a robin . . . cathartic.

Day 92

17 June 2020

*It is an unfortunate man or woman
who has never loved a tree.*
JOHN HAY

5:06 A.M. (sunrise same time tenth day in a row). 47 degrees, wind NW 0 mph. Sky: empty of clouds; rose wash in the south. A landscape photographer would cut out the sky; there's nothing there, just pale, barren blue. A magazine photographer might not, however . . . an editor could lay out a title or a lead graph in the vacant sky; that's about it. A blue void . . . except for a goose alone and silent, that passes southeast. Permanent streams: robin pair, like spotted sandpipers, hunt the emergent rocks in the lower stream; pick dormant insects waiting for rain. Wetland: veiled in anorexic mist. I can almost see individual droplets, which collectively blunt the crowns of spruce and fir that hem the far shore. Veeries spin music out of the moisture. Pond: outflow pipe no longer drips.

House wren back up to speed; rapid-fire song at machine-gun pace. An apportionment of resources: seven different warblers sing seven songs in seven different trees. Close to the road, pileated raps a hollow tree. Distant woodpecker answers, barely audible. Deer bounds through the woods, tail up.

Mid-marsh, red-shouldered hawk perches on the last snag standing, barkless white pine, limbs broken. The hawk's russet undersides perfect camouflage, an extension of the weathered, sunlit trunk. Hawk's incandescent vision fixed on reeds and muddy channels, looking for motion, a breath taken too deeply. Hawk retreats to pine on the western shore. Perches midtree, midlimb, and continues surveillance. Particular perches suit his interest, providing me with a level of predictability. Keeps me checking the same snag and horizontal limbs. Because red-shoulders are expansively mobile, favorite perches accrue over a wide area. When hawk hunts The Hollow, I know where to look. But he's not always here . . . plies several marshes and wet meadows, an itinerant warrior with sharp toes and sharp voice.

Timber rattlesnakes, which I've spent some time watching, are the epitome of predictability. During the snake's lifetime, which may stretch for half a century, there is a 99 percent probability it won't switch dens.

And year after year, females birth and shed almost always at the same site. Males know this. I know this. And hawks that hunt rattlesnakes know this. Red-shouldered hawk hunts a vast landscape, a bird of eminence who sees the world from an unrestricted perspective. Hawk and valley entwined. Hawk inhabits Coyote Hollow, as surely I do. Both of us transparently dependent on the same landscape . . . hawk physically. Me spiritually.

In the front yard, a pair of hairy woodpeckers idle on the trunk of my black walnut . . . a most personal tree. Thirty-three years ago, when Linny was pregnant with Casey, she decided that we should collect walnuts from a sizeable sweeping tree that grew on a nearby dairy farm. We were permitted to gather nuts that littered the yard like pebbled linoleum. We collected a bushel, the most magnificent walnuts I'd ever seen each one almost as big as a baseball with fragrant, yellow-green husks, like so many odd-shaped apples. Of the approximately 100 nuts we gathered, seven germinated. After Casey was born, Linny called the sprouts *Casey's trees*. She planted them in the yard and fussed over them. Four survived the first year. A deer ate one the second year; another died of unknown causes. When we moved to Thetford seven years later, the trees came with us; two feet tall—quintessential, slow-growing hardwoods— roots longer and stouter than trunks. During the three years that we lived on Houghton Hill, one of the saplings died. When we moved to Coyote Hollow, we had two boys and one tree. The walnut was now eight feet tall. We hired landscapers to transplant it.

When Linny died in 2000, the walnut was coming into its own.

Now, Casey lives in Colorado, and the tree—his tree, that his mother so lovingly tended—is over forty feet tall, more than a foot thick at breast height, and lords it over the compost pile and garden. Sapsucker holes like necklaces skirt the trunk. A rose-breasted grosbeak, bold among feathery leaves, its breast on fire, sings sweetly . . . a birthday tune. It's Casey's birthday today; he and his tree, a pair of thirty-three-year-olds. Even red-eyed vireos sound sweeter today.

The world's on fire. A flicker lands in the walnut. Yellow and white and tan, spotted and barred, black bib and mustache, red nape and gray crown . . . a birthday bird. I only wish Casey was here to see it.

Red-shouldered Hawk

Day 93

18 June 2020

Half the battle is just showing up.
STEPHEN HAWKING

5:06 A.M. (same sunrise time eleventh day in a row). 50 degrees, wind N less than 1 mph. Sky: light pink wash in the south that congeals on several long, wispy clouds, edges trimmed in chromatic brilliance. Blue everywhere else. Permanent streams: upper stream limps; lower not so permanent, absorbed by a gravel bed like a desert river. Then, reappears downstream as a series of pools. Disappears again. Sticklebacks couldn't survive the drought and skipped the breeding season (so far). Wetlands: sunlight descends on the softwoods across the marsh, a curtain lifting in reverse. Breath on a cool morning, light low-hanging mist across the marsh, a thin exhalation. Pond: water pulls away from the parched shore. Mist rolls over the surface, also going nowhere. A pair of great blue herons pass overhead in no particular hurry. Deep arcing wing strokes; slow-motion flapping compared to mergansers. Heron grunts, a low, guttural sound like steam escaping a radiator. Bullfrog belches.

Above the north side of Robinson Hill, the Lake Fairlee side, a loon yodels, a haunting call that makes the valley a notch wilder. A whole-body experience . . .

Parula warbler sings in the pines. Pair of agitated hairy woodpeckers chase each other, one begging, the other annoyed. In the alders, a couple of caterpillars clapped in his bill, yellowthroat speaks with a full mouth . . . *pic, pic, pic*. Plucks the third caterpillar off an alder leaf (reminds me of an Atlantic puffin with a bill full of capelin). Crows chase one another through treetops, noisy and reckless. Wings slapping leaves sounds like ripping paper. Veeries calling. Red-eyed vireo singing quietly (for a change).

Activity on the rim of the pond. Diggings. A tail drag in the sand. Did the snapping turtle finally lay her eggs? Then, a splash, followed by a bubble wake. Midpond, a painted turtle's neat oval shell transmogrifies into a river otter's head. Nostrils flare. Tail sculls. Black beady eyes fix on me. Dogs snort, noses combing the shoreline. Otter's ears are tiny. Face blunt. Fur dense, nearly four hundred thousand hairs per square inch midback. Looks better on otter than on us. A penchant for play. Back and forth, always hanging midpond. Dives. Rises. Dives. Rises. Dives again. Otter on a quest, en route through Coyote Hollow. Not too much here to eat. Minnows and catfish; shoals of green frog and bullfrog tadpoles. A frog. A turtle. Crayfish crawling along the bottom. A feast for me, if not for the otter.

Flicker drums on a metal fence post. Sapsucker issues a message, woodland Morse code. Then birds vanish. Eclipsed by otter, the second I've seen in the Hollow in twenty-three years. Fat tadpole gulps air. Otter dives, rises. Crown and arched tail break the surface. I turn an otter into an ichthyosaur.

Five painted turtles bask on the surface, but no otter. I examine spoor like the jeweler examines a diamond. Flattened reeds. More digging. Otter, an animal with time on its paws. A supreme predator, patrols miles of rivers and marshes and lakes. Senses fish at night beneath a pall of ice and snow. If the otter stays too long, nothing will be left to eat—a Pyrrhic victory.

Male otters live alone. Females raise pups. Otters are so good at fishing—invented catch and release . . . and catch again—that they have time for solitary and group play. Tobogganing. Chasing and throwing leaves. Tumbling in the water. A mammal my boys and I try to emulate . . . chronic immaturity. Casey and Jordan find humor in unexpected places. Both make a game of life. *Dad Jokes*, the worse the better, bring smiles (if not outright laughter). For example:

Who was the lesser-known knight who designed King Arthur's round table?

Sir Cumference.

Many years ago, I was given a copy of the 1977 Animal Control Agent's Report for Hanover, New Hampshire. Listed last, below 961 complaints, including one gerbil bite and two runaway jackasses, was a note that read, *Investigated a report of an otter chasing a mailman.* An unglued mail carrier had taken refuge in someone's home after being chased down the street by an otter. The Hanover Post Office offered no comment. E. B. White did, though. When my friend Patchen sent the report to *The New Yorker*, White responded in print, *Maybe that's what the Postal Service needs.*

How can a mammal three feet long and more than twenty pounds hide in a small pond with a mostly mowed shoreline? I linger. No luck. The otter cameo, a graceful moment, and all I did to receive the unexpected gift . . . get out of bed early and walk down the road.

Day 96

21 June 2020

Father's Day

We are formed by little scraps of wisdom.
UMBERTO ECO

5:06 A.M. (same sunrise time fourteenth day in a row). 61 degrees, wind-less. Sky: tissue-paper white, soft and foggy (tissue-paper thin), without clouds. Then, all at once, the lower atmosphere congeals to chowder. The entire valley is encased in fog, which hangs at treetop level above the marsh like a cloud that lost its buoyancy. Too bad I couldn't wring the air. Permanent streams need a transfusion. Their stone-studded interior looks like weathered bones. A fossil streambed. Moisture every-where . . . thickening, eclipsing, enshrouding; the big pines along the far shore, where the red-shouldered hawk consults with himself, are blotted out. I check the Weather app on my cell phone to verify what I see. In all caps, just below *Thetford Center*, is the word *FOG*. We're in sync, the phone and I. Where would I be without it?

Woods: green shade hums with mosquitos. Fortunately, they can't penetrate denim. Mountain maple flowers along the edge of the wet-lands, loose stems of upright or nodding clusters, individual flowers tiny and white and attended by thrips. Blue flag iris still flowers along the lips of the pond.

DOR: hairy-tailed mole; decapitated chipmunk; yearling milk snake; bullfrog, pancake flat and as large as a slipper.

AOR: White-tailed deer and robins.

Robins calling and singing, chasing each other through the woods. Time for a second clutch? Are first-clutch fledglings hungry? Is every-body lost in the fog? A pair of hairy woodpeckers tap an ill cherry limb. A clamorous mob of red-eyed vireos up and down the road, both sides, working too hard. Nothing dissuades them. Father's Day is a foreign concept. Yellowthroat, behavior subdued, calls from an alder branch. His sidekick, the chestnut-sided warbler, is nowhere to be seen or heard. Perhaps he has chicks to feed? The world is turning, ripening, dispersing . . . and ever-so-slowly darkening. Father's Day is late this year. Birds don't notice and carry on in idiosyncratic and unassailable ways.

A plump woodcock flies in front of me, wings whistling. Thick head.

Big, dark eyes set high. Knitting-needle bill pointed as though dowsing for earthworms. The color of the earth upon which it lives is mottled browns, blacks, and buffy orange. I've walked a short distance from an incubating female to fetch camera gear and never found her or her nest again.

Our truest, oldest, meanest-looking turtle floats midpond, her carapace an archipelago of spikes and points. Snapping turtles watched the dinosaurs live and die. They've been laying white, round eggs in sandy loam for eighty million years. They witnessed the drift of continents, the birth of islands, the drowning of coastlines, the rise and fall of mountain ranges, the florescence and decay of volcanoes, the spread of prairies and deserts, and the comings and goings of glaciers, rivers, and lakes. They've witnessed people cross the Bering Land Bridge, the arrival of Vikings, Columbus and the birth of globalization, Conquistadors and missionaries, Pilgrims, Dutch seamen, Russian whalers, the slave trade, too many wars to mention, the Spanish flu of 1918, the Stock Market Crash, polio, the sale of Babe Ruth to the Yankees, assassinations, the Beatles, the Miracle Mets, race riots, climate change (many times), the internet, protests and persecutions, Donald Trump and the rise of fashionable lying, and, now, Covid-19.

Snapping turtles: hatchet-faced and ill-tempered, their deep beauty that they endure and adapt. Not unlike my father commuting on the Long Island Railroad; one of four men sitting with knees interlocked, *The New York Times* spread between them as a card table. Twice a day, thirty-one years, pinochle for an hour each way. Bless them all.

SUMMER

2020

Day 99

24 June 2020

If one could conclude as to the nature of the Creator
from a study of creation it would appear that God
has an inordinate fondness of stars and beetles.
J. B. S. Haldane

4:02 A.M. (one hour and five minutes before sunrise). 68 degrees, wind SSE 3 mph. Sky: dark and brooding, slowly awakening, lumen by lumen. Air thick enough to slice. Rain is imminent (I hope). In the east, a hot orange glow precedes the sun. A cadre of fireflies above the pasture, marsh, and pond, and in the woods, blinking like slo-mo fireworks. One wanders the perimeter of a coltsfoot leaf; others crawl on the forest floor and lawn; staggered flashes of cold incandescence, bits of moonlight manufactured by beetles. Species recognize each other by the duration and pattern of repetitive blinks. I recognized nobody . . . just the beauty of soft-body phosphorescence.

It's an altogether different world when the curtains draw. With parabolic ears, dogs gather information (they know so much more than I). First woodland birds singing: ovenbird and red-eyed vireo, both constrained. First wetlands birds singing: yellowthroat and swamp sparrow, also constrained. Subdued hermit thrush and a pair of veeries set fireflies to music. Pond: full throated. Bullfrogs' deep belches are masculine and off-key. Green frogs' loose twang (needs tuning), feminine and expressive. Plops of unseen frogs retreat from the shoreline. Tadpoles gulp air and leave bubbles.

Pipette-mouthed mosquitoes out in force, a biblical plague. A female needs one drop of blood the size of a sand grain to make three hundred eggs. To get even, I have to kill three hundred for each successful bite. Unfortunately, successful bites increase exponentially, a number beyond counting . . . like our metastasizing pandemic debt. Marinating under a denim jacket, I have only hands, face, and neck to defend . . . at best a losing proposition, at worst an ill-fated expedition. Where are the bats? To console me, I recall that male mosquitos pollinate orchids, a thought that sustains me only so long. Then, slapping resumes. When British biologist J.B.S. Haldane, one of Darwin's earliest and most rabid supporters, claimed, *The universe is not only queerer than we suppose but queerer than we can suppose*, he could have been considering mosquitos.

Whirligig beetles and diving beetles zigzag across the pond like miniature bumper cars. Speak in waves, an ephemeral and forgotten language. I'm easily mesmerized. Scarab beetles, boldly black and orange, eat unidentified roadkill. Ladybird beetles eat unidentified aphids. Click beetle in the kitchen sink, clicking. Beetles of all shapes, colors, and sizes are a perfect stand-in for birds—which are just awakening—and an ideal antidote for mosquitos that cloud around me.

◠

When William and Jordan were in elementary school, they attended adventure spots across from the pond, on the downward slope of the hemlock knoll, where the wetland pinches together and pours through the ramshackle beaver dam, exiting as an unnamed congestion of wild water and stones. They'd ride their bikes downhill several times weekly, pitch them in the hemlocks, and bushwhack into the woods. The boys wrote poems and journaled, painted in watercolors, then stored their work in Tupperware buried beneath the leaves. Sometimes, William and Jordan caught froglets and tiny black toads, which they brought home to a fifty-gallon aquarium. Sometimes, they listened to the warble of catbirds, the broadcast of bitterns and red-shouldered hawks. Adventuring, the boys were unencumbered, alone and free . . . brushed by fingers of yellow light amid a wild world, unfinished and incomplete, sitting on their thrones of duff.

◠

A female luna moth lies on the stone steps; her green wings and streaming tail a banner of late June. Her body empty, literally. Like many rock 'n' rollers, luna moths survive on the charge of youth. Adults don't eat or drink. They have no digestive system. No excretory system. They're just a package of eggs or sperm encased in white pubescence, the most gorgeous moth imaginable. Gravid females inscribe night currents with pheromones. Then, from miles away, males read the message with large, white, feathery antennas.

Luna moths, enormous and gorgeous, bit players in the high drama of early summer. Like sockeye salmon, adults die after spawning.

Like a schoolboy writing, *How I spent my summer*, day after day, I chronicle my unforeseen pandemic staycation, now extending into the fourth month. I'm marooned at home in an emotional landscape, a narrow valley rife with memories that speak to me each morning in a language I nearly forgot (at my peril).

Every day bears abrupt and vast avenues of contemplation. At peace (for the moment) wandering among the poetry of The Hollow.

Day 103

28 June 2020

A Narrow Fellow in the Grass

The Grass divides as with a Comb . . .

But never met this Fellow
Attended or alone
Without a tighter Breathing
And Zero at the Bone.
EMILY DICKINSON

5:09 A.M. (sunrise one minute later than yesterday). 53 degrees, wind N 1 mph. Sky: mottled and highlighted, a whiter shade of pink. Eventually, long fingers of sunlight extend beyond Robinson Hill, an incarnation of a *Watchtower* cover. Permanent streams: upper on life support, not a murmur; lower, the wreckage of a stream. Rocks dumped by glaciers, polished by running water. Bones of a drought. I need a stethoscope to detect a flow. Wetlands: more haze than mist. Pond: light fog rolls off the surface and goes nowhere. Pine needles deposited and marshaled by wind, a floating mandala spiral outward, a concentric Etch A Sketch, or the sonogram of a veery.

Red-flowering raspberry in bloom petals on the darker side of red. Male flowers of white pine everywhere, light brown and weightless, sylvan dust. Iris gone to seed.

Annals of late June: volume turned down on most songbirds except for red-eyed vireos, which sing the entire walk. Summer's soundtrack, a simulcast along both sides of the road. Blue-headed vireos are more discrete and less abundant. Blue jays bicker. Tanagers, hushed and invisible, not a hint of scarlet in the oaks. Jailbird-striped, black-and-white warbler patrols the maples, silent as a fugitive. Three ovenbirds chase each other, no time to sing. Red-breasted nuthatch slowly repeats its tedious and nasal mantra. Pewee flies by, perches for a moment—then gone. Veery and hermit thrush, choral scholars, the morning's exceptions, sing duets with themselves; elegance rising. Music seeps through me like water through my hands.

Annals of sunflower-seed alchemy: evening grosbeak chicks camp near the bird feeders, toes grafted to cherry branches, wings drooping and quivering—bills agape, begging for more.

Annals of morbid amusement: using lilacs as cover, an immature red-shouldered hawk looms large and grim. Mourning dove panics. Hawk strikes. Dove escapes, leaving behind two tail feathers and a scrap of down. And me . . . breathless.

Phoebes fledged, hanging out in red oak by the barn door. Parents bring them moths, primarily white.

Department of Misplaced Accolades: In the spring of 1804, in a cave in Mill Grove, Pennsylvania, eighteen-year-old John James Audubon tied silver threads on the legs of five nestling phoebes. Hailed as the Father of Bird Banding for over two centuries, Audubon was given credit he may not have deserved. In the 1830s, many years after he ringed the phoebes, Audubon wrote that during the following spring (1805) two of the phoebes returned to Mill Grove wearing silver bracelets. In a recent article in the *Archives of Natural History* (a peer-reviewed journal published in Edinburgh University), a Pennsylvania biologist, who had studied the artist's diaries, reported that in the spring of '05, Audubon was in France—not Pennsylvania. In addition, a recent astronomically more extensive study of philopatry in phoebes demonstrated that less than 2 percent of banded phoebes return to their natal neighborhood—not the 40 percent Audubon claimed.

I'm not surprised. Audubon got timber rattlesnakes wrong. He painted one with round pupils and a set of teeth in the upper jaw. And in 1827, while lecturing in Edinburgh, he claimed a Louisiana rattlesnake chased a gray squirrel through the treetops, in the fashion of a limbless gymnast; and that the snake eventually killed the squirrel by constriction, not envenomation . . . pure fiction.

Milk snake skin in the stonewall, a sleeve of itself turned inside out. Late one April, while pruning apple limbs, a milk snake (maybe this one) slithered out of a mole tunnel. The snake felt cold, and I assumed she had wintered in the tunnel, below the frost line, and had just emerged for the season. She lays oblong, leathery eggs in the compost pile. In September, a dozen snakelets, brick-red hourglasses on gray background, rubbery and delicate, radiate from the compost pile, sometimes across the front lawn. Babies eat slugs. Adults eat white-footed mice and chipmunks, the two most important reservoir hosts of Lyme disease. Milk snakes advance through the tightness of stone walls—New England has 250,000 miles of them, enough to circle the globe ten times. For a chipmunk, there's no place to hide. For me, notwithstanding the brilliance of Dickinson, there's no . . . *Zero at the Bone.*

Day 106

01 July 2020

Until the flowers have blown away
And the branch is covered in fruit;
Until the heart, sated with childhood,
Has its rest
And confesses: it was full of pleasure, not for nothing,
This restless game of life.
HERMANN HESSE

5:10 A.M. (sunrise same time as yesterday). 62 degrees, wind SW 1 mph. Sky: saturated. Cloud clotted, thick, low, and without highlights. Fog columns and tendrils support a sunken atmosphere. Slight openings in the east. A wide river of fog traces the East Branch of the Ompompanoosuc. Truncated worldview. Leaves washed, shiny, and dripping, sounds like rain. Inside the woods, fairy-tale darkness. From crown to ground, trunks rain streaked, some wide, some narrow. Intermittent streams: braids of mud, seeping west (again). Permanent streams: infused and moving, but nowhere near April standards. Upper gurgles, a rhapsodic, hypnotic melody. Lower murmurs. Wet earth, a downhill ooze pirated by streams. Wetlands: the trees across the marsh, from where the hawk surveils, shrouded in mist. Pond: surface untarnished by the wind. Steam rises straight up.

Clusters of oxeye daisies bloom along the pond. White ash seeds litter the road, gathering in ruts. Lichens awaken, an intense aquamarine. Spiderwebs festooned with dew and rain, ephemeral necklaces.

DOR: two red efts.

AOR: two red efts and a millipede, legs waves of motion like prairie grasses against the wind. Slug drags westward. The lure of moisture.

Wet birds look bleak; songs just as lively. Juncos trill. Thrushes flute. Black-and-white warblers whisper. House wrens yell. Ovenbirds scream. Catbird—a mockingbird with imagination, inventive and not inclined to mimic—never repeats the exact phrase in succession. Crows caw. Chestnut-sided warblers ramble. Yellowthroats chatter. Hairy woodpecker in the uppermost branch of a skeletal birch, stone silent. Phoebes guttural, throat-clearing hacks. Tanagers and bittern, hushed and hidden. Pewees dispirited whistles. Jays complain; chicks beg. Red-eyed vireos, seasonal undercurrents of tedium (like shopping at Macy's), inexhaustible treetop Muzak. I may reconsider vireos in a month, when the woods fall silent. Rose-breasted grosbeak, full of beans, sings his heart out.

Doves coo. Out of the gloom, barred owl hoots. A crèche of turkey poults rises from a neighbor's driveway and scatters into the maples, an uncoordinated explosion. Three hens strut out of the woods and stand mid-driveway, quietly supervising.

The husk of a four-inch sphinx moth idles by the barn door, sharp wings angled back like a boomerang. Above the ocean of fog and mist, red-shouldered hawk hunts hilltop islands; razor voice fillets the morning.

Today's my parents' anniversary. They married the year the original *King Kong* was released. If they were alive, my mother would be 110, my father 105, and they'd still be wondering why I left the stability of the Bronx Zoo forty-six years ago after a series of random, inconsequential jobs for a rural life beneath dark skies and economic struggle. In an age where hyphens bridge words never before joined—*self-isolation*, *social-distancing*, the much overused *new-normal*, and baseball's frozenly enthusiastic *cardboard-spectator*—they'd understand I'm where I should be, where I was born to be, away from the strife and strafe of the suburbs ... masked like the yellowthroat, mapping my Green Mountain quarantine where passion, magic, and sense of belonging commingle under the shadow of a virus.

Day 108

03 July 2020

Nothing is more beautiful than the loveliness of the woods before sunrise.
GEORGE WASHINGTON CARVER

5:12 A.M. (sunrise one minute later than yesterday). 67 degrees, wind motionless. Sky: weakly overcast, breaking up, peach accents. Intermittent streams: muddy ribbons. Permanent streams: slow flow, more hum than babble. Wetlands: mistless, fogless, dewless. Pond: water level higher than yesterday.

Hallmark of Midwestern prairies, black-eyed Susan blooms amid oxeye daisies. A wreath of golden petals surrounds a dark disc. Jordan and Casey renamed the flower *black-eyed Aunt Susan* after their mother's oldest sister. Mountain maple keys are reddish and ready to launch.

DOR: unidentified songbird, pulverized.

AOR: American toad nicked by a car, destination DOR. I move toad into the ferns. Song sparrow gathers grit; three slugs cross before the sun catches them; one eft, neon orange; another transitioning to newt, an orange shade of olive, heading toward the marsh.

Red-eyed vireos, endless enthusiasm, feathered reliability. (If I find a vireo nest, I'll have something to consider other than a mind-numbing song.) Ovenbird shouts in vain, *teacher, teacher, teacher*. Of course all the teachers are home on Zoom. Brown creeper wanders up a maple trunk, tail pressed to bark; stops to sing, high and thin . . . *seee, seee, seee*. When Roger Tory Peterson could no longer hear blackburnian warblers, it was time, he said, to see an audiologist. My hearing yardstick, the brown creeper, confirms I don't (yet) need hearing aids.

Two note whistlers: chickadee high and titmouse low. Woodpecker broadcasts from a metal roof. Hidden in the thickets, a catbird meows softly. Chestnut-sided warbler, pausing on a naked branch, has nothing to say. Poses broadside as if for Audubon, and then resumes shopping in the alders for caterpillars. Turkey turns back the clock and gobbles.

Microfallout of yellow-billed cuckoos, a miraculous and provincial conspiracy. Four commandeer The Hollow, one so close to the house I look for him. No luck. Calls well-spaced, *coo . . . coo . . . coo*. More profound and not nearly as sad as a mourning dove. In late summer, when knots of webworms trash black cherry trees, Coyote Hollow hosts a couple of black-billed cuckoos. These are the first yellow-billed cuckoos I've ever heard in the valley, dinner guests without reservations, arriving on the heel of webworm outbreak.

The outer orbit of natural history: yellow-billed cuckoos occasionally lay eggs in the nest of other birds, most often black-billed cuckoos, and move on with chilly indifference. Unplanned adoption for the hosts and identity crises for the chicks. *Facultative* brood parasite. Not a no-other-choice *obligate* brood parasite like the cowbird. When a cuckoo builds a nest, it's a flimsy platform of sticks, a rudimentary home, daylight showing through the bottom like the side of an old barn.

Yellow-billed cuckoos pass through the valley. Stop to daven. And then gorge on hairy, treetop-grazing caterpillars. Swallow caterpillars one after the other. Spit up balls of irritating hairs that discourage most other species of hungry birds. Cuckoos, callus-throated and opportunistic, follow the tide of an unpredictable food source across the deciduous forest, as nomadic as buffalo hunters.

Department of embroidered facts: Confucian texts, circa 2600 BP, declared the hapless host of the Eurasian cuckoo, an obligate brood parasite (like the cowbird), paid *homage to an exemplary ruler*. The ruler, of course, is more shirker than tyrant, the original lousy parent. Brood parasites live by rules that both irritate and fascinate us. Who among us leaves her baby on someone else's doorstep? *Facultative brood parasites* like the yellow-billed and black-billed cuckoos may have taken a massive step toward becoming *obligate brood parasites*. Understanding the origins of a trait, submerged by time, rests with an avian tribunal and many thoughtful biologists.

A masterpiece of evolution, yellow-billed cuckoo, the occasional undevoted parent, mirrors life's complications. If a seemingly odd behavior benefits a species, the trait perpetuates itself into the next generation. The habit is discarded like yesterday's coffee if the response is deleterious.

Yellow-billed cuckoos may be gone tomorrow, off to greener pastures, never to return to The Hollow in my lifetime. Meanwhile, I listen and search for the sleek, retiring bird with the eponymous call. If I happen to find a parasitized nest, I won't need King Solomon to determine parentage.

Day III

06 July 2020

If a man [bird] does not keep pace with his companions,
perhaps it is because he hears a different drummer.
Let him step to the music which he hears,
however measured or far away.
Henry David Thoreau

5:14 A.M. (sunrise one minute later than yesterday). 59 degrees, wind SE 1 mph. Sky (and Earth): ceiling-to-floor fog, chowder-thick without highlights or texture. Visibility less than 100 feet, barn swaddled in vapor. Fog makes The Hollow more mysterious, hides imperfections, and stresses possibilities. (I once wandered out the front door and slogged for an hour in a fog, literally and figuratively, before I realized I was in the adjacent wetland, more than a mile from home.) Stimulates the imagination like a drug without the aftereffects. Bowl-and-doily spiderwebs pepper the lawn, dew covered and glistening. Intermittent streams: ribbons of mud. Permanent streams: upper, emaciated and limping; lower, retreats below the surface (again). Wetlands: far shore veiled in fog; jagged treetops softened, distant hills erased. Pond: mist becomes fog. It's night all morning, October without color. Milkweed pods open. Monarchs can't be far off.

DOR: red eft.

AOR: red eft, florescent orange cuts through the fog; bright enough to mark a runway, easily spotted and avoided by road-warrior robins patrolling the furrowed shoulders.

Fog has no bearing on vireos, who pour their voices into the soup, singing like there's no tomorrow. House wren effusive and creative. Three dueling veeries, all close to me and each other, voices sliding down the musical scale, arresting and enlivening. A fog song that transforms my walk into a mobile meditation. Dogs tug leashes, less interested in veeries than I am. Pileated drums in the fog, a lucid, inescapable rhythm, the morning tempo. Foraging in the alders, yellowthroat quietly calls, *pik, pik, pik, pik.*

Last night, I fell asleep listening to a yellow-billed cuckoo. I awoke to black-billed cuckoo (FOY) triplets, *cu, cu, cu.* Hollow, but softer, more haunting than yellow-billed. Both species lay an egg every fifth day; the duration from incubation to fledgling is a mere seventeen days. (By comparison, red-eyed vireo is twenty-four days; robin twenty-six; eastern phoebe, thirty-three; red-shouldered hawk, seventy-five days.) One cuckoo is on the verge of fledging and another is about to hatch. Siblings may be unknown to each other, well-spaced like the Chaplin children.

Besides hairy caterpillars, cuckoos track thirteen-year and seventeen-year periodical cicadas, abundant and predictable but geographically and temporally spaced across the eastern deciduous forest. I follow cicada outbreaks on the computer—2020, southwestern Virginia and adjacent West Virginia. Cuckoos follow a higher power.

Day 113

08 July 2020

There is grandeur in this view of life, with its several powers,
having been originally breathed into a few forms or into one;
and that whilst this planet has gone cycling on
according to the fixed law of gravity,
from so simple a beginning endless forms most beautiful
have been, and are being evolved.
CHARLES DARWIN

5:15 A.M. (sunrise same time as yesterday). 67 degrees, wind SSE 5 mph (delicious). Sky: colorless clouds horizon to horizon, a heavenly lid over an earthly terrarium. Permanent streams: upper, a faint ripple, on life support; lower, puddled, then subterranean retreat. Wetlands: a bowl of green reeds, hemmed by wall of green trees. Without fog, mist, or haze. Pond: also without fog, mist, or haze. Insects skate the surface, ride the wakes. Wind-driven current stirs reflections, an impressionistic painting like Monet's water lilies (but inverted).

Lots of milkweed flowers. No monarch eggs . . . yet. Terminal seeds of mountain maple dispersed.

DOR: slug, unintentionally bogged down by grit.

AOR: catbird, intentionally gathering grit.

Pockets of sound: house wren gushing in the pines; blue jay family in front-yard cherry eating green berries, all noise, all business. Ovenbirds holler. Juncos trill. Veeries and thrushes, woodland virtuosos. Catbird meows. Ravens converse. Chickadee on an old pine combs through the bark and stringy lichen limb by limb. Every pocket of sound has a vireo. One red-eyed crooning in maple; head back, face vacant, casually leaning into each phrase. Same poker face as hermit thrush. How different their voices. Now, in high summer, who's listening beside me? Vireo flies across the road almost directly overhead. Sees me. Executes a tight U-turn. Bill full of worms, robin responds to amped-up fledglings.

Female junco, pale brown, hunts caterpillars in hemlock needles, eating them on site. In the second edition of *The Sibley Guide to Birds*, David Sibley devotes two pages to the dark-eyed junco. He portrays five of the six subspecies, each with a description and a range map. (Some ornithologists believe several are suitable species.) I don't care whether the dark-eyed junco represents a group of subspecies or a group of sibling species. To me, their beauty resides in the dynamic way their ancestors colonized North America after the Ice Age. I watched volcano juncos last March in Costa Rica, picking through treeline rubble in the Talamanca Cordillera. The ancestors of these juncos retreated to Central American highlands during the glacial epoch and never returned. Volcano junco changed over the abyss of time and became a slightly different species. Eyes turned yellow. Bellies as gray as dusk. As breathtaking and eye popping (for cerebral reasons) as the resplendent quetzal.

A recent Gallup poll concluded that 83 *percent* of Americans reject Darwin's view of life. Of those, 45 percent believe God created human beings in our present form within the past ten thousand years; the other 38 percent believe we evolved over the past million years with God's guidance. A mere 13 percent of Americans agree with Darwin, far and away the lowest total in any technologically advanced nation.

And a recent online article published in *Science* stated that 13 percent of high-school biology teachers advocate creationism in class. Based on a nationwide survey of biology teachers, the report also claimed most teachers avoid conflict and don't make a solid case for evolution. Fewer than 30 percent take an adamant pro-evolution stand . . . Darwin relegated to the back pages of science.

Charles Darwin denied us special status. Species, he said, evolved from one to another. A biological arms race forged in the foundries of natural selection. As the product of competition and selection, humans, like juncos, are subject to the same trials as every other species. All life is related, past and future.

Darwin never used the word *evolution,* opting instead for the term *descent with modification,* the unifying theme of biology that reveals every living species as an ever-changing, unfinished work of art.

Black-billed cuckoos may have decamped the valley, like the quartet of yellow-billed cuckoos, which I haven't heard in several days. Secretive and unpredictable, cuckoos gave up philopatry for nomadism and abundance and stability for rarity and capriciousness. Topophilia is an alien concept for them, born and fledged without the urge to return. Shaped by eons of trial and error, by four waves of glacial congestion interspersed with four pulses of worldwide warming, cuckoos embody the mercurial aspects of evolution. Behavior: strange. Breeding habit: equally strange. That cuckoos survived and diversified is a testament to the creativity of natural selection.

Evolution by natural and sexual selection informed and formed Earth. I can't imagine physics without gravity, the constitution without the Bill of Rights, and ceramics without clay. Based on profound and repeatable observation, science transforms myth and nonsense into understanding, unlocking the secrets of a wondrous planet. Like gravity, junco and cuckoo convey that evolution is a planetary law—not a theory.

Day 115

10 July 2020

*I arise in the morning torn between
a desire to save the world and a desire to savor the world.
This makes it hard to plan the day.*
E. B. White

5:17 A.M. (sunrise one minute later than yesterday). 66 degrees, wind NNW less than 1 mph. Sky: light powder blue suffused with pastel pink, a wispy remnant of a cloud far to the south, and a vital, slightly more-than-half moon, bright and shiny as polished silver. Permanent streams: languishing, not nearly as stable as my persistence in calling them permanent; upper, a Sisyphean current, on groundwater life support; lower, reduced to a puddle with a faint flow, any connection to the marsh subterranean, deranged drainage. Wetlands: verdant, green and wet as possible without needing an umbrella; along the far shore, the sawtooth crowns of spruce and fir rise above a suspended bowl of mist. Pond: light fog rolls southeast like breath on a chilly morning. Tadpoles on the verge of being frogs gulp air. Deerflies and mosquitos . . . more persistent than the streams.

DOR: small green frog, newly minted.

AOR: grit-gathering robins and juncos.

Red-shouldered hawk, far to the southeast, piercing screech that carries valley to valley, vivifies the morning. Tanager in oaks, pack-a-day voice, prosaic song and dazzling color, bird with a tropical look and middle-latitude song, rubbed raw by competition with the more musically gifted. Juncos trill lustily and flit across the road. Ovenbirds are loud as ever; red-eyed vireos as persistent (such a surprise).

Blue jays in front yard cherry. Chicks beg . . . wings quivering, mouths open, bright red, a beacon in ground fog. Neither Casey, Jordan, nor William ever flapped their arms and chased me around the house, mouths open . . . begging for dinner. But there was no mistaking when they were hungry.

Veery and robin, a ritualized scuffle, rise straight up, breast to breast, wings aflutter. No contact. No sound except flapping; reminiscent of very agitated paper. Robin is much more significant. Veery holds his own and resumes singing, a gifted and descending spiral, corkscrew put to music on a misty morning. Reason for altercation: robin must be jealous. Compared to tanager, he's Sam Cooke; compared to veery, he's Louis Armstrong.

Yellow-billed cuckoo calls in the fog. I can't get enough of the cuckoo: elusive as a bobcat, drops subtle clues to odd movements and waives rules of avian protocol. Unpredictable. The mere suggestion of presence. Sits in the back of the woodland classroom, shy and still as a statue. In the late sixties, I saw my first-ever yellow-billed cuckoo in an apple tree, motionless in an Indiana front yard. Framed by blossoms, cradled in Midwestern morning. Then, years later, in mid-May 2019, in central Ohio farmland, a fallout of yellow-billed cuckoos, calling and darting through the canopy, exposing themselves. Loosest of flocks, a scattering of birds with rudimentary cohesion. Cuckoo, pointed on both ends, a feathered lance. Immaculately white underneath. Bright white spots on the long, dark tail. Rich rufous primaries. Foraging in oaks and hickories.

But Coyote Hollow cuckoos, all voice and no show (thus far), wild and provocative as the mist that hides them, invest a muggy July morning with promise. The little voice in my head says, *Let's find it.* My dogs, charmingly incompetent, disagree. Sit on the sidelines, paws to snout, rubbing off flies, until a deer bolts across the rutted road. Dogs rally, leashes taut. Searching for a cuckoo in the fog is like searching for a ventriloquist blindfolded. Voice everywhere and nowhere.

I surrender to the blissful ease of sunrise. Then, an ominous cloud of red-winged blackbirds and grackles, absent since early May, descend on my raspberry patch. (I need a goshawk.) Overcome inertia and start picking.

Day 117

12 July 2020

Natural history is a matter of observation; it is a harvest which you gather when and where you find it growing. Birds and squirrels and flowers are not always in season, but philosophy we have always with us. It is a crop which we can grow and reap at all times and in all places and it has its own value and brings its own satisfaction.

John Burroughs

5:19 A.M. (sunrise one minute later than yesterday). 72 degrees, wind S 10 mph. Sky: gray, overcast and indecisive. Begins as mist and ends as showers. In between, alternating drizzle, mist, and sprinkle. Gove Hill is in hiding, eclipsed by moisture. Leaves in motion, every branch hung with rain. Permanent streams: temporary infusion but sluggish. Wetlands: mistless and in sharp relief. Red-shouldered hawk above the reeds, circling and calling, much more robust, much louder, much longer than the blue jay's cover, and from a thousand feet in the sky—not from treetops or just above the canopy. A second hawk appears. The two fly in tandem, rising and falling on a whim, voices like lances piercing the valley. Pond: a fist-sized branch mistaken for the head of a snapping turtle. No mergansers. Thetford's version of *Make Way for Ducklings*. Although more secretive than mallard chicks that wander around Boston Public Garden, hooded mergansers follow their mother between the wetland and the pond, crossing the road once the curtain drops on day . . . otherwise, they'd contend with red-shouldered hawks, one now perched midmarsh in the pine snag, scanning the world.

Red-flowering raspberry sheds petals, magenta spots on the dark earth. I turn up my collar against mosquitos and deerflies that are everywhere and hungry.

DOR: American toad and pickerel frog.

AOR: hermit thrush pauses on the shoulder, looks both ways, and then flies across the road.

Tanager in full voice in oaks. House wren at warp speed in pines. Infectious laugh of pileated. Blue jays kvetch. Black-and-white warbler whistles quietly, thoughtfully, his voice hijacked by the wind whipping through the trees. Thrush and veery enliven dark woods. Only two ovenbirds sing. They've fallen off the sylvan version of this week's *Billboard's Hot 100*. Number-one spot occupied by red-eyed vireo for the eleventh week in a row. Three more weeks and vireos rival Queen's run with *Bohemian Rhapsody*.

Deer prances in the woods above the pond. Dogs come to life, eyes riveted and ears up. Bat behind the barn door, first time in more than a month. Grooms shadowy wings.

Yesterday, a friend in Vershire banded five kestrel chicks tucked in the bottom of a nest box. One fuzzy glutton, recently fed, had several inches of bright red tail sticking out of its mouth, the aftermath of a colorful feast. The tail belonged to a northern red-bellied snake, ventral scales overlapping like shingles. A splendid little snake, tan above, red below, an eater of slugs and snails, caught crossing open ground. Regardless of what the scientific literature says, the parent kestrel, the ultimate opportunist, took what was below it: an extended, thin package of protein for a developing chick. I think of kestrels eating grasshoppers, dragonflies, and meadow voles, but that's the beauty of natural history: just when you think you know something about something, another thing pops up that surprises you. Expands options in a direction you didn't know possible. Years ago, while watching hawks migrate over Fire Island, a fellow birder told me that when he was a boy in the 1920s, he saw a kestrel pluck a smooth green snake off the Hempstead Plains, near Garden City, miles of disjunct tallgrass prairie now occupied by shopping malls. And more recently, a friend sent me a photograph of a timber rattlesnake on the limb of an Iowa oak, a sapsucker in its mouth. Who would have thought a rattlesnake would climb a tree and wait for a bird to pass, the herpetological analog of *Waiting for Godot*.

Natural history: a mutating jigsaw puzzle. Each piece joins another for a moment, then changes shape to fit other circumstances. Circumstances, endless and pliant, are timeless, magical and profound, an antidote to boredom. The perfect companion for a Covid walk.

Day 119

14 July 2020

History is not what happened,
but what survives the shipwrecks
of judgment and chance.
Maria Popova

5:20 A.M. (sunrise one minute later than yesterday). 60 degrees, wind E 1 mph. Sky: congested and electrified. Atmospheric indigestion, thunder rolling above The Hollow. Tendrils of moisture rise everywhere and everywhere hold up the clouds like vaporous Greek columns. Heavens pour and rumble and flash. Branches hung with rain. Driveway needs therapy and roadside gullies run full. Road resembles an aerial view of Great Plains drainage, dendritically, with a main channel and scores of tributaries. Intermittent streams: yesterday disabled and dry, today arise from the dead, each a watery Lazarus pouring with renewed urgency. Earth-brown and leaf strewn. Permanent streams: full bore, gushing, loud, and as brown as the Mississippi. Main channels scoured and reamed. Water striders flushed into the marsh. Wetlands: lush and swollen, green with satisfaction. Pond: overflow culvert surges with fire-hydrant intensity. Raindrops dance on the surface.

Ancient big-toothed aspen, limb broken in the wind, hangs by a thread, straight down, awaits an appointment with gravity. Ash seeds litter the road. Lichens awaken, a saturation of gray-green, moisture swollen and soft.

No mosquitos. Birds are primarily silent and motionless. Pair of red-eyed vireos, stupefyingly tedious, song barely audible. Flashes of lightning pop behind the clouds, which glows for a hypnotic moment, eerie, scary, but spellbinding. A world renewed, washed clean, fresh and temporary as the yellow glow of sunrise.

Three days ago, the enormous female toad that hunts the garden and front porch, feasting on bugs chummed by lettuce and porch light, appeared in the barn soaking in the dogs' water bowl, head barely above the surface, legs splayed. My new yardstick for drought. Coyote Hollow, a parched landscape amid a deluge. Much too much water to be absorbed, runs down, over, and around, in every hillside crease, filling basins and footprints, flooding channels, overwhelming rivulets and tributaries, gathering behind beaver dams, water levels rising like the tide, every drop en route to the Connecticut River.

The river, 406 miles long, fed by 148 tributaries, of which thirty-eight are major rivers, drains 11,260 square miles. Pours into Long Island Sound at 19,600 cubic feet per second. The heart and soul of New England. Connecticut River. One long, brown pulse of water running downhill. Many obstacles intervene between aspiration and reality. En route south, water must negotiate sixteen dams on the main stem, more than three thousand on its tributaries, and forty-four thousand road crossings. Because water courses ceaselessly and carelessly along paths of least resistance, not all structures hold tight in floods. Tropical Storm Irene (2011) overwhelmed one thousand culverts and five hundred bridges throughout the watershed. This is no Irene, but Coyote Hollow fills and feels as though beaver are still aboard . . . yawning gulf, however, between illusion and reality.

As a distraction from the strange world of the Coronavirus, I began sunrise walks on March 18, several days after I returned from Costa Rica. A creative quarantine, a rediscovery of my home ground. Dogs, faithful but puzzled, reluctantly join me along the floor of the thunderstorm. Why can't I walk in the rain if John Muir glissaded down an avalanche? Off I go, footloose and possibly addled. By the time I reach the pond, three-quarters of a mile from home, showers metastasize to downpour, and thunder and lightning escalate. The sky flashes, clouds swell with electricity—a peal of thunder. Then, the ethereal song of a veery. A storm song cascading out of dark woods. Lightens a darker mood. Could there be a better finale?

Day 122

17 July 2020

The answer, my friend, is blowin' in the wind
The answer is blowin' in the wind.

BOB DYLAN

5:23 A.M. (sunrise, one minute later than yesterday). 58 degrees, wind SSE 5 mph (treetops in motion). Sky: bright, congested, without definition (the sort of atmosphere that detracts from a landscape photograph), a low, seamless sheet of clouds that alternates from drizzle to shower, steady and gentle. Intermittent streams: on life support, one a trickle, the other a necklace of puddles. Permanent streams: in motion but slowing down. Wetlands: luxuriantly green, recipient of seeps, dribbles, ground flow, and rain. If beaver were still here, there'd be a temporary pond, water from rim to rim, an aqueous crib for catfish fry and minnows and a deafening assemblage of frogs. Pond: mesmerizing sheet of dancing water, pocked and rippled, surface a blend of raindrops and air-gulping tadpoles. Unaccompanied bullfrog bellows, the counterpoint to the soft chips of yellowthroats and song sparrows.

Milkweed and Queen Anne's lace flower, Oxeye daisy and black-eyed Susan wither.

Fat toad left the dog's water bowl and moves into the tack room. A cloud of grackles descends on the raspberry patch. Arms stretched and waving, I become the scarecrow.

Out of a neighboring valley, a red-shouldered hawk screams, a high, drawn-out squeal, crystalline and sharp. Over and over and over, a rain of verbal arrows sounding like a blue jay on steroids. Or blue jay sounds like red-shouldered hawk on barbiturates. Red-shoulder, the scream of screams. Not the dispirited cackle of a bald eagle, not the nonstop yelling of a goshawk. No discordant notes. Like Miles Davis, the cry of the red-shouldered meant to be savored. Hangs in the air for a moment, tapers, and fades. Repeats. Fades. Repeats. Adds life to a world already alive. I don't have to see the hawk. Listening to him hurl his voice like a javelin is enough.

Tanager in oaks. Ovenbird in maples. Red-eyed vireo everywhere. Most warblers are hushed or gone. Song sparrow sings and stops abruptly midsong. Two rough patches of jays, family groups, separated by a half-mile, rip through the canopy. Rowdy. Full-grown chicks beg. Parents accede.

Black-billed cuckoo in the shadows across the marsh, voice a drizzle rather than a storm. A bird flies into big, decrepit aspen, the one with the widow-maker limb hanging straight down, its movements screened by leaves. A cuckoo? Maybe. It's the right size, and still as stone. Picks something off the back of a leaf. One of the inexhaustible supply of caterpillars? Perhaps a treefrog? Well hidden by fluttering leaves. I wait for disclosure, expectantly. A jay flies into the aspen. Another and another and another. Imagined cuckoo becomes a jay—right size, wrong bird. Five jays comb the canopy, a taciturn family more concerned with dining than chattering. Four jays leave. One stays.

Dogs disturb a nest of yellowjackets, which disturbs me. Chaos reigns. I drop leashes and run. Stings burn for the moment but itches last for days. Yellowjackets find me too attractive. Once, on a sunny July afternoon, Weedwacking in shorts and sandals, shirtless along the upper-pasture fence, debris sprayed my legs and chest . . . I blundered on, ensconced in headphones and safety goggles, merrily singing Dylan songs.

> *Yes, and how many times can a man turn his head*
> *And pretend that he just doesn't see?*

Thirty-five stings later, I dropped the Weedwacker and raced inside, my legs and chest peppered with burning welts, a character witness for my own stupidity.

From far away and high above, through a sieve of raindrops, a red-shouldered hawk flings his voice, a declaration of undisguised satisfaction filtering through the interstices of the old aspen, gliding down the columns of a July morning. When the world stagnates, when heat and humidity clamp down, and midsummer melancholy rises like steam, I'm reminded (again) that forces at work across the calendar make every day a unique adventure. Like fingerprints and iris scans, days are singular, each flung widely and indifferently across the wrinkled landscape. *Life*, claimed Forest Gump, *is like a box of chocolates. You never know what you're going to get.* I never know what I'm going to get . . . but 2020, unquestionably, is all nuts.

Day 125

20 July 2020

Hope springs eternal.
ALEXANDER POPE

5:26 A.M. (sunrise one minute later than yesterday). 71 degrees, wind S 5 mph. Sky: overcast with striations, then mackerel clouds, dappled and ribbed, ruffled and torn; openings basted pastel peach, fractured clouds mauve edged. Wretchedly humid, a marinating world. Dew-draped spiderwebs. A sprawling and moveable feast, an aerial landscape that belongs in Eliot Porter's portfolio. Intermittent streams: trickle and puddle. Permanent streams: more pulse than flow, took a hit in yesterday's heat. Wetlands: doe grazes the marsh, head barely above the surface, red-brown offset by green reeds. Somewhere a hidden fawn. Pond: whirligig beetles motoring in concentric circles, round and round as if stuck in first gear. Male kingfisher, the first I've seen here all year, stares down the pond; frogs and tadpoles, beware. Changes perches, rattling as though deeply disturbed. Maybe kingfisher hatched nearby, in an esker or the bank of the Connecticut River in the company of bank swallows and woodchucks. Or arrived from beyond, slowly working his way to Costa Rica. Either/or, he pauses for a snack along the road to elsewhere.

DOR: lousy night for green frogs. Scattered in huddled wreckage—one adult, four froglets.

AOR: pair of robins, always robins. Flattened frogs don't interest them.

Deerflies, little hollow tubes of hunger, desperate to be filled. Gorgeous rainbowed eyes and large transparent wings with dark bands. All the better to find me with. Like mosquitos and ticks, females imbibe blood to provision eggs. Her sling-blade mouth slices skin, an anticoagulant keeps blood flowing, and a spongy labrum laps it up. Males have weak mouths (like the husbands of many of my mother's friends), sip nectar, eat pollen, and *never* disagree (overtly). Growing up on Long Island, I faced the greenhead, the saltmarsh version of the deerfly. Emerald eyes and even bigger appetites, adding a *kamikaze* element to clamming or fishing the Great South Bay. The jumbo version of the deerfly is the horsefly, an insect big enough to hit with a shovel and a constant companion across the Everglades.

I need to commission a dragonfly (or two) to hover over my head, tethered to my binoculars. I'd send it across the morning, sweeping my personal space clear of deerflies and mosquitos. Unfortunately, the cloud of dragonflies that once patrolled the marsh decamped with the beaver, leaving me to slap, pinch, swear, and suffer.

The musical fabric of the neighborhood: crow shouts across the valley; ravens kibitz; four white-breasted nuthatches on white pine trunk, stutter (all at once); alder flycatcher, first I've heard in a month, an ascending *rrep, rrep*, sounds like angry phoebe; chickadee crowd in hemlock, one whistling, his two-note song sure to light up a February morning but out of place in the doldrums. Beyond the marsh, red-shouldered hawk screams, and barred owl barks. Yellow-billed cuckoo, soft, hollow note repeated at intervals, suggests an American bittern wearing a facemask. Tanager, breast and back still the color of molten metal until dowsed by the season, sings in the oaks, a series of hoarse, smoky phrases. Pack-a-day music makes similarly patterned robin sound like Jeff Buckley. A last look before he leaves, the last glimpse of indescribable red set off by coal-black wings . . . a secretive songbird espied in green leaves.

Loquacious blue jays, ten or twelve, a *mishpocha* on a Saturday outing, morsels of October in the bowels of summer. Chase each other around like kids on a playground. Wild troop enlivens the morning. Three red-eyed vireos by the lower stream engage in a cloying battle royal, each bird singing a phrase every couple of seconds, stupefyingly repetitive. *Here-I-am, up-in-a-tree. Here-I-am* . . . the dullest of musical messengers, but ho-hum songbird stands out as feathered metronome, setting the beat as summer drifts ineluctably toward autumn.

Full-throated and exuberant, robins everywhere rally. Drown out vireos, a monumental achievement. Parade earth-tone breasts around the road, in the trees, fearless and personable. Emissaries from the lawns of my boyhood. A bird that marks the travels of my life. We've crossed paths in Alaskan spruce glades; in Indiana soybean fields; on the slopes of the Sierras, the Rockies, the Cascades, the Black Hills, the Appalachians, the Ozarks; from coast to coast and along the rim of Hudson Bay and Bay of Fundy; along the margins of significant north-south and west-east rivers; in dark flocks constellating by the thousands in the Everglades. In city parks and cemeteries, playgrounds and parking lots. You can't go anywhere in North America outside the company of robins, which is why I'm devoted to them. Earlier this summer, robins nested in the basket of Nancy's scooter, high on a shelf on the back wall, deep in the cave of her garage.

For the past three years, Nancy has neutralized emotional isolation and softened rough edges (at least, those not already petrified). She's been a culinary and landscaping advisor, a department-store-field-trip organizer, and a walking and hiking buddy. Reluctantly, I swim with her. Enthusiastically, I lie in rivers with her, water pouring over us. We've attended Atlantic waves and stared at a condor above Big Sur. Nancy introduced me to the plight of the homeless and convinced me to volunteer at the local food shelf, most of whose volunteers had begun to self-isolate at the onset of Covid. She allowed me to partially unmake myself (no small achievement). We met on Match . . . nothing had prepared me for senior-dating and the unleashing of schoolboy giddiness. My parents bickered through sixty years, bombarding each other with assorted, petty grievances; starting over was unimaginable for them. Since Linny died and Annie left (twice), my emotional life has mirrored my geography, undulating and repetitious, feeling better and worse by turns. Desire still swells with possibility even if we kiss with our masks on and I can't see her indoors. Nancy and robins fill a void.

∾

Robins, like my girlfriend: consistent, dependable, attractive, of good voice, an intimate and cheerful bird, the ideal companion for a world awash in a mutating virus.

Day 127

22 July 2020

If you wish to make an apple pie from scratch,
you must first invent the universe.
CARL SAGAN

5:28 A.M. (sunrise one minute later than yesterday). 60 degrees, wind SE less than 1 mph. Sky: malleable clouds, swirls and layers; blue-gray with bright rims and shifting hints of mauve. A dynamic and mesmerizing Rorschach test. Last night, sitting in a front-yard lawn chair, I watched a cloud evanesce, become a trace of itself, dissolving into dusk like an

Alka-Seltzer tablet in a glass of water. Permanent streams: wait for rain (like everything else), lulled and unhurried, losing ground by the hour. Wetlands: lusciously green, the suggestion of mist. Across the marsh, far up the western flank, hermit thrush angelically vitalizes the morning. Green frog, in need of tuning, joins in. Pond: threads of exfoliating vapor quickly vanish (from the pages of the hydrologic cycle). Another critical portion of the cycle, rain, remains a promise. We need more than a thunderstorm . . . we need a revitalizing soak, something my driveway can handle. How many times am I going to mistake the same snag for the emergent head of a snapping turtle?

Rain of lavender raspberry petals. Jewelweed blooming, tiny orange trumpets, hummingbird goblets that eventually ripen into banana-shaped seedpods that curl and explode when touched. Unintended gift of a very small bird.

Two red-shouldered hawks screaming. Pass overhead, just above the green archway. On view for a nanosecond, voices lagging behind them. Pair of unhurried robins, pecking and picking, escort me down the driveway. High in oak, tanager's long, raspy-phrased song is dull compared to its plumage. Ovenbird, alder flycatcher, yellowthroat, and chestnut-sided warbler hushed. The list goes on . . . and on. Mnemonically, pewee whistles signal the next phase.

House wren, an audio sniper, rapid-fire from the pines. Color may be subdued but not voice. An effervescent crooner, a machine-gun minstrel. Much sound from such a little bird. Everyone should have a house wren in their neighborhood. There's never a dull moment, nor a silent one. Full of verve and mischief. I wish I had assigned the house wren as my boys' totem—the ideal bird to emulate. Every day's an adventure in sound, an excellent repertoire of trills, rattles, bubbly notes, and nasal whines. All flung carelessly from a thicket, never a sad, gentle acoustical ballad. House wrens nest from southern Canada to southern Argentina and on the Caribbean isles, the most widely distributed bird in the New World, a hemispheric bird full of life and unincorporated . . . ought to make every undocumented immigrant feel at home . . . even if we don't.

Insect chorus begins to replace bird chorus. Six-legged minstrels: crickets and grasshoppers. Dog-day harvest flies, big, green, and pop eyed, high-whining electrical buzz that overwhelms the afternoon. (I'd need headphones to endure seventeen-year cicadas.)

Last night, after ten o'clock, I stood on a bridge over the outlet of Lake Fairlee and watched comet Neowise, low in the northeast. A smudge in unmarred emptiness, a fuzz ball with a dimly lit squirrel's tail. Headed west toward Colorado, toward Casey and Becky. I watched the comet and thought of them, on the edge of Colorado National Monument, under star-spangled heaven, dark as my cellar. Comet-perfect landscape like a Vermont night. Comet Neowise last passed this way 6,800 years ago, just after the discovery of cheese. Back then, lions prowled the British Isles and leopards, Greece. Steppe bison roamed Alaska; dwarf woolly mammoths, Wrangle Island in the Bering Sea; jaguars, Florida; miniature elephants, the Mediterranean isles; ground sloths, Cuba. Hawaii was an unpeopled island chain. South Florida was underwater. Fresh from glacial refuges off the Carolina coast, timber rattlesnakes headed north. Back then, no one rode a horse or ate rice.

So much happened in 6,800 years . . . a geologic blink. So much happened in the past four months, a deplorable misstep. Where are the three men on camels?

Day 128

23 July 2020

My future is behind me.
STEPHEN B. RASHKIN

5:28 A.M. (sunrise one minute later than yesterday). 64 degrees, wind ESE 2 mph. Sky: fog-soaked and opaque. Off-and-on drizzle; pitter-patter of dripping leaves. Then Coyote Hollow reveals itself incrementally, a three-dimensional Polaroid snapshot. Permanent streams: refreshed and gurgling. Wetlands: morning's breath dispersing. Pond: mobile quilling, a hypnotic run of concentric circles.

Ferns and coltsfoot, upright and green.

Lead singers, morning chorus: robins, everywhere and boldly incessant. Background vocals (the avian versions of Darlene Love's *Twenty Feet from Stardom*): scarlet tanager, ovenbird (one), chickadees, white-breasted nuthatch (two chicks chase a parent), veery (calling), red-eyed vireos (hard to believe that they're self-effacing), woodcock (flushed from the road, wings whirring), pewee (soft and elegiac), crows, blue jays, yellow-billed cuckoo (once again), white-throated sparrow (clipped song), song sparrows, pileated (most percussive), barred owls (up late, carry on), house wren (pretense of song), goldfinches.

Deer bolts across the road fifty feet in front of us. Dogs alert. Leashes tighten. Another deer bounds across the marsh, shoulder-high in reeds, tail immaculate and erect, a beacon in dispersing mist. When Ken Kesey was asked about the 1969 Apollo Moon Landing, he replied that "we don't deserve to be in space until we learn to live on Earth." My boys grew up watching and listening to the kaleidoscopic assemblage of creatures that live or pass through Coyote Hollow. I encouraged them to embrace the world, to bond with their home ground, to track the seasons across the marsh and hills, landscape engorged with detail. I wanted muck to rise between their toes, the night to awaken their curiosity. I wanted them to contemplate the stars, the freedom of uncluttered time when hours pass like minutes, the magic of the world opening like a flower.

The other night, when Casey called and insisted I stay up to see the fuzz-ball comet, we had come full circle, the child now the father of the man . . . the father leaning on the warm hood of his car, childlike, peering into the unfathomable night sky.

Day 130

25 July 2020

We are like butterflies who flutter for a day and think it is forever.
CARL SAGAN

5:31 A.M. (sunrise one minute earlier than yesterday). 57 degrees, wind calm, 0 mph. Sky: who knows? Atmosphere spreadable, congealed to meringue thickness. Intermittent streams: current bearing. Permanent streams: aroused by rain, beds half full, speaking in faint aqueous lilt. Wetlands: fog makes the marsh appear endless, far shoreline erased.

Dew-pendant spiderwebs, stitched to reeds, sparkle. Pond: surface taut and brown. Fog appears confused. Heads east and then north and then east again. Painted turtle floats spread-eagle, poker chip with legs, shell barely above the water.

Joe-pye weed blooms and black-eyed Susan fades.

DOR: three-year-old garter snake. Flesh of pine cone, scales removed by a red squirrel, seeds eaten. What remains, scrawny like a corncob or a bald squirrel's tail.

AOR: hermit thrush; robin flogs helpless frog, maybe a peeper.

Front-yard freeloaders: chickadees, doves, jays, purple finches, and goldfinches.

Beyond the feeders: robins toned down (someone must have complained). Warblers, hushed or gone. Lone tanager in oak interrupts departure preparations and sings, farewell to summer. I can't find him. Pewee whistles. Pileated yells, a volley—*kuk, kuk, kuk, kuk*—full and wild. Sweet-voiced veery, a dulcet Rumpelstiltskin spins fog into music. House wren ignites. Filling auditory gaps, red-eyed vireos, vinyl records run amok, for a moment make me forget that warblers attend to pre-migratory chores . . . fattening up. Summer ripens.

Pond-outflow culvert similar to bathroom faucet, constant leak. I stare at the drip. A clatter of pebbles. Dogs stiffen. An otter emerges from an adventure in the marsh, scrambles up the bank, looks askance, and then passes under the drip, through the culvert, and into the pond, flat head just above the surface. Tiny ears. Black-button eyes. Black nose, wide like the dogs'. Back straight, and tail—a long, muscular cable— arched. Swims back and forth, a wake trailing behind. Otter submerges, leaving behind two bubbles and rings of concentric ripples, an impressionist. Surfaces with a fish and a gentle exhale more sigh than blast. Dives again. A crayfish. Repeats seven more times. Seven more crayfish, one so big claws stick out of its mouth. An imperial sportsman, an audible breakfast, crunching of bones and shells.

Above the otter: catbird cuts lose; kingfisher passes back and forth, ungovernable rattles. Bittern arrives from the marsh, stands motionless in the cattails, faces away from the water, bill skyward, swaying. Turns toward the water, spears green frog. A second otter walks out of a bank of ferns. Sees me. Walks back in.

Gift of a peaceful morning: otter's breath, kingfisher's rattle. Sunlight turns fog translucent. Time stops. Immersed in endless delight, I have no option but to stay.

Otter

I watched the comet again last night from the bridge over the outflow from Lake Fairlee. A crescent moon sank behind Gove Hill. Jupiter and its entourage of satellites rose in the southeast. The comet appeared midway below the Big Dipper's ladle, a woolly core with a million-mile debris trail, a cosmic dust bunny stretched across an unfathomable distance. Makes me feel small . . . ego reduction from the dawn of the universe.

Owl hoots. Loon wails. I leaned against the warm car, humbled by the illusion of distance and the tragedy of time . . . freeloading like birds in my yard.

Day 131

26 July 2020

*. . . but we have yet to verify any purpose in nature
beyond life's own persistence.*
Hal Borland

5:32 A.M. (sunrise one minute earlier than yesterday). 58 degrees, wind NNE less than 1 mph. Sky: mottled, white and dull blue-gray. As the sun rises over the eastern escarpment, a single peach-tinged highlight infiltrates other clouds, then spreads until most are silver buffed. Fog sits above half a dozen marshes, a serpentine ribbon above the East Branch of the Ompompanoosuc River. Permanent streams: soft hum and slow flow; predacious water striders skate on drying puddles, waiting for breakfast to drop in. Wetlands: bowl of green softened by gaunt mist, which vanishes above the treetops. Few dragonflies on patrol. Pond: two painted turtles idle on the surface; two hooded mergansers bolt, skittering across brown water, airborne, turn west, pitching into the marsh. Mother and one chick (down from eight). She's either an empty nester (I can relate) or parent in mourning, or both. Second-year tadpoles join the terrestrial ranks, hang on the shoreline, in the shadow of reeds, illustrating the 360-million-year-old first step fish took that eventually led to amphibians, then reptiles and mammals . . . to Charles Darwin, Albert Einstein, Mother Teresa, Zora Neale Hurston, Jonas Salk, Mahatma Gandhi, and Derek Jeter.

Queen Anne's lace blooms along the road. Overhead, in black cherry, the first fall webworm tents.

Red-shouldered hawk slings its voice out of a nearby marsh, up and over the western ridge, arrows of sound piercing the morning. Birds of intemperate song, red-eyed vireos and robins, vociferous opponents of the dog days, performing with early June enthusiasm. Pewee whistles, sad little darts. High in an oak guarded by leaves, scarlet tanager sings robustly. Needs a voice coach. Why so secretive? His pack-a-day voice, which is not his best attribute, draws my attention. His color . . . jungle incarnate, a raiment of Benjamin-Moore-red set against wings midnight black—a bird that needs to be seen. I search to no avail.

Fractured song of the hermit thrush, sheltered from the sky, emissary of deep woods. Chickadees. Titmice. A lonely crow. House wren sings a clipped version of the chart-topping hit, hurriedly, as though late for an appointment. Blue jay flies by with a caterpillar; speaks with a full mouth. Abridged songs: purple finch, goldfinch, song sparrow, white-throated sparrow, both nuthatches, catbird (no Charlie Parker today). Again, a yellow-billed cuckoo, an echo of itself . . . I can get used to monitoring sunrise. (Do I have a choice?)

⁓

Two bats behind the sliding barn door, the descendants of sixty million years of evolution, ambassadors of Deep Time, born in a temporal cleft left by dinosaurs. Radical mammals incorporated flight; also incorporated zoonotic viruses, including SARS, MERS, Ebola, Nipah, and rabies. We brought bats white-nose syndrome. Bats brought us Covid.

Bats tolerate viruses, a biological corruption. The elevated body temperature required for flights holds most germs at bay. According to a recent investigation, the physiological strain of flying produced leaky cells that release scraps of free-floating DNA. Bats tolerate wafting bits of DNA without a severe immune response, thus avoiding inflammation and possible grounding . . . hence, a hospitable environment predisposed to invading viruses, which linger indefinitely or are delivered to more susceptible mammals: pigs and civets. Or us. Our diet should not impinge on our welfare. Bats are not commodities.

As an undergraduate at Ball State University, I helped a professor who banded bats, which is like banding birds, except bats have sharp teeth and carry diseases. At twilight, more than a thousand little brown bats (*Myotis lucifugus*) and big brown bats (*Eptesicus fuscus*) left their nursery in a decrepit Indiana barn. Once outside, they trolled the night. Little browns ate little bugs; big browns ate big bugs. To leave the barn, they passed through a gauntlet of mist nets. We'd catch thirty or forty and then fix them with aluminum anklets. An eerie world of fidgety bats, a stuttering flight lit by headlamps. Sizzling and reeking, high-pitched squeals ... a discordant broadcast suitable for a nightmare. Pure Hitchcock.

Several years later, in Hancock, New Hampshire, I glued phosphorescent gelatin capsules on the stomachs of bats. Green capsules for little brown bats. Blue for big browns. I tracked their feeding frenzy over Willard Pond from my kayak, midlake on a dark night. Green looped lower over the water. Blue higher. Bats divvy resources, reducing competition. Like deranged fireworks, phosphorescent curlicues stitched the night. A psychedelic feast lasted until the water-soluble glue dissolved and the lake doused the lights.

My barn hosted a dozen little brown bats not too long ago. Half an hour after sunset, bats flew above the pasture, each the moving epicenter of an entwined oval. Some circled outside lights like fish to chum. I miss bats the way I missed butterflies and bees that visited my mother's garden in the late fifties—and then suddenly vanished into a sticky haze of backyard pesticides.

What's the moral of this Covid tale? Eating bats . . . barbaric. Watching bats . . . immense and purposeful pleasure. Long may they hawk mosquitos and pollinate bananas.

It's hard to say when—or if—little brown bats will return to vacant airspace above the pasture. I take solace in the two behind the door, survivors of their own crippling epidemic.

∽

In the act of extreme social distancing, crow calls into an empty landscape. I *caw* back, trying to make a lonely bird feel at home, black and shiny on a pine limb. What became of his flock? Like me, crow craves company ... just not mine.

Day 135

30 July 2020

Solitary the thrush,
The hermit withdrawn to himself, avoiding the settlements,
Sings by himself a song.

Song of the bleeding throat . . .
WALT WHITMAN

5:36 A.M. (sunrise one minute later than yesterday). 61 delightful degrees, wind calm, 0 mph. Sky: peach-washed lines of clouds in the south, spotless everywhere else, gradually lightening, lumen by lumen, heaven wiping the sleep from its eyes. Woods twilit, pastures and meadows warm sunlight. Permanent streams: emulating birdsong, both drying up. Upper, a detectable pulse. Lower, ratcheting scarcity; two puddles, otherwise, join the water table below the surface. Striders are long gone. Wetlands: suggestion of ground fog, soft brushstrokes thicken and spread. Green frog sole voice in a vast marsh. Beyond the far shore, webworm tents swelling and increasing. Yellow-billed cuckoo calls three times, celebration of an impending feast—hairy caterpillars by the gazillions. Pond: tendrils of mist, periscoping painted turtle, yellow stripes in brown water, dark as the Black Hole of Calcutta. No bittern. No otter. Great blue heron, pipe neck folded and stilt legs trailing, toes impossibly long, flushes from the south, where the fog convenes. Wings extended, curved downward like a long, narrow, gray umbrella. What scientists and architects call *camber*. An emblem of the outback, mythic and ubiquitous wading bird, patroller of the wetlands. Silhouette of nobility, the voice of indigestion. Mantled by mist. Circling, circling, circling.

Milkweed pods ripen. No sign of monarchs. Webworm tents mostly in black cherry; one in alder.

Knot of five little brown bats behind the barn door, second day in a row.

Born on a breeze, hatched amid a fortress of stone, turkey vultures are the essence of a hot summer day. For much of the summer, once the day begins to cook, I watch vultures cut lazy circles over the marsh, flight feathers fingering the wind. A gentle rocking flight, living kites adrift. Dipping over the reeds, rising over the eastern flank of Robinson Hill, and disappearing into rocky outcrops. The vultures search for carrion, flesh glued to hide. Perhaps deer, raccoon, or liquefying mouse, a morsel swallowed whole like an aspirin.

One April morning, eleven years ago, while hunting for timber rattlesnakes in the Bull Run Mountains of northern Virginia, I startled a turkey vulture hidden in a jumble of boulders. The bird ascended a hole in the canopy, circled a few times, then landed on the stout limb of an oak. In the boulder cave were two cream-colored eggs, decorated with a disarray of spots and squiggles as if Jackson Pollack had stood above them with a dripping paintbrush.

Later that summer, on the eastern face of Robinson Hill, Jordan and William, attracted by sibilant screeches and the smell of rotting meat, found a vulture nest. Inside a stone alcove, two nearly full-grown vulture chicks stood upright and pear shaped, two feet tall. Twilight gray, downy white shawls, and fuzzy as faux-fur pillows. A pair of pubescent teenagers and a couple of foul-smelling Big Birds. Quintessential adolescents . . . awkward, ruckus raisers, on the verge of leaving home.

⌒

In 1927, hermit thrush became the state bird of Vermont. There were more than a hundred other birds to choose from.

Morning of the hermit thrush, virtuosos at the dawn, distilling mist into scraps of song, hollow and haunting. A sextet of crippled flutes. Fragments of bittersweet music, ephemeral as summer sun. Maverick and solitary songbirds, back on stage for an encore performance just as the songs of others birds fade in the twilight. Thrushes sing midlevel in the woods, below the canopy and above the floor. Ovenbirds (muted now) also sing midlevel. Their song, loud and sharp, bludgeons. Thrushes soothe and quench, a trace of melancholy rolling out of hidden crags and recesses. Usher me into the moment, prisoner-of-the-moment for a moment, which is all I really have . . . as summer begins to slide ineluctably toward autumn. I'm spellbound.

I want to bottle the song of the blueberry-voiced bird, preserve it like summer jam, and then hit replay on a dismal November morning. Thrush song rising within me, a euphoric ascendancy . . . welcome counterpoint to Covid bleakness. Hermit thrush makes my world a better place.

Day 138

02 August 2020

If he were human, it would be the laugh of the deeply insane.
JOHN McPHEE

5:39 A.M. (sunrise one minute later than yesterday). 60 degrees, wind NE less than 1 mph. Sky: coagulation of clouds, a few with silver shimmer, opens reluctantly. Fogless. Intermittent streams: dents in the woods lined with pine needles and other woodland debris. Permanent streams: upper, hushed trickle; lower, retreats underground farther upstream, abandoning bed of water-abraded stones that, two months ago, hid blackfly larvae and sticklebacks. House wren and jay emote above dry bed. Wetlands: quiet and without fog; a tired shade of green dulled by summer's progress, more buff than verdant. In the hemlocks, on the far side of the marsh, owl barks, clipped version of midnight chart topper. Pond: thin, rolling mist, more exhalation than outpour. Two painted turtles sink below the surface.

Goldenrod blooming.

Old big-toothed aspen, sparsely leafed and leaning, serious widow-maker hanging down. Punky wood is easily excavated. Prospective tenement for cavity nesters. If I mirrored the tree, I'd be hooked to oxygen and clutching a walker. Uninterested in my opinions, chickadee finds caterpillars in the leaves. Plucks a few . . . then decamps.

August lull: pockets of birdsong framed by *long* stretches of silence. Delusional tanager, loud and hidden, sings as if it's May. Red-eyed vireo, unaccompanied soloist in the maples. Robin, with *chutzpah*, less than twenty feet away, leads dogs and me down the road; pause, hustle, pause, hustle, and then flies behind us and begins again. Hermit thrush, quelled by distance, song a suggestion of itself. Red-breasted nuthatch, a tricycle horn call, rising and tedious. Titmouse whistles.

Too high to have left nearby Lake Fairlee, loon angles southeast, trailing its voice across a tessellation of woods and marshes, tremolos raining on Coyote Hollow. If the call could be liquefied, streams would gush. Neck extended, back humped. Wide webbed feet extend beyond the short tail, calibrating the wind. Weighs up to fourteen pounds, bones robust, wings short by comparison. Constantly flaps, never glides . . . but fast, seventy miles per hour, arrow straight. In pursuit of fish, a loon may hold its breath for five minutes and dive more than two hundred feet into the cold abyss of a northern lake. A family of four eats more than a thousand pounds of fish in fifteen weeks. Long-lived, up to thirty years. Loyal, mates for life. But like many modern marriages, couples spend the winter apart, sometimes separated by more than a thousand miles, alone or with a raft of others, loons bunching and riding the rolling Atlantic.

Summer 1977. I surveyed nesting loons for New Hampshire Audubon, the best summer job ever—far better than answering the rare phone call in a carpet warehouse, reading Edgar Rice Burroughs, and perfecting a Tarzan call. Had kayak, would travel everywhere from remote Lake Umbagog to Lake Massabesic on the urban threshold of Manchester. One afternoon, I lunched with Judy McIntyre, a loon biologist from Syracuse University. At forty-five, while raising three children, she wrote a doctoral thesis on the common loon (*Gavia immer*), which remains the loon bible. A biologist with a sense of humor, McIntyre said,

> Anyone who has seen a loon egg is apt to remember it first for its size.
> Any female loon who has ever laid one no doubt remembers it for the same reason.

McIntyre also said that a species of blackfly that feeds exclusively on loon blood, a relationship honed over millions of years, was responsible for more than 20 percent of nest abandonments. Female black flies, which drive loons crazy, find the nest by the scent of loon semen dribbled everywhere. Loons may be the earliest known case of premature ejaculation at nearly forty million years old. I've not been able to verify or disprove the semen portion of McIntyre's story . . . I've not forgotten it either.

Overhead loon, bathed in yellow sunlight, laughing. At the quirkiness of evolution? Or at my gullibility . . . surprise me, morning, surprise me.

Day 141

05 August 2020

This
is not a poem about a dream,
though it could be.

This is a poem about the world that's ours,
or could be.

Mary Oliver

5:43 A.M. (sunrise two minutes later than yesterday). 62 degrees, wind SSW 9 mph—trees swaying and leaves in motion. Sky: mottled, bright with peach highlights. Air refreshed, leaves and needles spraying rain-drops. Intermittent streams: flowing and vaguely humming. Attenuated and shallow. Permanent streams: upper and lower bound for glory, flowing and gurgling (although not as loud as I had expected given yesterday's tropical storm), pirating the flow of the three intermittent streams . . . a portion of the woodland circulatory system that begins as mushy depressions on the western flank of Robinson Hill. Many depressions linger as seeps and springs. In a rainless day or two, the water table recedes. Wetlands: more vibrant than yesterday, a run of green and beige with *Spirea* flower heads pinking the drier rims, mist an afterthought. Pond: exhalations drift east across a faintly jiggled surface. Reflections of two black-eyed Susans, an upside-down Monet suitable for framing.

Rain of ash seeds torn from treetops, undiscriminating litter. Small limbs and twigs and a thirty-foot snag brought down by the high wind, a forest pruning. Colony of maidenhair fern, wet fronds, leaning and overlapping like snake scales. Goldenrod and jewelweed flowering. Old aspen still standing. My roadway footpath, more ruts than road, a candi-date for Pot Hole National Monument.

More cricket song than bird song. Webworm tents expand into town-houses and condos . . . cuckoo takeout.

Soundscape: three hummingbirds, hovering and chasing, wings con-versing; two robins quietly clucking (four others in the maples hushed); five blue jays and a forlorn crow. Red-breasted nuthatch cuts into the morning with a series of *yanks*. Fluty thrush deep in the woods. Red-eyed vireo in hardwoods sings his heart out. Stiletto cry of red-shoul-dered hawk. Tanager on a mission, pack-a-day in the driveway oaks.

Warblers, flycatchers, and most vireos too busy carbo-loading to sing.

Behind the barn door: little brown bats, the party of five, canceled reservations and moved on.

Several hundred feet above the marsh, flying due south, barn swallow en route to Peru. Graceful little bird, alone in a vast sky, heads toward the seaboard. I recall August gatherings of barn swallows above Cape Cod dunes and outer beaches of Long Island, gracefully and gratefully hawking greenheads over the salt marsh. All motion, like campfire sparks, twisting, turning, pivoting, mouths agape trolling for lunch. Occasionally, a merlin, also on the move, chased one straight up the sky ladder, where delicate birds—no matter how graceful—stagger in the turbulence and become vulnerable.

Enchanted, I watch the swallow arrow above sedge and cattail, above maple and beech, an envoy from beyond vanishing into beyond like a thought unleashed, a great unifier that binds seemingly disparate worlds, making a travesty of civilization. Swallow ignores boundaries, ideologies, religions, misinformation, political parties, and pandemics. Unveils the poetry of the natural world, reminds me that like the constellated, unfathomable sky, Earth carries the burden of its own history, enticing and ebullient. The price of admission: stop and look.

Day 143

07 August 2020

Between two pine trees there is a door leading to a new life.
JOHN MUIR

5:45 A.M. (sunrise one minute later than yesterday). 52 degrees (denim jacket to stay warm, not as a fortress against deer flies), wind W 1 mph. Sky: mostly clear, a few streaks and a tubular, white-fuzzy-caterpillar cloud lurking east of midsky. Ground fog. The moon, a smidgen more than half, leans west. World dew-brushed and refreshed. Bowl-and-doily spiderwebs pepper the lawn. Permanent streams: upper, less water than yesterday, volume turned down; lower, memory haunts the streambed, faintly audible, and then retreats underground, again. Parched landscape. Wetlands: a bowl of upwardly mobile mist; a world of silhouettes, by midmarsh green turns gray, brown turns gray, gray turns grayer and pale against the western sky. Crowns of evergreens in sharp relief. Pond: crickets keep pace with the temperature, barely audible. Very few monarchs and dragonflies. Cold forces deer flies and mosquitos into lockdown.

Overripe: red raspberries. Peaking: blueberries. Coming on: blackberries.

Morning belongs to goldfinches, everywhere. Pewee whistles less enthusiastically than in July. Red-eyed vireos reassure me they haven't left. Catbird meows halfheartedly.

Two birds, more significant than either robin or jay, move unhurriedly, high in aspen crown. Screened by leaves and frustratingly unidentifiable. I look into the green convergence, set in motion by slow-moving birds. Two minutes. Five minutes. Ten minutes. Birds in aspen, me on the road, chafing. I glimpse a cuckoo. What species?

Culvert stones damp from a water-dripping belly. A lithe, playful otter left the puddled marsh, crossed under the road, scaled the berm, and entered through the culvert, emerging into the brown pond. A narrow trail in the brush piques dogs' interest. We're all beside ourselves, jubilant, adrift in otter daydreams. Dogs, nuzzling wet grass, read a script I cannot possibly imagine. Breathe deeply, piggy snorts, basking in otter essence. Ten legs. Six eyes. Three noses, one of which is not up to the task of unraveling the mysteries of a roving otter. Excitement? Palpable.

The water surface, skintight and empty, veiled in a careless drift of fog. Nowhere an otter. An itinerant fisherman, wanderer of backwaters, otter crosses hills, summer and winter, perhaps miles from open water, coasting across the corrugated land. Making a game of life. I once saw one on the interstate, a royal but sad DOR, far from its natal element.

Otter may be in New Hampshire, dining in brutal elegance on bullheads, or nearby in the alders, asleep in the derelict beaver lodge. Crown prince of the watershed, the court jester of the reeds, gallivants across my imagination, touching me in absentia. A mammal to emulate . . . always game for a game. A solitary party or mother and pups. Play. Play. Play.

I walk among maples, over rolling terrain, far from rawboned and lofty. An invitation offered, a mystery to contemplate. Equal opportunities to lose myself in either the grand sweep of Earth or the simple flash of a moment . . . the sun always rises somewhere.

An otter skull sits on my bookcase. Teeth falling out. A talisman packed and unpacked more times than I can remember. May explain why the teeth don't stay put. The skull is a portal into a world of stardust and sunshine. Linny lived forty-nine years, a twinkle—I've known rattlesnakes that lived longer. She took her magnetic personality and infectious laugh, her ability to make everyone comfortable, down to the grave. She died at home in our bed, surrounded by friends and music . . . mementos of a well-lived life. Yoked by grief, I stepped into the batter's box, two boys in scoring position. And the hollow-eyed otter, binge-watching memories that follow me around the house.

Day 145

09 August 2020

Incredibly, yet again, circumstances—
fate, luck, Providence, the hand of God,
as would be said so often—intervened.
DAVID McCULLOUGH

5:47 A.M. (sunrise one minute earlier than yesterday). 62 degrees, wind NW 1 mph. Sky: fog blankets the ground, visibility less than a hundred yards. The sort of fog that hid George Washington's nine thousand troops on the morning of 27 August 1776, when they crossed the East River, from Brooklyn to Lower Manhattan, avoiding surrender to British General Howe, which would have promptly ended the American Revolution. Coyote Hollow fog not as historically transformative, but inventive and profound, and likely as bewildering . . . grinds down terrain with ephemeral moisture. Hides contours. Fades color. Cleaves tree crowns. Hawks blind; mergansers swim with impunity. Sober woods brood and drip, Hansel and Gretel grimness. Intermittent streams: resurrected. Permanent streams: refreshed by yesterday's thunderstorm, which dumped more rain in half an hour than Tropical Storm Isaias did in an entire afternoon. Upper, swollen and boisterous; lower, flows all the way home, water striders back, skating the water tension, graceful, quick, lethal. Wetlands: hidden in chowder fog. Pond: mist thick enough to slice. Painted turtle breaks the surface, neck stripes a yellow beacon. Snapping turtle patrols the eastern shallows, body submerged, head periscoped, a prowling isle of antiquity.

Bats, party of two, behind the barn door.

~

Yesterday, a bear visited my neighbor, high on the eastern rim of Robinson Hill, not far from the sadness of the goshawks. Having previously witnessed bears in the yard, the barn, and the garage—disassembling birdfeeders, tipping over pails of sweet feed and black-oil sunflower seeds—I moved the birdfeeders in last night. Dogs tell me when the bear comes around. They chafe to be loose. Barking, primordial, and chilling. Canine determination and bruin expediency were hallmarks of the Ice Age . . . black bears evolved in the company of giant short-faced bears (the largest mammalian land carnivore ever), saber-toothed cats, American lions, dire wolves, and grizzlies, which is why black bears take to the trees when frightened. Climb first, ask questions later.

Dogs drive bears across the valley, agitation lagging behind them. Often, the bear climbs a tree, then the dogs circle, anxiously barking. Eventually, overcome by boredom, they head home. Once, I followed a bear down the valley listening to my neighbor's dogs. A game of canine telephone. Bear left the valley, towing dyspeptic barks like a string of cans.

~

Two yellow-billed cuckoos call, a door-knocking, *ku, ku, ku, ku*. Drizzles out of the crowns of ash and cherry. If I walked at the pace cuckoos move through the canopy, I'd be home for lunch. I wait. And wait. Finally, a glimpse. Long, thin bird, yellow-brown as bleached leaves, belly immaculately white, hunched over like a computer geek. Nicknamed *rain crow* because of a supposed tendency to call before a storm. Cuckoos, black-billed and yellow-billed, disinclined to predict the weather in The Hollow, and probably everywhere else.

Yellow-billed cuckoo, seventeen days from egg laying to fledging. No bird is faster. Baby feathers erupt from the sheaths when less than two hours old. Cuckoo eats giant, slow-moving insects: smooth, spiny, or hairy caterpillars; katydids; grasshoppers; cicadas; occasionally treefrogs and nestlings. Eats so many bristly caterpillars its gut fills with noxious spines; then, like a cat spitting up a hairball, cuckoo spits up the entire lining of its stomach, a process frequently repeated during the year.

Spends summer skulking in Coyote Hollow, winter sulking east of the Andes. To get to South America, the cuckoo must expose itself. Exhausted birds feed aplomado falcons over the plains of Mexico. A tiger shark caught offshore from Sarasota, Florida, had cuckoo feet and feathers in its stomach. Furtive cuckoo veiled in leaves. I struggle to see the bird stroll through the canopy, once more . . . doubled over like an old man on the boardwalk.

2020: summer of the comet, summer of the goshawk, summer of the cuckoo. Memoranda from beyond the pandemic.

Day 147

11 August 2020

People connect to the land as their imagination allows.
WILLIAM LEAST HEAT MOON

5:49 A.M. (sunrise one minute later than yesterday). Wind NW less than 1 mph. Sky: ground fog, thick and mobile, rolls up the valley, often to the treetops. Clear above. Leaf condensation dripping, sounds like rain, feels like rain. In the east, the moon, a sliver less than half, peeks through the mist. Intermittent streams: moist, rock ribs slick. Permanent streams: inspired by last night's thunderstorms; upper, purls in the narrower, deeper segments, mumbles in the broader, shallower stretches; lower, puddle chain extends close to the marsh, then peters out. Wetlands: fog meringue; far shore a memory. Pond: misty, still, no sign of activity on the surface. Just beyond the south shore, red squirrel moves along an avenue of pine limbs, tree to tree, chattering. Spiderwebs sag with dew, concentric necklaces. Each bead an inverted reflection of The Hollow.

Joe-pye weed and goldenrod blooming; blackberries ripening.

DOR: small green frog (*Lithobates clamitans*), a flicker of terrestrial life; mosquitoes slapped, pinched, ground . . . compliments of me.

AOR: hermit thrush, hushed and hurried, hops along the road's margin.

In the dimness of dawn, three hummingbirds (no males) make chaos around the feeder. One red-eyed vireo, persistent as fog, prolongs the ebb of Neotropical songs. Pewee's slurred whistle, summer's saddest song. Woodcock flushes from damp gully, a maelstrom of flapping. Sapsucker whines. Crow caws loudly, a disturbed broadcast that renders all other music mute by comparison. Nagging catbird, the dissatisfied toddler sound. Yellow-billed cuckoo, swallow-voiced and hungry, ready for the horde of fall webworms, which multiply on cherries, lilacs, and apples. For the webworms, many leaves, very little protein, continuously eating, and continuously growing. For the cuckoo, a webworm bonanza. Casey's black walnut, a veritable apartment complex of webworm tents, at least thirteen on one side, some sprawling, in need of a cuckoo. Whenever I pass the bedroom window, I glimpse the walnut, hoping to see a cuckoo, hunched over, tweezing caterpillars from webs.

Provident red squirrels remind me of my own winter chores. Mouths like shears snip green pine cones, which splash through maple leaves. Cut and drop. Squirrel, cone in mouth, climbs down trunk. Lots of chatter. Lots of harvest. Lots of storage . . . one big seasonal alert. My agenda, overcome inertia: order wood, plant more lettuce, prune maples around the barn, make pesto.

Lisping cedar waxwing, a bird I haven't seen in The Hollow all summer. Flies into a tangle of blackberries. Eats ebony fruit; leaves coral berries to ripen. Following waxwing's example, I graze blackberries, the juicy sweetness of midsummer. In late June 1978, Linny and I biked across the Adirondacks. Up slope and down. Birded by ear, songs seeping through our helmets. Guessing (approximate) elevation by the chorus of thrushes and warblers we heard. One morning, waxwings flushed from the shoulder of the road. Curious about their activity, we stopped, parted the wet grasses, and found the ground speckled red, dense with wild strawberries, each no bigger than a pinkie nail. We ate until our lips and fingers were stained red, then gathered a cup for camp. Made world-class strawberry pancakes.

Memory unspools like a coachwhip. Strawberries and waxwings, an innocent time, embroidered in 1950s optimism . . . before homeownership, before personal computers and cell phones, when only people a bubble off plumb chatted into thin air. Before our boys, dreams danced unencumbered. Life was horse-and-buggy simple. The mutiny of cancer reconfigured life; ravaged the ground beneath our feet like a woodchuck in the peas. Now, as the light dims, I savor sunrise, being ushered into the new day. Morning's soft hand turns back my clock, brightening my mood like a fresh coat of paint . . . for a moment.

Day 148

12 August 2020

*The health risks in a natural environment
can be made worse when we interfere with it.*

RICHARD OSTFELD

5:50 A.M. (sunrise one minute later than yesterday). 66 degrees, wind NNE 3 mph. The bright moon in the east eroding, horns showing. Wispy clouds, a hint of peach. Ground fog defines streams, rivers, and marshes. A graceful sunrise that could have been included in Eliot Porter's large-format photographic classic *In Wilderness is the Preservation of the World* (1962), a romance with New England woods. Permanent streams: upper, pinched and silent, still on the move; lower, a puddle faintly pulsed, more shadow than substance, retreats below the ground well before the road. Wetlands: fog thick in the middle, thin along the edges, a topknot of moisture. Pond: more haze than mist, shallow, furrowed surface, breeze at work. An unattended parade of methane bubbles, bantam half-domes adrift, bubbles burst like random thoughts.

The steady drone of crickets. Here and there, a drizzle of caterpillar poop, tiny pellets splashing off leaves, what biologists call *frass*, spills out of maple and ash, a digestive storm, woodland fertilizer. Sounds like rain, looks like rain . . . *not*. Last of the red-flowering raspberries, magenta petals on dark earth. Blackberries ripen. Milkweed pods swell, leaves unchewed. Fall webworm tents abundant, more prominent by the day, a spectacle of caterpillars, each almost an inch long.

Both nuthatches call. One pewee. One red-eyed vireo (I linger). Jays are vocally robust—honk, holler, screech. Pileated tattoos tree trunk.

DOR: juvenile white-footed mouse, big ears peppered with nymphal blacklegged ticks (*Ixodes scapularis*), the vector for Lyme disease. Each summer, in the eighties, I removed one or two American dog ticks (*Dermacentor variabilis*) from our collie. Both German shepherds tested positive for Lyme disease, a bacterial infection, although both were asymptomatic. Before I began giving them chewable repellents, I'd pull dozens of dog ticks off them from March to November. I'd regularly vacuum engorged lima-bean-shaped ticks off the floor, tiny legs sculling the air like puppets on a string, one of life's most significant torso-appendage mismatches.

Recently, I asked Northern Vermont University biologist Allan Giese, a black-legged tick specialist, what accounts for the dramatic increase in tick species and tick populations in the Northeast. He answered unflinchingly, "Climate change," ticks spreading northward and into higher elevations.

Mild winters and wet summers favor black-legged ticks, which move on average twenty-eight miles further north each year. Hungry larva and nymphs catch rides on ground-feeding birds (robins, hermit thrushes, and catbirds, for instance). Meals and transportation included.

◦◦

In the 1970s, Gil Raynor, one of Long Island's premier birders, died of Rocky Mountain spotted fever, a bacterial disease delivered by the American dog tick and misdiagnosed by hospital staff. Besides spotted fever and Lyme disease, ticks transmit *babesiosis*, a protozoan infection of red blood cells with malaria-like symptoms, and *powassan*, a viral infection that triggers encephalitis, averaging seven reported cases a year, including a recent death in Saratoga. *Anaplasmosis*, like Lyme disease, is a bacterial infection transmitted by black-legged ticks and is the second-most-common tick-borne disease in Vermont; symptoms include headache, nausea, and confusion . . . the very manifestations of excessive living room quarantining.

Ticks move like zombies. One speed, one direction, a stiff, endless, methodical forward plod . . . best described as creepy. Small spiders—often mistaken for ticks—are animated, scurrying and stopping, eight-legged windup toys that feast on ticks and other tiny things.

A small vial of alcohol sits on my desk, an eternal bath for three pickled black-legged tick nymphs, each no bigger than the period at the end of this sentence, small enough to decorate a mouse's ear . . . tiny and alarming, a gift from Allan Giese. The Northeast has the country's highest incidence of Lyme disease per capita. Scary as that may sound, if we truly understood tick biology, we'd reserve the worst of our primal fears for the dark of night. Infected mother ticks do not pass to their eggs the spirochete bacteria that causes Lyme disease. Larvae hatch clean and only later pick up the spirochete from feeding on the infected blood of white-footed mice and chipmunks, the most competent reservoir hosts. Then, nymphs and adults pass the disease to us.

Spraying pesticides around the home has the unintended consequence of killing spiders, a principal predator of black-legged ticks. Ground-feeding birds transport ticks back long before the spider population recovers. Desiccation kills blacklegged ticks, which is why they avoid pinewoods and, on sweltering August afternoons, retreat under moist leaf litter. They avoid mowed lawns, even uncut meadows, the domain of the thicker-carapaced American dog tick.

Giese has never suffered Lyme disease, never been bitten. His secret: carry a change of clothes, and then cook your field clothes in the car carrier or at home in the dryer; take a shower and scrub.

∽

Hummingbirds chase each other around the feeder, in and out of the cherry tree. Red-breasted nuthatch calls (and doesn't stop). House wren sings in the pines, a rickety-rackety song. Pewee shortens his song, half a plaintive whistle. Goldfinches flashing yellow dominate the landscape. Red squirrels in the pines harvest cones ahead of crossbills.

Robin, silent but active, runs feathers through her yellow bill, the first line of defense against ticks . . . preen, robin, preen.

Day 151

15 August 2020

The longest day of sunlight . . .
comes at the beginning of Summer rather than in its midst.
In consequence, all Summer long we are inclining towards Summer's end
instead of building to a climax and then tapering off.
HAL BORLAND

5:54 A.M. (sunrise one minute later than yesterday). 54 degrees, wind NW 2 mph. Sky: cloud curdled in the south, hints of mauve. Ephemeral rubble. Transparent everywhere else. Very local ground fog. Permanent streams: upper, staggers to the finish line; lower, a barren channel, a muted eulogy delivered by water-smooth stones. Out of habit, I think of the stream as *stable*. The rock-studded bed, established long ago, grooved and scoured over millennia, but water, at least, flowing water this summer, in this valley . . . as scarce as a cerulean warbler. Wetlands: a single line of impoverished mist in the northwest corner. Sunlight strokes the far-shore evergreens, bright green. The marsh still shaded, colors saturated. Spruce, pine, and hemlock cone-laden, a feast for red squirrels; later, perhaps, for itinerant crossbills and siskins (if the northern cone crop fails). Pond: a rolling salvo of mist going nowhere, lifespan measured in moments, short lived as a mayfly. Vanishes several feet above the surface, called home by dry air.

Jewelweed gone to seed. I squeeze the green banana-shaped pods, marveling at the discharge of seeds. Eat blackberries. Detonate jewelweed.

Not precisely the *World Wide Web* (worm), but I add red maple and bigtooth aspen to my list of trees draped with silky tenements. Yellow-billed cuckoo swallows his voice, hollow and repetitive. Attends all-you-can-eat caterpillar buffet, cannot possibly keep up with the webworms.

Mid-August choral singers, a diminished ensemble: red-eyed vireo carols in the maples; three pewees; titmouse whistles, not loudly enough to provoke a band of four chickadees, which feed diffidently and quietly in the beeches. Jay honks; another apes a red-shouldered hawk. Red-breasted nuthatches.

Hermit thrush flits across the road. Joins robin in the leaf litter. The quest for food, the possible loading and unloading of black-legged ticks . . . a dance of millennia. Lyme disease did not magically appear in the backyards of Lyme, Connecticut, in the 1970s. Biologists in the Dominican Republic found evidence of a spirochete bacterium similar to the one that causes Lyme disease (*Borrelia burgdorferi*) in the gut of a tick frozen in amber. The tick and its cargo were more than fifteen million years old. And biologists from the Yale School of Public Health found evidence that *B. burgdorferi* had coursed through North America for sixty thousand years, since long before humans peopled the continent. After sequencing the genomes of 148 spirochetes, biologists determined that *B. burgdorferi* originated in the Northeast. Charitable birds brought them to the Gulf Coast and California.

On Sunday mornings, an insufferable twelve-year-old driven to distraction by bar mitzvah lessons (and everything else associated with puberty), I'd wait patiently by the front door for *The New York Times*. Not for box scores, which I eventually studied with scholarly devotion. I waited for the back page of News and Review, where Hal Borland's weekly nature editorial, short and tightly crafted, opened a window into my understanding of the natural world. I collected those essays as if they were baseball cards. Assembled them in a scrapbook, dates penciled on top. In one memorable piece, Borland compared the first crimson leaf to a lit fuse that ignites leaf by leaf, branch by branch, tree by tree, entire hillsides and watersheds. An otherworldly palette—red, orange, yellow, copper, purple—our original rainbow heritage, made a mockery of green. What my taciturn neighbor calls, *color*. I'd kept track of suburban trees, stared at chromatic wonder, and ironed wax paper on red leaves to preserve what could not be preserved. Once my baseball career ended, I reasoned, my legs too stiff to patrol center field in Yankee Stadium, I'd become Hal Borland . . . I'd travel the world with my puppy loves, Haley Mills and Annette Funicello, and broadcast from the fringe of civilization.

∾

Within the ocean of chlorophyll, four maple leaves blush. A busted branch hangs down, holds seeds of the coming season, embers once green. Earth leans.

Day 152

16 August 2020

Taxonomy is described sometimes
as a science and sometimes as an
art, but really it's a battleground.
BILL BRYSON

5:55 A.M. (sunrise one minute later than yesterday). 55 degrees, wind calm, 0 mph. Sky: mostly fog occluded; a hint of clouds, windrows like beach sand, cotton balls, and striations. Colorless. Sisyphean mist rolls up The Hollow softening the crest of the forest but going nowhere. Halted by the ridge. A seemingly endless run of vapor, a dream state, soft and safe, the perfect complement to a quiet Sunday morning. Except for the mechanical songs of katydids and crickets and the splashing of squir-rel-cut pine cones falling through maple leaves, I'm reminded of April's soundscape . . . quarantined silence. Everybody's home, engines off. At 6:30, Post Mills church bells punctuate the stillness. After a hundred days of near-endless repetition, even red-eyed vireos have nothing to say. Permanent streams: I need a stethoscope to hear the upper; lower, the discarded husk of a stream. Wetlands: visibility less than one hundred yards; a shallow bowl of fog spills over the rim and oozes up the valley and across the road. Pond: socked in, north end erased.

Birds: three pewees whistle summer away; young red-breasted nut-hatches tuning up; blue jays out there . . . somewhere; solitary chicka-dee, here a *dee*, there a *dee*; four song sparrows in the garden, gluttons for coriander; three hummingbirds; seven mourning doves under the feeders gathering seeds that goldfinches spill. Yellow-billed cuckoo, a knocking *ku, ku, ku, ku*, refused to swallow his voice; hopefully, he's eat-ing webworms, whose tenements hang like laundry on the black walnut.

Pickerel frog in the garden—gray brown with rows of hand-drawn square spots, yellow inner thighs; a froglet, an inch long, champion hopper, hatched in the marsh in May and transformed before summer's heavyweight drought.

A species' taxonomic or scientific name (aka *binomial nomenclature* or genus and species) reveals evolutionary relationships within the great family of life. Animals (or plants) included within the same *genus* are closely related and derived from a common ancestor. For example, the winter wren (*Troglodytes hiemalis*) and the house wren (*T. aedon*) are more closely related to each other than to the Carolina wren (*Thryothorus ludovicianus*). A wide-ranging bird like the red-tailed hawk may divide into several subspecies or distinct races and include a third identifying name (*Buteo jamaicensis costaricensis*). Thus, the Costa Rican redtail dif-fers somewhat from that found in Vermont (*B. j. borealis*).

Sometimes a scientific name reveals something in addition to evolu-tionary affinity. In 1984, James (Skip) Lazelle, Jr., discovered an unidenti-fied subspecies of marsh rabbit (*Sylvilagus palustris*) in the Lower Florida Keys. Lazelle named the rabbit *S. p. hefneri*, in honor of Hugh Hefner, in recognition of the generous support of his research by the Playboy Corporation. Barack Obama's name graces no less than fourteen organ-isms. Among them: a diving beetle; two fish; a bee; and a bird (*Nystalus obamai*), the western striated puffbird, a small but heavy-billed insecti-vore found in the sweltering Western Amazonia.

Recently, an unconfirmed caecilian species—a primitive, legless amphibian—was discovered in the jungles of Panama. The worm-like caecilian, four inches long, shiny and slippery as fake news, uses tentacles to find food and has edible skin, which young caecilians peel off and eat.

To fund future conservation projects, the Rainforest Trust auctioned off the naming rights, which were purchased by EnviroBuild, a Tampa contractor, for $25,000.

The new name? *Dermophis donaldtrumpi*.

Day 154

18 August 2020

*As naturally as the oak bears an acorn,
and the vine a gourd, man bears a
poem, either spoken or done.*
HENRY DAVID THOREAU

5:57 A.M. (sunrise one minute later than yesterday). 59 degrees, wind SW 1 mph. Sky: cloud bound and humid. Mist transitions to drizzle. Long tines of sunlight pinched by moisture. Intermittent streams: resurrected, puddle chain holds the promise of current. Permanent streams: upper, rain inspired, a lisping flow; lower, pools merge, more dribble than flow. Daylight flickering on tenuous ripples, a tranquilized light show. Wetlands: encased in fog and sprinkles; suggestion of the far shore. Flock of jays at the end of the marsh, heard but not seen. Pond: calm and foggy. Painted turtle suspended on the surface, smooth black shell, an island in the mist, yellow-striped head a hint of color in a brown world.

Goldenrod and Joe-pye weed, a run of yellow and purple, a late summer bouquet among dark green alders. A splatter of yolk yellow leaves, expanding traces of autumn—sugar maple, basswood (large misshapen circles), yellow birch, bigtooth aspen, black cherry—calico patches on the brown road. August tilts toward September, a sampler of autumnal color. Green leaves look worn and tired. Noisy red squirrels full of verve clip green pine cones, which make waterless splashdowns. Red-eyed vireos . . . still as stone. One male evening grosbeak, first I've seen in more than a month, joins the feeder crowd.

AOR: hermit thrush, deliberate and trusting, wanders ahead of the dogs and me. Investigates gullies without robins.

Yesterday's red-breasted nuthatches, the first audible pulse of fall migration—from the barn to the pond, like sonic beads on a necklace—packed up their voices and moved on. Nuthatches bailed on Canadian evergreens when spruce and fir seed crops failed and headed toward the coast. In alternate winters, red-breasted nuthatches would appear on coastal Long Island, often in stunted pitch pines along Jones Beach and Fire Island. Ate seeds and tried to avoid merlins and northern shrikes, both of whom left the same boreal forests, tailgating their lunch wagons south. A migratory chain reaction made winter walks on the barrier beach an eye-level glimpse of a boreal food chain.

One pewee, bitter end of the Neotropical chorus. Great crested flycatcher calls, the first since June. Wet catbird in the alders, calling not singing, shares a soggy post with juvenile Baltimore oriole, equally wet.

Background sounds: chatter of red squirrels, drone of crickets, splash of raindrops. Acorns bouncing off the metal roof.

At least once each decade, when the stars align, according to a constellation of variables—weather, soil moisture, geography, genetics, tree health, the standing of the Yankees at the All-Star break, and so forth—red oaks produce a shitload of acorns, an event known as a *mast year*. In the aftermath, what biologists call a *trophic cascade*, woodland mammals and wild turkey prosper. White-footed mice, the most abundant mammals in oak woods, breed throughout the winter. By the following summer, mice may have swelled their population from one or two per acre to more than fifty. And then, during the second summer, two years after the acorn drop, cases of Lyme disease rise, sometimes exponentially.

A more appropriate name for the black-legged tick ought to be the *white-footed mouse tick*—the cute, bug-eyed, soulful-looking mouse is the *most* competent reservoir host of Lyme disease. With apologies to H.D. Thoreau, *the mass of mice lead lives of quiet desperation.* A litany of midsized predators eat mice, depend on mice, their fortunes controlled by the expansion and contraction of the mouse population. During their short and brutal lives, white-footed mice eat, mate, and mate again . . . and again. No time to groom (ever). Cleanliness and godliness don't comingle. Tick larvae cluster by the dozens on white-footed mice. Around the eyes, the lips, and inside the big, soft, adorable ears. Because their immune systems do a poor job clearing infections, mice pass on spirochete bacteria that cause Lyme disease in 90 percent of the ticks that feed on them.

Mice are on the menu for owls and hawks, weasels and mink and fishers, coyotes and foxes, milk snakes and timber rattlesnakes. The moral of this ecological fable: make room for a milk snake in your stone wall. Befriend a fox. Spare a coyote. Praise a barred owl. Honor a weasel.

Little brown bats, party of three, behind the west-facing barn door. Third day in a row.

Day 156

20 August 2020

Or maybe it was . . . reverence? Yes, that was it;
reverence for a creature that, despite every obstacle
we as a species have placed in its path,
continues to hold faith with the wind and the far
horizon, with its genes and with the seasons.
SCOTT WEIDENSAUL

5:59 A.M. (sunrise one minute later than yesterday). 46 degrees, wind SSE 1 mph, a deathbed breeze. Sky: palest powder blue, pink wash across the south, a brushstroke of fluff in the north. Ribbons of ground fog rise above the east and west branches of the Ompompanoosuc, coalescing at Union Village, a treetop flow pinched, like the river, by oddly shaped hills. An ephemeral flow caresses the land, harassed by the breeze, converting a late-August sunrise into a dreamscape . . . until reclaimed by the sun. Permanent streams: upper, snail paced, a trembling flow, a shimmer of daylight, subdued reflections ripple gently and silently around polished rock; lower, one stagnating puddle above the culvert that even water striders avoid, damp earth everywhere else. Wetlands: pastel colors in an encasement of fog, pileated laughs on the far side of mist, as poignant as the church bell sounds floating in from Post Mills. Pond: sheds mist like a snake sheds skin; Lewis-and-Clark fog makes everything wilder. Kingfisher rattles . . . needs goggles to find minnows, divine help to find crayfish.

The murmur of crickets and katydids. White ash seeds spilled from trees pepper a patch of road with little green lances. Individual ashes must have their own seed-drop schedule; trees don't overwhelm seedeaters all at once (like oak and blackberry do). Too cold for cicadas, which hang in place, high overhead.

Summer's ebb: hairy woodpecker calls; flicker drills; pewee whistles, plaintively as ever; red-eyed vireo warbles, the first I've heard in three days, less repetitive, less imperative, drowned out by a chorus of jays. One mimics a red-shouldered hawk, others holler and bark, their voices carried on the cold air. White-breasted nuthatches, chickadees (several picking caterpillars in an aspen crown), and titmice singing and calling, segregated flocks up and down the valley—lots of chips and peeps, mostly the voices of the unseen. Like the coming of frost, flock integration not far off.

Another pulse of red-breasted nuthatches touched down last night, far fewer than the other day, off the end of the driveway. Small blue-gray birds dart in dimly lit woods. Like a tricycle rendezvous, tin horns honking. Bits and pieces of boreal Canada, driven south by hunger, en route to the outer beaches of Long Island and New Jersey, maybe as far south as Florida. Sharp bill, unique toes, and intuitive knowledge of the outer edge of the continent, where they assemble by the thousands, lulled asleep by the gray chop. An irruptive associate of herring gulls and sanderlings and wintering saw-whet owls, which eat unwary nuthatches . . . the blissful freedom of movement. How I envy the nuthatch.

A mixed flock of warblers in bigtooth aspen join chickadees, bits of feathered energy flitting around nervous leaves. It reminds me of playing Hungry Hungry Hippos, seasonal electrons frantically and frenetically zipping around the nucleus of August. Warblers cloaked by leaves that don't know how to stay still. Roger Tory Peterson, the father of field guides, called them *confusing* for a reason. Colors and patterns are more drab than prominent. Warblers do all the work—my neck aches.

Go to Jamaica, Cuba, Costa Rica. Go to Panama, Columbia, Ecuador, Argentina. Be safe as you face tropical storms and cross the Andes, the Pampas, the Pantanal. Be safe as you make a mockery of borders I can no longer cross.

Day 159

23 August 2020

*The first step towards getting somewhere is to decide
that you are not going to stay where you are.*
J. P. MORGAN

6:03 A.M. (sunrise one minute later than yesterday). 54 degrees, wind
NNE 1 mph. Sky: ground fog gives way to the rising sun; marbled vault
reveals itself; leaves dripping. Permanent streams: slightly nourished by
thunderstorm; upper, visible but barely audible; lower, a single starving
puddle. Wetlands: fog lifts; ashes along the far shore overloaded with
webworm tents, off white and misshapen; thin branches bent and
strapped together—end to end—constantly expanding silk tents, caterpillar metropolis supports astronomical numbers of hairy caterpillars,
the green leaves of summer reconstituted, as predictable as fall foliage
and bird migration. Caterpillars are targeted by parasitic wasps, which,
like the creature in *Alien*, lay a single egg in the caterpillar. Wasp larva
consumes webworm from the inside out, leaving behind the husk of the
caterpillar. (Where's Sigourney Weaver?) Survivors overwinter as pupae,
metamorphose to white furry moths, which bear no name of their own
but are known simply as . . . *fall webworm moth*. Pond: mist drifts west.
Painted turtles dimple the surface.

Interrupted and ostrich ferns wither, browning along the edges.
Goldenrod peaking, yolk-yellow fountains. The splash of green pine
cones, cut by industrious red squirrels.

Mixed flock of warblers—several Tennessee and at least one nattily
feathered black and white—drifting through the crowns of three towering bigtooth aspens, feasting and flitting, rarefied sparks of life that
draw me close to their hub in the nervous leaves. I can't turn away (like
trying to ignore a pebble in my shoe). I'm compelled to watch and try
to identify warblers, to tease birds from the flock, an effort that proves
futile. Bewitched, nevertheless, I'm pulled along their journey, an aerial
communion that lasts minutes, leaves me wanting more . . . a moment
that brings me closer to the pitch of the season. Hemispheric migrants,
here and gone.

Broad-winged hawks on the move, seeping through Coyote Hollow.
One perches in the open, mobbed by thrushes and robins. Ignores the
impulse of songbirds, sits, and takes the invectives, hurled like confetti.

Hawk poses, unflinchingly statue still, an impotent aerial hunter, waiting to pounce on toad or garter snake or chipmunk. Several years ago, along the Contoocook River, Jordan and I watched a northern water snake swallow a green frog. Moments later, a broadwing flew by towing a water snake, which trailed from its talons like an ad banner from a prop plane. Three-part food chain. Thrushes and robins have little to fear from broad-winged hawks . . . unless, potted on fermented cherries, they behave like teenagers.

◌〜◌

When I was twelve, I drank wine in the synagogue—half a paper cup. Everyone in bar mitzvah class attended Saturday morning services, a mandatory year's worth of Saturdays. At the reception after each service, no one seemed to notice (or care) that we drank Manischewitz, our personal rite of passage, instead of proffered Welch's grape juice. The wine was our unscripted reward for sitting three hours, enduring solemn rituals in a language read but not understood. Wandering home beneath a canopy of swaying limbs, leaves in perpetual motion, May sunshine blinking through . . . not a broad-winged hawk in sight.

◌〜◌

Another broad-winged, a juvenile, lands on ancient, leaning aspen. The tree doesn't fall. Hawk looks at me and leaves. Passes over the marsh, the slow road to Amazonia. A third broad-winged, another juvenile, perches above my neighbor's driveway, stares down at the gravel and waits with Biblical patience for a careless chipmunk. Compact and stocky, the broad-winged hawk has short, broad wings, and a short, wide tail . . . perfect shape to ride mountain updrafts and thermals, soaring on the columns of heated air that rise off rock outcrops and dark roads. Migrates to Brazil, mostly thermal to thermal. Feathered corkscrews—round and round, higher and higher, a hundred birds, a thousand, ten thousand—then, at the zenith, hawks glide to the next thermal, miles away. Thermal and updraft obligates that rarely resort to flapping. Migrating broad-wingeds skirt the Great Lakes and the Gulf of Mexico, avoid crossing open water. (Water heats uniformly. Not a thermal to be found.)

In metropolitan New York, stopovers for migratory broad-winged hawks run thin. One September, in the early seventies, when I worked at the Bronx Zoo—across Fordham Road, in the New York Botanical Gardens—a flock of twelve hundred broad-wingeds pitched into the hemlocks along the Bronx River. In the absence of thermals, the hawks moored along the river for several days, feasting on rats and mice. A mobile metropolis of hawks, the only time a migratory flock of broad-wingeds ever settled in my immediate neighborhood.

I'll celebrate hawk migration, an annual event that happens despite pandemics, despite virtual elections, despite social distancing, despite the collapse of the postal service, despite empty grocery shelves and rising gasoline prices, despite a disregard for science and the denial of evolution, despite racial intolerance, despite a ham-handed and transparently parasitic, Cheetos-headed actor in the White House, who scoffs at environmental regulations, who denies climate change and favors prehistoric energy sources, who doesn't understand that the Arctic National Wildlife Refuge, the largest intact ecosystem left in North America, a bequest of the Ice Age, means more caribou and musk oxen, more polar bears, which means more to Earth than golf courses and hotels. Broad-winged hawks will freckle the sky in a couple of weeks, passing over the Gile Mountain fire tower, kettles of hawks above The Hollow. Bring on the hawks, please bring on the hawks . . . tuned to the vestigial anthems of Earth.

Two coyotes howl, a forlorn, mist-piercing emote. Peps up the morning. I'm hooked. An auditory rapture, fifty shades of wildness, one for every intruding thought in my head . . . for the moment, abidingly thrilled with animals I can't see.

Day 162

26 August 2020

*If I had to choose, I would rather
have birds than airplanes.*
CHARLES LINDBERGH

6:06 A.M. (sunrise one minute earlier than yesterday). 51 degrees, wind WNW 5 mph, treetops in motion sound like cars on a dirt road. The stutter and slur of leaves, the passage of a cold front followed by gentle northwest winds, a recipe for migration. Sky: no ground fog, a refreshed atmosphere, an invigorating sunrise. Long, slender clouds across the south shaped like a blue whale, the color of a blue whale. Beyond whale cloud, tufts and patches, wooly white brushed by pale rose. Everywhere else, bright and clear. Fifty years ago, on a morning like this, I'd salute the candy-cane Fire Island Lighthouse and watch the vanguard of hawk migration, mostly kestrels, merlins, sharpshins, and marsh hawks. Rarely, an Arctic peregrine. (In the late sixties, before Heinz Meng (SUNY New Paltz) and Tom Cade (Cornell University) pioneered captive breeding and hacking, *native* peregrines were extinct east of the Mississippi River, victims of pesticides— principally DDT, the upwardly mobile food-chain assassin.)

Permanent streams: upper, a rippling current; lower, rebounded, transports freight. Wetlands: the marsh stretches before me, flat and worn as a Kansas prairie. Shaded and pale, primarily greens, yellows, tans, and grays. Lone pine stub, limbs pruned by time, waits for a hawk. Pond: coffee-colored waters driven by wind. Two hooded mergansers swim by me, skitter across the surface, take off, wings strumming air, over the road and alders, pitch into the reeds, then lost in the lineated wilds.

Unwary junco, almost invisible all summer—cameo roles around the barn, the roadside, the woodland underbrush—walks me down the driveway. Crows loud and loquacious. White-breasted nuthatches, a slow, southern drawl, as if waking up. Turkeys in the lower pasture gorge on cold-stunned grasshoppers, gobbling. Jays, sharp voices cleave thin air, conversing in the oaks, yanking green acorns, petulant and persistent. Pewee mourns the passage of summer, gives hope to autumn, lurking dreamlike just below the surface. Another pulse of red-breasted nuthatches arrived on the red-eye, navigate The Hollow.

Sparks of color, red and yellow, smoldering leaves . . . The seeds of autumn: in the trees, sparks of color, red and yellow, smoldering leaves and, high overhead, on the wings of southbound birds, whose voices spill out of the night sky. Birds drift by day through my familiar landscape, shards of sunlight in the east, the same sun and half-hidden moon that greets them in the jungles and islands far away.

Warblers comb through the canopy, feast on caterpillars, inch south tree by tree, valley by valley . . . until nightfall and then, under the cover of darkness, move—a broad front of little birds, an outpouring of wings above a rumpled landscape. In May, when leaves were smaller and birds brighter, I tried to identify every warbler that passed by. Now, I'm left with a mobile feast of chips and buzzes and peeps. Mostly silhouettes and vague field marks. Little birds whose behavior, shaped by the last Ice

Age, mean more to me than who they are. I believe in things wild and free, in the urgency of life, in vital messages carried on the wind.

On the cusp of September, chickadee whistles. A caroling red-eyed vireo reminds me of what's been missing for the past two weeks, Earth's most monotonous song, now *cherished* as summer pushes away from the table.

Day 163

27 August 2020

Turtles are a kind of bird with
the governor turned low.
EDWARD HOAGLAND

6:07 A.M. (sunrise one minute later than yesterday). 43 degrees, wind ESE still as death. Sky: painterly. Ribbons, sheets, and balls of fluff . . . broad brushstrokes of peach and rose, ablush. Not destined to last, heaven on the verge of ruin. Permanent streams: waiting for rain; upper, slowing down, the wear and tear of summer; lower, water desolate, a lonely puddle, last stop on the surface. The bleakness of drought. Wetlands: below the far canopy, an emaciated cloud, more haze than mist, hovers like a ghost. Pond: fog machine, westbound vapor following Horace Greeley's advice, then gone. Pair of hooded mergansers paddle leisurely, veiled in mist. Snapping turtle, head, tail, and spiky shell barely breaking the surface, an archipelago of antiquity.

Lethargic and long-lived, snapping turtles hibernate six or seven months of the year, dreaming turtle dreams, tucked beneath a blanket of anoxic mud, in the basements of the marsh's main channel or the pond, their pilot light barely flickering. The ability to endure prolonged exposure to low levels of dissolved oxygen permits snapping turtles to overwinter in sites off limits to wood turtles, which need much higher oxygen levels during dormancy.

As is the case with rattlesnakes, reports of the snapping turtle's nature are addled by exaggeration, and no characteristic is more hyperbolized than its bite. When I was a boy, suburban legend claimed that a sizable hatchet-faced snapper—common in the sluggish waters of Long Island's

South Shore—snapped broom handles in half. Years later, I tested the hypothesis . . . *false.*

Snapping turtle, whose jaws are more clamp than guillotine, does occasionally take birds. According to a note in volume 108 of *The Wilson Bulletin*, in late summer, when Lake Ontario's shallows heat up, large mats of filamentous green algae rise off the bottom and drift. Teeming with invertebrates and small fish, the mats are a floating buffet for migratory shorebirds. Snapping turtles, classic ambush predators, lurk beneath the algae; pull hapless lesser yellowlegs through by their feet . . . a fatal interruption for a sandpiper bound for the mudflats of Belize.

A shower of pine cones. Pewee's farewell whistle. Just off the road, a male turkey herds a flock of females and juveniles through the woods. Erect and bulbous, wings waving as though conducting an orchestra. In a month, when color engulfs the hills, turkeys will be under the clothes-line eating acorns, under the feeder eating sunflower seeds, in the pasture eating numb grasshoppers.

A flock of warblers, unstoppable whispers, unbroken activity, unknown identities. I stand in the driveway, accompanied by the warm thought that many warblers turn the Western hemisphere into personal roadmaps. Beneath a canopy of stars, they cross the Gulf, island-hop the Caribbean, or pass down Mexico's long spines . . . international borders be damned, their lives a collaboration with Earth, a covenant with mystery and the magic of time.

Day 167

31 August 2020

Autumn is a second spring
when every leaf is a flower.
ALBERT CAMUS

6:12 A.M. (sunrise one minute later than yesterday). 46 degrees, wind less than 1 mph. Sky: pastel-pink brushstroke across the west, otherwise white or blue and cloudless. Ground fog. A dew-laden world. Permanent streams: upper, flow steady and shallow. Evaporation does not take a severe toll. Lower, flows within twenty yards of the marsh, then retreats underground, a surface evacuation leaving behind damp earth and slippery rocks. Wetlands: a bowl of dissipating mist, hazy treeline, opaque colors. Blue and yellow hot-air balloon above the reeds. Burner off, sailboat silence. Burner on, ocean liner tumult. Midballoon, thick black stripe with yellow letters, big enough to read from the ground ... *SPAM*. Pond: drifting mist, unknown surface disturbance, ripples and bubbles.

Rain loosed a scattering of yellow and red leaves—yellow of basswood and cherry, red of maple. A scattering of green acorns loosed by jays. A large, broken maple branch hangs from a strip of bark. Holds a hundred red leaves, chilled sparks in green woods.

Red squirrels persevere; a constant rain of pine cones bouncing on the road, splashing through a sieve of leaves. Dogs are alert and confused. Cones land all around us, dull green with a veneer of sap. Squirrels too busy to chatter move through the pines like wraiths. Squirrels could replace industrious ants in *Aesop's Fables*. I could replace the grasshopper—there's wood to stack, lawn to mow, trees to prune, garden to harvest.

Jays and crows, feathers soaked, active and loud as ever, flying across the marsh and the pond, roving through the oaks, tree by tree, intolerant of prolonged silence, fill the blank spaces. One crow follows another, ink spots across an empty sky. Two pileateds on either side of the marsh, reverberating laughter, a crisp message, then stop. Two groups of red-breasted nuthatches, a lusty tin-horn serenade, pass through the canopy, drifting south with the season. Over the road, pewee lands on a horizontal branch, whistling a sad tune, the summer lingering. Second and third pewee fly in, and only the first bird sings ... then all three leave, taking summer along for the ride.

Having shaken off a night of torpor, male hummingbird visits the feeder, hovers, feeds rapaciously, fattening for a miraculous adventure. Weighs less than a nickel, flies nonstop across the Gulf of Mexico. A summer farewell, like the last blackberry, soon to withdraw into the velvet night.

Quiet, ever so peaceful, holding of tongues. Stopover red-eyed vireos move through bigtooth aspen, methodically harvesting caterpillars. Diurnal fattening, stop and shop before the Amazon Basin. Nocturnal flight. One vireo, its trip cut short by my bay window, a fatal migratory breach, rests in my cupped hands. Short, stout legs. Blunt, hooked bill, long for a small bird. Dark-bordered gray crown. Long, flat head. White eyebrow, black eyeline. Greenish gray above. White below. Pale yellow undertail coverts. Wings unmarked and long, greenish, extend nearly to the toes. Red eyes gone dull. Reassigned to a plastic bag, tossed in the freezer to idle amid pesto cubes, tubes of garden kale, and a pygmy shrew in a film canister.

✤

One cold December evening, several hours after sunset, my friend Jeannie came for dinner. I lit the grill in the mouth of the garage. Jeannie rocked on the porch, beer in a gloved hand, while across the frozen marsh, a long-eared owl called from inside a dark knot of hemlock. Deep, well-spaced hoots—*hooooo . . . hooooo . . . hooooo.* I put on Boca Burgers for Jeannie and what I thought was a frozen rib eye for me. Breaking away from the owl, I checked our dinner with a headlamp. As the heat of the grill thawed my steak, my dinner had morphed into a skinned, tailless gray squirrel. Astonished, I shouted to Jeannie and the owl, alone in December darkness, *My steak has legs.*

✤

Vireo's little body, still warm, once a palace of promise, the seat of a hyperbolic voice, now silenced. An ephemeral treasure, admired and displayed, and then sadly scrapped . . . bird lost in the transparent tragedy of my window.

Day 168

01 September 2020

*Sometimes you will never know the value
of a moment until it becomes a memory.*
DR. SEUSS

6:13 A.M. (sunrise one minute later than yesterday). 50 degrees, wind NW less than 1 mph. Sky: light ground fog below; sweeps of tattered clouds, pink bloomed and silver edged. Brighter in the east. Across the marsh, sunlight ignites the western cap of Robinson Hill, two F-stops more brilliant than the reeds below. A world waking up. Permanent streams: upper, a creeping current (making the most of what it has)—if I hold my breath, I hear a trickle; lower, shy and retiring, water receding daily—the illusion of flow. Wetlands: lushly colored under a canopy of clouds. The soft mist slowly rises and vanishes; morning dissolution. Beyond the marsh, barred owl roosts in a wall of dark spruce. Called all night, an ebullient hoot flung haphazardly against the constellated sky. Pond: still surface, the suggestion of mist, slowly drifting nowhere. Catbird in tangled shrubs meows.

On the road: sprinkle of basswood leaves, first-light yellow like errant bits of sunshine; a bumper crop of pine cones, work of unflagging red squirrels, up since dawn, clip and drop.

Tufted titmouse pair in crab apple pulls webworms out of a tent. Jays and crows inherit the airwaves. Ungovernable tongues: loud, louder . . . loudest. Above the upper stream, broad-winged hawk on a pine limb flushes west over the lower pasture. A flood of red-breasted nuthatches works limbs and trunks. Tin horns ringing, a flock of migratory tricycles. Pewee whistles repeatedly, last in the neighborhood . . . arrived in June, departs in September, an indifferent voice, the saddest note of summer . . . a seasonal sendoff.

Pair of red-shouldered hawks above the marsh, adult and offspring, circling, primary feathers finger the air . . . the calculus of flight. Voices harpoon the morning. Then, follow each other over the upper pasture, the bramble patch, in and out of the aspens. Adult lands. Then the juvenile. Up again, high above The Hollow. Announcements and pronouncements are charged with meaning. A September tribute, an unraveling of the unwritten rules of dependency. For the juvenile, a final moment to pester. A lifeline severed . . . I understand.

Jordan, twenty-four, leaves for Boston, wavy brown hair swept back as though released from a hockey helmet, the last of a small flock of boys to fledge. Linny died the day before he turned five, not before choreographing his birthday party. Friends fulfilled her wishes. The party proceeded. Casey played a significant role, playing parent to his little brother. I sobbed when the candles were lit, the cake cut, the presents opened. I had to leave the room. Friends kept me afloat.

Around and around, like a fish in a bowl, I tried to swim beyond relentless sadness. I found footing raising the boys. Jordan turned five. Turned ten. At twelve, we traveled to Cuba. He played baseball, ate mangos in the outfield, and opened beer bottles for coaches with an opener on the sole of his flip-flops. He stood at second base when I argued a call with the opposing coach, who spoke only Spanish, an interpreter between us. Jordan turned fifteen. Turned eighteen and left for college. Graduated. He has his mother's eyes, her hair, and her disposition. He embodies empathy. He has my appetite, but no longer likes ketchup. After breakfast, he flexed his wings. Goodbyes are never easy.

Day 171

04 September 2020

Let it be known there is a fountain
that was not made by the hands of men.
ROBERT HUNTER

6:16 A.M. (sunrise one minute later than yesterday). 54 degrees. Wind E less than 1 mph. Sky: moon, slightly less than full, leans west and supervises dawn. Venus, east of midvalley. The morning begins fair, an inkling of peach and pink brushed across the center; clouds slowly germinate, wispy at first, then grading into shape-changing balls, ovals, patches, and a small windrow that slowly drifts north. A few clouds merge, a kaleidoscopic atmosphere that becomes a blank slate within a couple of hours. Leaves dripping, moisture dispersing. Permanent streams: upper, thinning, flows lonely to the marsh; lower, puddles in retreat, surface recall. Wetlands: dewy spiderwebs strung across the reeds. Four blue jays play follow the leader; fly blue, black, and white above the marsh. Back and forth, voices plunder the morning, then atrophy in the distance. Pond: a parade of mist, straight up and gone. Small pickerel frog leaps away from the dogs, an explosive hopper.

On the road, tires pulverize green acorns into green flour. Bumblebees pollinate jewelweed, hanging black and gold from orange trumpets.

DOR: tire-tenderized chipmunk.

AOR: tiny red eft, an inch and a half long, cutest amphibian of the morning. Escorted off the road.

Last night: the triumph of a shooting star; the misery of a fallen tree. Sitting on the porch, speaking on the phone to Nancy. A meteorite blazed an arc across the sky, west to east. She saw it too, high above the pasture across the street . . . same sky, same meteorite, a binding bit of stardust, a cosmic message linking two lonely hearts: man with soap seeking woman with hand sanitizer for good clean fun.

Later, walking the dogs, a mature tree moaned, creaked, swayed, disconnected from its roots, and collapsed, taking out neighboring branches. Maybe neighboring trees. Resounding crashes and then silence, as though nothing untoward had happened. When to let go, a decision made in collaboration with the wind . . . I struggle with the concept, too.

Casey left home flawlessly in 2006. Went to college and graduate school. Passed his licensing exam, packed up his sense of humor, and hit the road as a traveling physical therapist. Mankato, Minnesota. Bennington, Vermont. Brookings, Oregon. Grand Junction, Colorado, an itinerant PT who visited patients in their homes. In Grand Junction, he met Becky, a second-year resident in primary care medicine. Their first date: a sunset hike up Palisade Rim, a blanket, and a couple IPAs. On the way down, they got lost . . . in each other's eyes.

A quintet of gray squirrels—mom and four nearly full-grown kits—pause on a maple trunk. Group huddle. Plans cemented. Up the tree and across a horizontal limb, deeper into the woods. Gray squirrels are more attractive away from the garage, the lawn chairs, and the feeders. Red squirrels wander north in The Hollow, itinerant pine cone harvesters invested in the industry, drawing closer to my home. Cones hang in clusters like long, thin grapes. Without pausing on the ends of slender branches, expeditious squirrels cut one after another. A rain of pine cones, tricking, splashing, pouring through the maples and beeches. Reds hyperactive; greys buttoned up. Speed verses barbiturate.

Pileated derisively laughs, wild and resounding. Defines a landscape like an owl or a loon. Speaks for the trees and mist, adding remoteness and mystery, erases complacency. Jays. Three red-breasted nuthatches, on the move, their nasal calls following the route of hundreds of others that passed through The Hollow last week. Unknown *Empidonax* flycatcher poses on a leafless alder branch; perfect posture, straight up (take note—not the hunch-over from sitting at a computer too long). Eye ring and faint wing marks . . . maybe willow or alder. Two catbirds sulking. Vagabond crow on the compost pile, a quick hollow call, like clicking sticks together. Flushes. Changes tune to ringing *caws*, denouncing my return home.

Eye level in the alders, mixed flock of chickadees and warblers. Black-throated greens. Cape Mays. And . . . one Connecticut warbler, the first I've seen since two detangled from a mist net, circa 1974, on the Tobay Bay side of Jones Beach. A biggish warbler with a gray hood, complete white eye ring, faded yellow undersides, olive back, a bird not in a hurry, just above the ground. I watch, thrilled, until the warbler flits deeper into the alders, closer to the marsh.

Named for the state where it doesn't nest, where it's not a common migrant. Heads for the jungles east of the Andes, the humid heart of Amazonia. An ambassador of the unexpected. A delicious surprise . . . keeps me smiling long after I leave the alders.

Bat, a party of one, behind the barn door. The blissful ease of sunrise.

Day 174

07 September 2020

*Nature is not a place
to visit. It is home.*
GARY SNYDER

6:20 A.M. (sunrise one minute earlier than yesterday). 52 degrees, wind NNW 0 mph. Sky: The low cloud ceiling blocks everything but a pair of black, boisterous, low-flying crows. The moon, a day closer to half, and Venus, unseen, leans in obscurity toward Ohio. Somnolent woods in free-fall shade, not awakening any time soon. Permanent streams: upper, inflammation at the source, groundwater deprived, slowing and drying, laryngitic tributary struggling to be heard; lower, a boneyard of water-smoothed rocks. Wetlands: reeds along primary channel green, everything else blanched like an overexposed print. Pond: juvenile broad-winged hawk, stubby, egg-shaped bird on a broken birch limb— stares at brown, unrippled water. Big head, short tail, far from Amazonia. Buzzed by a chickadee. Hawk moves to maple, one tree back from the shoreline.

Scolding, a hairy woodpecker lands on the maple trunk. Displeased chickadee resumes pestering. Hawk has enough, leaves for Brazil . . . *take me with you, hawk. I crave a road trip.*

Spotted sandpiper, winter plumage—unspotted, brown and white—teeters along the shoreline, a narrow mud skirt. Butt up, butt down, out on a narrow, tapered peninsula. Bill to the water touches its reflection; two birds, one natural, the other an illusion. Holds eloquent pose; the appearance of pervasive self-absorption . . . the narcissism of hunger. Unique among birds, female spotted sandpipers arrive on the breeding grounds earlier than males. Stake out territories and mate with as many as four males, providing each a clutch of eggs to incubate. Liberated of reproductive responsibilities, females roam the shorelines of the continent while males hatch the chicks.

Red-breasted nuthatches (again) took the red-eye and pitched into The Hollow early this morning, the first bird I heard when I stepped out the front door. Groups are on both sides of the road, around the marsh, and vocal. Tin horn flourish.

Labor Day fanfare: red-shouldered hawk rips a hole in the morning; winter wren on fallen birch, brown bird on white bark, pecking at the trunk and larger branches; catbird kvetching; crows and jays loud and repetitive; pileated laughs, a jungle cry straight out of *Tarzan*. Red squirrels are all business, silently harvesting green pine cones. Follow crop north, morning after morning, approaching my driveway pines.

Saying goodbye to summer: phoebe on the pasture fence, tail bobbing, back turned to the wind. Every morning is different; every hour is different. Sparks of vermilion. Specks of yellow. Flecks of gold. The tranquility of impermanence, the rhythm and conspiracy of existence. The gift of being homebound . . . the opulence of a September sunrise.

Day 176

09 September 2020

One day the dragonflies appear sudden
as the sun. Speed and softness,
they lash sky to air in silent seams.
KEN CRAFT

6:22 A.M. (sunrise one minute later than yesterday). 61 degrees, wind SSW less than 1 mph. Sky: half-moon overhead, Venus down in the west; ground fog constricts visibility; small diffuse clouds pinked by an unseen sun. Permanent streams: upper, silent and thirsty, easy to the marsh; lower, lightly seasoned with basswood leaves, yellow disks on dry gray stones. Wetlands: mist in thin layers, the sediments of night. Pond: hazy and still, coffee brown.

Two nighthawks fly back and forth the length of the marsh. Long, pointed falconine wings arched deeply as if rowing; broad white wing bars, one per wing, just beyond the crook, flash. A semaphore flight. Mouths open, trolling for flying ants. Every year, from late August through mid-September, nighthawks by the hundreds pass south through the Connecticut River Valley, an annual ritual. An old friend that no longer nests in the neighborhood.

〜

24 May 1983: Male nighthawk above Dartmouth College's Wilson Hall and the Hopkins Center. Then, warm weather ushered in more nighthawks later in the week through campus—six or seven in the glow of Baker Library Tower. One male rose above the floodlights and then plunged with an audible *snap*. I stood, mid-Green, a voyeur fixed on the courtship flight of another species. First one nighthawk, then another flew straight up into the blackness and dove earthward beyond the library like kamikaze pilots.

Only the male nighthawk plunged for love. Each time he reached the end of his dive and checked his descent, his stiff primary flight feathers snapped and vibrated like a tuning fork, long and tapered, extending from the outer half of his wing. The air boomed with love notes. The object of his attention sat like a stone on the gravel roof of Kiewit Computer Center or the old Mary Hitchcock Medical Center, watching, listening, internalizing each participant's performance. After several swoops toward the female, the male landed, out of view, next to her. Fanning his white-banded tail, rocking back and forth, and inflating his white throat, he tried to seduce her.

But the courtship ritual only bored the female, who flew away without acknowledgment or fanfare. Not to be denied, the male pursued her back into the lights of Baker Tower, calling incessantly . . . *peent, peent, peent*. The entire performance, repeated more than a dozen times, eventually ended in connubial bliss on Kiewit, either that night or a few days later. Once their bond solidified, the female laid two eggs on the gravel roof and began incubation—and her mate, fresh from nuptial triumph, continued diving and booming until the eggs hatched.

Nighthawks are not always gravel-roof nesters. They nest, on occasion, in gardens, on bare patches in the middle of meadows, and in areas recently burned. I once heard them calling in northeastern Maine, above the spires of spruce and fir north of Lubec. A forest fire had cleared a tract of land in the Moose Horn National Wildlife Refuge, and nighthawks had found the site. I have discovered nighthawk eggs in the cobbles of West Texas and watched birds coursing above South Dakota shortgrass, where they nested in bison wallows. Along the wooded Connecticut River Valley, however, I found them in town, on rooftops, raining their nasal notes down on the urban landscape.

Nighthawks belong to the family of birds called nightjars or *Caprimulgids*, which consists of sixty-seven species distributed across the globe; eight species are found in North America. Although they superficially resemble the whippoorwill (another *Caprimulgid*), nighthawks can be distinguished from other members of the family by their long, pointed wings and lack of rectal bristles around the mouth. The name nighthawk is the Standard English name for three species of *Caprimulgids* in the genus *Chordeiles*. The common nighthawk, circling Baker Tower, nests from southern Yukon to Newfoundland and south through north-central Mexico.

I used to walk across the Green every spring in the middle of May to see if the nighthawks had returned from the Neotropics. I looked forward to our meetings, the annual homecoming. If the evening was cool, few flying insects loitered around the floodlights, and certainly no nighthawks, which are drawn to the light out of crepuscular skies. As June approached, though, the season would ripen and the nighthawks would arrive.

One evening, in the eighties, Linny and I met the nighthawks on their own terms, high above the Dartmouth Green in the crown of Baker Tower. The sky darkened as the hands on the clock moved to eight and twelve. We braced ourselves for the clock bell, for the crush of sound, my back against the tower, my feet wedged in the white railing, every muscle in our bodies tight, as though waiting for an injection. Then, the bell rang. And rang . . . but the sound was not nearly as crippling as we'd expected (the blare, in fact, seems louder when heard from below, say at mid-Green, having somehow gathered perspective as it races toward town). Neither the nighthawks nor Linny and I flinched.

Later in the evening, a sudden drop in temperature scattered the birds, forcing them to forage closer to the ground, away from the tower. I heard *peent, peent* out of the blackness. I imagined they swept above the treetops, their mouths wide, swallowing insects. Once I thought a bird was headed for my perch, its voice close, over nearby Rollins Chapel. I sifted through the night with binoculars and found nothing. *Peent, peent,* and *peent* again, the voice faded away from campus, away from Hanover.

Now, when crossing the Green on a spring evening, I still look north, hoping to see amorous nighthawks rising and diving against the incandescence of Baker Library Tower. Sadly, I'm always disappointed. Nighthawks stopped nesting on Kiewit and the hospital when the roofs transitioned from gravel to standing seam; by 1990, they vanished from downtown Hanover, Lebanon, and Windsor. Spring nights have lost expression and a feast. But in early September, from the scorched earth of recently burned northern forest, nighthawks still trace the Connecticut River south. Commandeering twilight in pursuit of flying ants.

Another autumnal fuse lit, sparks catching, color advancing. Several red maples smolder . . . torch the southeast border of the marsh. Red squirrel, late for work, scoots across the road.

DOR: small toad.

AOR: wood thrush and two robins.

Barred owl signs off for the day, a drawn out *whooo*. Two yellow-billed cuckoos, the sound of knocking sticks. Amid scores of chirps and peeps, three pewees whistle. Red-shouldered hawk calls, a bold, emphatic scream that no blue jay ever perfects. Red-breasted nuthatches, less than yesterday, busy in the pines, surround sound.

Yesterday afternoon, shortly before sunset: a perfect day for dragonflies, warm and still. Above a corner of the yard, partially confined by the kitchen and sunroom, half a mile from the marsh, multiple species of dragonflies circled and dipped like grains of rice in a rolling boil . . . dragonfly frenzy. Only a handful coursed above the pasture and the garden, where white cabbage butterflies fluttered from broccoli to broccoli, laying eggs—slow, edible, seemingly easy-to-catch butterflies. But dragonflies had eyes—gorgeous, round, compound eyes that transmitted a hundred images simultaneously like a curved wall of flickering televisions—only for a small corner of the front yard. Stirring otherwise still air. A cloud of ancient insects, long, transparent wings brushing blueberries and windows, cedar clapboards . . . and me.

Perpetual motion. I recognized one of the dragonflies, *common green darner*, by its flashy blue abdomen, the darning needle of childhood, a mother's ally. It would—my mother claimed—sew my mouth shut if I kept annoying her, a lingering bit of her rural Ohio roots, where Ashkenazi refugees gathered wives tales as well as freedom. Green darners are perhaps the most abundant dragonfly in North America and their arrival in the front yard was purposeful, competitive, and short lived.

I noticed a swarm of winged ants rising from the edge of the slate walkway. To confirm my suspicions, I tossed an ant into the air and watched it disappear amid a swirl of long wings. An hour later, when the ants' exodus ended, the dragonflies left, a roving band of aerial predators in search of another windfall.

The sandy soil of the Connecticut River Valley, a residue of glaciers, favors ants, which attract migrating nighthawks, as well as dragonflies. (Sandy soil is scarce in western Vermont; so are southbound nighthawks.)

Threads bind, shape, and are shaped by an unforgiving world, whose players, major and minor, are the products of natural selection, the embodiment of objective vitality. I could just as easily praise winged ants.

Day 178

11 September 2020

Perhaps no other tree in the world has
had so momentous a career. Certainly no other
has played so great a role in the life and
history of the American people. Fleets were built
to its great stands, and railroads bent to them. It
created mushroom fortunes, mushroom cities.
Donald Culross Peattie

6:24 a.m. (sunrise one minute later than yesterday). 57 degrees, wind NNE 8 mph, combing through leaves like a river; trees sway, moan, knock together. The Hollow, fresh and refreshed. Sky: clouds consolidated, bruised and brooding; a depressed ceiling keeping pace with the leaves. Permanent streams: upper, like leaves on a still morning, a silent creep that borders on stagnation; lower, large, heart-shaped basswood leaves, yellow and brown, decorate the rocks and wait to wash into the marsh, which may be a long wait. Wetlands: straw-hued reeds and goldenrod in motion, swaying like an Iowa prairie (sans coneflowers); across the marsh, an orchestra of sounds, evergreens whistle, the original woodwinds, and lean southwest; flat light encourages barred owl, whose voice chides the restless morning. Pond: wind cleans the surface and pushes leaves into the shallow south cove.

I can't help but dawdle.

Woodbine (Virginia creeper) on fire; snakes up alders; red leaves ember bright in an ocean of green, alerting migrant and native thrushes to the presence of edible fruit, blue as the brooding sky. *Foliar fruit flags,* the forest billboard announcing with detached compassion, *Eat at woodbines.* A wand of blackberry leaves, purple, thorns like cat claws, arches over nothing but green, berries gone, eaten by dogs and me.

Red-squirrel-cut pine cone lands at our feet. Dogs startle. A big, crooked pine, a hundred cones, a thousand cones, squirrel's idea of paradise. Naturalists in the eighteenth century described pines growing in veins, pure stands, as though representing deposits of gold, which the pines turned out to be for the colonists. Towering white pines two hundred feet tall, segregated, exclusive, blotted out the sun. Light, durable wood, arrow straight. Perfect for the masts of clipper ships. Squirrels had stiff competition. Everywhere, white pine fell victim to the crosscut saw and the long-handled ax; en route to mills, logs clogged rivers, congested bays, gouging out banks, dismantling aquatic food chains . . . an ecological root canal. The permanency of defeat.

For a red squirrel, history means nothing except its own. Cut and drop. Cut and drop. I try to catch a falling pine cone. No luck, too many deflecting thoughts.

Sunrise constants: wind dominates the soundscape. I strain to hear crickets hum and nuthatches toot. Nearby sapsucker, Morse code. Razor cry of red-shouldered hawk slices through the wind. Crows and jays.

On the nineteenth anniversary of a world spun apart by social centrifuge, all I can say is what I remember. Jordan drew pictures of leopards in kindergarten, fingers stained yellow. Casey, in eighth grade, performed on the Hanover High School ropes course, then sat in silence in the gym. I stood by the kitchen sink transfixed to Vermont Public Radio, struck dumb as on the afternoon of Kennedy's assassination. William was not yet in our lives. Linny had died the year before. She would have cried at the turn of the morning's news. Yet, on 11 September 2001, a billion birds headed south above the grieving continent . . . and kept going like they always do. Beyond pandemics, cruelties, and Pyrrhic victories, beyond our fraying relationship with Earth's biota, lies a reassuring constant, the seasons come and go despite us. The slow, gorgeous, unsupervised procession of autumn.

I walk on the rim of the morning when veils of darkness roll back. Birds headed to places I've never been drop into green and yellow trees. Wander along branches that blush. My cellphone notifications chirp like a tree cricket, but when crickets peep in the gray light of dawn, I don't think of my cellphone . . . I think of night fading, summer giving way to autumn, sunlight warming the muzzle of Robinson Hill. In the cool breath of September, I savor the sun, warm against my puckered skin. Night dissolves, and the hawk hurls his voice across The Hollow. The world ripens with possibility . . . again, despite the anniversary.

Day 181

14 September 2020

*What was wonderful about childhood
is that anything in it was a wonder. It
was not merely a world full of miracles;
it was a miraculous world.*

C.K. Chesterton

6:28 A.M. (sunrise one minute earlier than yesterday). 59 degrees, wind N 7 mph. Sky: clouds foraged out of thin air, blue-gray drifting south, eventually carpeting the heaven, fogless and *dark*. Permanent streams: upper, puddles and threads of water barely leaning west, a slow journey to a parched marsh; lower, *Desolation Row*, desert-dry. Decorative orange maple leaves join yellow basswood on parched rocks. Wetlands: color-rich, shallow water. Pond: a flotilla of leaves pushed into the south cove. Future bedding for tadpoles.

Yellow creeps through the trees on all levels, white ash with a hint of purple. Hundreds of cones litter the road below a tall, crooked pine. Only the thinnest branches hold cones, which hang like banana bunches, ripe and ready for squirrels. If I stand long enough, anywhere, a leaf floats down, a loose speck of color . . . arrests my attention on a quiet morning.

DOR: yesterday's gray squirrel, killed en route home from the feeders, gone.

AOR: chipping sparrow, first winter, clean breast, trusting and casual.

Loon and raven call beneath the canopy of clouds, one guttural and expressive, with a vocabulary to match its brain; the other with a wail so haunting I stare at the wild heart of the clouds, lost for a moment in the richness of the morning. I see neither. But does that matter?

Porcupine waddles across the driveway, down the bank, and into the woods. Climbs aspen, bunching-of-the-body climb, expanding and contracting like a squat Slinky. Having had pliers remove quills from their nostrils, lips, and gums, dogs are interested but cautious. Some lessons stick: porcupines and skunks, slow and easy, are meant to be seen. Bobcats and rattlesnakes, patient and camouflaged, are not meant to be seen and rarely are. Mountain lions, the essence of secrecy, conjure out of the landscape of the imagination . . . sightings in Vermont far too numerous to be credible. I heard the loon, saw the porcupine, flesh and blood and prickles, now on a limb. What more do I need to start the day?

Two pewees pass through The Hollow, trim their summer song, as melancholy as the unabridged version. Two red-breasted nuthatches, a smattering of chickadees. Drum roll of pileated. Soft probing of hairy woodpecker. A small group of magnolia warblers in the alders; one pauses, delivers a hoarse, nasal *enk*. Then, gone. Red-shouldered hawk screams into the morning.

Three blue jays in adjacent hemlock crowns, one bird per tree. Silent for the moment. Peer into the marsh with the intensity of Hebrew scholars pondering the Kabbalah. Eventually, discuss the mysteries in bell tones and squawks. Suddenly, jays appear everywhere and enthusiastic, flying in from the pines, over the marsh, the pond, and the alders, joining the trio in the hemlock canopy, rocking in the breeze like so many wind vanes. Alerting the world to their presence, blue-feathered alarm. Rarely do jays keep their thoughts to themselves.

In the early eighties, I watched a sharp-shinned hawk chase a mob of jays into hemlock. Desperate and terrified, jays went silent. Sharpie tore into hemlock and exited with a crumpled jay in its talons. Then, blue jays loosened their tongues. A blue storm of screams poured out of the tree and chased the hawk (to no avail).

I watch jays the way I watch baseball. I look for nuanced expressions, the subtlest clue that might reveal the immediate future. Are jays passing through? Staying for the winter? Quebecois on Covid holiday? Natives of The Hollow? Maybe they visited my front yard feeders, fattening on sunflower seeds grown in Kansas, before departing for Maryland or North Carolina. A band of rowdy blue threads that cinch the morning . . . utterly familiar, utterly wild, utterly free to come and go. Lucky jays.

Behind the barn door, two bats (fourth day in a row) brace for the coming cold.

Day 182

15 September 2020

*The connections we make in the course of
a life—maybe that's what heaven is.*

*We speak with more than our mouths.
We listen with more than our ears.*

FRED ROGERS

6:29 A.M. (sunrise one minute later than yesterday). 37 degrees, wind SSE less than 1 mph. Sky: last night, star studded and bird filled; this morning, pale orange wash in the east. Haze from California wildfires does little to hide Mount Ascutney, forty miles away, my visibility yardstick. Permanent streams: upper, stickleback's nightmare; lower, needing a eulogy. Wetlands: cold pocket; mist above the reeds, frost on the reeds, crystalline and white. Pond: ice crystals on shoreline grasses. Too early to reach my garden.

On the doorstep of September, in the late seventies and early eighties, to deny frost, Linny covered the basil and zucchini with newspaper. Mid-October 2000s, the garden thrived, and I'd busy myself making fresh pesto. Last night the cold settled into the marsh and gilded the reeds but not my garden, which has enough problems coping with drought.

The night sky holds far more than a billion stars. And this time of year, an equally unfathomable number of migrating birds. The unseen pageant moves south above the face of the continent, patterns established since the Ice Age, a watershed of feathers. An outpouring of birds head toward ancestral homes, adding meaning and color to a season in transition. And loose predictability in an unpredictable world. Colorado State University's AeroEco Lab, a leader in the new science of radar ornithology, predicted that more than four hundred million migratory birds would be aloft over North America last night. Fifty million over the Northeast, which includes more than two million over Vermont. I think I heard *seven* thin peeps, chirps, much softer than cricket chirps, an audio drizzle from a thousand—maybe ten thousand feet—free-falling out of the firmament. More distinctly at predawn, when chilled crickets fell silent. A friend, lying on her picnic table, claimed to have heard an ocean of sound, the soft whoosh of busy wings, as though the entire flight of songbirds and cuckoos and whippoorwills and hummingbirds passed over her. A wonderful image . . . but more likely, she suffered tinnitus. I have suspicions.

Amid the noise of blue jays, crows, chickadees, and nuthatches, bands of warblers and vireos, mumbling incoherently and screened by yellowish leaves, pass through the canopy, refueling on numb insects. Four wood thrushes, the first I've seen since late May, erect and synchronized, patrol a neighbor's driveway.

Every fall, most species of warblers fly more than a thousand miles to crowd into a fraction of the landmass they occupied during the summer. Upon arriving, they face a different suite of predators—bird-eating snakes and spiders, among them—and competitors—antbirds, manikins, and so forth. They must adapt to a vastly different forest structure and climate. Take the lonely eastern kingbird, a hunter of bumblebees and dragonflies over pastures and marshes. A kingbird aggressively defends its summer turf against other kingbirds, robins, tree swallows, and even broad-winged hawks and bald eagles, which they escort from their home turf with gusto. (Their Latin name is *Tyrannus tyrannus*.) But, wintering in a New World jungle, kingbird transforms into a gregarious and peaceable berry eater, a Fred Rogers among flycatchers. For me, the capacity to change is a repeatable lesson. And continuous striving.

Another Covid project. Winter's coming. Arrive at amicable solutions. Follow kingbird's example.

Day 184

17 September 2020

Two roads diverged in a wood, and I—
I took the one less traveled by
And that has made all the difference.
Robert Frost

6:31 A.M. (sunrise one minute later than yesterday). 46 degrees, wind NNE 2 mph. Sky: cloudless and hazy, fog along the East Branch of the Ompompanoosuc. Sunlight filtering through California wildfire smoke, third day in a row. I stood in the front yard last night staring at the smoke-occluded Milky Way, analogous to stargazing through gauze . . . dim stars, barely detectable twinkle. Permanent streams: more of the same, dry, drier, driest; upper, puddles and dribbles; lower, water-table withdrawal, leaf-littered, rocky channel—yellow, red, brown. Wetlands: hovering mist, tight to the ground. Swamp maples, red-hot leaves on the southern edge of green basin. Pond: water recedes, shoreline expands, escaping heat rises straight up.

Phoebe on the fencepost, calling. Flicker on the lawn, anting. Several blue jays, here and there, others dispersed or moved on. Red-breasted nuthatches, numbers down, still noisy. White-breasted nuthatches in the pines above the south corner of the marsh, wandering up and down trunks, calling and chasing. On the move? Maybe?

Adult peregrine falcon perches midmarsh on the red-shoulder's snag, surveying a domain of reeds. Flies off, long, tapered wings swept back, deep strokes, a sixty-mile-per-hour air-churning flight. Returns to the snag. Scans for a careless songbird. And then heads south, perhaps to the outer banks of Long Island—where I first met them above the dunes of Jones Beach. Coyote Hollow sits between two peregrine eyries: one on Fairlee Cliffs, six miles north; the other, across the Connecticut, on Winslow's Ledge, ten miles east. During Little League games, falcons passed over the field in Post Mills, circling. Sometimes screaming, calling attention to themselves. Lured to the fecund marshes of Lake Fairlee. One summer evening, two adults and a fledged chick convened high above the outfield. Loudly, sharply, over and over, the chick begged. I stopped the game and delivered a brief natural history lesson. Behold the fastest animal on Earth. Usain Bolt with feathers. Casual flight: sixty miles per hour. Dives (or stoops) at well over two hundred miles per hour—a feathered, teardrop-shaped missile plunging from a thousand feet.

By 2020, more than twenty thousand peregrines spent part of their lives along the coastlines of the United States. In Vermont, nesting peregrines had risen to over forty pairs, more than the entire eastern United States supported in the 1950s when pesticides like DDT had brought the birds to their knees, softening their eggs by interfering with calcium deposition in their shells.

The peregrines' reversal of fortune traces back to the federal ban on the domestic use of DDT. More generally, it links to the birth of such nonprofit watchdog groups as the Environmental Defense Fund and to

Nixon-era legislation—Clean Water Act, Clean Air Act, Endangered Species Act. The peregrine's comeback can be traced back fifty-eight years, to 16 June 1962, the day *The New Yorker* published the first of three installments of Rachel Carson's landmark *Silent Spring*, which birthed the modern environmental movement. It was not an easy delivery.

Silent Spring, which Kenneth Galbraith described as one of the most important books of Western literature, ignited a worldwide debate on the direction of technological progress and the degradation of the quality of life. *Perhaps not since the classic controversy over Charles Darwin's* The Origin of Species, wrote Carson's editor and biographer Paul Brooks, *had a single book been more bitterly attacked by those who felt their interests threatened.* An argument still rages over issues such as climate change and genetic engineering.

The final chapter of *Silent Spring*, titled "The Other Road," references the Robert Frost poem "The Road Not Taken." Carson begins by reminding readers that we had been traveling the smoothest, straightest interstate, and then eloquently articulates the debate over short-term gain versus environmental health.

Her final paragraph could have been written yesterday.

> The 'control of nature' is a phrase conceived in arrogance born of the Neanderthal age of biology and philosophy, when it was supposed that nature exists for the convenience of man. The concepts and practices of applied entomology for the most part date from that Stone Age of science. It is our alarming misfortune that so primitive a science has armed itself with the most modern and terrible weapons, and that in turning them against the insects it has also turned them against the earth.

Pileated fractures the morning reverie, hollering across the marsh, an unmeasured profusion of spirit. I stand, listening, wild voice, culled and savored, a gift in troubled times, thinking of Rachel Carson and the falcon that ripped through wildfire haze. I wonder about my behavior in the age of metastasizing climate change. About gender reveal parties and pyrotechnic displays amid western evergreens, driest of woodland timber, I think about my patterns of travel. My levels of consumption. My contribution to everything that's ailing Earth; and as much as I hate to admit to being part of a global problem, I am . . . and sadly, in spades. My life is filled with residual uncertainty. Change has to start somewhere, and actions have consequences.

AUTUMN

2020

Day 189

22 September 2020
First Day of Autumn

Another fall, another page turned.
WALLACE STEGNER

6:37 A.M. (sunrise one minute later than yesterday). 28 degrees, wind SE less than 1 mph. Sky: valley-fog gridlock, mainly from the Connecticut and Ompompanoosuc Rivers and Lakes Fairlee and Morey. Frost: in the pastures, raspberries, the garden. Zucchini and tomatoes burnt; last night, eleventh-hour basil rescue . . . pesto production. Permanent streams: upper, the memory of flow—three puddles and a damp channel; lower, catch basin for furloughed leaves, mostly basswood and ash. Wetlands: hard frost, fog suspended at treetops. Marsh sand colored and dull, without highlights; spiderwebs hung with crystallized dew, droop like chandeliers. Pond: water level down, pulling away from the shore, a steep bank like the winter beach on Fire Island. Muddy rims tracked by a raccoon foraging the shallows, preparing for winter. Tendrils of summer rise and spread; shoreline, an exhalation of juncos, a shade of twilight closer to black. Across the road and into hemlocks, cascades of tinkling notes, the residue of passage.

Ash leaves yellow and purple tinged, open late, fall early, everywhere, and slowly, leaflets spin down. Floral smolder, red and yellow descending. Light scrapes of color, the sound of ricocheting leaves; a counterpoint to squirrel-trimmed pine cones falling through the branches. If this keeps up, ashes will be bald by noon. Ostrich fern, brown and withered. Christmas fern, green and listless. Milkweed leaves droop, a field of limp umbrellas.

Five jays head south above the ruin of summer. Robin on neighbor's lawn, close at hand, still and cold beneath a white birch. Fluffed like a stuffy, watches the dogs and me pass. Hawk delivers the morning's news faithfully and poignantly. Fluffed chickadee pulls a webworm out of a tent; another plucks a big, chilled caterpillar off a maple leaf, bangs it against a branch, and then swallows. Pauses a moment, composes itself, blinks, and flies off. Red-breasted nuthatches could be my constant companions over the next six months. They're everywhere and off key—a discordant concert. Red-shouldered hawk hurls a salvo across the bow of autumn, a loud, long, piercing cry, over and over. Summer's epitaph.

Warblers in the woods. I hear them in the maples. I imagine tiny birds squatting around their naked legs, puffballs against the tyranny of the morning, continuously titrating their feathers . . . waiting, like me, for an invigorating sun.

Warm dogs rub my legs. The garden lies in ruin. It's a lackluster sunrise . . . but behind the pale curtain, I see a world in endless edit. Birds and bats are coming and going. Mammals harvest, fatten, and move through the night on velvet feet. Across Robinson Hill color unfurls, spreads—a season unto itself embedded within autumn—a cold, chromatic fire. A wonder of Earth slowly turning my hermitage into a visual amusement park.

Behind the barn door, bats, a party of five, chilled and motionless. Am I ready?

Day 191

24 September 2020

*To the attentive eye, each moment of the year
has its own beauty, and in the same field, it
beholds, every hour, a picture which was never
seen before, and which shall never be seen again.*
RALPH WALDO EMERSON

6:39 A.M. (sunrise one minute later than yesterday). 46 degrees, wind ENE less than 1 mph. Sky: half-moon, a beacon last night, absent this morning, somewhere over Ohio. Ground fog, above the marsh and distant rivers, hovering on the hillside above empty streams and the memory of flow. Permanent streams: water lonesome, leaf cordial, peppered with color. Wetlands: opaque fog, thick enough to spoon, sufficient enough to hide an *Apatosaurus* knee deep in muck. Pond: brown, unmarred surface releases mist so thin I'm not sure I'm looking through mist at all.

Little kingdoms: sarsaparilla, puddles of butter-yellow in dark woods; New England aster flowers, discs of yellow bound in purple; seedling ashes, naked, yellow and brown leaves decorative patches of ground cover. Color three weeks ahead of 2017 (landscape chromatically matched from a series of cell phone pictures). Hermit thrush, mute as molasses, flips leaves and then poses on a roadside branch, dull red tail amid a foliar tide of crimson and vermilion, rich colors softened by fog. Bathed in red, red shade. No thrush song, not today, just the hushed valor of migration.

DOR: gray squirrel, sans head and shoulders. Short-tailed shrew, a hummingbird among mammals, genetically caffeinated, perpetually jazzed. Life ended on the road, from twelve hundred heartbeats per minute to zero. A fatal burnout.

AOR: crow feeds on squirrel, morsel by morsel; stays put as dogs and I approach, its goitrous throat crammed with meat. Nearby, raven in pine watches crow, an unfulfilled dream of squirrel for breakfast—eventually, both crow and raven flush. Robins in the gully.

Red-shouldered hawk screams in the rolling white . . . long, loud, fog-piercing screams that revamp the morning. Who needs a dinosaur when you have a hawk? Blue jay unable to contain himself mimics the hawk . . . fools no one. Turkey tracks in road dust.

Four robins in my neighbor's front yard. Go to my compost pile. Please. You'll enjoy your time there. The pile sits west of the garden, two ripening mounds of table scraps, grass clippings, expended garden plants, and hand-pulled weeds. I turn the pile once in a while, releasing sweet aromatic steam that rises from the interior, the black, organic welter of my recent history. Worms love it here and convene by the hundreds, maybe more. All are exotic and dangerously so. Robins eat all day, an uninterrupted feast.

North of the southern boundary of the last glacier, New England rocks were scrubbed bare, and earthworms were obliterated. Today, every earthworm in Vermont is an alien invasive, fourteen European species, two Asian. Several species arrived in the seventeenth century, others more recently. The pedigree of every worm laced on a fishhook, every worm yanked by a robin or a woodcock, traces to England or France. Or Japan.

Not exactly Magellans or Balboas, earthworms colonized approximately thirty feet of turf yearly. Left to their own devices, earthworms might reach Coyote Hollow in fifty thousand years. New England woodlands evolved without them; our forests depended on soil fungus and arthropods to slowly decompose organic matter into valuable nutrients. Invasive earthworms digest leaf litter so rapidly that they threaten the very stability of the hardwood forests. They also increase soil emissions of leading greenhouse gases—carbon dioxide and nitrous oxide—by more than a third. So, one might say earthworms have a role in climate change, the worldwide soap opera with vast and negative implications across the Northeast. Earthworms and fossil fuel . . . who knew?

In early summer, milk snakes lay eggs in the compost pile. It's the perfect place. The heat of decomposition incubates the eggs, and snakelets feast on the burden of small worms. A hatchling milk snake moves across the path in front of me, a spinning barber pole of brick-red and white-cream bands, nine inches of sensuous curves. A waterless flow. Loose spine, shingled belly hugging the ground, swimming. Tiny tongue flicking. Fits in my hand, a rubbery toy of a snake, and never stops moving or biting. Invisibly small teeth catch a knuckle, dig in—a painless bite, mouth wide like an open book, breathing and biting. A newborn off to see the world, unexpectedly and momentarily detained. I set the snakelet down. It swims through gravel and sand into a fortress of withered goldenrod.

The little milk snake unspools into the weeds, belly deep in the huddled wreckage of summer. September darkens toward October. Leaves stain the earth. I anticipate a seasonal harvest of good books on long nights. What would make me smile today on a solemn sunrise? I want to take the snakelet inside to keep me company, to make a life for him in a glass bowl with earth, leaves, bark, and a plate of water.

Then, desire spontaneously combusts. Belly scales scratching gravel, a faint ambivalent sound, the sound of risk and . . . freedom. He seems to know where he's going.

Day 194

27 September 2020

The heat of autumn
is different from the heat of summer.
One ripens apples, the other turns them to cider.
JANE HIRSHFIELD

6:42 A.M. (sunrise one minute later than yesterday). 64 degrees, wind S 4 mph, feels like summer, looks like autumn, an inconsistent morning. Sky: as confused as I am; mounds of black and blue across the west suggests an umbrella; air and levitating sun suggest Coppertone; at home, windows and doors wide open, my house freshening. Permanent streams: upper, puddles sheathed in fallen leaves, primarily yellow; lower, leaves, also mostly yellow, the speckled bones of flow. Wetlands: woods off the western shore, an artist's palette of color, sunlit against a backdrop of bruised clouds. Marsh, sand colored and brittle, a thread of green reeds framing the main channel. Pond: a leaf flotilla; catbird sounds like a spoiled child, mopes in the underbrush; house wren in a tangle of grape fires off like a Smith Corona, the sound of manual typing (something I never mastered).

Yellow leaves of ash and sugar maple browning on the twigs, the color of overheated butter. Red maple leaves burn, cold incandescence, hot enough to notice. Striped maple leaves blanched a pale yellow. Bigtooth and quaking aspens (popple) and red oak conspicuously green . . . wait their turn.

AOR: a full-grown eft, a chromatic transition, the interplay of orange and olive, on the way to becoming a newt; a slow-motion migration. I escort the eft off the road. Another eft, tiny, is removed from the road and released under maidenhair ferns.

White-throated sparrows, with white crown and tan crown stripes, work the lower streambed. Pod of red-breasted nuthatches in the pines. Red-shouldered hawk announces his position in The Hollow; he doesn't call; he swears. A hairy woodpecker taps on a basswood limb, then calls a sharp *peek*.

When I was a boy, I asked my Nana, born in Brooklyn in 1890, how far back her memory went. She recalled the sound of scuffling through fallen leaves, holding her parents' hands, and walking through Central

Park. I think of her as I walk through a tunnel of color, shuffling my way through fallen leaves. Dogs don't see much color; they don't share my enthusiasm for fallen leaves. (Fortunately, we're on the same page for running and eating.)

Color and leaf fall are the opulent byproduct of water conservation. A kaleidoscopic landscape, a pageant of red and orange and yellow and purple, changes by the day, hour, especially when the sun shines. Although I'd be hard pressed to tease a male blackburnian warbler or an American redstart out of the flushed congestion of maple leaves, black-throated blue and Tennessee warblers, and female redstarts, drab gray sprites, stand out. Migration fallout, more sprinkle than a downpour, hunt through the smolder of driveway maples.

༄

I imagine warblers in my house flying in and out of rooms filled with trees. A live version of the children's book *Salamander Room*, which I read ad nauseam to the boys, but my dream doesn't include streams, marshes, puddles, or cascades dribbling down the walls. I'm too old to be sliding across floors. I want my house full of birds the color of summer and leaves the color of fall.

༄

Some trees have a presence, often the reciprocity of size or shape, but in late September, color sometimes calls attention to a once-anonymous tree. This morning sunlight settles into the crown of the citrus-colored sugar maple; a tall, neon-bright tree stands in my neighbor's front yard, just below the ledge, limbs sweep up at forty-five-degree angles, most on the south side, and the main stem rises and splits a dozen times until the crown splays out into a filigree of twigs, each bearing a bouquet of leaves. Chickadees convene in the branches, animated as ever, hobnobbing amid an amusement park of leaves. I stop and consider a tree I walked by a thousand times but never really noticed. Chickadees, black and white against tangerine, a gift of shortening days. By early October, the maple recedes to obscurity, and the chickadees, inchworms gone, reengage the feeders . . . a gluttonous matinee, a lifeline that buoys me all winter.

Day 195

28 September 2020
Yom Kippur
Year 5782

28 September 1978
The Highest of Holidays

Gray Atlantic, driven by September winds
Eats the summer beach.
Sand dunes bleed woodbine
Crimson streaks across their faces.
A gentle breeze whispers from the northwest
Wafting a multi-colored robe of monarch butterflies
From a twisted cedar.
A murmuration of shorebirds,
Tightly packed,
Flash black and white,
Flung down the beach, bound in a
Single mind.
Blue-gray merlin slices the wind
On scimitar wings.
A hapless warbler explodes into
An ephemeral rain of olive down.
A thousand voices herald autumn
New Year 5738.

6:44 A.M. (sunrise two minutes later than yesterday), 68 degrees, wind
WSW 2 mph. Sky: a disheveled blanket, gloomy gray, torn and frayed;
powder blue inside the holes, a slow northeast drift. Permanent streams:
rained for less than an hour last night, not that the streams noticed.
Wetlands: rain and overcast deepen color—tan reeds grade to brown,
brown reeds darken. Across the marsh, the wall of maple and ash, a saturation of red and yellow, becomes an otherworldly pronouncement of
the proximity of ordinary to extraordinary . . . leaf rendition of the caterpillar into the butterfly. The dogs, colorblind, noses to the ground, are
more interested in the passage of a deer than in a Frederic Edwin Church
landscape. Pond: floating leaves coalesced into islands, each arrayed with

raindrops, equally spaced droplets that host an inverted image. Macro- and microcelebration, a *free* inspirational display. And, as birds migrate through the vibrancy of late September; I sense the beveled Earth.

An ethereal and ephemeral season: many ashes and black cherries already leafless, gaunt branches raking the sky, clothesline limbs hung with empty webworm tents, which dangle like worn socks; along the road, parallel windrows of rust and umber leaves organized by passing cars. As other trees dim, red oak begins to blush alongside aspens, green as the Blarney Stone, their leaves in perpetual motion.

Five crows in the pines perch in the open. Catbird in the alders flies to a pine limb directly in front of me, calls four times, and drops out of sight, its voice like summer weather lingering. Red-shouldered hawk screams, The Hollow's crier. One day very soon, he'll take his voice and chilly stare to the Carolinas. Pileated disassembles a maple branch; sounds like someone hanging clapboards, flies over me, an undulating flight, black and white flashes, sharp red face. Off to another ant-infested tree.

༄

Yom Kippur, the Day of Atonement. The yearly forgiveness for bad behavior, the most solemn of Jewish holidays (if you're pious). If you're a nonreligious Jew and you grew up in the New York metropolitan area, it was the time of a Yankee pennant race, bird migration . . . summer on the lam. Remember your loved ones, confess your sins, and ask God to be penciled into the Book of Life for the coming year, my mother would say, mascara running with tears down her face. All these years later, I try to be thankful for what I have and try not to be an asshole.

I've lost, and I've loved, tamping down sorrow and rejoicing in the free harvest of the wild and in my own anniversaries. Sadness may shadow me . . . but when daylight breaks, the moments are enchanted. Another Yom Kippur, my calendar advances, it's time to remember . . . 28 September 1978, the Jewish Year 5738; the day hawks took me with them.

༄

Windswept and (mostly) desolate, Fire Island runs thirty-seven miles off the South Shore of Long Island, a narrow island of sand, fragile in the gray face of the Atlantic. East of Democrat Point, I stood on the largest sand dune between the ocean and the bay—from the dune, I could see both—staring at the Fire Island Lighthouse, which had stopped blinking several years earlier. My landmark for describing the position of migrating hawks, the lighthouse—an alternation of weathered, black and white stripes—dominated the view. (An oil painting of the lighthouse hangs in my office.)

An hour before sunrise, I met Jimmy Meyerjack at Long Island Railroad Station in Wantagh. Jimmy was a New York City fireman, a Buddhist who lifted weights in the station, waiting for the alarm to ring. He was a big, robust, thoughtful, excellent, dawn-to-dusk companion who wanted to see hawks above the beach. For Jimmy, everything was miraculous, and this day would be especially so.

Dawn flowered. Hundreds of songbirds pitched into the pines that ran west from the lighthouse to the bay. Red bats lingered overhead. Once the sun levitated out of the ocean and the land heated up, butterflies and dragonflies, their wings freed of dew, rose from the swales. Flickers appeared everywhere, back and forth. Above the surf, a lash of cormorants headed west. Then, loons. Offshore, terns hawked baitfish pushed up by a feeding frenzy of bluefish, which mangled the surface. To the east, beyond the lighthouse, the first kestrel appeared, wings fanning, rufous tail spread, hovering above a distant dune. Then, another and another, until a jittery line of kestrels, tiny orange and blue-gray falcons, tacked the wind east beyond the village of Kismet. Merlins arrowed by. One turned a hapless warbler into a rain of olive down. Others picked off dragonflies and ate fast food at sixty miles per hour while they flew. Overhead, ospreys, some towing fish. Marsh hawks. Sharp-shinned hawks. More and more kestrels. Some so close I felt the displaced air rush by. All day, Earth hemorrhaged birds.

By dusk, nearly six thousand hawks (a conservative count) had passed our lookout, more than a few at or below eye level. Monarch butterflies, en route to Mexico, paused on our knees and shoulders. And . . . on our heads. Three-thousand-plus kestrels. Two-thousand-plus sharp-shinned hawks. Hundreds of merlins and marsh hawks and osprey. The odd Cooper's hawk and peregrine. Many unidentified raptors. And below, just Jimmy and me, the dunes to ourselves, beneath a watershed of migrants.

I wrote of that day for Newsday's Sunday magazine, *Long Island Magazine*. Then, two years later, I brought Linny to *my* dune on a bright, late September morning. In front of the lighthouse, people crowded. An organized group called FIRE (Fire Island Raptor Enumerators) had gathered to watch and count southbound hawks. Someone had read my story, visited the site, and organized. Still going strong, FIRE built a railed-observation platform to protect the dunes, which was essential. I was pleased to have contributed to the public appreciation of the drama along the outer beaches. But I also learned a lesson: keep sensitive locations geographically vague. Through the years, rattlesnakes, goshawks, and snowy owls profited.

∾

Science begins with observing the world and noting the repeatability of what we see. Think gravity or boiling water or the appearance of migrating hawks in late September. Science is not magic or intended deceipt. It does not embroider or embellish. In Vermont, red-shouldered hawks most often migrate in October, on the heel of a cold front, when a gentle northwest wind ushers them south. Evolution, the unifying principle of biology, is not benevolent. Evolution is about reproduction and survival; in that context, viruses, garter snakes, and people are bound by the same considerations. Science is the *only* way to douse the pandemic when a novel coronavirus looms with unavoidable grimness. Epidemiologists are disease-tracking heroes.

Home alone during Covid, on the morning of Yom Kippur, I'm a self-assigned scribe, noting the comings and goings of the seasons and my emotions. My fodder is *color*, senescence of woodlands, and noises that lead me through The Hollow. The spin and drift of thoughts. I lounged beneath a dust-ball comet and said Kaddish for a trio of goshawk chicks. Listened to the sweetness of winter wrens and hermit thrushes. Endured red-eyed vireos. I coveted a snakelet; removed a snapping turtle from my front lawn. Unexpectedly, unavoidably, and thankfully the virus brought me closer to home.

Not burdened by a lack of self-regard, their tongues ungovernable, blue jays cuts lose. Three chickadees join in . . . a celebration in the year 5782.

Day 198

01 October 2020

I don't try to describe the future.
I try to prevent it.
R AY B RADBURY

6:47 A.M. (sunrise one minute later than yesterday). 46 degrees, wind SE 2 mph. Sky: a long, mauve-edged cloud in the west, embossed in blue; in the east, a congress of more minor, whiter clouds scud north. Intermittent streams: dry again. Permanent streams: less emphatic after yesterday's deluge—less turbulent, less water, less babble—flowing at approximately half capacity. Wetlands: light ground fog, wide bands higher; along the far shoreline, jagged evergreens and gaunt hardwoods softened by mist, framed by long (now much darker) mauve-edged cloud. Pond: sparsely carpeted, pine needles and yellow leaves, primarily black cherry.

More on the ground than in the trees, leaf attrition, a Jackson-Pollack-sprinkling on the road, primarily yellow. Red and orange across the marsh, the last embers of autumn. Maple has had its moment. Some, a blend of brown and orange, like a vestment of monarch butterflies, shed the condensation of a season. Bigtooth aspen leaves, a trace of yellow. Beech, a hint of copper. Color is short lived, now more memory than substance. Brown the new orange.

AOR: red eft, cold and motionless, an orange salamander en route to a tan marsh, escorted off the road.

As the leaves fall, bald-faced hornet nests appear in the woods, unmasked by a downpour of red and yellow, hanging from branches like Christmas ornaments.

❧

A few years ago, a hornet nest dangled from an oak that grew between the stone wall and pasture fence. The boys and I collected garter snakes under the nest. Then the leaves fell. Apparently, I never raised my head.

Stark against the setting sun, the nest was eighteen inches long, tapered on both ends like a peeling, gray football. Although pregnant queen hornets wintered in mouse burrows and crevices, those still in the nest had been killed by frost. I wanted to filet the nest, peel back the translucent layers, the way I'd undress an onion. I wanted Casey, Jordan, and William to feel the texture of hornet paper; see the horizontal layers of brood cells that the paper covers, each cell a perfect hexagon. We'd find pupae, larvae, eggs, incipient queens, and incipient drones, one per cell. Harmlessly frozen *in situ*.

I needed help to retrieve the nest, perhaps a cherry picker and a Green Mountain Power linesman. Unexpectedly and unwittingly, an ally appeared. One October afternoon, while I lunched in the dining room and gazed out the window, I saw a pair of black wings flicking on either side of the nest. Standing precarious on spindly branches, a crow tore off pieces of the hive, which floated like confetti into the pasture. When the hole was large enough, the crow ate the entombed hornets.

A second crow appeared and pestered the first, which flew off with a chunk of the nest. The crow dropped its booty, which I retrieved. The boys acquainted themselves with the hive's inner workings, the catholic diet of crows—and serendipity.

In the alders, a Lincoln sparrow, a sulky bird with a finely streaked breast, first described by John James Audubon in 1833, and named for his travel companion, Thomas Lincoln, not for the president. In August, the governing body of bird names, the American Ornithological Society, voted to change all common North American bird names that commemorate people, renaming the McCown's longspur, a plain-colored grassland songbird, *thick-billed longspur*. John P. McCown, a bird collector and amateur ornithologist, had also been a Confederate general.

Audubon, John Muir, and Theodore Roosevelt. The National Audubon Society, the Sierra Club, and the American Museum of Natural History grapple with the dark side of their respective heroes. If these men were alive today and behaved as they did in their lifetimes, they would unquestionably be labeled *white supremacists*. They were men of their times, not ours. We're products of our time, not theirs.

Although I don't condone their behavior and beliefs, as a lifelong naturalist whose boyhood was unburdened by salt air and gray waves, I am sustained by their contributions to the understanding, depiction, and protection of the landscapes that I love. In 1901, if Roosevelt had not acceded to the White House, we wouldn't be rallying against President Trump's endorsement of industrial tourism in the Grand Canyon because there would be no Grand Canyon National Park; uranium mining would have seen to that.

Last night, the voice of a lonesome snow goose floated through an open window.

Day 201

04 October 2020

*Whenever I find myself growing grim about
the mouth; whenever it is a damp, drizzly
November in my soul . . . then I account it high
time to get to the sea as soon as I can.*
HERMAN MELVILLE

6:51 A.M. (sunrise two minutes later than yesterday). 43 degrees, wind
less than 1 mph, a raw morning, the sort that steered Ishmael to sea.
Sky (and Earth): a vaporous bundle. Low clouds, high fog. Permanent
streams: refreshed by last night's rain, but not up to par. Wetlands:
less than mid-marsh visibility. Fog muffles vision and hearing. Pond:
wind-organized pine needles crowd the south cove. Form beautiful patterns tightly arrayed like iron filings to a magnet. I break through the
roof of a mole tunnel and then follow the excavation with the toe of
my shoe to the water's edge . . . maybe the work of a star-nosed mole, a
wetland insectivore with a tentacled nose.

Color: single bigtooth aspen leaf, red and orange lines across yolk-yellow background. Alder leaves, green grading to brown like apple leaves.
Male black-throated green warbler on tarnished alder. Chickadees probing lichen on the branches of white spruce.

There are three hundred species of oak in North America, sixty north
of Mexico. One in my backyard, northern red oak.

Red oak acorns take two years to mature. Every three to five years,
depending upon a litany of variables—including weather, geography,
genetics, and tree health—the Northeast produces a bumper crop of
acorns, which bounce off my standing-seam roof, tumble into the backyard, collecting below the clothesline. Day and night, nutritious packages
of protein and fat, a sleep-depriving downpour like prairie hail. Every
morning the ground is cobbled with acorns. Hanging laundry requires
flip-flops.

Blue jays fly in and out of the oaks, squawking and yanking acorns
off stout trees. Crops bulge, four or five acorns per bird. When acorns
flood the woods, animals prosper, a phenomenon called trophic cascade.
Jays gather only healthy acorns and plant them, one at a time, here and
there, just under the leaf litter. Jay-planted acorns left uneaten sprout
90 percent of the time, those that fall off the oak only about 10 percent,

which may explain why oaks spread north so quickly after the Ice Age—according to pollen analysis, three hundred yards per year on average. (Compare that rate to various species of spruce, whose wind-blown seeds moved north approximately two hundred yards per year.) Jays travel miles between roosting, feeding, and storage sites, circulating cacophonous notes and acorns. The red oaks of Coyote Hollow symbolize collective decisions made by communities of blue jays—selecting, dispersing, caching, retrieving (or not)—over the past century. The distribution of oaks in eastern North America represents an alliance between jays and trees that exceeds human memory.

Gray squirrels, which join the backyard harvest, are not nearly as well traveled as blue jays and receive too much credit as foresters. Unlike jays, squirrels pile their cache deeper in the ground and not nearly so far from the parent tree.

Following a trophic cascade, white-footed mice and chipmunks may swell from two to more than fifty per acre. Mice breed straight through the winter; chipmunks begin earlier in the spring. Two years after an acorn drop, timber rattlesnake births increase, hawks and owls fledge more chicks, foxes and weasels more kits. Along highways, gray squirrels are killed everywhere.

∽

Calculatingly nonchalant, five chickadees tear beaked hazelnut catkins off twigs, small paired, sausage-shaped male flowers, set in place for next April. Each bird takes a catkin to another perch, holds it in place with its toes, and then pecks off the anterior end. Surfeited or bored, chickadees eat for a few minutes. Move on, their voices lingering behind them.

Post-*color* in overcast Vermont, drizzle oozing out of damp air. An ineluctable truth: living things manifest the intricacies of the world around them . . . chickadees and jays, ordinary and companionable, do a lot for me, animating the darkest, dankest, most dismal morning.

Day 203

06 October 2020

*I'm so glad I live in a world
where there are Octobers.*
L. M. Montgomery

6:53 a.m. (sunrise one minute later than yesterday). 48 degrees, wind SSE 2 mph. Sky: a smooth continuous sheet, clouds tucked and drawn tight along the horizon. Permanent streams: leaf clogged but moving, the sweet sound of motion. Wetlands: somber, brown theme, collapsed, reeds weighed down by rain and wind; vague suggestions of green (except main channel and alders, which still sport summer look). Three flickers fly northeast over the marsh, white rumps flash over brown reeds, semaphore flashes. Pond: glass surface disturbed by hooded mergansers, one nonbreeding male and two young-of-the-year females, in tandem. Scull to the north, rippling the water. Then dive, one after the other. Bob up with food. Beetle larva? Crayfish? Chicken salad sandwich? Morsels are too small to identify.

Pale blue asters bloom in the woods along the edge of the road; milkweed leaves turn yellow, some seedpods open; seeds beaten by rain clump on the ground, vegetative dust bunnies. Goldenrod flowers wilt, dogs unwitting seed dispersers. A world of wet, matted, dull-colored leaves that stick to everything: upright trees, boulders, rocky streambeds, roadside patches of hay-scented fern, lawns, driveways. Summer's funeral, autumn's chore, winter's insulation, spring's nourishment. Red oak and beech: rust and copper.

Red-shouldered hawk flies up the Hollow; leads with his voice, which lingers like shards of glass. Crow rapidly clucks, like the banging of hollow sticks; suddenly switches to a familiar *caw*. Hermit thrush in lilacs. Woodpeckers: pileated, downy, hairy. Two woodcocks flush, wings whistling.

Department of broken records: red-breasted nuthatches, tooting fills woods.

Six or seven hyperactive golden-crowned kinglets join chickadees in white spruce, hovering, probing, pecking, crowns radiant. Chickadees probe; kinglets hover nearly vertically, just above the twigs, like hummingbirds but with slower flaps. Is there a bird with a more gorgeous head? Golden crown, black and white facial stripes. Otherwise, a rather plain and quiet songbird.

Nearly as tiny as ruby-throated hummingbirds, kinglets do not go into torpor during cold winter nights, as chickadees do. Capable of enduring temperatures down to minus forty degrees Fahrenheit, golden-crowned kinglets bunch together to stay warm and feed all day on soft-bodied insects, spiders, and insect eggs. In winter, I find them with flocks of chickadees and nuthatches. But one winter morning, several years ago, from a bridge over Goose Creek in northern Virginia, I ran past a flock of several dozen golden-crowned kinglets that enlivened a stand of cottonwoods and box elders, the largest kinglet gathering I've ever seen. Mostly, I hear a few drizzling, thin, unconsolidated notes from a density of spruce or hemlock.

Kinglets and chickadees move into the alder for a food fest, harvesting tiny caterpillars from the back of green leaves. Then a ruby-crowned kinglet pops into view, leaves spruce, and joins golden-crowned and chickadees. Ruby's crown is well hidden, but the eye ring and wing bars are a dead giveaway. Kinglets are jazzed and energized, sprites of the North animating a sober October landscape.

∽

In 1972, Penguin Books published Eliot Porter's *Birds of North America: A Personal Selection*, a coffee table book culled from a lifetime of large-format photography that gave Porter rock-star status among would-be nature photographers. *Birds* included a photograph of a ruby-crowned kinglet (taken circa 1945) at its nest in the spindly crown of a New Mexican Engelmann spruce. To get the picture, Porter, the Ansel Adams of color photography, hired a cherry picker to cut off the top of the tree, nearly a hundred feet above the ground. Day after day, the cherry picker lowered the crown by increments until the kinglet nest was at eye level. From a blind, Porter got his landmark photographs, and the kinglet chicks fledged.

Oh my, times have changed.

Day 206

09 October 2020

*The leaves are all falling, and they're
falling like they're in love with the ground.*
ANDREA GIBSON

6:57 A.M. (sunrise two minutes later than yesterday). 30 degrees, wind E 2 mph. Sky: half-moon overhead, alone in an unsullied vault. Air crisp as a Northern Spy. Permanent streams: creeping around their foundations, trickling mazes of leaves—maple or birch or basswood; one leaf escapes the mat and goes for a ride, a tiny lifeboat with a petiole rudder, journeying to muck. Wetlands: marsh and alders frost-glazed and hushed, except for the scream of a red-shouldered hawk, hurled down the Hollow like a javelin, undermining distant church bells. Rolling mist above a settlement of leaves, a pond carpet, a turtle blanket. Unmoored isles of pine needles adrift, a transitory echo of plate tectonics, splitting and uniting, an accelerated illusion of geology. Lone whirligig beetle scoots on the surface, stirring the inverted reflection of three flying crows that land in a shoreline red pine; an image in turmoil, an upside-down world, implications and analogies . . . endless.

Some milkweed is still green. Color, mostly off yellow and orange fading to brown; one red maple on fire, a waning vermilion blaze. In the afterglow of autumn, nothing left to ignite, just cold, gray, bleak branches. Red-breasted nuthatches jabber in the hemlocks. Hyperactive golden-crowned kinglets hover at the tip of white spruce twigs and tweeze caterpillars from bouquets of needles. Mellow chickadees inspect ash branches or hang upside down and probe webworm tents. Crows and jays announce their arrival on the scene. I hear myrtle warblers in the woods, the lucid, inescapable rhythm of my boyhood in the dunes, a run of sharp, unmusical *chek, chek, chek, chek*. I can't find them. A motley duo of discontent, my dogs ignore the warblers for the red squirrel that comes down a maple, scales the stone wall, and broadcasts a stream of invective. Interest piques, leashes tighten. Now a test of wills, me with binoculars, the dogs with taut leashes. A trio collectively enmeshed in unsustainable self-interest. Eventually, we lose track of the squirrel and the warblers.

Yellow-bellied sapsucker, the first I've seen in more than a month, *mews* from a maple trunk. Walks up the tree. Several half-hearted taps. Then, flies south over the pastures and marsh toward the coast, perhaps to a banquet of beach plums. Years ago, when I still lived at home with my parents, a sapsucker pitched down the beach, its long, white wing patch as evident as the white tail of deer. A companion identified the bird and told me how to recognize it at a glance. Some things you never forget.

I want to join the sapsucker on a journey to the dunes, to arrive on the doorstep of the ocean, the sea smelling of salt, the marsh of sulfur, terns frolicking above the waves, marsh hawks coursing above the cordgrass, tossed by the wind, tilting and turning like feathered kites on invisible strings. Instead, I'm home in Vermont, my travels on indefinite hold, waiting for a viral tide to turn.

Butterscotch sunshine gilds the shoulders of Robinson Hill . . . things could be a lot worse.

Day 208

11 October 2020

Autumn leaves don't fall, they fly. They
take their time and wander on this
their only chance to soar.
DELIA OWENS

6:59 A.M. (sunrise one minute later than yesterday). 45 degrees, wind NNW 7 mph, aspen crowns in perpetual motion, air streaming through rivers of yellow-green leaves. Spindly trees are astir. Sky: cloud islands full of shape and promise, rimmed in rose and peach, mobile. In the east, hollowed-out half-moon, bright as porcelain, emerges behind a cloud. Permanent streams: refreshed, infused by last night's thunderstorms, which entertained and then interrupted a front-yard, socially distanced picnic—the first time Jordan had been home in six weeks, and I couldn't hug him. Wetlands: deer and coyote paths through brown reeds; merlin above the north end, no-flap soaring, tight ovals above a stand of aspen, then arrowing south, assisted by the wind. Pond: shoreline attended by juncos, surface attended by the wind. A mother asleep in her car while her son bowhunts, just waking up. The boy, dressed in camouflage and high boots, seems ready for the apocalypse. She likes birds, she tells me, and mentions robins, which have flown by her car since dawn. I mention kinglets.

Aspens, more yellow than green, a rich buttery tone. Big-toothed aspen leaf floats down in front of me, lands face up on the dirt road, palm sized, seasonally embroidered and embellished—yellow, gold, crimson, orange, three shades of green, browning on the margins.

8 November 1956. Third grade. I wrote a limited-edition book, *Why Leaves Change Color*, held together by brass split pins and illustrated with original crayon drawings, mostly goldfish and flowers. While producing the short, hand-printed book, I spelled *vegetable* three ways—*vegitable, vegatible, vegetible*—and shoehorned the letter *n* into twigs more than once, as in *kinglets hover at the tip of* twigs. I discussed apples and potatoes, flowers and groundwater, and described the kitchen fishbowl at some length. Nowhere did I mention fall foliage.

Two years later, in a futile attempt to preserve color, I ironed maple leaves between sheets of waxed paper. Some leaves singed along the margin and began to smoke. Others faded. Wax melted, hardened, cracked, escaped. The ironing board and floor were a big mess. My mother, a house wren of nerves, was not pleased.

Quiet morning. The air feels like departure time, dashing through the Hollow at a steady clip—the red-shouldered hawk may have hitched his star to the wind. No sign of the hawk. Geese honk in the marbled sky and pileated calls from inside the eastern shadows, a faint and haunting laugh. Three chickadees inspect a curl of yellow birch bark; white-breasted nuthatch peels cherry bark. Titmouse lands on stone wall. I haven't heard the wren in a fortnight, the catbird in a week.

The silence that began in March seems so long ago. A Covid quietness that kept most everyone at home. No cars. No planes. An unmarred sky. The church bells of Post Mills never sounded so sweet. Apparently, people are not the only species that recognizes the absence of noise pollution. Recently, *Science* reported that white-crowned sparrows in San Francisco sang more softly than before lockdown, at bandwidths more typical of the 1970s. Without the constant hum of land and air traffic, sparrows hit higher notes and sang at wider bandwidths. This past April, male sparrows, reported *Science*, likely heard each other from twice as far away as before the pandemic—and, unerringly and accordingly, adjusted their songs.

If sparrows accommodate new realities . . . can't we?

Day 209

12 October 2020

The caterpillar does all the work,
but the butterfly gets all the publicity.
GEORGE CARLIN

7:00 A.M. (sunrise one minute later than yesterday). 30 degrees, wind W less than 1 mph. Sky: in the east, a crescent moon gleams through torn and frayed clouds, not yet white; sunrise enriched by remaining yellow leaves; otherwise, woodlands gloomy and cold and filled with robins. Chickadee bouncy, enthusiasm for a frosty morning. Three crows, black below the gray canopy. Permanent streams: puddle prone and barely a pulse. Wetlands: glazed and still. Pond: reeling mist, calm surface. Although not much to look at, the alders between the pond and marsh are still green and leafy. Bird lure: chickadees, both nuthatches, both kinglets, song sparrows, and a lonely dyspeptic blue jay, constantly complaining.

Kinglets make chickadees look big. Three days without a red-shouldered hawk make every other Hollow bird look small and fragile.

Yesterday, a monarch sipped goldenrod nectar in the lower pasture, then fluttered south, pushed by a northwest breeze. Up above the pasture fence and the dimming wall of hardwoods . . . away.

The butterfly follows the Connecticut River toward Long Island Sound from Coyote Hollow. It may cross the Sound, joining Island hoppers from Martha's Vineyard, Nantucket, and Block Island. When it reaches the forked tail of Long Island, the butterfly may travel west, from Orient or Montauk point, along the outer beaches—the Hamptons, Fire Island, Jones Beach, Long Beach, the Rockaways—across New York Harbor and south down the coastal plain. On 14 October 2000, a monarch banded fifty-seven days earlier in Essex Junction, Vermont, landed on the South Fork of Long Island. The butterfly had flown 250 miles, averaging four-and-a-half miles per day.

The alternative route: butterfly skips an ocean crossing and follows the Sound's north shore, west along the Connecticut coast, and crosses the Hudson River close to the Tappan Zee Bridge. Both routes merge over the Jersey Shore, and the monarchs fly toward the Gulf, feeding the whole way to south-central Mexico. Once at the overwintering site, the butterflies fast.

What's the difference between maple leaves loosed by wind and monarch butterflies? Monarchs know where they're going, three thousand miles to a remote forest in the mountains of Michoacán, Mexico, undiscovered until New Year's Day 1977. So astonishing was the news that more than one hundred million, maybe a billion, Halloween-colored butterflies wintered in Mexico that *National Geographic* and *Natural History* ran competing stories, and *The New York Times* announced the discovery on page one.

In 1996, by some estimation, a billion monarchs overwintered in Mexico. By 2014, the population had collapsed to thirty-three million.

For a Vermont butterfly to reach Michoacán, having negotiated tropical storms, cold fronts (and frosty mornings), hungry mice and shrews, and an altered climate accompanied by out-of-sync blooms . . . nothing short of miraculous.

∽

In 1543, Polish astronomer Nicolaus Copernicus drove a stake through the heart of conventional thinking when he published *On Revolutions of Celestial Spheres*, stating that planets orbited the sun rather than Earth, a truth now held to be self evident. For fear of reprisal from the church, which believed Earth was the center of the universe, Copernicus delayed publication for three decades and dedicated the book to Pope Paul III. For his revelation, the church banned the book and excommunicated the author.

Another critical thinker, Darwin showed that humans don't reside at the center of the universe. He included us with everything else in the struggle of life, but also delayed publication for more than twenty years.

What exactly did Darwin say? Like Copernicus, he denied us special status.

Darwin thought species evolved from one to another. *Natural selection* is a process in which traits for survival and reproductive success pass to the next generation. Humans are subject to the same trials and tribulations as monarch butterflies and viruses. All life, past and present, extends into the unknown future.

Like gravity, evolution is an earthy law, not a theory.

Kinglet hovers at the tip of a spruce twig, dislodging frost crystals.

Chickadee

Day 212

15 October 2020

In Walden wood the chickadee
Runs round the pine and maple tree,
Intent on insect slaughter:
O tufted entomologist!
Devour as many as you list,
Then drink in Walden water.

RALPH WALDO EMERSON

7:04 A.M. (sunrise one minute later than yesterday). 39 degrees, wind N less than 1 mph. Sky: clouds, ephemeral but evolving kaleidoscope of color and shape. Pink, rose, mauve, and a lavender rinse above the marsh. Cotton cylinders, cotton mounds, and a nautilus-shaped cloud that curls and fractures into a pinwheel of soft colors . . . an October morning meant for a landscape painter. As the sun rises, aggressive light turns pastel clouds bright silver, almost white hot. Permanent and intermittent streams: on the move, gift of a far-off hurricane, gravity, and saturated ground. Flow orchestrated by ledge, above and below the surface. Wetlands: a line of malnourished mist above tans and browns and the green thread of central channel; below, the far shore's last copper and rusted leaves; a landscape anchored by a stunning palette of atmospheric color. Two geese circle the marsh, raining honks; three crows pass in silence . . . they let the sky speak for them. Pond: the faint rise of moisture, more haze than mist.

Eight crows fly north, followed by a ninth, a laggard, pitch black beneath pale tangerine.

Ideal morning for a sharp-shinned hawk to leave for Cape May.

Cascades of sound. A mile-long chorus of robins, nuthatches, chickadees, titmice, jays, crows, ravens, woodpeckers, juncos, sparrows, and kinglets. Chattering, peeping, chipping, deeing, cawing, screaming, zeeing, kvetching, croaking, rattling, tapping, laughing.

Of them all, I love chickadees the most. If the Hollow were a manuscript, chickadees would be the verbs that conjugate the woodlands. Is there a more companionable bird? Unburdened by weather and everywhere active, in the crowns of maple where the last orange leaves overcook to brown, in the alders and hazelnuts, the goldenrods bend under their weight. Chickadees deliver the morning news in a language easily understood. The number of *dees* reflects levels of excitement. An owl or a hawk gets a barrage of *dees*, a call to arms. In the front yard, I get two or three widely spaced acknowledgments of my presence.

Pioneer of integration, the glue that binds the flock: chickadees attract titmice, nuthatches, kinglets, sometimes a myrtle warbler or Carolina wren. Their voice . . . the voice of inclusion. Patient. Tolerant. Accessible. Convivial.

When color fades and the decorations come down, chickadees linger, uncompromisingly cheerful, little voices easing into the frigid air— plumes of breath, micro mist on a cold morning. This winter, far more than most, I need chickadees.

Day 213

16 October 2020

You don't always whittle down,
sometimes you whittle up.
GRACE PALEY

7:05 A.M. (sunrise one minute later than yesterday). 54 degrees, wind SSE 2 mph. Sky: gray and overcast, misty, drizzly, foggy, steady and fluent, builds to rain. The constant sound of dripping leaves mostly burnt orange and auburn. Permanent and intermittent streams gathering and canalling. Wetlands and pond receive what the sky and earth offer.

Leafless black cherry and white ash reveal a metropolis of webworm tents. One cherry hosts thirty-one, an ash thirty . . . no wonder cuckoos arrived this past summer and stayed for the smorgasbord. Done for the season, milkweed beaten down by time and rain. Beech leaves, the color of old pennies, are tenacious and thin. Oak leaves, the color of rusted nails, are stubborn and thick. Both echo tropical origins, trees that have not fully embraced the deciduous idea. Yellow maple leaf, a zigzag descent. Yellow birch leaf tumbles. Black cherry leaf floats. Others spin and drift. More bare branches rake the sky, and more leaves spot the road.

DOR: two tiny green frogs, a fatal exodus, smashed en route from pond to the marsh, intestines empty and unspooled.

AOR: rain-soaked robins and juncos, gather grit. In no hurry to leave.

Hairy woodpecker, sharp tongue in dim light. Then a second and a third. Two crows pass over. A song sparrow, several chickadees high in spruce. No sign of kinglets.

⸺

Since I was twelve years old, blowing up balloons for the dart-throwing booth of a traveling carnival that passed through Wantagh, I've had a vast array of jobs: National Park Service and museum naturalist; loon biologist; sanctuary manager; busboy at the Ahwahnee Hotel in Yosemite National Park; dishwasher at a crepe restaurant in Aspen, Colorado; both ocean lifeguard, where I studied the sky and gray chop, noting birds and bobbing heads, and pool lifeguard; councilor at a very depressing and abusive boys' home in rural Indiana; teacher at an overnight environmental center; leader of nature and walking tours around the hemisphere; and photography workshop leader. One September, I polished copper trim on a government building.

I've also been half-time college and adjunct faculty, guest lecturer, substitute teacher, and tutor. I wrote a syndicated newspaper column; recorded radio commentaries; wrote essays, book reviews, children's books, and adult books; dug fence holes; set fences; stained houses; caddied; shoveled snow; mowed lawns; loaded carpet on a truck; handled the telephone in a grim warehouse; provided security at a stereo show—wearing a badged uniform and twirling a nightstick—and at American Airlines Corporate Headquarters. I also roofed a few houses and hung aluminum siding, neither of which I was cut out to do.

My favorite job was teaching at the Bronx Zoo. The menagerie was my teaching tool. I had a mountain lion kitten named Carlos confiscated by federal agents at the Port of New York. When we met, Carlos was seven weeks old, soft and spotted.

Together we invented a game played in the auditorium during lunch hour. I'd unleash Carlos, and he'd disappear under the rows of bolted-down chairs. Then I'd jog up and down the aisles, and Carlos would ambush me, springing from behind a row of chairs, tackling me repeatedly until I was too sore to play. As he grew, his spots disappearing with age, he turned tawny as a summer whitetail.

I took Carlos to assemblies at inner-city schools. He traveled well and was tolerant and trustworthy. He'd sit by my side when I spoke and let children pet him (one at a time). Carlos was the hit of every gathering we attended, even when preceded on stage by a *Mad Magazine* cartoonist.

Some days, I'd walk Carlos around the Zoo on a metal leash. He was aware of everything: overhead ducks, elk grazing in their pavilion, bison on exhibit along the Bronx River, an errant rat or squirrel, children and their parents. Anything that moved held his interest. He was, after all, a big curious cat . . . a very significantly curious cat. He kept his razor claws sheathed and mouth closed when we played, except to lick my hand with a sandpaper tongue. Carlos was iron tough and independent, and when he turned eight months old, the Zoo put limits on his contact with the public.

In the fall of 1972, I left the Zoo for graduate school. When I returned home, Carlos was on exhibit in the Lion House, part of a group of mountain lions that wandered the artificial rocks or stared for hours into the unfathomable spaces of captivity. For the remainder of his life—at age three, Carlos died of pneumonia—whenever I visited his exhibit, he climbed down from the rocks, sat in front of me, and purred, a full-grown mountain lion, one-hundred-plus pounds. An interspecies bond, Jewish boy and big cat.

In 1997, when we moved to Coyote Hollow, Vermont's first conservation license plate featured a peregrine falcon. The second conservation plate, released in 2006, featured a catamount, the northeastern alias for the mountain lion *Puma concolor*. (This beast that roams two continents—from southern Alaska to Patagonia—has collected many names, including panther, puma, cougar, and painter.) On Thanksgiving morning in 1881, a catamount was shot in Barnard: the last reliable documentation of a Vermont lion, stuffed and exhibited in the statehouse in Montpelier. (I visited the lion once—a rather ratty taxidermy job.) In the future, if the state wants to decorate our license plates with an animal that no longer lives here, I'd nominate the woolly mammoth or passenger pigeon.

Last year (2019), Vermont added three new conservation license plates: white-tailed deer, common loon, and brook trout. I'd prefer less-charismatic animals like pine marten, lake sturgeon, common tern, or Jefferson salamander. My preference: timber rattlesnake, making its last stand on the Champlain ledges east of Rutland.

∽

The tilting Earth: seven days without red-shouldered hawk; three weeks without snake or bat; five weeks without vireo; seven weeks without bittern. Leaves fall in waves, lifting the veil from the woodlands. There's a slick hillside and a crowd of naked hardwoods, branches raking the sky. Accepting the faith of change, enduring and never ending.

Day 216

19 October 2020

We're all wind and dust anyway . . .
We don't even have any proof
that the universe exists.

Bob Dylan

7:09 A.M. (sunrise one minute later than yesterday). 39 degrees, wind N 1 mph. Sky: nearly empty, baby blue except for a single rose-colored cloud, spindly and frayed. Intermittent streams: mute but moving. Permanent streams: upper, water song from yesterday's babble to today's lullaby; lower, less reliable water source than the upper, barely carries a tune; a line of leaves caught in rocks, coiled like a snake. Wetlands: thin ground fog, a remnant of weekend rain. Remaining green fading to brown. Alder leaves burnt by yesterday's frost, blackening (still of some interest to chickadees, which work the sparse foliage). Across the marsh, pileated laughs, a long, rollicking salutation to the rising sun. Pond: mist rises and vanishes; mergansers, hooded, cut paths across the surface, telegraphing ripples that spread in every direction. Winter attire, brown and gray, could be males or females, adults or first-year birds. Too far away to identify.

Yesterday's elegant yellow-orange stripes, sinuous lines of roadside leaves, erased by passing cars; leaves reassembled on the edge of the woods, enmeshed in quotidian details . . . brown by degrees.

Two sparrows, white-throated and Lincoln's, dainty as daisies, perch on goldenrods, eat seeds as stems flop. Robins in small groups, noisy and busy. Chickadees, sparrow-like, eating goldenrod seeds as well as insect eggs pried from frayed bark, and numb spiders gathered from under the overhang of the porch roof. Along the edge of the driveway, hermit thrush picks through a cluster of fallen colored leaves, mostly aspen. An October hush, a dilute version of his April debut, when he threw back his head and set The Hollow on fire for two months producing hauntingly beautiful music, flung carelessly and dispassionately as the wind. Flipping yellow leaves, flipping yellow silence. The frenzied pace of life subdued. I can't take my eyes off the thrush . . . one more song, please. One last piece to ward off the decay of summer.

Thirteen doves under the feeders, scavenging seeds. Tiny heads. Rush to flight. Sometimes into the picture window. I think of doves as simple birds, fast, powerful fliers but not keen problem solvers. Chickadees they're not.

Even within their family (Paridae), a pert and perky group that includes titmice and Old World tits, the black-capped chickadee is an Albert Einstein stand-in. Regular visitors to my feeders, chickadees take one seed at a time, pound it open on a nearby cherry limb, or hide it unshelled in tree-branch lichen or a cluster of conifer needles. With a map in their heads, chickadees find what they hide—nearly eighty thousand seeds—up to twenty-eight days later. Their *hippocampus*, the brain region associated with spatial memory, enlarges during autumn and is proportionately larger than those of related species that cache less food, making black-capped chickadees darlings of *cognitive ecologists*.

On bone-chilling, subzero nights, despite weighing less than half an ounce, a black-capped chickadee survives by lowering its body temperature to conserve energy, entering self-induced torpor (or regulated hypothermia), a sort of nocturnal hibernation. Then wakes up latte fresh, ready to exercise its brain and uncover its trove of hidden seeds.

Chickadee: default bird of the Northeast. Black bib, throat, and crown; white cheeks and belly; buffy sides; gray back. A bird of total recall. Is there a more recognizable, personable, front yard or wilderness bird? State bird of Massachusetts and Maine. The bird of birds in Coyote Hollow. A trusting bird, indefatigable and captivating. Feeling down about self-isolation and the trail of rubble in its wake? Feeling blue about the evil wind in the White House? Consider the chickadee, another of life's creative uses of stardust. Chickadees may not suppress the spread of the Coronavirus, but they'll help you forget about it for a moment.

Day 219

22 October 2020

A man can stand anything except
a succession of ordinary days.
JOHANN WOLFGANG VON GOETHE

7:13 A.M. (sunrise two minutes later than yesterday). 46 degrees, wind ESE 2 mph. Sky: clear in the east, hints of pink; in the west, a diagonal megalink of bright oval clouds, peach rinsed. Fog is more pronounced than yesterday; thicker above water; rolls uphill, creeps into pastures. Permanent streams: noisy in the sinuous narrows, sprawling and quiet in the flats. Wetlands: rising mist softens far shoreline textures, eclipses shoreline color, and accentuates sausage clouds, which dominate an otherwise empty sky. Pond: four mergansers rush to judgment, disturb the lull, bolt on caffeinated wingbeats, capsizing reflections. Pitch into the marsh. An aisle through matted goldenrod and aster, a trail up the bank and into the water. Dogs are keenly interested. An otter, I think. Noses to the grass, dogs know but aren't saying.

Everywhere in weeds, bowl-and-doily spiderwebs, jeweled by dew. Blueberry leaves are bright red, blackberry dull purple. Biscotti-colored beech leaves are paper thin, Merlot-colored oak leaves leather thick.

AOR: adult female green frog (*Lithobates clamitans*), small tympanum, eye sized. Throat white (not yellow like the male), a frog the size of an oak leaf, upright on the road, as cold and slimy as raw chicken. Stays put in my hand, puffed up. I put her in the woods aimed toward the marsh. Dogs sit patiently, wondering what's happening.

Roosting mourning doves coming and going, loosening yellow maple leaves, which float into the garden. Brown creeper wanders up yellow birch, long tail pressed to trunk, picks through peeling bark, thin voice loud as mist, a faltering delicacy. Three or four off-key nuthatches toot tin horns, all red (and gorgeous). White-breasted nuthatch on a pine, small bird on a massive tree, wandering down the trunk, blood rushing to its head; almost hidden by bark furrows, a creeper in reverse. Along the hem of the pond, white-throated sparrow—cream-colored crown stripes and throat, canary-yellow lores—reaps seeds, eats them on the spot from doubled-over stems.

Pileated hollers. Everywhere . . . chickadees, chickadees, chickadees. Above the crippled beaver dam, a clique of robins call, a rapidly repeated chirr in the crowns of hemlocks and pines. Not a predator alarm—none around that I can see. Several years ago, on the Jones Beach dunes, an immature goshawk killed a luckless robin and flew to the rotted frame of an old observation tower. While the hawk plucked lunch, nearby robins went ballistic, rapidly screaming . . . sharp, caustic notes, far different from the mellow notes I hear this morning.

Crows cawing softly from the next valley. Others gather at the compost pile, picking and probing. The premier crow-feeding station. One flies off with an eggshell; another with a slice of stale bread. I flip the compost with a pitchfork, a jewel-eyed toad napping below the surface, swaddled in unconsolidated food scraps.

Deliciously alive red squirrels play tag, one after the other. Up and down pine trunks, across limbs, racing and leaping, screaming, hemorrhaging energy while utterly disregarding social distancing.

Below the summit of Robinson Hill, sunlight ignites an aspen globe, yolk-yellow in naked woods.

Day 220

23 October 2020

You don't need a weatherman
To know which way the wind blows.
Bob Dylan

7:14 A.M. (sunrise one minute later than yesterday). 55 degrees, wind SW 2 mph. Sky: thick and overcast, a remnant of a half-hearted rain; sunrise as dark as the dawn, a disarrangement of gray, highlighted by a passing red-tailed hawk. Permanent and intermittent streams: without chronic evaporation, volume and volume, a xerox of yesterday, a peaceful, joyful babble. Wetlands: green thread of tall reeds that marked the main channel now brunette in a buff-colored marsh; green isles of sweetgale, where deer birthed and red-wings nested, now dark chocolate. Alder leaves drop; chickadees harvest seeds from tiny cones. Pond: four mergansers linger for a moment—two juvenile males, two females—swim in tightening circles, then skitter across the surface and flush. Fly low over alders and cattails, arrow into the marsh.

AOR: plump woodcock lands along the edge of the road in front of me; orb head and whistling wings; knitting-needle bill a dimly lit silhouette. Two robins flush. One lands on a flimsy, horizontal grapevine, a woodland teeter-totter; thinks the better of it and leaves, the vine bouncing like a springboard.

Scat-on-the-road (SOR): mink, very fresh. Dogs and I are interested in the same item, which still glistens. With apologies to William Shakespeare: *That which we call a nose/ By any other name would not smell as sweet.* Although mammals have five hundred different odor receptors, not all noses smell alike. We have about five million olfactory sensory neurons; my dogs have more than two hundred million. They change inhaling patterns, called *focus sniffing,* to detect different odors, just as we focus our eyes. Deep piggy snorts, nostrils flaring, the dogs read messages and gather knowledge far beyond my limited understanding. They smell a coyote days later. Know the fitness of a bear from its tracks. What do the dogs deduce from this glistening scat—other than it's recent and the mink a bit lighter on its feet?

Aspen leaves litter the road, sunshine yellow and burnt butter. Stammering crickets, a throwback to September. Most robins have moved on, but voluble nuthatches and blue jays make up for their absence . . . chattering, tooting, screaming as though on holiday.

∽

The word *topophilia* means *love of place,* a complex multilayered emotion echoed in the poems of Mary Oliver and the essays of Edward Abbey and Aldo Leopold (without the word itself being mentioned). Landscape memories evoke a jubilee of sights, sounds, smells, and textures of days gone by. In my case, those *lazy, hazy, crazy* summer days on the beach. I grew up a bike ride from the salt marsh, daily flooded by tides, and Jones Beach, a skinny barrier island—seventeen miles of dunes and swales, scarcely half a mile wide—relentlessly pounded by the surf. Going to the beach meant swimming . . . and seeing birds from the four corners of North America.

One bird stood out from all the rest. Marsh hawk (a.k.a. northern harrier) was the first hawk I identified on my own. Long-winged and slender. Sexually dimorphic. Males (always the smaller of sexes in raptors) pewter colored above, white below, with ink-dark wing tips; females mud brown and with streaked chests; juveniles, colored like females, with a rosy bloom on their chests. Light and buoyant as kites, marsh hawks coursed endlessly and effortlessly above the salt marsh, wings held in a shallow V. Long, rudder tails fine-tuning flight. On any given trip to Jones Beach, I'd spot five or six, maybe more.

Sadly, climate change triggered higher tides and more frequent flooding, which significantly reduced the number of marsh hawks inhabiting Jones Beach since the ubiquitous and marsh-loving meadow vole, a principal food source, had been flooded out by rising tides. When I return to Jones Beach, a once-visible and visceral connection to my boyhood has become noticeably scarce. The absence of marsh hawks, a frayed strand in the fabric of memories that tether me to my coastal roots—green-plumed marshes and snow-white clouds, bare feet, carefree summer days, time pausing. Ambitious hawks that drift with purpose.

Casey and Jordan grew up in Coyote Hollow. William spent eight years here. Then color peaked in the third week of September, and snow arrived in November. Peepers filled the marsh in late April and remained into July. Robin or bluebird in winter was a big deal. In late fall, evening grosbeaks arrived in the front yard, and some stayed all winter. Almost every year, we'd see a moose. We never saw opossums. Cardinals, titmice, and red-bellied woodpeckers stayed close to the Connecticut River.

One yardstick I use to track Vermont's weather patterns, grimly fascinating and wretchedly unpredictable, is the appearance or absence of dooryard birds. Simple enough. Birds are a malleable window into an evolving climate and an emasculated landscape.

༄

23 October 2020: temperature in the midsixties. I haven't filled my wood stove in two days.

I am the steward of my boyhood memories, and climate change and environmental degradation have exacted a toll, a displacement of a source that bonded me to a shifting strip of sand. A loss rarely considered. I may no longer live near the wild surf . . . but the gray chop and kiting hawks frequent my dreams.

༄

Every morning I face a serious choice . . . get out of bed and walk, or stay put in my Covid hermitage and miss life's pageant. My dogs have some say in the matter. The ease of each morning varies. But once outside, I'm rarely disappointed—a thousand lifelines, haphazardly and unpredictably, strewn across The Hollow. Each morning I grab one or two—distant goose, late yellowthroat, wary merganser. An itinerant mink leaves a token, the story of a life and a time. The price for admission to the inclusive world beyond my doorstep . . . go outside. Cherish boyhood memories . . . but immerse in the here and now. It's all I really have.

Day 223

26 October 2020

There are worse crimes than burning books.
One of them is not reading them.
RAY BRADBURY

7:18 A.M. (sunrise one minute later than yesterday). 37 degrees, wind SSE 2 mph. Sky: off-and-on drizzle; cloud mass horizon to horizon, drifts northwest in line with the wind. Intermittent streams: leaf-clogged leakage. Permanent streams: congestion of rain-matted leaves, mostly oak and aspen, an obstacle course for the current. Wetlands: sober shades of brown; deer paths through cattails obvious now that alders have shed their leaves. Pond: far end blended into the brown shoreline, three hooded mergansers diving; one surfaces with crayfish; unlike the past three days, ducks don't panic and flush . . . too busy feeding. (An aspect of natural history I deeply understand.)

Farther up the road, between my driveway and the north end of the marsh, significant leaf drop, aspen and oak, a carpet of burnt butter and dried blood, color as ephemeral as the weather.

DOR: female America toad, strings of eggs like maple buds, in place for spring.

AOR: grit-picking robin, flushes.

Last communiqué of the night: barred owl barks at the break of dawn; a single disarticulated hoot.

First communiqué of the day: blue jay at the break of dawn mimics red-shouldered hawk, long gone. (Jay needs to expand his repertoire to a seasonally more appropriate echo.) Nineteen turkeys in the yard. Ten under the oaks, gorging on acorns; nine under the feeders gorging on sunflowers. In anticipation of spring, one male rehearses, tail fanned, wings low and quivering, strutting . . . a student of multiplication. Raven bellows from a nearby pine, an overflow of sound like a car without a muffler. Dogs look up. Robins flush from limbs, repeatedly, consistently landing in front of me. Last weekend, walking with Nancy across Bragg Hill in Norwich, one town to the south, bluebirds on a power line flushed over and over, chaperoning us down the road. And whenever I kayak or canoe, kingfishers do the same, moving in front of me, downriver limb by limb, repeatable and predictable flushing. In 1998, in Big Cypress National Preserve, a mangrove cuckoo led me through a mangrove tunnel . . . land, watch, flush. Repeat. All four species easily bewildered.

∾

Growing up in the fifties and sixties, three books changed my life, confirming that I had a path to follow. Roger Tory Peterson and James Fisher's *Wild America* (1955) and Carl Kauffeld's *Snakes and Snake Hunting* (1957) were eye-popping narratives for a naturalist, a young prisoner of the suburbs. Reading them, I understood that Major League baseball players were *not* the only men who made a living doing boy things. Peterson and Fisher birded and Kauffeld caught snakes across the face of North America . . . and ebulliently described how much fun they had doing it.

The third book, Donald Culross Peattie's *A Natural History of Trees of Eastern and Central North America*, an American classic, a doorstop of a book, was published the year I was born, 1948. Peattie imbued trees with personality in contagious prose, weaving the fabric of our own history into each account. About bur oak, a rare resident of the Champlain lowlands of western Vermont (though reasonably expected in the Midwest), he said, *A grand bur oak suggests a house in itself . . . No child who ever played beneath a bur oak will forget it.* Makes me want to rush to Addison County to find one to play under.

When the male flowers bloomed in the illimitable pineries, he wrote about the white pine, *thousands of miles of forest aisles were swept with golden smoke of this reckless fertility.* Something to think about next June when I hose pollen off the car.

Peattie saved some of his most eloquent writing for a two-page essay on balsam fir, favored by The Hollow's passing kinglets:

No harm, but only good, can follow from the proper cutting of young Christmas trees. And the destiny of Balsam, loveliest of them all, would otherwise too often be excelsior, or boards for packing cases, or newsprint bringing horror on its face into your home. Far better that the little tree should arrive, like a shining child at your door, breathing of all out of doors and cupping healthy North Woods cold between its boughs, to bring delight to human children.

Every December, pruning saw in hand, Casey led his younger brothers on a Christmas-tree expedition along the western rim of the marsh. They'd be gone for hours. After all, trees had to be compared. The finer points of the shape, height, and color had to be debated ... the Kabbalah of the Christmas tree. They stood knee-deep in snow, only their tight ski caps moving, deliberating as though in front of the Supreme Court. Finally, a tree was chosen (God only knows why), sawed, and sledded home, branches radiating like a bottlebrush. Invariably, the tree had to be trimmed to fit through the sunroom door. Often, it was too tall for the room and had to be topped. The furniture had to be rearranged. The room smelled like the Canadian muskeg. I loved the ritual of the Christmas tree—even if I am a Jew—and celebrated by making latkes.

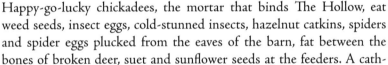

Happy-go-lucky chickadees, the mortar that binds The Hollow, eat weed seeds, insect eggs, cold-stunned insects, hazelnut catkins, spiders and spider eggs plucked from the eaves of the barn, fat between the bones of broken deer, suet and sunflower seeds at the feeders. A catholic diet that promotes abundance, vitality, maybe even cheerfulness. A possible contingency of climate change: more narrowly adapted species (blackburnian warbler, let's say) may perish in the dark hole of extinction, while bibbed and bonneted chickadees radiate into new species that (hopefully) continue to entertain their neighbors, whomever they evolve to be.

Effervescent chickadee, a Christmas tree among songbirds, spreads joy across the grim—in newspapers, on computer screens, on television, and on the receiving end of disembodied phone calls. My anodyne for the ills of 2020. Me and chickadee, the stuff of stars.

Day 226

29 October 2020

*It would be easy to show that within the same group
carnivorous animals exist having every intermediate
grade between truly aquatic and strictly terrestrial;
and as each exists by a struggle for life, it is clear that each
is well adapted in its habits to its place in nature.*
CHARLES DARWIN

7:22 A.M. (sunrise two minutes later than yesterday; desperate for Eastern Standard Time). 34 degrees, Wind NE 1 mph. Sky: morning swaddled in fog, dim and somnolent, and so joyously damp, an owl hoots in the hemlocks, where midnight lurks undiminished. Condensed fog drips from branches and twigs. (An under-the-covers morning, if only I could). Intermittent and permanent streams: after yesterday's rain, a slight volume increase, crystal clear, filled with music. Wetlands: across the marsh, density of fog suggests evergreens and bony-branched hardwoods, pressed against the possibility of limitlessness. A flat, seemingly unmarred landscape, a two-dimensional mural accented by an owl, a disembodied voice in the loneliness of late October. Pond: juvenile male merganser, crest slicked back in a pompadour, a Little Richard duck, hugs the eastern shoreline, glances at the dogs and me, and then glances toward the cattails. Keeps glancing. I look, too. Mink, moving like an expanding and contracting slinky, enters the cattails, slips into the water, barely a ripple. In and out, three times. Four times. Five times. Unlike summer's otter, mink avoids the middle of the pond. Stays put in the shallows, diving and swimming, catching tadpoles and crayfish—all business.

A mammal on the cusp of two worlds, aquatic and terrestrial. I've watched mink catch sunfish in a lake and voles in a woodpile and climb the lower limbs of silver maple. So unique the mink, Darwin affords it a cameo in chapter 6 of *On The Origins of Species*:

> Look at *Mustela vison* [now, *Neovison vison*] of North America, which has webbed feet and which resembles an otter in its fur, short legs, and form of tail; during summer this animal dives for and preys on fish, but during the long winter it leaves the frozen waters, and preys like other polecats on mice and land animals.

Now I see it. Now I don't. Now I do, long and thin. Cute but toothy. A water weasel, sleek and brown, the mammal that kept my mother fashionable. Eventually, mink leaves the pond and vanishes into a robe of fog, and I head home . . . momentarily unmoored.

Merganser, freed of concern, drifts back toward the cattails.

∽

Pileated cracks, loud, repetitive laughter. Robins and red-breasted nuthatches are conspicuously absent. Seventeen turkeys, foraging around the garden and the raspberry patch, chatting.

This valley, this life, both specks on the North American theater. But . . . they're my specks. And every morning, no matter how dismal the weather or how urgently lazy I feel, I choose motion and enrichment and go outside. Rarely am I disappointed. Something—chickadee capering in the hardwoods, mink, rose-breasted grosbeak, yellow aspen on a bleak hillside—takes my breath away, arrests my attention, and makes me appreciate life beyond my doorstep. Makes me understand life beyond myself. A moment alone with Earth's vast, impartial, glorious, precarious nature. What more could I ask for? To be part of the pale green fragility.

A barrage of honks spills out of a leaden sky. Two flocks of geese— one a wavering line, the other a small V. On an evergreen teeter-totter, chickadee, unabashedly buoyant, tweezes something other than the scent of Christmas out of tufts of balsam needles.

Mink

Day 228

31 October 2020

Halloween

*There are nights when wolves are silent
and only the moon howls.*
GEORGE CARLIN

7:24 A.M. (sunrise one minute later than yesterday). 19 degrees, wind E
1 mph. Sky: clear and wintery, fog and frost, ice-sealed puddles. Tonight,
the second full moon of October, a Halloween Blue Moon, the first Blue
Moon since March 2018, and the first Halloween Blue Moon since 1944,
five days after the United States and Australia won the largest naval
battle in history (three hundred ships and four hundred planes). Next
Blue Moon, August 2023. Next Halloween Blue Moon, 2039. NASA
rates tonight's full moon a *micro moon* because it's approximately fifteen
thousand miles farther from Earth than average; supposedly, the moon
appears slightly smaller. Good luck noticing the difference. Permanent
streams: fuller by the day, rocks ice free but leaves frozen and crusty.
Wetlands: bright marsh glazed, frost rimes on alder branches and withered leaves, featherings of tiny icicles. Pond: three female mergansers
bunch and dive. One catches a crayfish, the others nada.

Out of the woods and into the water . . . mink, sleek and dark brown,
torpedo of a mammal. Sinuous swimming, back and forth along the
shore. Dives. Catches a bullfrog. Ducks complacently bold and apparently apathetic, swim past mink, which mounts the bank and disassembles the frog . . . the epicurean's delight. Mergansers carry on, diving and
huddling, unfazed. Foolish ducks. Finished with the frog, the mink flees
into the woods and disappears behind the stone wall.

AOR: junco flock, white-rimmed tails flashing.

Yesterday afternoon: six red crossbills high in the pines, competing
with the squirrels, tweezing seeds from dangling cones. They appeared
to be wrestling the cones.

This morning: a crossbill flies over the road. A bumper crop of cones,
clustered like grapes on the end of branches, have been attended by red
squirrels since 15 August. I've been waiting for crossbills since before the
maples blushed. A friend in southwest New Hampshire had them six
weeks ago. Now they're here.

Myrtle warbler, female, lands on pasture fence. Eats a small red berry, yellow rump flashing . . . then off to New Jersey. Grouse pair explode along the north end of the marsh, a heart-pounding exodus. Three ravens overhead. Three red-breasted nuthatches toot in the pines. Chickadee investigates the broken end of pine branches. Finds something to its liking. Jays everywhere and rowdy, back and forth across the road, screaming from the tops of pines, aspens, fences, feeders, the invisible avenues of the sky.

～

For anyone not already convinced:

1) We no longer have to look at images of a hapless (and helpless) polar bear treading water or a collapsing Antarctic glacier to see the effects of climate change. Forty years ago, black vultures barely crossed the Mason-Dixon Line. They first nested in Massachusetts in 1999, in Connecticut in 2002, and now have been seen as far north as Bangor, Maine. I've seen them above Hadley, Massachusetts, drifting north with an air of triumphant ascendancy. Fashioned in the crucible of sun and rock, black vultures depend on rising columns of heated air to stay aloft, moored to thermals as sailboats to wind. This past spring, a pair of short-winged, short-tailed vultures nested in a dilapidated barn near Burlington, Vermont, a sign of climatic trauma.

2) In the past decade, Lake Champlain froze over three times, and in January 2020, Vermont temperatures ran 7.4 degrees warmer than normal. Curious about Lake Champlain's freezing records, I checked the NOAA website and discovered that from 1816 to 1969, portions of the Lake remained ice-free *six* times, approximately 4 percent of the winters; then, between 1970 and 2016, the Lake remained open twenty-six times, approximately 57 percent of the winters. This spring, nearby Lake Fairlee was ice-free on 15 April, eight days earlier than in 2017, sixteen days earlier than in 2018, and eleven days earlier than last spring.

3) The rattlesnakes I monitor responded to a warming world. In the eighties, I visited dens from mid-to-late-May, when snakes basked near their den under a filigree of nearly leafless branches. Now, viewing season begins in mid-April and ends well before Memorial, when most dens are in the full cool shade.

Suppose we continue to drag our collective feet and remain reluctant to change our lifestyles. The arrival of black vultures in Vermont suggests a rapidly warming world. In that case, our bipolar climate will only worsen . . . who's to say I won't see king vultures and Andean condors above the Connecticut River soon?

Day 230

02 *November 2020*

Second day of Eastern Standard Time

*We need the tonic of the wilderness . . .
to smell the whispering sedge where
only some wilder and more solitary
fowl builds her nest, and the mink crawls
with its belly close to the ground.*

Henry David Thoreau

6:27 A.M. (sunrise one minute later than yesterday). 30 degrees, wind W
5 mph, the toe of a cold front. Sky: a composite of white and blue, silver
highlights and a southerly mauve rinse; then, snow (out of where I'm
not sure) spits and flurries, the world suddenly streaked with flakes, wet,
midsize, not sticking . . . won't last. A moveable and mobile feast, clouds
and snow. Permanent streams: fuller than yesterday, merrily on the move
over a carpet of drowned leaves; a few stirred by the current. Sodden
banks slippery but rocks ice free. Wetlands: slender mink leaves the
pond and runs across the road, disappearing in the cattails, swallowed
by the immensity of the marsh. Fits perfectly between slender reeds, a
thin mammal on life's narrow path. Not a stem out of place. Pond: nine
hooded mergansers, all females and juvenile males, dillydally on the far
end, swimming and diving, bunched. One catches a small crayfish. No
hasty retreat this morning.

Mink reappears in the outflow culvert, a dark brown tail flick. Sweet
face, a stuffy with a mouth full of teeth. An amped-up carnivore speaks
directly to the dogs with a pair of devastatingly foul anal scent glands.
A century ago, pioneering field biologist C. Hart Merriam said the odor
was *one of the few substances, of animal, vegetable, or mineral origin that
has, on land or sea, rendered me aware of the existence of the abominable
sensation called nausea.* I raised three mink kits, which were adrift in a
motherless world. I recall that their scent glands smelled like compost,
intense but not nauseating. However, I released the young mink on the
bank of the White River before life got too out of hand.

In the culvert. Out again. In. Out. A quick peek—a furry periscope
with a confined perspective. Around the rocky berm, the goldenrods,
the willows, then vanishing like a David Copperfield prop into thin
air. For me, a savory encounter. For the mink, an apparent roadside

distraction—two dogs and a man . . . of which nothing good can come. I walk home backward, hoping for another glimpse. I'm disappointed, the dogs confused, the mink engaged, somewhere, in the helter-skelter of life, away from prying eyes, an actual proponent of social distancing.

Pileated rocks in the morning, an ear-splitting laugh. Two red-breasted nuthatches join a group of chickadees in balsam fir. Nuthatches work the trunk, chickadees the needles. Raven and crow, a guttural duet in a world streaked by snow. Black against white lines, crows over the marsh, an avian afterthought. Female hairy woodpecker on pole-sized maple, demurely tapping . . . Woodland Western Union.

Coyotes in the lower pasture, pitching voices to the waning moon and rising sun, sealing a bargain with night. Like us, an animal *not* built for social distancing.

Day 231

03 November 2020

Election

Falling short of perfection is a
process that just never stops.
William Shawn

6:28 A.M. (sunrise one minute later than yesterday). 30 degrees, wind WNW 7 mph. Sky: clouds like eskers, long, thick undulations embossed on blue, an aerial landscape; a transitory hint of peach in the south. An inch of snow last night—the first since Mother's Day, May 10—blows off branches and beech leaves. Musical woodland, clacking limbs, creaking hardwoods. Pole-sized pines, rocking crowns combing the currents of a charming but wobbling world. Permanent streams: snow-covered rocks accent clear, cold flow. Water carols with wood . . . an upbeat melody on Election Day. Wetlands: snow highlights the western wall of conifers that lords over the marsh. Faded reeds streaked and dusted white. Dark isles of sweetgale pepper a bleached-out landscape. Three crows fly through the squall, silent as the snow. Pond: five hooded mergansers, two females and three juvenile males, huddle at the far end. One duck dives and surfaces. Another flushes. A short run across the water, and then airborne, wings churning. Three of the four remaining follow suit, complaining as they go, a series of guttural quacks. Alone on the pleated surface, the fifth duck reconsiders his options . . .

Lots of deer tracks. No sign of mink or otter. Three red-breasted nuthatches wander around black cherry trunk, picking up and down in defiance of gravity. A pensive communiqué. Perhaps, election jitters (like mine). Chickadees remain upbeat and stay that way.

Goshawk flies over the marsh and pond, arrows through the flurries, up and over the eastern rim of The Hollow, a solitary warrior in a cold world—a thrilling nanosecond—a mood enhancer without an aftertaste.

Seized by a goshawk again. The nest on the rim of the Hollow last June was an exception. Away from a nest—through the years, I've visited three—goshawk encounters are serendipitous, like an electrifying homerun that ends an unremarkable ballgame. I never leave home expecting to see one.

$\curlywedge$

Fifteen years ago, early on a Saturday morning, I stood in the garage, stomping down trash bags in the garbage pail, when I heard the distress cries of our barred rock hen. Tea Cozy ran up the driveway toward me, feather-duster tail askew, screaming like a banshee. Right behind her, an adult female goshawk, blue-gray and single minded, wings board straight, gliding just above the ground.

Hawk chased the chicken right into the garage. Tea Cozy scrambled past me, wobbling from side to side in a cartoonish way as though running across a trampoline. Panicked, she dove into the coiled garden hose, which lay on the ground behind me. Goshawk, followed ember eyes fixed on the hen. When she saw me, the goshawk banked around the garbage pail, executing an aerial pirouette, and flew back out of the garage. I felt her displaced air. Heard her wingbeats. Looked into her alien eyes, all in a matter of seconds.

I've watched November goshawks migrate above and below the North Lookout, at Hawk Mountain, along Pennsylvania's Kittatinny Ridge. But that Saturday morning, I stood in the garbage pail, not on a granite slab. The goshawk landed several feet away. Perched in a driveway maple, she stared into the garage, chest heaving, long enough for the boys to come out of the house and see her.

This morning, for a few moments, the only thing that stirred by the marsh was the wind and my memory of a hen and her hawk, an event that lasted seconds. Maybe less. Still, all these years later, I replay the scene, carefully studying each frame until reality becomes myth; the hen, the goshawk, the garage, the pail with me inside, and . . . the hen's transparent terror, my iridescent exhilaration, the hawk's relentless pursuit. All bound in a frozen moment, memory lasting a lifetime.

This morning's goshawk didn't whip around me, didn't overwhelm my senses . . . but did for an enchanted moment arrest my thoughts and evoke a memory, a welcome distraction on a disquieting Election .

Day 233

05 November 2020

When despair for the world grows in me
and I wake in the night at the least sound
in fear of what my life and my children's lives may be,
I go and lie down where the wood drake
rests in his beauty on the water, and the great heron feeds.
I come into the peace of wild things . . .
WENDELL BERRY

6:31 A.M. (sunrise one minute later than yesterday). 30 degrees, wind calm, 0 mph. In the west, potbellied moon chaperones a fleet of pink-trimmed clouds; elsewhere, mist lingers over low spots in the valley, linear above tributaries and rounded above marsh and pond. In depressions, relics of snow on the north side of trees and boulders, shaded leaves, limbs, and seed heads. Permanent streams: water swirls around snow-covered rocks, sans ice. Wetlands: lightly frosted reeds, dissipating fog. Noisy jays commute north against the flow of vehicular traffic, which has yet to recover from the pandemic, likely to my sunflower feeders, where they'll join an odd quail, seventeen turkeys, a dozen doves, and the fluidity of chickadees, titmice, juncos, nuthatches, and woodpeckers. Pond: mostly closed by a skin of ice not thick enough to support thought. Three mer-gansers, two females and an immature male, swim in tight circles on the north end, freedom circumscribed by the limited open water.

Mink ballad: in the shade, along the edge of the pond, line of paired tracks with the author standing on hind legs. Curiously watching me watch him. Big, poker-faced male, cream-white chin, everything else pro-foundly dark against a backdrop of waning snow. On an otherwise bleak morning, a supple wild mammal, two days post-election.

Sexual dimorphism: variance of size between the sexes; the hallmark of raptors and *Mustelids* (weasel family), but in reverse. Female hawks and owls, on the frontline of nest defense, dwarf males, the dutiful providers. Male minks dwarf females. Mating mink like a World Wide Wrestling Federation death match. The male chases the female, grabs her, and pins her by the scruff of her neck. Abuses her like a tempest, vigorously and expeditiously. A breeding ritual honed over millions of years has yielded fascinating dividends: weasels, ferrets, martens, bad-gers, wolverines.

One morning, after Little League practice, Jordan and I watched mink mate, mostly a breathtaking battle royal, more a Texas Death Match than a tender caress. Much the more significant, the male chased the female out of a Lake Fairlee marsh, around the grassy land-ing strip at the Post Mills Airport, across the road half a dozen times, and around a stand of hillside pines. He finally pinned his betrothed down by the neck, in the same way he might have dispatched a musk-rat . . . and mated. Two long bodies interwoven, a ball of luxuriously brown fur, scratching and flopping. An encounter (seemingly) devoid of romance or passion. Repeated half-a-dozen times in the woods on both sides of the road. The word rape comes to mind . . . nevertheless, such a chillingly chaotic ritual yields results. Had my mother only known the true nature of the beast whose fur kept her chic!

Five sober crows high in a vacant sky; three fly west, two north. Pileated laughter passes through the open canopy, red crest swept back. A ptero-dactyl of a bird, rising and sinking in flight.

Oblivious to absentee ballots, three chickadees hang upside down from the ends of hemlock twigs, prying tiny seeds out of little cones. Their specialized leg muscles, which permit dangling, would impress Bo Jackson . . . maybe Jim Brown. In the neighborhood of acrobatic chick-adees, a chorus of red-breasted nuthatches and a trio of chattering red squirrels. One squirrel launches from maple to pine at a forty-five-degree angle, limbs extended, similar to the nascent glide that an ancestral flying squirrel must have taken more than thirty million years ago.

I walk through a cold tunnel of nuthatches—post-election fanfare under a compassionate sky. The toy horn chorus is a celebration, a message of tolerance, forgiveness, and hope for a rickety world. Upbeat in the pines and maples, chickadees are still busily exercising leg muscles, ignoring leaping squirrel—a strategy that ought to be used for political polls.

Again, pileated rakes the Hollow, a loud, vibrant proclamation, a chuckling boundary marker, an audible locator. Maybe he's laughing at himself . . . as I do during times of unmitigated stress.

Day 235

07 November 2020

The chickadee and the nuthatch are
more inspiring society than statesmen and
philosophers, and we shall return to
these last as to more vulgar companions.
Henry David Thoreau

6:34 a.m. (sunrise two minutes later than yesterday). 41 degrees, wind ENE 1 mph. Sky: half-moon above the marsh shines through a pastel wash, the pink and peach of a nearly bright dawning; the birth of several clouds, condensation points, some grayish-purple; in transition to springtime white and blue. I peer into the vastness, where comets roam, hope and aspirations are born, and dreams go to die. A pocket of thin ground fog, the breath of night, slowly dissipating. Permanent streams: a pair of watery ribbons allows rock-hopping mink to reach The Hollow's eastern wall and into the next valley, eventually to my friend Ford's trout pond, where he'll dine in solitude on the most delicate, most expensive fish in the neighborhood. Both streams, steady flows; the magic of summer, which sleeps as soundly as a woodchuck, has lost its evaporative clout. Wetlands: half a bowl of mist on the west end, east end clear. The western wall, a dark and jagged mix of evergreens, now softer and lighter in diffusing fog; more ethereal, less bleak . . . a simple illusion. Pond: lonely merganser, a female, brown frosted crest erect, a tomahawk head, works the far edge, the mink's realm, diving, surfacing, circling, slipping back underwater, barely a ripple, feathers a tightly linked water-repellent unit—rachis, barbs, barbules, hooklets—the original Velcro. Surfaces again, a small crayfish clamped in her serrated bill. A shake. Two slaps against the water surface. Then, down the dark gullet, toward a lethal bath of stomach acids and digestive enzymes. A slight current of mist drifts in from the marsh.

Milkweed seeds, like scraps of cotton, litter the berm, the grass, the shoreline; peeling off pods; seeds sowed for next year's monarchs, whose immediate ancestors cross the Rio Grande and the Wall, the international border, their leveraged migration built on summer's milk-weed crop. Aspens release yellow-brown leaves, drift and litter, a final foliar rain.

Nowhere to be found in The Hollow, robins disperse across southern New England and Mid-Atlantic states. Three clusters of red-breasted nuthatches keep up their end of the vocal bargain, enlivening the woods with lighthearted—if colorless—toots. In defiance of planetary law, one descends a pine, picking through pleated bark. Investigates a tuft of brown needles, the ceaseless hunt for insects and insect eggs, spiders and spider eggs. Finds something to its liking. And a second something. Claws on bark, a soft, scratchy sound like belly scales of homebound rattlesnakes brushing against brittle leaves.

The whisper of brown creepers. The sibilance of pine siskins. The lamentation of mourning doves. The yawp of crows. The thrill of a southbound red-shouldered hawk that passes over the marsh.

The enthusiasm of chickadees. Comprehensive feeders: on the end of fir twigs; the seed heads of asters and goldenrod; the crotch of beech branches; banging open galls; scavenging from spiderwebs. Back and forth, all over the place, from drooping stem to branch and back. One chickadee visits the forest floor, something of interest in the sodden leaves. Hopping, hopping, hopping. Spider eggs, aroused insects, coma-tose pupae, egg clusters. Nothing's safe.

I'm alive and alone, ambivalent, dogs on leashes; the 2020 presidential count goes on without me as I straddle that thin line between rhapsody and despair, out and about in the desolation of November. My agenda in our bipolar world . . . see the light in the nuthatch's eye, watch the falcon stoop, listen to the coyote sing all night in the dark, beneath a diamond sky. Welcome the chickadee, be a good neighbor. Is that asking too much?

Day 237

09 November 2020

*There is only one solution if old age is
not to be an absurd parody of our former life,
and that is to go on pursuing ends
that give our existence a meaning . . .*
SIMONE DE BEAUVOIR

6:36 A.M. (sunrise one minute later than yesterday). 36 degrees, wind SSE less than 1 mph. Sky: pink in the south, pale blue in the east. At less than half, the moon hollows out, its horns the straps of a silver, shining Covid mask . . . an old-man-in-the-moon mask for astronomers. Sprawling ground fog, a serpent flow through lowlands. Permanent streams: merrily rolling along, the same as yesterday and the day before and the day before that. Wetlands: dark isles and pale reeds frosted, vanishing fog and fingers of sunlight. Ansel Adams landscape: intimate yet alluring, a feral potato field brought back by time and beavers, hemmed between hills and a lake, within soundscape of church bells and traffic. A twenty-first-century wildness, which called out to Linny, all those years ago . . . I dutifully followed, an only child, a watcher of birds, a catcher of snakes, the son of a haberdasher and an energetic mother, sloughing suburban rust. Pond: motionless and empty.

Milkweed pods split, seeds dangle like shredded cotton. Scraps everywhere.

DOR: gray squirrel en route to the bird feeders.

AOR: slug moving at a snail's pace.

Blue jay performs a medley of greatest hits: shrill scream; incessant squawk; cry of a red-shouldered hawk; descending holler of a red-tailed hawk; high note of a broad-winged hawk; key-in-the-ignition tooting; pumping water, clear and musical; and an odd assortment of whirrs, chortles, rattles, buzzes, twitters. A female downy woodpecker draws attention to herself and hops along a familiar cherry branch—spring podium where a trusting chestnut-sided warbler sang his heart out last June.

Robin in an apple tree, surrounded by withered apples. A chorus of red-breasted nuthatches. One picks through lichen on a pine limb then investigates the end of a busted branch. Eventually, flies to the ground. Repeats steps one through three. Pileated calls, a heartfelt laugh.

❧

On New Year's morning 1978, a pileated was our New Year's bird; the first bird Linny and I saw that year. Since then, New Year's birds are mainly blue jays and chickadees. Once, a common redpoll.

This morning, of all mornings, I could use a chickadee to cinch my mood, to rewind my heart.

Linny died twenty years ago today. Seems like yesterday. The melting and congealing of time: slowing down, speeding up, inverting, minutes passing like hours, hours like minutes, eventually to vanish into the void of memory loss. Linny asked me who had won the Bush-Gore election in the wee hours of 8 November 2000. Political symmetry.

If she knew of our current political imbroglio and that *Fox News* has replaced *The National Inquirer* as the premier purveyor of fake news and that lying everywhere has become fashionable, she'd be saddened. School shootings would break her heart.

The following morning, close to dawn, she whispered, with a hoarse confidence, *I know the boys will be all right* . . . in no small part because of the foundation she had built. Those were the last words she spoke. Casey was thirteen. Jordan turned five the next day; she planned his partying flat on her back.

I want to tell you that your boys are stellar, a tribute to your legacy and that our friends pitched in. That your sisters stood by us. That the raspberry patch you planted produces more fruit than twenty people could eat, and every July, throughout Jordan's childhood, he gathered berries before breakfast, his fingers and face stained with summer. I want to tell you that I've taken on pesto-making and Key lime pie, and that merlins nest along the Ompompanoosuc River and bald eagles along the Connecticut, and that, sadly, as the world heats up, your beloved Alpine Gardens—where we scattered most of your ashes and built a cairn of white quartz—withdraws from the summit of Mount Washington, flower by tiny flower.

I want to tell you that you were the moral cortex of our household, the soother, the master planner, and that I'm still here, my eye on The Hollow, my hair white as the snows of Kilimanjaro and still disheveled. That the beavers are gone, but the bittern and rakish-faced owl still haunt my nights.

Oh, how the modest trees have grown. Your little boys have become men. They carry you with them—Casey didn't inherit my phobia of power tools and engines; Jordan listens with empathy. Both love beer and hot sauce, and mountain biking. Both laugh deeply and with assurance. Both stand erect under challenging times.

A merlin harries a jay in the compost pile . . . the jay bolts, bagel in bill, squawking with a full mouth. I light a *yahrzeit* candle, the candle you made with Casey from birch bark one summer in Minnesota. Back outside, solaced by chickadees, I keep track of the vagaries of November; and all that you loved.

Day 238

10 November 2020

I wish the bald eagle had not been chosen as
the representative of our country. For truth, the turkey is
in comparison a much more respectable bird,
and withal a true original native of America.
He is besides, though a little vain and silly,
a bird of courage.

BENJAMIN FRANKLIN

6:38 A.M. (sunrise two minutes later than yesterday). 34 degrees, wind calm, 0 mph. Sky: clear with a peach wash, ground fog creeping through the lowlands. Moon in the east hollowing out, horns prominent. Intermittent streams: reduced to puddles, in need of a transfusion. Permanent streams: five days in the sixties have taken a slight but noticeable toll, a shallower, softer lullaby in concert with nuthatches and chickadees, a woodland whisper. Wetlands: rising bands of ground fog.

Flyover flock of red crossbills, distinctive flight calls above the reeds, disappear into shoreline pines, branches laden with cones. Pond: mist, like chickadee breath, barely visible.

AOR: six slugs, slow-motion migration, headed west. One leaves a crooked slime trail.

Wraithlike deer walks through crisp leaves, ratcheting dogs' attention. Leashes tighten. Deer runs across road, tail up . . . all hell breaks loose.

Busy red squirrel, the sound of tiny feet shuffling through dry leaves. After more than two months of attending squirrels, white pines still have enough cones to attract nomadic red crossbills, which pause to tweeze seeds from between the scales. Red-breasted nuthatches are conspicuous by their absence. Not white-breasted nuthatches, which haunt the hardwoods with a low, hoarse, dyspeptic *yank, yank, yank*. Two hairy woodpeckers, unseen, call loudly and sharply. Downy woodpecker, a faint avian telegraph.

The sleepy internal rhythm of the morning is interrupted by the merriment of chickadees. One fastidiously forages through the loose bark of honeysuckle, a run of muted taps . . . woodpecker wannabe. Titmice calling in the hardwoods, a clear, two-part whistle like an amped-up spring peeper, far less common than chickadees, their trusted associates.

Out of the northwest, circling above the canopy, a red-tailed hawk. An adult, rust-red tail teasing the breeze. Hawk gathers itself in a teardrop, tail feathers pinched together, wings against flank, and pours south over pastures and marsh.

Three male turkeys strut under the feeder admiring each other, vainglorious boasting of unhinged game birds, the *very* self-absorption archers prey on. Aztecs domesticated the turkey, a local race called Gould's turkey the most significant and southernmost of five subspecies of wild turkey *Meleagris gallopavo*. A concise history of domestication: Conquistadors brought the turkey to Europe in 1519; reached England in 1524, Henry VIII was the first British king to eat turkey. Edward VII made turkey fashionable for Christmas dinner. In 1969, Neil Armstrong and Buzz Aldrin ate turkey sandwiches on the moon. In 2020, my Covid Thanksgiving plans imploding.

Benjamin Franklin should see the trio under my feeders. Pompous. Arrogant. Oblivious to the doves and lonesome quail forced to shuffle around their heavy feet. A purple rinse of light pours down the hills, ignites the morning, encourages me to pause, sun on my face, and think of Jordan. It's his birthday today, a five-star November morning. The next generation, my boys are perpetual gifts. I am thrilled . . . except for the fact that I'm stuck at home, footloose, fancy free, socially distanced from everything but chickadees, standing on the threshold of an opalescent morning—prisoner of the obvious and the mysterious.

❧

Later in the day, as chill and velvet darkness seep in, I sit with Nancy around her fire pit in Pomfret. A barred owl perched on a telephone pole decamps, flies over the driveway and above the flames. In silence, silhouetted, long wings rise up and back like a cardboard mobile on a string. Like the bird décor above Jordan's crib, flapping in the lamplight as I pulled the string. Jordan's twenty-four today, in Cambridge, opportunity on his doorstep. Without a string to pull or a boy to feed, I watch an owl in flux, soft, silent flight in the waning light. The agendas of owls and boys are *not* so different . . . everyone has to eat.

Day 240

12 November 2020

Give me your tired, your poor
Your huddled masses yearning to breathe free,
The wretched refuse of your teeming shore.
Send these, the homeless, tempest-tossed to me,
I lift my lamp beside the golden door!
Emma Lazarus

6:40 a.m. (sunrise one minute later than yesterday). 54 degrees, wind NNW 6 mph (the nuthatch red-eye, on the heels of a cold front, filling familiar and remote evergreens with disembodied toots). Wind, like traffic, roars; sheltered beech leaves in motion, a foliar sibilance. Pine crowns stirring, whisk the air. Sky: ashen, textured, damp. Yesterday's rain motivated several peepers, which trilled in the privacy of the leaf litter, the tiny bells of spring. Pockets on the road, puddled. Permanent streams: refreshed, fuller, louder, more mesmerizing . . . still far from capacity. Wetlands: staid. Above the marsh, flying north, raven pair, black between gray ceiling and tan floor, an occasional croak, leisurely flapping. One raven barrel rolls, an unquenchable joy for life. Off to breakfast on a disemboweled deer? Pond: surface rippled and empty. Impressionistic reflections, *matin couvert*.

Pine crowns are burdened with cones. A mast year. Today, however, no sign of crossbills. Two chattering red squirrels chase each other up and down and around three pine trunks, toenails scratching bark, louder than the twittering beech leaves, a dizzying pursuit. Dogs sit, watching (hoping one falls nearby). Next spring should produce a bumper crop of red squirrels. Two litters per female, up to six kits per litter. Songbird nestlings, beware. Raptors prepare.

My mother, one of eleven children, was born to Russian parents, neither of whom spoke English when they arrived at Ellis Island. My grandfather taught Hebrew, didn't handle money whenever he read the Torah, about twice a week, and got around in a horse-drawn carriage. My grandmother had a cow, chickens, and a large garden. Somehow, they managed on the outskirts of Toledo, Ohio. They put away borscht and brisket. Made latkes. As far as I know, neither responded to a mast year.

This autumn's bumper crop of acorns and pine nuts, littering lawns and hanging from trees, should trigger a trophic cascade, a food chain flowering of white-footed mice, red and gray squirrels, chipmunks, and flying squirrels. Next spring, an abundance of small mammals well fed on eggs and chicks stolen from songbird nests will in turn feed Cooper's hawks and goshawks, both midsized terrorists—spirited, relentless predators. Mast, a three-year cycle: from nuts and seeds to rodent outbreak (and more cases of tick-borne diseases delivered to us) and fewer songbirds fledged. More rodents, more hawks fledged, and weasels weaned. And if you enjoy rattlesnakes (as I do), in two years, late summer 2022, there will be more rattlesnake births on the ledges above Lake Champlain . . . but that's another story.

My grandparents, tending garden and barnyard, far removed from the bounties of a mast year, never had it so easy.

Day 242

14 November 2020

My birthday

*For the first time in 4 billion years a living
creature had contemplated himself and heard
with a sudden, unaccountable loneliness, the
whisper in the night reeds.*

LOREN EISELEY

6:43 A.M. (sunrise two minutes later than yesterday). 34 degrees, wind
SW 3 mph. Sky: a bouillabaisse of shape and color, pastel pink, shades
of gray, white, and blue. Highlights and bruises. Rising ground fog. The
forest floor is crisp to sloshy. Intermittent streams: puddles linked by
drizzle, temporarily bridged and flowing. Permanent streams: bolstered
by an all-day rain, the soft, soothing voice of water. Wetlands: frostless
and soggy, a deep pool of cold air, fed by a half dozen spigots that channel
Siberia down every crease in the hillsides, a bitter watershed made less
bearable by the past week's glory, six days in the sixties and seventies.
Crossing the marsh over the spongy ground, puddle to puddle, past narrow otter trails and wider, unevenly trampled deer trails. And oval beds
where deer spent the night . . . drinking and playing cards and whatever
else deer do when the lights go out. Truancy of birds. Pond: nano waves,
like windrows of sand, a subtle undulation. In the shallows, drowned
leaves blanket tadpoles and frogs for their six-month nap, metabolism
reduced to a tic. Underwater, in winter, turtles breathe through the lining of their throats and cloacae, frogs and tadpoles through their skin,
a seasonal adjustment fine-tuned over two hundred million years. The
unwavering nature of reptiles and amphibians. There's a lesson here,
somewhere . . . I'm sure.

Across the marsh, astronomical bushels of pine cones dangling.
Check for crossbills. Nothing. In the absence of crossbills, like a whale
watch without whales, I rely on narration and stories. I begin a crossbill
dialogue with myself, staggering through unconsolidated muck. Eleven
races of red crossbills in North America, possibly eleven different species,
each with a different bill size and body size, each with a different evergreen preference and geography. Each with a different call. A vagabond,
Type 1, southern Appalachians, wanders widely in the East. Northeast,

Types 1, 2, and 10, some years Type 3, cashing in on the cone crop, wherever that may be. Type 8, Newfoundland, a homebody. The rest are out West (Type 6, Mexico, Sierra Madre Occidental, wanders north into the Southwest; Type 11, southern Mexico and Nicaragua). Type 10 might *actually* be Type 7. Who knows? Not me. Quizzically and patiently, the dogs look off into space.

Back on the road, a squirrel ignores us. Red squirrel, sitting beside a pine, handles a cone the way we might manage a three-foot corn on the cob, held in the palms of both hands. Happy squirrel spins the cone. White eye-rings set off coal-black eyes. A facial lamplight. Dogs more interested in squirrel than my crossbill musings.

Jay, the town crier, announces a new day. Chickadees keep to themselves, hushed in the woods. Woods lightly seasoned with nuthatches, a soft fanfare. In defiance of Newtonian Law, three wander down a sugar maple trunk, picking through tufts of moss and lichen, flit to adjacent maple for an encore performance. Jay heads northwest, fractures the dreariness, and rushes to feeders.

Today's the first day of rifle season. I don't hunt, nor do I own a gun. But I don't post my land. I welcome deer hunters; there are plenty of whitetails to go around. For predators and furbearers, however, I insist on a no-shoot policy. Several men who hunt Coyote Hollow grew up on Robinson Hill and have hunted the hill and marsh since boyhood, often in the company of their fathers and grandfathers. Their history here is deep, deeper than mine, topophilia passed down the generations. I won't disrupt those bonds because I own the property and pay the taxes. I remember the moon rising into the night, the surf washing over my feet. An owl tracing above the shoreline. The beach held my childhood together. And besides, it's my birthday and I don't want to be an asshole.

Sunlight spills down Robinson Hill, cold and bright. I pause to hear the jay proclaim the feeders full, and from all directions, they come.

Day 246

18 November 2020

The main thing is this—when you get up
in the morning you must take your heart in
your hands. You must do this every morning.
GRACE PALEY

6:48 A.M. (sunrise one minute later than yesterday). 21 degrees, wind
NW 10 mph (an ominous, frigid blow, trees swaying). Sky: murky. In
the north, a rating of 6 on Ansel Adams' Zone System, a shade of gray
that leans whiter than black; in the east, Zones 2 and 3, textured dark,
highlights bright enough for sunglasses. Permanent streams: soft dancing light, more waltz than horah, ice on the ends of emergent sticks.
Wetlands: flushed by unabated wind, loud enough to hijack the voice
of a nearby chickadee, everything else hunkered down. Pond: ice-sheet
blooms in the south cove, shards and panes unite and spread north,
sealing off a third of the pond . . . not quite ready for hockey. Two jays
overhead, one following the other. Both scream, cut through the wind.

Roving red crossbills, in and out of the pines, chatty flight, eight
mobile dots, a tight grouping, silhouettes against the gray, from one tree
to the next, from one valley to another, nomadic diners that occasionally
stay in Vermont to breed. Lives devoted to the geography of cones. For
crossbills *philopatry* is a bond not to a location but to evergreens, a deep
relationship with North America's green sweep of pines, firs, spruce,
hemlock, larch—from the subarctic south around the Great Lakes and
down every mountain range—North Carolina to Belize, Oregon to
Baja, Alaska to Colorado. I enjoy them while I can; they may be absent
for years—the nature of crossbills: the story of sporadic food abundance,
a dietary migrancy, the original vagabonds.

In the late sixties, when I studied wildlife biology as an undergraduate,
our class subdivided Delaware County, Indiana, into a grid system. On
designated mornings, I drove my grid and counted roadkill—raccoon,
fox squirrel, red fox, long-tailed weasel, thirteen-lined ground squirrel,
and so on. Back in class we used a formula (long since forgotten) based
on the number of casualties to determine each species' population.

Unfortunately, I don't believe the formula applies to fallen pine cones.
Since late August, a shower of cones has littered my walking route, cut

and dropped by red squirrels. Most of the cones are gone, retrieved by squirrels or pulverized into the dirt road, reduced to a white resinous stain—a reminder of natural cyclical overproduction. If I need further evidence that 2020 is the *Autumn of the Pine Cone*, I listen to chattering crossbills and watch red squirrels visiting cone caches or raiding each other's larders. Lots of helter-skelter rushing, whirring voices like tape decks run amok.

Brown creeper slowly, methodically wanders up a dead, pole-sized pine. Checks crevices for spiders, cocoons, and insect eggs. A slender, curved bill scrutinizes bark like a water-witcher scrutinizes the ground, probing, probing. Tail, woodpecker stiff, braced against the tree. Around and around, always up, a nuthatch in reverse, a corkscrew search for food. A dainty, delicate bird. Looks like a piece of loose bark. Colored like a dried leaf, brown and streaked. Light underneath; ochre band on wings. Sounds like an errant hearing aid, high and thin, barely audible, in the vocal range of kinglets and blackburnian warbler . . . louder than thought, quieter than a twittering beech leaf. Compared to blue jay or chickadee, the creeper is antisocial, a loner—Covid poster bird—an unorthodox little bird that keeps to itself.

Brown creeper flits from one tree to the next. Wanders up and around. Now I see him, now I don't. Now, I see him again. Nearby, four chickadees are in flux. Dashing and calling, investigating everything that isn't a brown creeper. Branches. A mat of frozen leaves. Stone wall. Pine needles. Twig tips. For the moment, I stick with the creeper . . . it may be months before we cross paths again.

Two crows, silent beneath the unfolding sky, usher up the sun. Black birds above the marsh. Headed into the wind. Below the crows, chickadees, at peace in atmospheric and Covid chaos, patrol microhabitats on limbs. Feeding. Calling. Pausing, now and again, to fluff out like animated stuffies, the indefatigable defenders of the joy of life. I want to live the remainder of my life with the sparkle of a chickadee. I lean on chickadees often . . . and do again as the virus torches my Thanksgiving plans.

Day 247

19 November 2020

Childhood is measured out by sounds and
smells and sights, before the dark hour
of reason grows.

JOHN BETJEMAN

6:49 A.M. (sunrise one minute later than yesterday). 18 degrees, wind NNE 1 mph. Sky: dense rose and mauve in the east, a hint of pink in the south, everywhere else a tangled blue, white, and gray. Permanent streams: ice on backwaters and along the hem of the main channels, more closed than open. A strand of song, occluded by ice, dubbed over and hollow. Wetlands: without frost, quiet except for two furious red squirrels high in a shoreline pine. Pond: sealed shut, ice thickest in the south cove, a curved white border near the middle. Elegant feather patterns on thinner ice. Dogs curiously sniff an otter trail, a trough in the frozen grasses and weeds plastered by a dripping coat. Ends in the water, now closed off by ice.

The chase: two red squirrels up and down the pines, scratching of bark, maddening chatter, a leap from one tree to another. Tails in play, instruments of balance, flicking and twitching. The thief and the pursuer. I close my eyes and listen. Toenails strike bark. Everywhere pine cones hang like holiday ornaments. Red squirrel freeloading is a twenty-first-century crisis.

Hairy woodpecker calls from the bleak, granite outcrop where a hermit thrush electrified the month of May, obediently infatuated. Thrush's voice intoxicating. Woodpecker's not so much.

Cardinal under the feeder, a male, only the fourth or fifth time in more than twenty years—red among the gray squirrels.

～

In 1771, when William Bartram wrote *Travels through North and South Carolina, Georgia, East and West Florida, the Cherokee Country, etc* (now shortened to *Bartram's Travels*), the cardinal was a bird of the moss-clad South, splashing color from canebrakes, thickets, and river edges. At the time, cardinals were unknown in the Northeast. By the late 1800s, they had become fashionable cage birds. Thousands were sent to the Northeast and Europe, imprisoned like canaries in wire baskets, a sad vestige of wild America. Their incarceration ended with the passage of the Migratory Bird Treaty Act of 1918.

Over the last century, cardinals expanded their range northwest along the Mississippi River and its tributaries, and northeast along the Atlantic Coast. Some ornithologists suggest the bird's range expansion is a sign of climate change—nonmigratory, cardinals don't store fat. Others suggest a response to the popularity of bird feeders and two centuries of habitat change; thickets and clearings—cardinals' preferred habitat—replacing old-growth woods. In 1886, cardinals were casual north of the Ohio River. By 1895, they had reached the Great Lakes; by 1910, Ontario. In 1914, they nested on Staten Island. Cardinal sightings were documented in Connecticut in 1943, Massachusetts in 1958, Vermont in 1962, and Maine in 1969. Today, cardinals nest in Nova Scotia.

In the 1960s, cardinals zipped in and out of my mother's flowerbeds, brightening the most dismal winter morning. They gathered sunflower seeds beneath the backyard feeders; males waged war on their reflections in the living-room window and side-view mirrors of my father's Lincoln—breath condensing on cold glass.

Named for the robes worn by Roman Catholic cardinals, cardinals caught the American public's attention. They became the official state bird of seven states: Illinois, Indiana, Kentucky, Ohio, North Carolina, Virginia, and West Virginia. Missouri, home of the St. Louis Cardinals, chose the bluebird.

❧

The pandemic's silver lining is the joy of staying home for eight months and being entertained by nuthatches, chickadees, and blue jays . . . back to basics. Casey and Becky, three months from their first child. I am with birds and clouds. Popi's training wheels.

❧

I cup my hands to my ears, gathering in nuthatch calls, slowly rotating left and right, a self-made parabolic reflector, an owl with external ears, or an elderly Mouseketeer. The soft swish of air, more of a conch-shell experience, does little to amplify the nuthatches . . . but I do hear memories echoing in the parlor of my hands. A little boy on the beach. My father hands me a moon-snail shell, round and white as a sunbeam. Fills a tiny hand. I believed I heard the ocean in the deep, spiraling interior, that endless roll of surf—boyhood on the beach, blind obedience to the cadences of life. Impressionable, too.

Day 250

22 November 2020

Going nowhere . . . isn't about turning your
back on the world; it's about stepping away
now and then so that you can see the world
more clearly and love it more deeply.
LEONARD COHEN

6:53 A.M. (sunrise one minute later than yesterday). 25 degrees, wind WSW 1 mph. Sky: clear and cold, pink rinse across the south. Permanent streams: dwarf cascades and minirapids, infused and iceless, pulsating light and flow. Wetlands: heavier glaze than yesterday, a whiter shade of tan. From somewhere in the pines, beyond the marsh, the *kip, kip, kip* of crossbills. Pond: a tighter, thicker seal (not that I'm about to walk across). Shards and slivers froze into a jigsaw—stained glass without the stain—mosaic of ice, adorned with milkweed seeds, eye-catching white plumes, tassels in the breeze.

Across the marsh, midway up a shoreline hemlock, a barred owl, bright as fresh snow. Globe-headed bird, motionless and silent. Staring into the reeds, telescope eyes appraising patterns, ears awry, measuring sound. Reads a world I can't comprehend. Then decamps, launching through a cleft in the hemlocks. Absorbed by green.

Years ago, when *I wore a younger man's clothes* (to borrow a helpful line from Billy Joel), I stood on a boardwalk in an old-growth cypress swamp, on the south end of Fakahatchee Strand, a barred owl perched ten feet overhead. A smaller barred owl, a pig frog dangling from his bill, landed next to the larger owl. The small owl gave the large owl the frog. Then, betrothed, mounted her, tails askew . . . connubial bliss lasting seconds. Done, they headed into the generosity of the swamp. One laughing like a maniac, the other dining alfresco on frog legs.

༄

The International Ornithological Committee estimates that eleven thousand species of birds inhabit Earth, classified into 44 Orders, 253 Families, and 2,384 Genera. Of those, only 3 percent evolved to hunt at night. The retinas of daytime hunting birds are packed with color-sensitive *cones*, including ones that detect ultraviolet light. The retinas of owls, huge and tube shaped—eye-tubes, not eyeballs—are packed with

93 percent light-sensitive *rods* and amount to 5 percent of the body mass of some species. By comparison, writes Jennifer Ackerman, our eyes account for 0.0003 percent of our body mass. The large round head and substantial forward-facing eyes of a barred owl see by starlight. Hear footfalls miles away, hunt with unerring accuracy on the darkest, quietest nights.

It's no wonder thirty thousand years Before Present (BP), on the wall of a cave in southern France, an artist painted the image of an owl. If our eyes were as big as theirs, writes Ackerman, they'd weigh four pounds and be the size of an orange.

◦◡

I love the mystery of owls. I've raised barred and saw-whet chicks. Chickadees may brighten my mood, but owls affirm the unknown.

A far-off pileated laughs. Nearby, the tricycle horns of red-breasted nuthatches. A *Duck Soup* melody . . . Harpo Marx, his feet submerged in Edgar Kennedy's lemonade. Debonair titmouse and six raucous jays. Red squirrels: shy introverts on the ground, extroverts emoting on a limb.

Five chickadees investigate white birch. Two others fly into the skeletal crown of aspen. Check under curls of bark and the ends of broken twigs. Pick at leaf buds. What's in it for the chickadees? Insect eggs? Buds themselves? Hard to tell from below. On frigid winter nights, chickadee lowers its metabolism—self-induced hypothermia. Winter temperatures may drop more than fifty degrees Fahrenheit between day and night. The internal chilling conserves fat and reduces oxygen consumption. May also evoke the sound of sleigh bells and dreams of Christmas . . . though this remains unproven.

Fingers of freshly minted sunlight run down Robinson Hill.

Chickadee

Day 252

24 November 2020

I'd just climbed out of the car and there
it was, eye-level, looking at me, young,
bare blue, the crest and marking jewelry
penciled in [. . .] It seemed to wait for me,
watching in that superciliary way
birds watch too.

STANLEY PLUMLY

6:55 A.M. (sunrise one minute later than yesterday). 34 degrees, wind NNW 8 mph, howling and whispering. Pine trunks sway; branches in motion, a landscape in flux. An orchestra of trees, the original woodwinds—creaking, moaning, yowling. A triumph of noise, enough to drown out crows and jays . . . a deed indeed. Sky: empty of birds. At first, occluded, atmospheric topography, primarily blues and grays. In the east, a hint of peach. Spits tiny, bouncy, milk-white hail that sticks to metal roofs and every low spot on the road. Melts elsewhere. As I wander, clouds break up, dividing into islands and archipelagos. Permanent streams: enhanced by yesterday's rain, clearer and fuller. Wetlands: marsh dreary, vault vibrant. Luminous shape-changing clouds, with pink suggestions. Wind as a sculptor smooths, tears, teases, welds. Pond: yesterday's rain, today's ice. A stratified surface has two weak layers. Wispy lines of hail, a cold smoke, muscled by wind. Then, stops. Momentary windrows, ephemeral stripes across transparent ice, until set in motion again. I skim a rock, long slide, wake and twang, throbbing ice.

Soggy milkweed seeds dangle out of pods, limp laundry on the meadow line.

Twenty feet away, red squirrel tends a cache of pine cones. Bored with the morphology of clouds, dogs focus on squirrel. Sit and stare, hoping it strays across the road.

Jay flies past. Blue of the blue jay, an optical illusion. A structural color, a scattering of light. Not a pigment. Transparent, gas-filled spaces (called *vacuoles*) in the barbs—collectively the vane on either side of the feather shaft—bounce light back at the viewer. Me, in this case. The result? A festival of blue: indigo blue, madder blue, china blue, porcelain blue, Gobelin blue, Dutch blue, sky blue, baby blue. Paul Newman's eyes. Turn off the sun, take away the light . . . a gray bird. Without light refracting off the vacuoles, nearby *melanin* cells, their pigment darkish brown, render the jay (or bluebird or indigo bunting) an uninspiring gray. Today's jay: dripping wet, drab as twilight (although a lot more animated). Even the expressive crest . . . an ashen gray. What's not an optical illusion: white cheeks, black wraparound scarf, eyeliner, barred tail and wings, white-tipped wing feathers. And the gray of the breast, unbroken like the sharp jeering that spills across the marsh.

There are colors I don't see, sounds I don't hear. And then there's the blue jay, an illusion, a chromatic Penn and Teller trick. Now blue, now gray, now blue again . . . the nonchalant rendering of a small star.

Day 253

25 November 2020

*Life is what happens to you while
you're busy making other plans.*
JOHN LENNON

6:57 A.M. (sunrise two minutes later than yesterday). 25 degrees, wind SE 4 mph. Sky: taut, uniformly gray, featureless as an unrumpled sheet. Snow, eye-stinging microflakes, whitens the forest floor and marks the open air. Chills my cheeks. Gathers on the dogs, a light, regular dusting, absent since the first week in May. An untainted whiteness. Permanent streams: water rushing around snow-capped rocks. Wetlands: white on beige, reduced visibility. Pond: snow on ice, trackless. A half-moon of open water against the eastern shore, gift of a leaky hillside.

Three ravens, ambassadors from another valley, preceded by their voices. Growls. Croaks. A percussive knocking. Corvid dialogues, complicated discussions. Doppler effect, into the morning beyond Robinson Hill. Louder and louder and louder. Then the birds, coal black and inquisitive. Miss nothing. Reading the world from aloft . . . above the marsh, the pond, the eastern flank, toward the Connecticut River, whitened by snow. Big-brained birds, avian Mensas. And gone, voices trailing off like yesterday's news.

A fourth raven appears and plays catch-up. Follows the narrative thread, black wings like an awning, stretched and barely flapping. Although buoyant chickadees and nuthatches fill nearby pines and maples, I watch the raven, alone in a sky brushed with snow, a commanding bird, bigger than a redtail. Barrel roll, a patented maneuver. Calling. Wanting. Seeking companionship, three minutes behind his cohorts, having dawdled at the evergreen roost.

∾

Comeback birds. In the spring of 1976, on an ornithology field trip, I visited a remote raven nest high on a cliff in Stoddard, New Hampshire, at the time, the only known nest in the state. Now, rarely a day passes when I don't hear or see a raven. They nest on the nearby Fairlee cliffs, sharing the wall with peregrines and turkey vultures. One winter, several years ago, more than thirty roosted in a pine grove on the north end of The Hollow, just up the road from my driveway. Ravens have returned to New Jersey, Pennsylvania, Maryland, and down the spine of the Appalachians to South Carolina. In the New York Metropolitan area, they nest on water towers, buildings in Queens and the Bronx, and secluded Long Island beaches. In the Chelsea district of Manhattan, somebody spotted a raven eating a bagel.

Department of Teamwork and Planning: during the summer of 1980, on our honeymoon along the shores of Hudson Bay, Linny and I watched a pair of ravens steal whimbrel eggs from a nest. One raven drew both whimbrels from the nest; then, the other stole an egg. Easily duped, whimbrels never caught on. Four times, two whimbrels chased one raven, while the other raven made off with an egg . . . until the nest was empty, a lonely scape of tundra.

We marveled at the ravens' strategy, the planning, the relentless execution, and the uncompromising success. We heeded the ravens, mapped out our own future, and imagined the trajectory of our lives. We'd introduce our children to the moon and stars, lose ourselves in the continent's vast folds, and eventually become white-haired and bent over, worn down by time. Perhaps we'd end our days as campground hosts in a national park, Death Valley or Yellowstone, rocking on the porch under Panama hats, itinerant naturalists sharing their harvest. Dreams drove us forward . . . reality was a fly ball off the Green Monster.

∾

Does the fourth raven see the trio, distant dots against the gray? Raven, a triumph of vision and will, flaps over the hill and out of sight, a dark kitchen sink of a bird with a wedge-shaped bill. Black as the Queen of Spades, voice receding like static. Last night, I heard that a college friend, a linebacker on the football team, matinee handsome, had died of Covid alone in Texas. An unhinged year grows unimaginably darker. A deeper shade of raven.

On the eve of Thanksgiving, I seek what the Hollow offers. Life in the open air, on a bleak Wednesday morning, an unconquerable joy . . . loosed from the pandemic, if only momentarily—something to be grateful for.

Day 254

26 November 2020

Thanksgiving

For the animal shall not be measured by man . . .
They are not brethren, they are not underlings; they are
other nations, caught with ourselves in the net of life and time,
fellow prisoners of the splendor and travail of the earth.
HENRY BESTON

6:58 A.M. (sunrise one minute later than yesterday). 36 degrees, wind W 1 mph. (turkey, brined and patted dry, lounging in the refrigerator). Sky: an iteration of yesterday, gray fitted sheet of clouds releases the proverbial wintery mix . . . snow, rain, sleet. Road: a path of frozen slush. Permanent streams: above the culvert, the road glazed and treacherous. I'm wearing the wrong shoes, slipping and sliding. Dogs take charge. Wetlands: evergreens on the far shore softened by rising mist and falling rain. Deer trails, ribbons of flattened reeds, marshland sutures, running lengthwise from alders to hemlocks. Blue jay, grayer than blue, heads north, trailing his voice behind him. Just before seven-thirty, the town sanding truck passes. Pond: puddles on ice. Time-lapsed geology, a glimpse at the formation of sedentary rock (sandstone, limestone, shale). Locked within the ice a brief history of the week, evanescent sedimentation . . . surface ice, snow, rain, freeze, more rain—the Pleistocene writ small upon the pond. Like stray mammoths, milkweed seeds and maple leaves submerged in cold rainwater, soon to harden.

At eight-thirty, nineteen turkeys mill in the yard (one in the oven). Three practice masculinity, pompously strutting, wings drooped and quivering. The rest ignore the out-of-season histrionics, gorging on spilled sunflower seeds and acorns. I step outside and all disperse, a troop of feathered bumblebees, big bodies and tiny wings—pear-shaped birds, more glide than flap, into oaks and maples, dark knobs on distant trees. Branches sag, lumps on limbs.

❧

When the Pilgrims disembarked, wild turkey ranged across the deciduous woods of eastern North America west to Arizona and south to central Mexico. By the nineteenth century, they were gone from New England. In 1969 and 1970, Vermont released thirty-one wild turkeys from western New York. Originally native only to the state's four southern counties, the wild turkeys prospered. Today, Vermont's population approaches fifty thousand, residents of every county, every woodlot and forest, every ensemble of farmland and pasture and meadow. Releases didn't stop here. Turkeys thrive in several western states, southern Canada, Hawaii, Germany, and New Zealand.

During the past half-century, while the wild turkey prospered, the domestic turkey floundered, growing fatter, weaker, slower, and dumber. Overbreeding to satisfy our craving for white meat has left domestic turkeys so pathetically plump that they can't make little turkeys without help. When attempting to mate, domestic turkeys look like love-struck footballs, rocking and rolling—legs too small, chests too large, tapered at both ends.

Selective breeding left turkeys flightless and witless. But while they're a bubble off plumb with the IQ of wood chips, it's a myth that they drown looking up at the rain. Turkeys can't look up; their eyes are on the side of their heads; they lack binocular vision. Still, the birds can't be too bright for such an unflattering rumor to catch on. Darwin chose pigeon breeds to demonstrate the analogy between artificial and natural selection. If he were alive today, he might have fun illustrating his thesis with domestic turkeys.

Turkeys in the naked oaks hold their position, rain dripping off their beaks. I approach. They flee, again. Glide across the upper pasture, land in the lower pasture, and rush into the woods, ambulatory, unlike the bird browning in my oven.

Day 257

29 November 2020

The fact that we are connected through space and time
shows that life is a unitary phenomenon,
no matter how we express that fact.
Lynn Margulis

7:01 A.M. (sunrise one minute later than yesterday). 27 degrees, wind E
1 mph. Sky: pale blue and empty, a faint rose infusion. Last night, dense
fog. This morning, frost. Frozen dewdrops fixed to twigs like a confec-
tionary glaze. A bleached and crystalline world. Permanent streams:
although the lower stream carries more water, it's quicker to shrink and
dry than the upper, which has a deeper, more dependable source. Both
babble on a cold morning, voices carrying far up the road—both are
windowpane clear. A patch of fallen birches, roots loosened last night by
rain—white on brown earth, a graveyard of tree trunks. One straddles
the lower stream, a squirrel bridge, a gleaming, peeling femur of a tree.
Wetlands: a catch basin for dense, cold air draining downhill like rain
and settling with iron confidence. Glazed marsh. Glazed alders. Glazed
isles of sweetgale. Red squirrels, more shiver than chatter, a rustling
of the teeth. Pond: frozen over, slush to ice. Some portions polished
smooth; others, jigsaw pieces with raised edges, frozen sutures stitching
the lid together—nine circles of varying diameters, with thinner, clearer
ice. A moment of mystery, a question raised . . .

An otter paid a call last night. It likely arrived from the marsh via the
culvert under the road. Up the rock-retaining wall, dense fur dripping.
Through the black-plastic overflow culvert and into dark water, sealed
shut. Surfaced nine times, each hole bludgeoned open from below. Skull
thick as a brick. Ice shards fixed to the surface like broken pieces of glass,
abstract tangrams. Swimming in circles, the otter authored the ice, now
glass clear. At one hole, midpond, crayfish scraps: two claws, frozen and
frosted, embedded in ice . . . residue of a midnight snack.

Dogs engage otter spoor, noses to the ground, snorting. Otter might
be miles away. The Ompompanoosuc, East Branch or West; below the
Union Village Dam, where the branches couple and flow flatly to the
Connecticut. Perhaps, the Connecticut itself, north or south. Maybe
Lake Fairlee or the three linked ponds on the eastern rim of the Hollow.
Or the necklace of marshes to the west. Perhaps Ford's pond for fish filet.

Shellfish and trout under the cold steel of November. That's the best The Hollow has to offer.

Pileated laughs at a private joke. Red-breasted nuthatches diligently inspect icy twigs and birch bark flagging, where curling paper meets tree. One walks down birch and forages in frozen leaves, the tinkle and crinkle of tiny feet. Titmouse prospects the creases of a maple limb, a dignified, solitary bird. Crest erect, taking his time. More formal and less hurried than nearby chickadees. Hairy woodpecker tapping pole-sized pine snag . . . woodland Western Union. Fourteen crows commute north, a rain of caws. The delicate whisper of brown creeper. Raven, loud and expressive, high overhead, well behind northbound crows. Ruffed grouse startles, an explosive exodus, a whirring of wings. After 257 days of looking, I've only seen one owl. I still look across the marsh, hoping to see a big bird perched in the raw, stoic as a monk. Nada. I look anyway, wistfully, like a boy at the ballpark, hoping for a homerun whenever Mickey Mantle stepped into the batter's box.

Like the *Sunday Times* crossword puzzle, my valley poses an assortment of questions, a few answers ironclad, many inaccessible. Several questions, like the otter's lingering gifts, evoke educated guesses. I am witness and participant, stenographer and painter. I render impressions, note questions, and seek answers. I speculate. An otter and I crossed paths hours apart. Eyes wide, I remain awed by the simplicity and mystery of home—absentee otter enchanting like silent chimes.

Day 259

01 December 2020

All grownups were once children—
although few of them remember it.
ANTOINE DE SAINT-EXUPÉRY

7:04 A.M. (sunrise two minutes later than yesterday). 57 degrees, wind ESE 5 mph. A throwback to spring sans leaves, flowers, the cacophony of peepers, and the sweet melody of thrushes. A bipolar climate: eighteen degrees on November 19, twenty-five degrees on November 25. Water is on the move, everywhere. Sky: overcast with dazzling highlights. Earth is the pearl suspended inside the curvature of a celestial oyster. Luster and surface dissipating as I walk . . . an emergence of blue. Permanent streams: fuller and louder after a day of rain, at times torrential. Eastern slope of Robinson Hill, an aquatic circulatory system, an anastomosis of water-swollen creases and folds, most emptying into the two permanent streams, the hillside's twin aortas; a few reach the marsh on their own, others empty their freight into intermittent streams, now burdened with water. I feel a thread of cool air swept downhill with the current. Wetlands: in the heart of the Hollow, everything empties into the marsh, including cooler, heavier air. Western bank, a serration of hemlock, spruce, pine, and fir, an evergreen potpourri. Not as somber as yesterday, shades of green alive and well. Inside the shadowed wall, a barred owl, soft of feather, silent of flight, a voice that floated through the rain yesterday afternoon. Pond: surface do-over, melted. Ice-embedded otter sign erased, a meteorological Etch A Sketch moment.

AOR: an earthworm, thin, brown, string bean of a worm on December 1.

Chickadees and titmice under the barn overhang remove spider eggs from tattered webs.

Blue jays bury acorns and sunflower seeds. Raven, a gravel-voiced bird, black under a mother-of-pearl sky. Downy woodpecker on suet.

Above the pond, a flock of thirty (or so) red crossbills. For a moment, crossbills fill the airwaves. Flight calls rapid-fire *kip, kip, kip*. All seem to call at once. Then, silence.

They land in crowns of adjacent pines. These itinerant seedeaters, tamest of wild birds, attack the pine cones. In the winter of 2013, on the northeast side of Boston Harbor, I watched crossbills from my knees, eye level, five feet away, extracting seeds from pitch pine cones beneath a parade of commercial jets. Today, crossbills are in the crowns of white pine, a hundred feet above the valley floor. Big-headed. Short-tailed. Beaks like pliers, twisted at the tips. Crossbills rocking on the southern breeze.

Each of the eleven red crossbill types specializes in extracting the seeds of a different conifer. Seed predators, biologists call them. Crossbill wedges its weird bill between the scales of a ripe (open) cone. Closes the crossed tips with powerful jaw muscles and twists, turns, and pulls the seed loose from the cone scale. Then husks the seed on the roof of its mouth. More general seedeaters (pine siskin, for instance) are held at bay by the tightness of the cone scales and cannot extract pine seeds.

Each type of crossbill evolved a twisted bill best suited to harvest and husk seeds from a particular evergreen. Tree and bird conjoined. Think Darwin's finches, evolutionary radiation driven by food competition over a suite of limited resources. In the case of crossbills . . . conifer seeds. A stunningly august work of natural selection molded over deep time. Like monarchs and milkweed, bill and cone together forever.

⌒ᴗ

Back home. Ernie, the Hungarian partridge, runs around the front yard, a plump wind-up toy, geographically out of its element. A native of the steppes and pastures of Eurasia from Ireland to Scandinavia and eastern Russia, south to Spain, Italy, Greece, and Turkey. Ernie escaped from a breeder two valleys to the east. He crossed the valleys into the Hollow, avoiding everything that eats plump, slow-moving, and tasty fowl. Ernie arrived under the feeders two months ago and roams the front yard. Spends nights alone in the raspberry patch. Wary of me, but not afraid.

I fashioned Ernie a bed, a pile of hay in an old, wooden apple crate wrapped in plastic to keep the rain out. Looked perfect. An ideal roost, I thought. Cozy. Facing sun and shielded from the elements. What more would a partridge want? Something. Ernie roams the front yard in the company of gray squirrels. Avoids the heavy feet of turkeys. Survives on black oil sunflower seeds spilled by jays and woodpeckers—an incomprehensible bird keeping his own counsel, alone in an alien world.

Ernie walks the stone wall, feathers ruffled by a southern breeze. Unsupervised and out of place, Ernie . . . could be Ernestine.

Day 263

05 December 2020

I want to be light and frolicsome.
I want to be improbable and beautiful and afraid of
nothing, as though I had wings.
MARY OLIVER

7:08 A.M. (sunrise one minute later than yesterday). 34 degrees, wind S 1 mph. Sky: cold, taut pewter. At the moment, void of animation. Permanent streams: loudest voice in the woods. Wetlands: dull of color, absent of sound, mute testament to a suspended world that holds its collective breath. The secrecy of the marsh, nothing revealed (to me), reflecting the weight of leaden clouds, heavy with sleep. Abruptly, a red squirrel races across the road, rushes up a pine and out a limb. He stands on his hind legs, facing me, and emotes. Pond: a do-over. A regression of ice, fourth freeze coming apart, north and south end open. Where the feeder stream that curls down the slope of Robinson Hill enters, a tongue of dark water, black as a sable, slices through delicate ice. Elsewhere, ice thin skinned, feathers and panes, brittle water . . . jigsaw stage. Clearest ice becomes a window into the pond and its motionless bottom.

෨

In the mid-seventies, I found a narrow, thickly frozen pond on the West End of Jones Beach while searching for winter owls in a swale between parallel dunes. A muskrat swam beneath the ice; a profusion of bright bubbles rose out of its fur, long lines of cold, silver fireworks. I lay on the ice and slid after the muskrat; pearly bubbles gathered under the surface like a discharge of rowdy boys, pushing, merging, popping.

෨

Raven screams, a loud disruptive call, then silence. A moment later, above the marsh, another raven and a crow transcribe an aerial X. Raven, below, heads northeast, crow northwest. Black dots receding.

Closer to home, a mixed flock of nuthatches and chickadees hijack a humdrum morning in the woods beyond the upper stream. Feed. Call. Flit from tree to tree. Harvest tidbits from bark and twigs and tufts of pine needles. White-breasted nuthatch lands on an unconsolidated mat of leaves, a reassuring presence on the dark floor. He flips a leaf as big as he is. He flips a second leaf and then flies to an ash trunk. Investigates furrows, tail pressed to wood. One chickadee pins down something with its foot and hammers away. Swallows, blinks, flies off.

I wish to dine out like the birds. The intoxication of communion, to relax with kindred spirits. Chickadees and nuthatches remind me of what life was like before Covid and what it has become afterward. I long for a pause from interiority, the endless self-evaluation of a life lived alone. Covid reality: three families exchange Thanksgiving potluck on a porch and then everyone drives home and eats alone. I crave touching and holding, the intimacy of soft breathing . . . I want to see the full contours of a face that belongs to someone else.

A gathering of jays, paragons of busyness, heads toward the feeders. Woods and yard awash in discord. Mostly off-key scolding. Prospects for my day immediately improve. Common, indefatigable songbirds repair the fabric of the morning, erase gloom and melancholy, and echo the potential of my own feelings.

Day 264

06 December 2020

We get into trouble these days because
we think the only magic is what we do.
JOHN HAY

7:09 A.M. (sunrise one minute later than yesterday). 27 degrees, wind WNW 13 mph, sounds like traffic, tall pines stir the air above half an inch of snow. Several trees need lubricating; one needs Pepto-Bismol. Sky: low clouds, gray, disheveled, and charmless, straight out of the barren lands. Pruning wind releases a deluge of rotted and brittle limbs, a few thick as a thigh. Slippery road tracked by a wandering coyote. I walk the crinkled edges. Permanent streams: high water, clear and cold. Rocks decorated with frozen leaves. Mink tracks, paired prints bounding, follow the upper stream, disappearing into woods. Wetlands: three crows flap silently north over the marsh, buffeted by a headwind—a slow, methodical progression. The wind seeps around the eyepieces of my binoculars, watering my eyes and rendering the reeds an impression of beige, green, and white. Pond: half frozen, grainy ice in the south; open and wind-stirred in the north. Between the two zones, a wavy border of ice slowly annexes open water. Like scar tissue, older, frozen undulations mark former open-water boundaries, perhaps the passage of mere hours. Ice reaches out from the eastern shore and a hidden pocket in the north—a conversion that spreads in all directions. Coyote tracks along the western shoreline, a straight, thoughtful line of prints, one after the other. Beast on a mission. Unlike the dogs, which step left and right for every forward step, there's no veering. Less interested in ice formation than I am, chickadee flies past. Lands in alders. Tilts his head back and calls, an unanswered, oft-repeated broadcast—unspool-
· ing *dee, dee, dee, dees.*

A red squirrel bolts across the road, pine cone in mouth. Climbs a pine, settles on an eye-level branch, wedges the cone between radiating twigs, leans back, mouth open and lips slightly curled, a revelation of self-sharpening, pinking-shear incisors . . . and chatters.

A flock of seventeen red crossbills, treetop height, a chorus of *kip, kip, kip*. Beyond the pines, calls fade quickly, victims of the wind. Classic Doppler effect. From inside the woods, several nuthatches and jays chime in. Proxies for the unseen.

Under the feeder a forlorn turkey. My neighbor on the eastern flank of the Hollow had fifty-four. Not a flock, a herd. He texted me a progression video, a long, sinuous line of wild turkeys, fifteen- to twenty-five-pound birds, marching out of the woods and downhill into a meadow, dark and oval, parading across a carpet of snow. Several hours later, forty-three reached my yard, out of the pines and over the stone wall (one at a time), creating a boulevard of trampled snow. A battalion of hungry nomads assembles under the feeders, across the lawn, in the garden, the raspberry patch, the upper pasture, and the compost pile. Three investigate the garage. More than six hundred pounds of birds sweep through, ingesting sunflower seeds, acorns, mummified raspberries, and scraps from my most recent meals—an all-morning binge. One male displays and struts. I may be the only one paying attention.

As I look out the bedroom window, turkeys disperse into the pines, an oblique departure, front yard exhalation. Another morning unsullied by barking electronics, political denial, and vaccination protocol. Personal freedom, the business and busyness of turkeys.

Day 267

09 December 2020

*Trees are an invitation to think about time
and to travel in it the way they do, by standing still
and reaching out and down.*
Rebecca Solnit

7:12 A.M. (sunrise one minute later than yesterday). 21 degrees, wind WNW 1 mph. Sky: in the east, a waning moon, a sliver less than half, brightly glowing, a tungsten filament inside a thin bulb of rose-colored clouds, the incandescence of sunrise. Color drains, leaving the impression of the moon, fading into blue white. Snow sprinkles the landscape. Intermittent streams: sections retreat beneath mats of frozen leaves, a hollow-sounding flow. Permanent streams: rocks in riffles iced over, others dusted. In the dogwoods and alders along the upper stream, male cardinal trims a dull landscape, candy-apple red in a weft of brown branches, calls softly . . . *tik, tik, tik, tik.* Crest erect. Black face sets off a mass of scarlet feathers and lipstick-red bill. In twenty-four years, I've seen fewer than ten cardinals in the Hollow, all on the ground foraging below my bird feeders. Lower stream, backwater freezing over. Wetlands: the weight of cold settles in. Dark brown sweetgale spots on the beige fur of the marsh. Pond: sealed and dusted, immaculately white, wind patterns across the snow. Where the stream drains into the pond, a shorter, narrower lead of open water, black as obsidian.

Lower pasture, a red-tailed hawk perches in black cherry, straight up, amber eyes smoldering. Scans meadow and upper marsh. Tail more rust than red, like an October oak leaf. Default hawk in most of North America, as varied as the weather. Light phase. Dark phase. Intermediate phase. Krider's redtail, a pale prairie bird. Harlan's redtail, a redtail without red. Costa Rican redtails, red bellied and thighed, sail over the highest mountains, in the company of low-hanging clouds.

Red-tailed hawk not the default hawk here. Coyote Hollow—a mosaic of marshes and open water—is red-shouldered country, but they're gone for the winter. Redtail down from the north. Maybe the nearby north, Orleans or Chittenden counties. Perhaps the far north, Labrador or Newfoundland or the raw rim of James Bay. May stay until driven south by snow.

～

In North America, redtails hunt from perches, in the tropics often from the air. Always looking for movement. Any movement. Vole. Gray squirrel. Cottontail. A careless dove or grouse. Maybe a weasel or a mink. Some redtails develop a fondness for rattlesnakes, loitering above traditional birth sites and snake dens, statue still. One September morning, several years ago, I found the severed head of an adult timber rattlesnake on a boulder along the shore of Lake Champlain. The stone had been clean when I walked past earlier in the morning. I imagined the hawk had plucked a basking rattlesnake off the talus, killed it with needle-sharp talons and a bite behind the head, then flew to the edge of the lake and decapitated the snake with a guillotine bite. Swallowed the body piecemeal, leaving me the grim head to contemplate.

ɔɯ

Back in the lower pasture, chickadee appears. Pesters the redtail, buzzing around its head, scolding and pecking. A rain of *dee, dee, dee, dee, dee*, the language of agitation. Lacking inducements, hawk leaves. Soars high into the awakening day, leaning progressively eastward. Drawing circles around the morning, wingtips and tail feathers teasing the wind. Mission complete, chickadee returns to the feeders, full of cheer. Thirty turkeys gather in the front yard, scavenging what the chickadee spills. When the dogs and I appear, they explode into the air and head southwest, a discharge of enormous birds. Labored flaps, then glide on bowed wings. Reassemble in the pines—blobs on branches.

ɔɯ

When I was a graduate student forty-five years ago, I took a forest ecology class taught by a professor with a spiritual bent who remarked (more than a few times) that a *forest was really one organism with many trunks*, a point taken in both the recent documentary *Fantastic Fungi* and Richard Powers's novel *The Overstory*, winner of the 2019 Pulitzer Prize for fiction. As I waited for the sun this morning, I read "The Social Life of Forests" in the December 6 issue of *The New York Times Magazine*. The essay highlighted the research of Suzanne Simard, a professor at the University of British Columbia, who demonstrated that within six Douglas fir stands, each stand about ten thousand square feet, all trees were connected underground by a network of fungi, none with more than three degrees of separation. One giant Douglas fir linked to forty-seven others, perhaps as many as two hundred and fifty. Trees share carbon and nitrogen and water. Nutrients are passed in either direction, depending on the season. Dying trees, purposefully stripped of needles, transfer carbon to neighboring trees, not necessarily their own species.

Forest socialism: the sharing of underground resources between trees through a fungal pipeline referred to as *The Wood Wide Web*, an underground symbiosis that includes everything with roots and mycelia. One tree rejuvenates another; dying trees disperse stored resources; hardwoods benefit conifers; conifers benefit hardwoods. Trees benefit fungi. Fungi benefit trees. White pine seedlings, for instance, growing in full sun on infertile soil, have a symbiotic relationship with mycorrhizal soil fungus, which aid in nitrogen and phosphorus uptake. One species of fungus kills tiny springtails; the decomposing hexapods provide up to

25 percent of the pines' nutrient uptake. The fruiting bodies of the fungi (mushrooms) are eaten by red-backed voles, which disperse the spores in their fecal pellets. And voles depend on downed, rotting trees for shelter . . . a three-way symbiosis. A woodland library, books without pages. Stored information, shared, flows in all directions.

In the yard, facing the sun, chickadee and I, a union of breath . . . members of the community of the miraculous.

Day 270

12 December 2020

Third night of Hanukkah

Owl was telling Kanga an interesting anecdote full
of long words like Encyclopedia and Rhododendron
to which Kanga wasn't listening.

A.A. MILNE

7:14 A.M. (sunrise one minute later than yesterday). 27 degrees, wind NW 1 mph. Sky: baby blue, hosts thin white clouds and a postsunrise hint of peach. Permanent streams: ice caps on rocks, tight like yarmulkes, some with visors that extend above the splashing flow. An oblong island of grit in the lower stream, submerged until the next drought, slowly expands. Like a trumpet mute, ice formations contribute sound effects—a hollow-sounding flow. Wetlands: whitened by frost, deer trails winding through the reeds; pathways of the unforsaken in the waning days of archery and muzzleloader seasons. Four crows, framed by blue and peach, head into the wind, a hushed and crooked flight. Wetlands: frosted and silent, a three-dimensional museum diorama, working title *Mid-December, Vermont Marsh: Everything Quarantining.* Pond: like a clam shack at the beach . . . closed for the season. Ice supports a coyote, whose muddied tracks around the delta in the southeast cove froze, fossil footprints dating back to midnight.

Red crossbills on hillside pines, a rain of chatter. Pileated calls, truncated laughs from a phalanx of hemlock. Hairy woodpecker on maple administers woodland telegraph, barely audible—a whispered message from the threshold of sunrise. On a maple, white-breasted nuthatch walks up trunk. Tree not to his liking, he finds another and repeats. And repeats again. An enigmatic search for breakfast. Raven, a joyful volley of baritone croaks. Crows and jays, so many, many blue jays. *Winter of Red-breasted Nuthatch*, everywhere and vocal. Chickadee in birch twiddling strips of curled bark. No turkeys. No red-tailed hawk.

Red squirrel on pine limb, palaver turns to music, a surprisingly sweet trill. Dogs show no interest.

∾

Last night, shortly after sunset and before the crescent moon rose, an owl dismantled the silence, an echo out of the void. A tuning fork in the brittle air, cold, crisp, unforgiving. I faced the sound, cupped my hands to my ears, and listened. Who else listened? The soft-furred, bug-eyed flying squirrel gliding through the gloaming? The white-footed mouse gathering seeds under the feeders? For the squirrel or the mouse, the barred owl reaps grimly. Soft of feathers, a hushed nightmare glide, silent as smoke. All talons and beak seeking incautious rodents.

I imagine the flying squirrel's blood runs cold when the owl makes pronouncements. Owl measures movement, his every glide purposeful. For squirrel and mouse, the night is unforgiving like winter itself. A restless, hungry ball of feathers, the owl penetrates darkness, every night another challenge, survival never guaranteed.

Barred owl: round-headed and slightly larger than a crow. Back, gray-brown. White horizontal bars on breast. Vertical streaks on belly. Swivel headed. Asymmetric ears track sound, twitch like radar, a one-bird triangulation unit. Moon eyes, dark as dusk, see remarkable detail in dim light, mostly in grades of black and white, devouring night, even those of the blackest pitch. Black and white mouse in a black and white landscape.

Last night, when the owl left his perch, he floated across the marsh, dark bird over dark wetlands, shadow beneath the diamond sky. Once the owl completed his business, night drew quiet. Then, hooting resumed from a distant corner of the Hollow, staccato barks, seven hollow hoots rising at the end. Owl moved to the shoulder of Robinson Hill, above the marsh, along the eastern apron of the valley, where weasels hunt the brush piles. Unwary hunters may become the hunted.

Before I went to bed, I opened the window. Owl called again. Captain of the gloom. A feathered wraith punctuating silence and animating night. I cannot imagine Coyote Hollow without an owl. One March, a saw-whet owl lingered for two days, and twice a long-eared owl made deep-winter one-night stands. But always the barred owl, nocturnal counterpart of the red-shouldered hawk. December shadows breathe whenever the fugitive predator trolls for dinner.

Sunshine spills down the slope of Robinson Hill, spreading across the marsh. Tonight is the third night of Hanukkah. I lit the candles alone last night and wore Casey and Jordan's green felt yarmulke, rimmed in gold, the one my father brought home from Jerusalem. In 1997, the year we moved to Coyote Hollow, my father died at eighty-two, stricken on a Florida golf course. After he was buried, I sat Shivah deep in the Everglades, amazed that pink spoonbills flew across a fruit-bowl sunrise, gathering in the shallows, swinging their bills as though nothing had happened.

Last night, I ate too many latkes, the next best thing to being with family . . .

Day 272

14 December 2020

Fifth night of Hanukkah

After you have exhausted what there is
in business, politics, conviviality, and so on—
have found that none of these finally satisfy,
or permanently wear—what remains? Nature
remains; to bring out from their torpid recesses,
the affinities of a man or woman with the open
air, the trees, fields, the changes of the seasons—
the sun by day and the stars of heaven by night.
WALT WHITMAN

7:16 A.M. (sunrise one minute later than yesterday). 30 degrees, wind NNE 2 mph. Sky: overcast and damp, the sun appears unnoticed (by me, at least). Permanent streams: swollen from yesterday's downpour;

loss of ice, except for a birch limb still partially encased, an ice tube with a core of wood, cream white. Deer bolts across the road along the south side of the lower stream. Wetlands: rain-rich colors, reeds yellow-brown, dark isles of sweetgale almost black. Raindrops sag from every twig and catkin, an astronomical number of jewels. From the far-shore evergreens, pileated laughs across the marsh. Two ravens head east, a single, loud baritone *croak*. I answer, my voice shoehorned into the morning. An echo of an echo bounces around the Hollow. Woodpecker ignores me (like most everyone else during Covid). Not the red squirrel. He sits on a limb, releasing a public denouncement, an off-key scolding.

Pond: closed over again. Undulating ice lines, sutures binding new ice to old. Pine limb on ice broken into a dozen pieces and flung carelessly as the stars. Hockey solitaire played under the secrecy of night. I play the outdoor version of *What's My Line*. Close to the inflow is a round hole in the ice. Chips and slivers on the surface. By the hole, flattened grass and forbs, a frozen pathway into the water. Noses embedded in odor, dogs know the identity of the athlete. Then, the image gels into certainty. Otter played hockey alone—shenanigans on ice—one limb bitten into a dozen misshaped pucks. Otter equipment: body for hockey stick, face for blade, feet for skates, tail to pivot. No defending against an otter, the Wayne Gretzky of the animal kingdom.

If the moon watched, he must have smiled.

❧

Back home, a mixed flock of chickadees and nuthatches constellate the feeders and the oaks, an undercurrent of lively chatter, morning metronome . . . ad infinitum. Blue jay in the backyard picks up an ice-cold acorn. A pair of woodpeckers, one hairy, one downy take turns on the suet.

In the front yard, septic man, hose out, motor on. Map in hand, searching for the tank on the wrong side of the garden. Disperses jays, woodpeckers, nuthatches, and gray squirrels. Even Ernie, the partridge, leaves. Not chickadees, which have a high tolerance for our little foibles.

Day 275

17 December 2020

Last night of Hanukkah

Do you need a prod?
Do you need a little darkness to get you going?
Mary Oliver

7:18 A.M. (sunrise one minute later than yesterday). 16 degrees, wind NW 4 mph. Sky: small-flake snowstorm, twelve inches and falling, a peaceful world. Visibility less than two hundred yards, a Christmas-card landscape streaked in white, far-off trees vague illusions, hillsides rendered seductive and suggestive by a screen of snow. Nearby trees, dark branches outlined in white. Here and there, puffs of snow slide off pine boughs, the morning's frosted breath. Permanent streams: snow on ice muffles sound, the trace more a sigh than a gurgle. Wetlands: almost a whiteout. Reeds merge into a beige-white mat. Across the marsh, a hint of the evergreen shoreline. I imagine that inside the hemlocks, an owl, head cocked, listens for red-backed voles, and outside, the red-tailed hawk moves south ahead of the storm. (Deaf to footfalls, it's tough for the hawk to hunt rodents under deep snow.) Pond: an expanse of undisturbed white.

No cars, a snow lockdown.

Red squirrel bounds across the unplowed road, vulnerable until it reaches a tree. Old deer and coyote tracks fill in. The second morning in succession, no red-breasted nuthatches—possibly bailed ahead of the storm. White-breasted nuthatch walks down white ash, white on white through a screen of white. Chickadee in the alders, unperturbed by falling snow. Alone on the edge of the marsh, effervescent as ever.

At the feeders: hairy and downy woodpecker on opposite sides of the suet bag. A mob of eleven jays gather in the front yard, belligerent, rowdy, crests erect, rude but beautiful. Acorns are unavailable under deep snow. Jays chase each other off perches. Cherry and ash limbs. Off the ground below the sunflower feeders. Off the suet cage. Off pine boughs, which discharge cottony puffs of snow. Patiently, three chickadees and two titmice take a turn on the feeders. Tolerant. Well-mannered. Everything blue jays aren't . . . but a world without jays would be a dull world indeed.

Chickadee

Chickadees, flying back and forth, sunflower seeds in bills, hiding up to a thousand a day, more than eighty thousand a winter—one reason I've gone through forty pounds in the past ten days. Called a *scatter hoarder*, one seed here, one seed there, tucked in a crevice, inserted under bark or lichen. In tufts of pine or spruce needles, in the crotches of twigs, in the barn overhang and windowsills. Remembers the location and quality of each seed—a bird with a very high IQ. To aid in relocation of the (my) hidden sunflower seeds, the chickadee's hippocampus, on the floor of its brain, the center of memory and emotion, enlarges in the fall, then shrinks in the spring. Fortunately, the shrinkage doesn't affect a chickadee's state of mind—jovial and tolerant year round.

Untethered magic in the front yard is always welcome, particularly during a pandemic—worth the price of sunflower seeds.

After I light the menorah and wolf down the last latke, I trudge across the marsh, sinking through more than a foot of snow and into the air space below an awning of folded reeds. Dogs make me break trail.

4:13 P.M. (another show-stopping sunset, same time as yesterday). Sky and its clouds like the flank of a fish, more brook trout than mackerel. Tangerine and lemon bloom in the west, gilding every cloud that isn't already orange. The crescent moon, also citrus colored, leans southwest—the DreamWorks' logo minus Fishing Boy. Jupiter and Saturn, *very* close to each other, attend to the moon and play peekaboo behind the mobile topography of clouds.

I look and listen for an owl, to no avail. I take solace in a cosmic rarity of circumstance, a conjunction of planets not seen this close together in eight hundred years. The last time Saturn and Jupiter appeared in the night sky a dime's width apart, Charlemagne was emperor in the West and Genghis Khan in the East; and many more bison than people roamed North America. Pausing below the two enormous and distant planets, I flounder in the snows of a third, significantly minor, significantly bluer world, my home . . . my signpost in an ambiguous universe.

Day 277

19 December 2020

No winter lasts forever;
no spring skips its turn.
HAL BORLAND

7:19 A.M. (sunrise one minute later than yesterday). -6 degrees, wind calm, 0 mph. Sky: cloudless, baby blue with a pale rose wash in the south and east. My heat rises into space unimpeded—fingers in mourning, roof of mouth throbbing. Permanent streams: upper, a mountain range of snow, conical peaks and conical valleys; water flows through a tunnel, barely whispering. Frost blooms on honeysuckle branches. Lower, two oblong openings iced over and rimmed in hoarfrost, long, feathery crystals. Shape-changing air pockets slide along the undersurface of ice windows. Stream makes a hollow, echoey sound like singing inside Central Park's Greywacke Arch. Wetlands: settlement of cold air disarms everything but stray thoughts: the marsh itself, a white and beige floor, distant green and white walls. Surface animation suspended; below, voles and red squirrels roam dark snow tunnels of their own making, while weasels, quick as sparks, hunt the unwary. Chickadee in the alders. Pond: smooth white surface; the only tracks are my own and the dogs.

Red squirrels keep to themselves. Chickadees, of course, ambitious, a cascade of *dees* out of the alders and bittersweet. What are they eating? Frost crystals? Hairy woodpecker on ash, a percussive, stuttering tap—a self-initiated dialogue with the tree. Two ravens, wing tip to wing tip, black in the blue, their hoarse and hollow volleys suspended in the frigid air.

In 1621, the Pilgrims brought barnyard turkeys to North America, descendants of a Mexican subspecies domesticated by Aztecs more than two thousand years prior and brought to Europe by the Conquistadors in the fifteen hundreds. (Anasazi of the Desert Southwest, scions of the Aztec, domesticated a second subspecies circa 700 BP.) The seventeen turkeys in my yard know nothing of their species' history. Nor do they care. Too busy scratching through the snow, searching for acorns and sunflower seeds. Turkey tracks loop around the house and radiate into the pines and oak groves. Hungry turkeys, all fluffed out, on the move. Feet scratching, constantly scratching through the snow . . . a gallinaceous twisting and leaning that would make Chubby Checker envious.

Turkeys see me and scatter, a spewing of stout birds. Short, round wings stir the air. Turkeys sail into the pines—perch in the open. Feathered knobs. In fifteen minutes, they return, trampling and plowing and twisting.

What's the most common bird in North America? Not turkey. Answer: robin, at approximately three hundred million. Most common nonnative bird? Answer: chicken. Two billion, of which one-and-a-half billion are destined for ovens, soups, and grills and the other half billion for eggs.

Joining the turkeys under the feeder is a single tree sparrow, an Arctic songbird with an uptown look. Bicolored bill. Rufous eyeline and cap. Whitish breast and belly with a dark, cosmetic spot. Otherwise, mottled brown and rusty like the withered leaves of bearberry. Our honeymoon bird. Forty years ago, tree sparrows entertained newlyweds along the icy edge of Hudson Bay. Linny and I stood slack-jawed in the presence of substantial white bears and dainty brown sparrows that fed chicks through the midnight twilight, around-the-clock foraging. This morning, recall, as much as birds, flares up on a glacial sunrise.

The fondness of memory, a bridge into a big lonely house.

WINTER

2020—2021

Day 279

21 December 2020

Winter Solstice

People don't notice whether it's winter.
Anton Chekhov

7:20 A.M. (sunrise same time as yesterday). 28 degrees (thirty-four degrees warmer than two days ago), wind NE 2 mph. Sky: closed off by an October fog, the byproduct of warm air on snow. Permanent streams: upper, dark, fish-shaped openings engraved in deep snow, salmon and rays, possibly a molly. All openings are loquacious. Lower, water between the road and marsh, still closed, still silent; above the road, emerging holes babble, acoustic ballads . . . among *Billboard's Top Aqueous 100*. Wetlands: across the marsh, the evergreen fortress reduced by mist to a mere suggestion, vaguest of outlines. Red crossbills are unperturbed. For them, a hint is quite enough. Out over the reeds, ebullient chattering, a conversation in triplets: *gyp, gyp, gyp*. Pitch into tree crowns, grappling with pine cones. Pond: deer spoor across the surface crisscrosses, bows, and loops as if unspooled. Weasel tracks, paired prints seven or eight inches apart; tiny feet—maybe a short-tailed weasel, an ermine white as snow—along the berm, up the bank, and into a snow tunnel, an inch-wide portal into another world. This subnivean tunnel, so called, where mice and squirrels convene, is a northern lifeline, particularly for small mammals. Darker, warmer, more humid than the snow surface.

Road wanderings: deer down the middle, along both shoulders, back and forth. Red-backed voles, on and off the snowbanks, prints like stitches, twisting everywhere. Knots and bows of footprints, the work of a drunken tailor or surgeon. White-footed mouse tracks are also clusters of four, with a long tail dragged down the middle of each set, like the aimless stitching of a sewing machine.

Bobcat came out of the marsh and walked along the road. Neat round prints, almost but not quite a straight line. Four oblong pads in front of a tri-lobed heel pad. No claw prints, lethal weapons retracted. Maybe the same bobcat that pulled the goshawk chicks out of the pine nest last June and stole my homebody cat, Roberto, a week later. A warrior wandering in search of food along *Desolation Row.*

Low-flying raven, resonant croak. Small clusters of red-breasted nuthatches, first appearance since the snowstorm on the seventeenth (other than one or two at the feeders). Turkeys hunched over, a herd of elderly men strolling along the Coney Island boardwalk; two in the front yard scratching for sunflower seeds, five in the backyard scratching for acorns and standing on one foot, scratching with the other. With a backward kick and shuffle, oak leaves scatter. Then, turkey steps back and examines—Peck, peck, peck. Acorns swallowed hole, stored in the crops, an interior grocery bag—an outgrowth of the gullet (esophagus), and then pulverized in the gizzard (muscular stomach). No teeth, weight eliminated . . . one of life's many accommodations for flight.

Bobcat should visit my front yard and crouch under the Adirondack chairs. And wait for turkeys, a breakfast of drumsticks my nana called *polkes,* Yiddish for dark, richly oxygenated and well-developed thighs. So much walking. So much muscle. Squadrons march up and down the Hollow, often single file like the Seven Dwarfs (without the *heigh-hoing*). Propelled by future holiday drumsticks.

◦◦

In the late afternoon, Nancy and I walk the back roads of Pomfret, unmasked. I hear pine grosbeaks' soft warbling whistles for the first time in many years. Males crab-apple red; females grayish-greenish golden yellow. Beaks are more sparrow-petite than cardinal-gross. Pine grosbeaks visit from the subarctic and boreal woods. Very approachable (if you see them). In winter, pine grosbeaks fancy apple seeds and frozen, withered fruit in Vermont.

◦◦

24 October 1975, Short Beach, Fire Island: five pine grosbeaks, a life bird, gorging on Russian olives. Behind them, the Atlantic, gray and rogue. The relentless onshore wind ripping off the tops of waves and making a farce of gulls while grosbeaks calmly overwhelmed the olives.

◦◦

It's good to be walking with someone other than myself. To dine away from home, around Nance's firepit restaurant, first (and only) seating by the warm stones, smoke plumes curling into the night sky. The winter solstice, light deprived, the Great Conjunction of Jupiter and Saturn . . . the planets seeming to touch. The ancients ascribed meaning to heaven's rare events. For me, the planetary conjunction coincides with being outdoors, away from home. I grab Nancy's hand, glove to glove, and squeeze. The timelessness of touch. My shell cracks, and for a moment, I'm *not* alone.

Day 283

25 December 2020

Christmas

My true religion is kindness.
14TH DALI LAMA TENZIN GYATSO

7:22 A.M. (sunrise one minute later than yesterday). 55 degrees (sixty-one degrees warmer than six days ago), wind SSE 11 mph, whistling and roaring. Sky: overcast and steadily raining. Then, steadily pouring. An unbearable deluge, snow in full retreat, from two-feet deep to nearly gone. Feels like April, replete with mud. Warm air on melting snow spawns rivulets of ground fog that flow into the marsh and vanish. Permanent streams: upper, iceless and rushing, loud as ever; lower, churning through ice tunnels, over snowless rocks and frozen patches. Brown water freights silt and random maple leaves. Wetlands: marsh mostly snowless, beige with splashes of white. All creases and folds on the hillsides, and all gullies along the road, funnel water and cool air into the basin. Deeper in the middle, getting deeper by the moment. Pond: overflow gushes out of the culvert, under the road, and into the alders. Rain and snow melt, puddles on ice. Feeder stream rushing and loud, a ten-foot-wide cut through the surface ice. Old deer tracks, cervid calligraphy, are ice-gilded and underwater.

Crossbills off to feed in the pines, limbs bent with cones—birds and their chatter fade in the drizzle, displacing raindrops as they land. Crossbills tweeze pine seeds out of cones like a flock of mothers removing splinters from their children. I can't recall the last Christmas I spent with crossbills . . . must have been long, long ago. Possibly never. Who knows when an evergreen seed failure in Canada and a seed bonanza in Coyote Hollow will coincide?

Everything else must be home opening presents.

At the feeder: Ernie the Hungarian partridge, a smooth, oval, water-repellent bird, under an Adirondack chair, faces south into the wind and rain. Like a grouse but smaller. Like a bobwhite but larger. Blue jays soaking wet and bedraggled, more gray than blue, dull light draining color.

Secrets of the front yard. Chickadees and titmice select one seed at a time, then hide the seed nearby, well above the ground. Jays fill crops, which bulge like goiters. Hairy and downy woodpeckers spill more than they eat. When the *right* seed appears, woodpecker flies off, leaving the lawn littered . . . an accessible harvest for turkeys, doves, gray squirrels, chipmunks, and Ernie. Chickadees and titmice occasionally fly down and grab a seed.

I'm in the sunroom eating Christmas cookies a neighbor left on my doorstep, watching the woodland food bank, captivated by the spirit of unintentional giving.

～

Day 285

27 December 2020

If Galileo had said in verse that the world moved,
the Inquisition might have let him alone.
THOMAS HARDY

7:22 A.M. (sunrise same time third day in a row). 27 degrees, wind SE 3 mph. Snow lingers in parallel ridges along the road's edges and shady creases on the hillside. Otherwise, gone. Sky: mottled, pink blush in the east. A mistless, hazeless sunrise. Mount Ascutney is visible in the distance, a blue-gray bump in the clear air. Intermittent streams: flow and hum with a false sense of durability, provisioned by two inches of rain and two feet of melted snow. Permanent streams: ice laminates low, overhanging branches, fragile and decorative, the consequence of energetic water. Wetlands: marsh silent as a tomb, a snowless expanse of bent reeds, the main channel sprawled and iced, an episodic lake.

Chickadee in the alders. Creeper and nuthatch in the pines. Busybody red squirrel delivers soliloquy. Pond: closing up again. New ice, thinner and grayer. The dark oblong lead of water from the feeder stream is shorter and narrower. Old deer tracks become amorphous dimples. Five otter holes full-moon round, windows into a hidden world, all on the northern half. Each hole sports a branching avenue of open water like the old version of a phylogenic tree; one pair splayed like caribou antlers. An undulating crack runs north to south, cleaving the surface, the stillness point of a yin-yang pond.

Blue jay drinks from a roadside gulley, a clear, whispering flow. Red squirrel, framed by the marsh, chastises me from a pine limb. I haven't had a red squirrel at the birdfeeders in months. They don't favor sunflower seeds when packages of turpentine-flavored pine nuts dangle in spades. Gray squirrels, on the other hand, travel to the beat of a different drummer—only deep snow keeps them from my sunflower seeds. A convocation of seven assembles on the Adirondack chairs as if posing for a family portrait.

I'm enthralled by a raven . . . black bird beneath the blue sky flies north, trailing his voice behind him. Two crows palaver, harsh and loud. Two crossbills, several times back and forth, engage in less spirited discussions—more schmoozing than crowing.

Male hairy woodpeckers in the cherry and on the suet. On the lawn, a male downy woodpecker under the cherry gathers loose seeds dropped by chickadees and nuthatches. Hairy chases downy, then both resume their previous positions. Although both are in the genus *Dryobates* and look almost identical, hairy and downy are not as closely related as ornithologists previously thought. Downy is more closely related to Nuttall's woodpecker, a California bird, and to the ladder-backed of the Desert Southwest. Hairy is more closely related to the Arizona woodpecker, a bird of the Mexican highlands and southeast Arizona, and to Strickland's, a Mexican species.

Similarities in plumage may confer respect from other birds for the daintier downy, whose range overlaps that of the more robust hairy throughout much of Canada and the United States, a phenomenon called *social dominance mimicry* or *competitive mimicry*. It means little to Cooper's hawk, which rips after either one with gusto.

෴

Thoughts at warp speed: Everything has meaning. Everything connects. I live in a world of colors I can't see, sounds I can't hear, scents I can't smell, and sensations I can't feel. A world of pedigrees, tens of millions of pedigrees, all lines radiating from a common ancestor 3.5 billion years ago. Part of an ancient, mutable tapestry, interwoven strands of life I barely understand. In a 2015 paper in *Proceedings of the National Academy of Science* titled "Moth tails divert bat attack: Evolution of acoustic deflection," the authors determined that the spinning tails of a luna moth, the twisted streamer off each hind wing, fracture a bat's echolocation, hiding the vulnerable palm-sized, white-bodied, green-winged moth within the transparency of night. There are so, so many questions I don't know to ask—another day of unalloyed fascination with our *pale blue dot.*

Sunrise's muffled heartbeat, subtlest of gestures, barely tangible, soft and faint like owl down. The new day, welcome and reliable, an early morning dose of optimism. Winter sunshine pours down Robinson Hill, spreads across the valley, warms boulders, melts snow, and rewrites my morning. For me, there's no second-guessing. I abide by an ancient code . . . loyalty to place. Facing south, I pledge allegiance to the sun. On the cusp of 2021, amid chickadees and jays, I'm reinvigorated—Covid be damned. There're chores to do, a future to imagine . . . a stolen kiss, holding Nance's hand.

Day 288

30 December 2020

Second to last day of the year

Year's end is neither an end nor a beginning
but a going on, with all the wisdom
that experience can instill in us.
HAL BORLAND

7:23 A.M. (same sunrise time, third day in a row). 10 degrees (forty-five degrees colder than Christmas morning), wind WNW 1 mph (beech leaves chime in, a twittering melody). Sky: in the east, hints of peach quickly leach away. A few filamentous clouds tease apart, otherwise mostly clear. Granular snow, dustings of tiny balls like upholstery stuffing. The crest on Mount Ascutney, forty miles south, cold granite and dark spruce, rises above the flat Connecticut River floodplain like the Rocky Mountains out of the Colorado prairie. Most days, Ascutney is screened by haze. Today, however, it's a smudge on the horizon. Permanent streams: wherever water hesitates, even for a moment, ice. Deep tunnels and submerged sheets, *far* more than I expected. Main channels sandwiched between metastasizing ice shelves that jut from both banks, convoluted margins like tidewater Maryland, serrated, crenulated, pinched. Ice laminates emergent rocks, thick and reflective, and stratifies nearby twigs and stems. Flow, babbling loudly on a frigid morning. Wetlands: Frosted reeds lean south, marsh a bowl of cold air. Noisy crossbills above a sleepy marsh. I scour the sky and pines to no avail. Red squirrels keep to themselves, hushed and hidden. Pond: the delta's closing, three feet long and a foot wide. Bound by frozen sutures. Delta ice oldest to newest: thin, thinner, thinnest. Thaw lines fit inside each other like two-dimensional Russian dolls. Four pine cones embedded in the surface. Old deer tracks devolve into iced-over dents. Dogs and I lurch along the shoreline, hoping for something beyond yesterday's news.

A morsel of joy on the penultimate morning of 2020: a lonesome red-breasted nuthatch sounds reveille. No response. Even chickadees sleep, a descent into torpor—a world in the thrall of a cold front.

Last night, I opened the freezer to grab a bag of tortellini. My dinner idled on the lower shelf of the door, next to a hapless pygmy shrew in a transparent film canister, frozen circa 1997, and a red-eyed vireo in a Ziploc bag, a victim of a window strike, which I froze last August to show my sister-in-law the vireo's thick legs. What lurks in the bowels of the freezer, beyond pesto cubes and raspberries, is anyone's guess.

Nearly at an end, this lonely, stressful year. In mid-March, when I returned from Costa Rica, empty roads and the astonishing grace notes of hermit thrushes (otherworldly tunesmiths), carried me through the first month of the pandemic. Then, as time crept by and Covid worsened, I became hobbled by the constrictions of restriction. How do I touch the people I love when I can't leave home? My boys, beyond the doorstep. Midsummer, I'm pleasantly distracted by a squirrel-tailed comet. On the fringe of winter, I'm saved again by the conjunction of Jupiter and Saturn but repeatedly distressed by a bipolar climate and a leader in denial. Where would I be without my daily dose of chickadees? Day in and day out, they carry on regardless of human tragedy, regardless of my longings: their voices, their jaunty antics, convivial and inquisitive, a preamble to almost every sunrise of 2020. Snippets of their lives ground me (for the moment, anyway). Chickadee, a bird to be thankful for, silences my internal dialogue with endless threads of *Hey, sweetie* and *dee, dee, dee, dee, dee, dee.* Guide me into the New Year, delicate songbird, and remind me (often) that there's more to Earth than empty grocery shelves, overcrowded hospitals, restricted air travel, and shuttered restaurants. Literally and metaphorically, chickadees have become my Covid confidants . . . I lean on them.

Day 290

01 January 2021

Another year begins

In the early days of the English sparrow in this country,
while they were being protected, northern shrikes
became so abundant on Boston Commons men were employed
to shoot them lest they destroy the sparrows.
Arthur Cleveland Bent

A fine start to 2021. 7:23 A.M. (same sunrise time, fifth day in a row). 23 degrees, wind S 3 mph. Sky: moon, a chip off full, setting platinum in the west. A flotilla of pink-infused clouds drifts eastward across an ocean of blue. Permanent streams: upper ice, deep tunnels and submerged sheets, an aqueous photocopy of yesterday; lower, a fluted voice, notes rising out of cavities in the ice. Wetlands: frosted reeds and somber pines. The chatter of passing crossbills. Pond: a desolate oval, gelid and lidded, hemmed in boney trees, cold as iron. Feeder stream, sealed.

High over the marsh, raven calls attention to himself. Far below, red-breasted nuthatches answer, muffled toots from within the shadowed pines, vague as an afterthought. Crow with an unusual accent caws.

Tick-ticking off the sunrise metronome, chickadees everywhere, gathering in the maples, hemlocks, and cherry. Off the trail into the lower pasture, wild alders and tired goldenrods overrun with chickadees, thankful afterthoughts. Passing from feeders to the forest. Ferrying seeds, one per trip. An outpouring of *dee, dee, dee, dee.* Chickadees look alike to me, nattily attired . . . black bib, black cap, immaculately white cheeks, grayish, whitish, beige-ish elsewhere. To a female chickadee, each male looks different and bears a unique ultraviolet signature. Where I see white, a chickadee sees ultraviolet, the color beyond purple . . . beyond my detection.

∾

Late in the day, en route to Nance's home, a drive I've made so many times in the past four years I must have inscribed ruts over Howe Hill like wagon wheel tracks across the Great Plains: a northern shrike, a mouse or vole clamped in hook beak, passes in front of the car. First thought: *What's that jay carrying?* Then, forty-mile-per-hour insight . . . blue jays are blue in the sunlight, not gray, and rarely fly around with mice in their mouths.

Northern shrike, a bull-headed songbird with attitude. Except for the inability to carry prey with its feet, a shrike looks and behaves like a falcon—big head, a spike on either side of the upper bill and a corresponding notch on either side of the lower. Spikes and notches—the *tomial tooth*—force apart the vertebrae of mice and birds up to the size of grosbeaks and jays, killing them quickly. Last February, along the edge of the Colorado River, in the happy-go-lucky pre-Covid days, I watched a smaller, more thickly masked loggerhead shrike leave its sagebrush perch and grab a western harvest mouse ten feet in front of me. The shrike bit the mouse at the base of the skull and returned to the sage, jamming it between two twigs. Then, the shrike took the mouse apart, piece by piece.

Despite its scarceness—rare as an Indian Head penny—people still persecute shrikes because they impale songbirds (mice and lizards, too) on thorns, sometimes in front of birders. Predation may be gory, but predators lift a veil from the planet that reveals a miracle of life . . . survival of one animal (or plant) at the expense of another. A natural history lesson played out by snakes, wolves, owls, hawks, spiders, and much-despised blue jays, which occasionally reach into bird nests and swallow hatchlings alive. Predation, viewed without bias as part of the whole landscape, is a window into natural selection, the continuous process of planetary self-regulation, not flawless, but perfect. Paul Errington, author of *Predation and Life* (1967), noted that most predation attempts fail. Teeth, talons, and venom don't guarantee success. Errington's lifelong studies of mink and great horned owl suggested that most predators succeed less than 6 percent of the time. It would be easier for a relief pitcher to get a base hit than for a peregrine to snag a morning dove.

℘

No matter how much I want a crossbill or an owl to be my first bird of 2021, on the threshold of sunrise, standing in the kitchen, opening a can of dog food, out of the corner of my eye, I see chickadees against the dawning sky. Back and forth, already indulging in the day. Chickadees take me with them, a slave to their disposition.

Day 292

03 January 2021

Scars have the strange power to
remind us that our past is real.
Cormac McCarthy

7:23 A.M. (same sunrise time, eighth day in a row). 27 degrees, wind SW less than 1 mph (too subtle for beech leaves to notice). Sky: in limbo. Flurries settle on a half-inch fluff that outlines every branch and peppers every trunk—a zillion white lines. Hemlock limbs sag, Christmas ferns collapse. Eventually, several rolls of white clouds separate from the blue-gray, unspool and then merge again. A dull sky lightens, lumen by lumen. Blue white replaces blue gray. Ruffled replaces taut. A hot, orange sun climbs above the eastern hills. A cold half-moon sinks in the west. Permanent streams: babbling incoherently, water hurrying to the marsh, leaving me lulled by the flow. Wetlands: glazed and glorious. Reeds more white than beige. Evergreens more white than green. Marsh, silent under a rolling cloudscape, now separating into isles of cotton white. Pond: airtight, corked by snow and ice. Three errant oak leaves blemish an otherwise trackless, pristine surface. Where deer wandered over the pond, loops and lines, north to south, back and forth, mammalian calligraphy penned by split hooves. Certainly, hunger didn't drive the deer onto the snowy, icy surface—the only food, a couple of leaves, brown and dry as dust. I believe the deer enjoyed itself, dancing under the gleam of a half-moon shrouded by clouds on a white night in winter.

For a magical moment, the Hollow becomes a Hallmark greeting card or the backdrop for an Andy Williams Christmas Special.

Dogs investigate a tapered two-inch-long scat in the road, sinking into a drunken canine stupor. Deep breaths grade to snorts—scat too small for a coyote. Maybe a fox, red or gray, both conspicuous by their absence this past year.

More deer tracks along the road, dragging of heels like a child scuffling in oversized boots.

Stereophonic red-breasted nuthatches, two groups on either side of the pond. All are calling at once; *ink, ink, ink, ink.* The most nuthatches I've seen or heard since 15 December, when a cold front (7 degrees, wind NW 9 mph) swept through the Hollow. Chickadee on a hemlock twig, up and down, up and down . . . a spindly teeter-totter, playground in the trees. Bellicose jays. Seven crossbills, overhead and hushed. Two curious, tolerant crows watch the dogs and me walk beneath their maple crown.

Idyllic Vermont purged of ills. Vermont as the world imagines it, a byproduct of the Department of Tourism: rolling green hills and white snow; a Crayola landscape lit by October sunshine. A confined perspective: no opioids, no homelessness or rural poverty, no hunger, no domestic violence, no suicide, no alcoholism, no racism, no Confederate flags tacked to rustic barns, no self-appointed militia with a Trumpesque mandate and MAGA caps. A world of rich syrup and sharp cheese, of designer beer and handmade gin, of VRBOs and impeccable ski slopes . . . a ruptured reality.

Day 294

05 January 2021

*Memory whispers someplace
in that jumbled machinery.*
KEN KESEY

7:23 A.M. (same sunrise time, ninth day in a row). 30 degrees, wind NNE 2 mph, less snow on branches and trunks than yesterday; otherwise looks and feels like yesterday. Sky: disheveled gray blanket, the sun rises unnoticed (by me, at least). Permanent streams: it's yesterday, all over again, tediously repetitive like the voice of a red-eyed vireo—the tributaries version of *Groundhog Day*. (No sign of Bill Murray in the woods, however.) Wetlands: dull lighting, a suspension of visible activity (red squirrels and chickadees, prominent marsh-rim ambassadors, muted on a listless morning). Overhead, four crows and a raven break the ice—four *caws* and a *croak*. Pond: feeder stream melts through the surface (again), the black tail of a white dog. The heat of flowing water melts snow, a gray oval patch, more slush than ice in the delta. No new deer calligraphy. Yesterday's tracks convert to pockmarks hemmed by snow. Elsewhere, tracks widen and sink into slush, becoming progressively less distinctive.

On the way home, from deep within the maples, pileated laughs, a rollicking cackle, the first outpouring in more than a month. Hairy woodpecker politely drills spindly ash, barely whispers, and then backs down the swaying trunk; tail pressed to wood. Crows and jays call. Crows, high overhead. Jays, low in the treetops, flashes of noisy blue and white. Off the beaten path: white-breasted nuthatch, soft, nasal calls. *Yank, yank, yank.* Not the metallic tooting of red-breasted nuthatches, conspicuous by their absence. Twenty (a rough count) red crossbills call attention to themselves, passing over the road, vanishing into the pines. Ernie, the Hungarian partridge, on the walkway leading to the porch, coat inflated like a miniature Teletubby, scooting around the yard, a windup toy of a bird. Ernie's not fond of gray squirrels, to which he gives ground, over and over, day after day.

Seven evening grosbeaks, all banana-yellow males, first of the season, crowd the feeders, spilling seeds.

~

I remember spring 1998, two months after Linny was diagnosed with inoperable, stage-four breast cancer: One evening, at the dinner table, she said *I have an idea that would be good for the whole family.* Oh no, I thought, she wants us to visit her sister in Dallas for spring break. Fortunately, her proclamation did not include a trip to Texas. *The boys need a dog,* Linny said, *to distract them from my struggles. There's a border collie for sale in Woodstock, the last puppy in the litter, and—you'll love this, Teddy—the breeder owns the Norwich Navigators.* (The New York Yankees Double-A affiliate). *Maybe the breeder knows Joe Torre and Don Zimmer. Maybe Bernie Williams and Derek Jeter played for him.* Plying my weakness with the absurd possibility that this puppy was one degree removed from pinstripes. *Teddy, please keep an open mind.*

Brief background on the boys, then ten and two. Casey was a cross between Alan Dershowitz and Derek Jeter. When he wasn't playing ball, he would negotiate the finer points of allowance rates and parental discipline. He was focused, alert, but sometimes when friends were around, my commands morphed into pleas, fell on deaf ears. On the other hand, Jordan still was too young to have discovered the superpower of selective hearing. In his trimmed view of the world, the thinnest of lines separated toys and living things.

Linny assured me that she and Casey would help raise the puppy. Our previous dog had died four years before—a tall, princely mix, Afghan and collie, an obedient homeboy that would walk off leash in Manhattan or the Green Mountains. Reggie adored children and whined with excitement (without becoming maudlin) whenever old friends stopped by. He loved to run and swim and was loyal to a fault. Reggie once climbed the rickety seventy-five-foot Gile Mountain Fire Tower when he heard my voice. (Once on top, he was so frightened I had to carry him down, head bumping the steel frame on every turn of the staircase.) Reggie would be a tough act to follow.

For a naturalist, life without a dog, however, had its good points. After Reggie died, our property morphed into a wildlife sanctuary. Grouse drummed from backyard stumps and hermit thrushes and juncos nested in the front yard, at the interface of lawn and woods. Mammals and birds scavenged deer carcasses I had placed in the side yard. One spring, lured by venison, a pair of gray foxes stayed and raised six kits in the brambles, less than fifty feet from my studio door. They caught squirrels in the front yard and mice and woodchucks in the garden. Nursed on the lawn. Fox family ate donations of watermelon and roadkills, often dining on our deck while we reclined in patio furniture. Friends came for barbecues and fox watching.

Relentlessly, Dershowitz and Mother Theresa exercised their opinions. I caved, defenseless under burgeoning pressure. (Casey and Linny granted me the naming rights to sweeten the deal.) The following day, we drove to Woodstock. I named our puppy Yogi after Lawrence Peter Berra, the Yankee's Hall-Of-Fame catcher. Yogi the dog was bright-eyed and intelligent, a canine Einstein, with traditional border collie fur, long and black and white. Paws the size of squash balls.

After exploring the house for ten minutes, Yogi relieved himself on the living room rug. Then, Linny reported that her white blood cell count was still low and that she shouldn't clean up after the dog, *I don't recall you having mentioned that yesterday*, I mumbled, heading to the utility closet for disinfectant. Once Yogi settled into life in the Hollow, he had two primary missions: herd Jordan and chew upholstery.

Every morning at sunrise, I walked Yogi to the pond (the very activity Covid has reinstated). When he was six months old, I enrolled Yogi in obedience school. Near the end of each session, participants simultaneously unleashed their puppies. A few minutes later, the owners, one at a time, called their puppies to their sides. Once a puppy reported to its master, it was given a treat and freed to resume play. One evening, Yogi, who had been responding well to the drills, became discombobulated during free play. *Come, Yogi, come,* I called, *Yogi, come, Yogiiii,* my voice transitioning from exuberance to urgency. Finally, he arrived. *Who's a good boy, Yogi?* (Certainly not you.) *We'll do better next time.*

Later that night, on the long ride home, Casey, reclining in the front seat and on the verge of sleep, announced, *Yogi and I are a lot alike. When friends are around, we're easily distracted.*

I'm on board, Casey. Birds have distracted me for more than sixty years, especially during these past pandemic months. Why stop now? Birds brighten an otherwise dark world, remind me that there are golden voices and scarlet robes beyond my dooryard, that my life is my creation regardless of epidemics in politics and health.

❧

4:26 P.M. (sunset one minute later than yesterday). 35 degrees, wind N 3 mph. Walking the dogs in the gloaming along the snowmobile trail between the upper and lower pastures. Night drops like an anvil: cold, heavy, dark. A series of deep, muffled hoots ride the night currents north of the marsh, out of the lower end of the saddle along the base of Robinson Hill, where pine yields to maple and birch. *Hoo-hooohoo-hoo-hoo.* Great horned owl. I first met horned owls on the pine barrens of Long Island and have seen them across the continent, from Alaska to the Everglades, including the suburbs of Los Angeles and New York City, and found nests in the Roosevelt Elk Pavilion at the Bronx Zoo (1972); in a caliche canyon above the Dog Fork of the Brazos River, in West Texas (1973); forty-five feet up a pitch pine in Dutchess County, New York (1975); on a railroad trestle over the Connecticut River between Brattleboro, Vermont and Hinsdale, New Hampshire (1976); and the Hanover (New Hampshire) Sewage Treatment Plant (1978 and 1979). This is my first horned owl in Coyote Hollow. The owl tugs at me and I follow, hopelessly and helplessly afflicted by a wild, unscratchable itch.

Great horned owls nest the length of the hemisphere, from the Aleutian Islands to Tierra del Feugo. Fifteen subspecies, all varying shades of mottled brown. From Arctic pale to jungle dark. Describing morphs is like ordering steak: pale, medium-pale, medium, medium-dark, dark, *very* dark—a massive bird, big and bold. A grapefruit-size head and expressive face punctuated by bright yellow eyes. White bib and feathers for horns. Great horned owls eat anything they want—from mice to great blue herons, red-tailed hawks, osprey, peregrine falcons, porcupines, timber rattlesnakes (a major predator), fox kits, raccoons, skunks, and feral cats. I found a mink's tail, a woodcock's bill, and a sucker's dorsal fin in a nest in lower New York State.

A random evening walk becomes vastly more interesting. Dogs and I wander into the saddle. Listen patiently and quietly—more deep, solemn hoots. Tuba hoots. Then, a single eerie barking note, also deep. I'm so close. I call back, hoping to engage the owl in conversation. Only beech leaves answer.

Day 296

07 January 2021

My mother's 111th birthday
The morning after democracy stumbled

While preachers preach of evil fates
Teachers teach that knowledge waits
Can lead to hundred-dollar plates
Goodness hides behind its gates
But even the president of the United States
Sometimes must have to stand naked.

Bob Dylan

7:23 A.M. (same sunrise time, eleventh day in a row). 23 degrees, wind NNW 9 mph (raw and oceanic, shrieks through pines, a grim disturbance). Sky: overcast and dim, somewhere between nautical and civil twilight. Permanent streams: icicles like teeth or stalactites grow from sprays and splashes; extend from the mouths of episodic caves. Flow harmonizes with the weather. Mesmerized by the outpour, I pause and listen. Waiting for my recovery, the dogs sit down. If I rearranged rocks, I could recompose the melody. Wetlands: colors dull, cold wind sharply out of the north races across the marsh, bending and stirring reeds, which speak in tongues. I face the wind like a chickadee, fluffing imaginary feathers. Red squirrels avoid the elements, probably under the snow, visiting food caches, stoking internal fires. Chickadees and titmice, an integrated party of eight in the alders, the pines, back and forth across the road. Pond: hermetically sealed. Feeder stream frozen shut, black watery tail now docked by ice. Deer exhibits exceptional artwork. Hoof prints like half-filled balloons unwind across the surface. New tracks loop through old, sensuous and immediately appealing. Why would a deer wander around the frozen pond at night, supervised by a waning moon and peek-a-boo stars?

Lonesome red-breasted nuthatch tooting in the pines, the winter analog of red-eyed vireo, monotonously repetitive. Very high, raven strokes the gelid air with slow, leisurely flaps. Bird on a mission, heads south. No sign of great horned owl last night or this morning; the vagrant wanderings of a bird looking for a homestead. A Billy Graham journey . . . *I'm just passing through this world.*

Darkness at the break of noon: Yesterday's purposeful assault on the Capitol was shameful: a sad attempt to erase truth, prune democracy, and break the sod of justice. Fueled by misinformation about the result of the 2020 presidential election, thousands of citizens loyal to the outgoing president, many armed and carrying inflammatory banners, breached the Capitol . . . an insurrection disavowing the outcome of the election. Three hours of chaos. I watched time hurtle by, overcome by the same feelings I had when someone shot President Kennedy, and I sat in seventh-period German drugged by disbelief, unable to conjugate thought, let alone verbs.

This morning's purposeful riot: flush with activity, a horde of eleven jays mob the feeders, flashes of white and cerulean. Ironclad and cranky. Jays recap and translate the neighborhood mix of birdsong, a raucous rendition. One broadcasts an out-of-season parody of a red-shouldered hawk. Three mourning doves waver, waiting in mottled sunlight. Titmice and chickadees displaced. Woodpeckers disrupted. Sunflower seeds rain on the lawn benefiting two hen turkeys, three gray squirrels, and Ernie, the Hungarian partridge.

Chickadees, everywhere and busy, diligently and merrily pick through pine bark and chat up a storm, patiently waiting for jays to leave the feeders. Then, they come, six bundles of energy. A sign of continuance. Chickadees berth in the here and now like Old Testament prophets, their world untouched by political chaos. Little totems in the front yard: gray-feathered rays of hope. From neighbor to neighbor, chickadees deliver the morning news. While the fortress of our own democracy appears frail, chickadees carry on and remind me to face the wind and persevere . . . ever so slowly, a bitter morning ripens.

Day 300

11 January 2021

But if in your thought you must measure time into seasons, let each season encircle all the other seasons. And let today embrace the past with remembrance and the future with longing.
KAHLIL GIBRAN

7:21 A.M. (sunrise one minute earlier than yesterday, two minutes earlier than on Insurrection). 9 degrees, wind ENE 1 mph, a polar breath. Pines need lubrication, creaks and moans a whispered dialogue. Sky: baby blue. Clouds in lines, puffs, and mare's tails, cream white and on the move. Here and there, a pale pink wash. Permanent streams: upper, the passage of a mink, transcription in the snow; lower, ice bridges hide flow zones, amplify sound. Behind icy curtains, under icy floorboards, amoeboid air bubbles split, a lesson in mitosis, the magic of shape changing. An intersection of tracks: deer heading south jumped over the lower stream, and three coyotes headed east to supervise daybreak. Wetlands: visually and audibly dull, under an arch of the sky, now drained of pink. To the west, far away, crow commutes to Post Mills. Pond: feeder stream zipped shut. Yesterday's deer hoof prints, artistic loops and sensuous curls melted and refroze—now a nearly unidentifiable mess. Crystalline bouquets sprout on the ends of withered meadow flowers—goldenrod and aster sag under the weight of hoar frost.

Red-breasted nuthatches, three, maybe four, deep in the pines. Crows high, jays low through treetops, crossing the road from one feeding station to another. A pair of hen turkeys under the feeder, in the company of a trio of gray squirrels. Fussy titmouse chooses a *particular* sunflower seed based on an arcane calculus understood only by titmice. Disappears into a configuration of walnut branches. Returns to the feeder. Selects another seed. Over and over. Always to the walnut, who's furrowed bark-like pantries accommodate birdseed. Noisy flight of doves, a whirling and whirring exodus. Everyone notices.

I have not seen a crossbill in a week, a junco or a goldfinch since November, a warbler since the maples blushed. I rely on chickadees, jays, and nuthatches; they accompany me through the seasons, dependable and entertaining neighbors. I hold them close. Moreover, when a crow or a raven appears, dwarfed by the vast sky, or an eagle on long, broad, table-straight wings, I pause and watch. Without them, the light would dim.

Numbingly cold, but high on spindly ash, a male chickadee tilts toward spring. Sings a simple two-note *whistle: fee-bee, fee-bee, fee-bee*, the *fee* higher than the *bee*—a territorial proclamation out of sync with the weather. An early sign that chickadee flocks—the democracy of winter—will eventually rupture into spring autonomy. A single bird audibly casts a mating lure on a frigid morning, a tiny sprout of the coming season. An undeterred little bird that reads the stars, measures the ambient light, sings a sweet, simple tune . . . a newsworthy event. The announcement warms me.

Day 303

14 January 2021

Ravens are the birds I'll miss most when I die.
If only the darkness into which we must look
were composed of the black light of their limber intelligence.
If only we did not have to die at all.
Instead, become ravens.
LOUISE ERDRICH

7:20 A.M. (sunrise one minute earlier than yesterday). 31 degrees, wind calm, 0 mph. Sky: a flat, ghost-gray sheet, tightly fitting. Sun arrives unnoticed (by me). A stray flurry or two nearly lost against eyelid mist. Permanent streams: Excellent example of Ansel Adams' Zone System with the benefit of musical accompaniment—black water, Zone I; cloudy ice, middle tone gray, Zone V; a dusting of snow, Zone X. Water purls through an obstacle course of stone and ice. Shape-changing air bubbles, fewer than yesterday, more like a lava lamp than fish school. Wetlands and pond: a visual and audible holding pattern; deep, repetitive malaise. January, like August, is gripped by the doldrums.

Cacophony of chickadees, nuthatches, jays. Solitary crow, high above the marsh and far to northwest—*caw, caw, caw, caw*—a digestive rumble. Stuck at home in the depths of January, birds remind me that no matter how tired and monotonous the Hollow appears, no two days are the same.

The ambivalence of sunrise: loosened from hemlock, barred owl sails across the road, a silent discharge like breath on a cold morning. Big bird. Soft feathers. Inhaled by a dark stand of pine. Vanishes. A true denizen of the winter woods. Shelters in place, knows what January offers. No retreat to gentler climes. Waits above the road, the trail, the patch-cut woods, the rim of the marsh, and the pond edge for slight movement and faint sound. Then, phantomlike, pounces. Sometimes through deep snow, feet first.

∼

Raven pair high over the marsh, black against gray (Zone I flying below Zone V), wings rowing, effortless, deep strokes. A downpour of baritone croaks. Maybe a couple. Feels like a couple, flying wing tip to wing tip. Tantamount to holding hands. Ravens mate for life. Sensitively, couples preen each other's heads—those hard-to-get-to places—one tiny feather at a time. Social and bright. Charter members of Avian Mensa. Solve complicated problems . . . pulls string with suspended food, holds string in place with foot, pulls up more with beak. Leads wolves and coyotes to frozen carcasses. Oversees Tower of London, a living fable from the book of Aesop. May even understand baseball.

In Vermont, in the 1960s, ravens were rare as a 1952 Topps Mickey Mantle card. In the spring of 1976, during a graduate-school ornithology class, I took a field trip to Stoddard, New Hampshire, to see a raven nest high on an inaccessible cliff. Today, these birds nest on remote Long Island beaches; Co-op City in the Bronx; a water tower in Forest Park, Queens; and at the Brooklyn Waterfront. Several years ago, more than forty wintered in the Hollow, in a stand of pines on the far north end of the valley, less than a mile from my front door.

∼

Nineteen robins flush from a stand of white pines, a burst of sharp clucks. Circle. Land. Bolt again and circle. Fourteen peel off to the northeast, well below the conjugal ravens.

Every winter I see a few robins (never nineteen till today), a byproduct of warmer winters and an incursion of berry-producing invasives— honeysuckle, buckthorn, and bittersweet. In the spring, my waterlogged front lawn is a diurnal diner, mostly earthworms, another exotic, a colonial-era donation to the Northeast's fauna roster. For migrating robins, meals to-go. In one day, one robin may eat fourteen feet of worms. Since the sixteen hundreds, we have revamped the continent into a robin food shelf.

Five robins linger in the pines; the dogs and I linger on the road, all of us patiently waiting for spring.

∽

The charity of birds: one owl for less than five seconds, two amicable ravens, and nineteen robins in the bittersweet . . . for those moments, drinking it all in, I am relieved of the desire to travel (anywhere). Freedom. Enthusiasm unbridled. The simple pleasures of January on an affluent winter morning . . .

Day 304

15 January 2021

*And above all, remember that
the meaning of life is to build a life
as if it were a work of art.*
RABBI ABRAHAM JOSHUA HESCHEL

7:20 A.M. (sunrise same time as yesterday). 27 degrees, wind SSE 1 mph. Sky: clear with a peach wash. October fog, November temperature, late March feel. Permanent streams: overnight dusting of snow speckles ice. In the flat woods, where water in a level run enters the marsh, layered and growing ice shelves extend from the shoreline, squeezing ephemeral canyons tighter and tighter. Wetlands: residual beige reeds in a bowl of chowder-thick fog, which extends midway up the evergreens on the far shore. Crowns of pine and hemlock poke through a band of mist. Tiny crystals. Pond: feeder stream barely reopens, otherwise a carbon copy of the past several days. Deer calligrapher elsewhere, old tracks hardly suggest deer.

No robins today. Yesterday, they visited the roadside bittersweet, the vines that lace pines together. Now, flecks of berries decorate the snow, the red scraps a reminder of that brief encounter. Freeze-dried berries keep robins alive.

An overnight influx of red-breasted nuthatches and chickadees heading either north or south. Hard to tell. A riotous outpouring of *toots* and *dees*. One nuthatch wanders down a pine, blood rushing to its head. Explores the scaly bark, probing like a man with a metal detector. Eats something too small for me to recognize. Others forage in lichen tufts and pine-needle clusters, on suet cages.

Morning brightens. Sunshine devours fog. Jays argue and crows scream. Standing in the front yard, the sun on my face and dogs by my side. The sound of church bells floats over Robinson Hill, a colonial sound more in step with rural New England than my suburban roots. Jews do not ring a bell; they blow a horn, a primordial sound, the wildest I know . . . like a Viking call to arms or an Arawak on a conch shell or Tarzan yodeling from a jungle tree. The blowing of the ram's horn was the gift for enduring—when I wasn't actively suffering—hours on a hard bench, for reading a book written backward in a baffling alphabet one step removed from hieroglyphics. At home, facing the sun and a new day . . . the tolling of distant bells, the recalling of distant memories. I lean into a modest morning.

Day 305

16 January 2021

*I try to bear witness that we are living
in a beautiful, ordered world,
and not in a chaos without pattern,
as it sometimes seems.*

M. C. ESCHER

7:19 A.M. (sunrise one minute earlier than yesterday). 36 degrees, wind N 5 mph (hums with authority). Sky: in need of a decongestant, gray and thick, with no sign of the sun. A rotation of drizzle, rain, and snow. Occasionally, tiny white ice pellets bounce on impact. Raindrops on twigs. Under a dusting of snow, the road is frozen and slippery, a micro-spike morning, the first time this winter. Permanent streams: upper, an absence of ice; lower, open below the wooden snowmobile bridge, but closed and silent on the rock-studded, west-facing slope. Wetlands: saturated colors. Beige turns brown. Seen through the wind-driven rain, marsh and shoreline in surprisingly sharp relief. Pond: figure eight several shovel widths wide cleared by a skater (or an overly ambitious deer).

I stand in the road, spikes digging into the ice. Coyotes on a mission, three lanes of tracks run down the middle, stopping for nothing. Footprints: coyote's middle toes slant inward; dog's slant outward. I follow the coyotes from my driveway to the marsh, where they headed west, flanked by cattails and rushes, easing through muck and mire under cover of night. Dogs tug on leashes, urging me to follow. From one side of the road to the other, white-footed mice tracks cut coyote tracks at a right angle. A quick crossing. No bold midroad trek. Then, the second set of mouse tracks closer to the pond. Stitchwork. Snow turns to rain. Mouse spoor erasing.

Pair of red-breasted nuthatches works the pines to the west. A white-breasted nuthatch to the east, alone in the maples. Jays, here and there, to and fro, back and forth, subdued, the product of cold rain and a north wind. At the feeders, a sparse gathering busies themselves in inclement weather. In the backyard, jays excavate buried acorns, looking bedraggled. Feathers matted and more gray than blue, dull as the sky.

A male pileated woodpecker (red of the crest extends below the eyes) disembowels a pine—soft taps and chips, flying bits of wood just off the driveway. Stops. Chases a hairy woodpecker, which squeals, hitting the high notes. Pileated returns to pine, claws dig in—two toes in front, two behind—stiff tail pressed to trunk. Leans back and hammers, crested head a blur. No concussion here. A spongy cranium (*cancellous* bone), a shock absorber at the base of the upper mandible, consumes the blow. A slightly longer lower mandible strikes wood first, straight on, directing the force of each impact to another spongy bone (*hyoid*), which anchors an elastic, inquisitive tongue. Pileated jackhammers all day and still gets a good night's sleep.

Morning cannot make up its mind. Snow turns to rain, turns to snow, turns to rain. Abruptly, five chickadees fly into the front yard cherry. Silent and graceful, the elegance of indifference. Two visit the feeders. Others pause in the tree for a nanosecond, a raindrop on the tip of each bill. Then, off for sunflower seed and back . . . again. Once the sanding truck leaves, my driveway becomes a grit station for five mourning doves. Ernie, the Hungarian partridge, has been missing for days. Doves' sad cooing takes on added meaning . . . a dim day grows dimmer.

Back indoors, I wander from window to window, eating toast and sipping coffee, cocooned in wood heat, and watch birds being birds, exuberant and nonchalant on a gray, messy morning.

Day 308

19 January 2021

*The thing to be known
grows with the knowing.*
Nan Shepherd

7:17 a.m. (sunrise one minute earlier than yesterday). 14 degrees, wind ENE 1 mph. Sky: light cloud ceiling cracked open, pastel blues and gray-pink; low humidity unveils Mount Ascutney, a dark lump forty miles south. Room for the sun to break through, at least in the morning. Permanent streams: ice reappears in the broader, shallower, slower-moving sections. Elsewhere, churning water holds ice at bay. Wetlands: cold sink with frost. Across the marsh, spruce and hemlock have shed some snow. Pond: a quiet sameness.

Short-tailed weasel: delicate five-toed footprints, silent footfalls on soft snow. Paired tracks, short bounds; out of the woods, across the road, into the alders. Maybe to hunt voles in dark tunnels beneath the snow. Always hungry. I have a hyperactive thyroid and need plenty of food, too. But the weasel is hyperactive and high-strung, a furry tube of perpetual motion. A hummingbird of a mammal. Heartbeat, four hundred times a minute. A long, thin body sheds heat. The surface area to mass ratio is very high. Curls in a disc to stay warm. Weasels are born almost embryonic. Fuller development would be lethal to the mother, a restless hunter who would stick like a cork in rodent burrows. Weasels kill more than they eat . . . and they eat a lot. Store hapless prey (primarily mice) in stone walls and cavities, a frontline defense against Lyme disease. Lines temporary den with victim's fur. Always on the move, a small itinerant hunter, itself vulnerable. Particularly to an owl.

Weasels caught our imagination and colored our language. Noun. Adjective. Verb. Theodore Roosevelt called political jargon *weasel words*. A shifty, untrustworthy weasel of a person gives the animal a lousy name. One can (and has) weaseled out of responsibility or into forbidden quarters.

∽

One winter morning in the mid-nineties, a long-tailed weasel chiseled frozen venison off a deer carcass I had positioned close to my studio door. While I watched the weasel, a barred owl—wings up, feet extended, talons spread, smoke silent—swooped down as though on a pendulum. No pause. Owl grabbed the weasel by the shoulders, digging into its chassis, and then looped back up . . . one fluid motion. Weasel dangled, an airlift of vital resources. A pestering raven dive-bombed the owl to no avail. Then, the owl entered into the secrecy of pines, dark and somber, where one predator ate another.

Raven, foiled, stuck with venison.

∽

Crow over the pond, two ravens over the marsh. Both calling. Nuthatches call: white-breasted from maples, a muffled pileated of a call; red-breasted from the pines. Both visit the suet cage until dislodged by a hairy woodpecker. Chickadees and jays are busy and noisy.

Quietly tapping, pileated eviscerates roadside maple. A semi-circle of woodchips, some six inches long, litters the snow. A roller-coaster flight, black and white wings flashing, flushes over the driveway. Lands on the trunk of a skinny maple. Hops higher up the tree until he reaches the top and then launches to another hardwood closer to the house, the same tree I saw him in yesterday. Red crest erect, a beacon of color in dim woods. A second pileated calls, a loud nuthatch of a call, a derisive laugh hurled in the face of January.

Day 309

20 January 2021

Inauguration

United States rejoins the Paris Climate Accord

'Hope' is the thing with feathers –
That perches in the soul –
And sings the tune without the words –
And never stops – at all –
EMILY DICKINSON

7:17 A.M. (same sunrise time as yesterday). 19 degrees, wind S less than 1 mph. A dusting of snow last night. Sky: hopeful in the east, silver clouds embossed on morning blue. A rumor of pink. For the moment, a sunny and buoyant Inauguration . I am thankful for both. Permanent streams: level stretches sealed and silent; sloped stretches, a composite of ice, snow, and gushing (not plunging) water. Brown creeper whispers in ash, barely audible above the purl. Wetlands: across the marsh, dark wall of evergreens—hemlock, spruce, fir, pine—trimmed in snow. Out of the green and white wall, the derisive laugh of pileated. Bird with a one-track mind, again and again, and again. Dogs sit down and chew various body parts. At the same time, I listen intently for a revelation, a secret that might otherwise be disclosed if I hadn't paused, fingers numb, cheeks stinging, to consider something other than the swearing in of Joe Biden as the 46th President of the United States. Purpose achieved, pileated stops laughing. Dogs keep chewing. Staring at an empty marsh, my morning embellished . . . but I am no more enlightened than before. Pond: inlet frozen shut. I strain to hear the flow.

Shrew trail zigzags back and forth, woods to marsh. Inside the shrew trench, itsy, bitsy footprints. Its face serves as a plow, its legs too short to either jump or hop, like dragging a thumb through the snow. Then, the shrew appears. Baffled, twilight-gray mammal runs from one side of the road to the other, crossing its own track, like animation from Nintendo. Starts and stops, changes direction, eventually disappears into a snow tunnel on the marsh side of the road. Shrew eats every three or four hours. Heartbeat eight hundred to a thousand times per minute. By comparison, a weasel is a couch potato.

Far away, a raven calls. Draws closer. Passes overhead, towing his voice behind him. A pair of crows. A hairy woodpecker demurely taps a maple limb. A gentle decree. Another pecks fat from a bag of kidney suet. Titmice and chickadees, fluffed out, take turns at the feeder. Jays and doves elsewhere engaged in purposeful activities . . . likely to do with food.

∽

Yesterday, coyotes hurled their voices at the crescent moon in the gloaming. First serenade I have heard in months.

∽

On our way down the road, female pileated in roadside maple quietly chips away, then flushes when I pass. On our way home, she's back at work, deep inside the tree, tapping and spraying wood chips. She remains hidden, cocooned in wood, twenty feet up. The dogs and I stand next to the tree. Pileated looks out. Flicks chips. Softly hammers. More chips. I see her ant-seeking tongue, a flesh-colored flash. Unspooling or reeling? Hard to tell the direction.

I watch until my neck aches. An unimpeachable emissary of the wild disassembles a tree on a bright, beautiful, *hopeful* morning . . . an overflow of optimism.

Day 313

24 January 2021

Two days after the death of Henry Aaron

Whether I was in a slump or feeling badly
or having trouble off the field,
the only thing to do was keep swinging.
Didn't come up here to read.
Came up here to hit.

HENRY AARON

7:13 A.M. (sunrise one minute earlier than yesterday). 9 degrees, wind NW 12 mph (almost feels like January in Vermont, a drafty walk on the doorstep of Siberia). Oak and beech leaves in perpetual motion, a seasonal performance below the swaying pines. Sky: swept clean and clear, pink along the southern and eastern perimeters, elsewhere blue. Winter sunshine spills down Robinson Hill, radiant and inspired, an elixir of the Gods. Permanent streams: upper, several small windows on otherwise hidden flows, raccoon on a midnight walkabout; lower, leaves twitter, water more gasp than mutter. Wetlands: the repository of cold air. Unobstructed, brutal winds rip across the marsh and vibrate limbs, stirring trees, which chatter and creak like hard teeth. Squirrels stay home, bundled in leaves, swaying to the rhythm of the wind. Pond: inlet closed, feeder stream icebound, surface scarred by a snow machine. Shoreline red pines speak, everything else quietly frozen.

Hatched for mornings like this, raven courses high above the marsh. No flapping, just a partial inward squeeze of the wings. Then, full extension, tilting, turning, gliding. Rides the wind above the reeds, playing on and in the frigid air. An occasional *croak*. *Melanin*, the dark pigment in bird feathers, does not direct absorbed heat to the body and does little to warm a bird (several desert birds, including ravens, are jet black). Melanin is a tough protein that protects feathers from wear and tear. Think the tip of seabird wings—gulls, terns, albatrosses, puffins, and so forth.

Two ravens together, wingtip to wingtip. The tandem flight of lovers. Rocking and rolling. A courting couple. Their voices, deep echoing honks, louder than the wind, animate the Hollow in the depths of winter, a heartwarming show of affection, which apparently my dogs don't recognize.

Female pileated standing inside roadside maple, a closet of her own design. Tongue patrolling ant tunnels, chips everywhere.

❧

The memory of baseball and brown bears, summer 1997.

Although I dream of vistas and seaboards of the East, I love the visibly rugged West. When Casey was ten, Linny and I wanted him to experience the full sweep of the American landscape. (Jordan was only a year and a half.) How else could he appreciate how America grades from one bioregion to the next? Perhaps, we reasoned, with that understanding, he would have a fresh view of the Connecticut River Valley, his own home ground, an integral valley in the ensemble of American landscapes.

To show Casey the splendor of the far Northwest, in the summer of 1997, our family visited Kodiak Island off the Alaska coast. A floatplane dropped us off at a remote cabin on the south end of Frazer Lake, a long, narrow body of water hemmed by green, dripping hills. Early one morning, Casey and I rowed across the lake and hiked a mile to the upper falls on the Dog Salmon River. The river twisted like a serpent through a lush valley of grasses and lupines and towering cow parsnips, and spilled from stony ramparts in a swirl of mad water. Sockeye salmon swarmed against the current, red fish in blue water. Eleven brown bears fished the river between the upper and lower falls. Late in the afternoon, three bears walked out on a weir. The largest bear stopped and leaned far over the railing, scanning for salmon. Smiling, I turned to Casey and said, *If those bears were boys, the smaller ones would push the larger one into the river.* Almost as soon as the words left my mouth, the smallest bear shoved the big one in.

Casey and those seemingly otherworldly beasts had a common ground, a shared behavior—whatever the bear's actual intention—that brought him ineffable joy and closer to the heart of Kodiak Island.

A week later, we visited Katmai Peninsula, among another knot of Alaskan brown bears. Standing on the edge of a glacial lake, in the national park, about to go salmon fishing, Hank Aaron signed an autograph for ten-year-old Casey, an aspiring shortstop, who said, *Thank you, Mr. Aaron.* Said Aaron, *Not everyone remembers to say thank you.*

The following day, still marveling at the brief exchange of ballplayer and boy, I stood on a wooden platform adjacent to a stream and photographed airborne sockeyes jumping a small waterfall into the mouths of bears the size of Volkswagens, my face buried in the viewfinder. Sometime later, Hank Aaron arrived, inadvertently nudging my tripod and knocking my composition askew, the subject taken out of play like a runner picked off base. Aaron apologized. I have no recall of the misaligned photograph, though I'm sure it included a bear. If Aaron had bumped my arm, I would have framed my T-shirt. Fishing and looking at bears in the middle of nowhere, he took time to acknowledge a ten-year-old who said *Thank you*. Two days after his death, I'm thinking of Henry Aaron: spectacular ballplayer, quiet humanitarian, humbled by Jackie Robinson, enamored by Martin Luther King, a star athlete for whom every life mattered.

Well . . . Thank you, Mr. Aaron.

Day 315

26 January 2021

Place and a mind may interpenetrate
till the nature of both is altered.
Nan Shepherd

7:12 A.M. (sunrise one minute earlier than yesterday). 12 degrees (cold lurks inside my jacket), wind WSW 2 mph. Sky: a faint blush across a rolling aerial landscape, mostly silver-white and grandbaby blue. Southern and eastern horizons trimmed in pastel pink. Permanent streams: flowing water and air press against the undersurface of ice, shapes dynamic and endless, an army of squiggles and blotches, colorless but gorgeous descent through the lungs of winter. An adult pacifier for the easily amused. (Apparently bored, dogs sit in the snow.) Wetlands: across the marsh, deep in the evergreens, pileated jackhammers a pine (or spruce or hemlock). One or two volleys per minute, ten or twelve drumbeats per volley. Faster in the beginning and in the end. Carries a mile or more and may be delivered by either sex. Second pileated answers, derisive laughter from up the road near the disemboweled maple. Pond: hardened and mum, thick ice under a crust of snow. Even the feeder stream keeps its voice under wraps. A seasonal holding pattern until March, lentic malaise.

Pileated Woodpecker

Red-breasted nuthatch on barkless aspen. Brown creeper on cherry. A squad of chickadees, squalling in the alders and hemlocks, recover stashed seeds and torpid insects. Three doves pick grit in the driveway. Flush when I appear, an over-amped exodus on noisy wings. Hairy woodpecker drums on a resonant pine limb, faster volleys issued more frequently than pileated's. Garbled-voiced crows and piercing jays.

Female pileated chisels deeper into the roadside maple, an artist immersed in her work (literally). Wood chips everywhere. The tree may fall before she's done. Likely, her mate wallops the evergreens across the marsh. Pileateds do not migrate and maintain territories year round. Like beavers (alligators in the Everglades), pileateds are a *keystone* species that provide life-sustaining cavities for other animals: American marten, both species of weasels and flying squirrels, wood duck, saw-whet owl, and kestrel, among many others. Plenty of holes to go around. Every spring, woodpecker couples excavate a new nest cavity; every summer, a new roost site; and every winter, each grown chick has a separate roost hole. Although pileateds may reuse an old nest as an evening roost, they rarely nest a second time in the same cavity.

Pileated in maple responds to her partner's drums . . . a delirious burst of *wok, wok, wok, wok, wok.* She cares not that the dogs and I stand twenty feet in front of the tree, watching little clouds of breath rising from her mouth. The Hollow belongs to the hardy. As January peters out, the pileateds proclaim ownership every morning.

Two weeks ago, the chickadee began to sing. Now, pileated and hairy woodpeckers drum daily. Dusk and dawn, daily, light stretches in both directions, minute by minute. In the jungles of western Amazonia, scarlet tanagers must be molting, stirring, and overeating. Responding to circannual cycles, mysteries triggered in a tropical landscape where photoperiod has a mere cameo role . . . a subtlety known to tanagers, imagined by naturalists, and anticipated by anyone with oaks in the backyard.

Above the southeastern edge of the marsh, just beyond the hammering woodpecker, a raven calls loudly and persistently before the sun, a black bird dwarfed beneath the cloudscape. Floating over Robinson Hill, a hot-air balloon, quilted patches of black interspersed with a rainbow palette of other colors, joins the raven in an otherwise dull sky. Balloon's engine, a flurry of combustion coughs, and then silence. Floats dreamlike above the evergreens. A lone man stands in the basket, dressed like me—a brown bear of a coat, balaclava, and mittens. Man and raven look down on the threadbare landscape, white with ragged snow, the pretense of an endless winter. I wave . . . grateful for human contact.

Day 317

28 January 2021

We can know only that we know
nothing. And that is the highest
degree of human wisdom.

LEO TOLSTOY

7:10 A.M. (sunrise one minute earlier than yesterday). 25 degrees, wind NNW 7 mph. Sky: gray, scalloped edge to edge, spits snow, which floats like wood ash. Permanent streams: distorted lyrics leak from cracks in the ice, a high-pitched gurgle, the afterthought of flow. Wetlands: an amphitheater of bent reeds and frigid air. (In summer, a replica of the Everglades writ miniature; in winter, an echo of the tundra.) Yesterday's velvet snow, which trimmed the evergreens, has blown or melted. West of the marsh, shrouded by hemlock, pileated drums in privacy (again), a percussive message hitched to the north wind. I listen. Dogs wait. No answer. Pond: suspended animation, like an on-deck batter after the third out. Old tracks transformed into pockmarks. Living poles with crowns, red pines rock in the wind. A green bench straddles the plowed loop; a seat for a young hockey player to lace up skates; an obstacle for deer to vault; a bridge for an otter to slide under; a surface for ravens to play cribbage.

Female pileated absent from roadside maple. Snow fills the rim of the cavity; snow-covered chips litter the ground. Raven, voice spilling over Robinson Hill, a guttural outpour. Overhead, wings barely moving. A colossal songbird slowly patrolling its domain. Two much smaller, vigorously flapping crows hurl sharp-edged voices across the Hollow. Jay mimics a red-shouldered hawk; makes me look. The whining of dove wings as six flush from the driveway, a choreographed exodus. Small heads, long tails, easily disturbed. Angelic flight. A huntable commodity in Texas. A cherished dooryard bird in Vermont. South of El Paso, in spring 1972, at a biological station in the northern edge of the Chihuahuan Desert, just beyond Kermit, a tiny town so dry that trucks delivered water twice a week, I ate dove for ten consecutive days. While I collected pocket mice and kangaroo rats for reproductive analysis, my faculty advisor, Dr. Packard, collected doves, everywhere by the thousands, for dinner. Surprise, surprise . . . mourning dove tastes like chicken, fit-in-your-hand chicken.

In and around the alders, adjacent to the marsh, two red-breasted nuthatches toot. Chickadee calls an abridged version—*dee, dee*. I whistle the chickadee's song, two notes, the second an octave higher than the first, encouraging spring to bloom in his syrinx like quickening pussy willows in a vase. Sedated by boredom, dogs lie down. Chickadee, unheeding, ignores my encouragement, ignores my goading, and continues *dee, dee*. A consolidated measure of day length, thawing, and planetary elixir, spring cannot be forced.

Back home, chickadees being chickadees, full of urgency, flash past on silent wings, voices under wraps, like static electricity. I wait for a cold front to fall like an anvil; Arctic air will orchestrate the weather and turn the Hollow brittle for three days. Nevertheless, there will be sunshine, delicate winter sunshine; caramelized sunlight across a quasi-Siberian landscape . . . and my porch faces south.

Day 320

31 January 2021

-6 degrees
Chickadee

One part heart
Three parts feather

How big is the spark
That beats in you

And doing so
Warms us both?
Claudia Kern

7:07 A.M. (sunrise one minute earlier than yesterday). -6 degrees, wind NW 3 mph, an ecological treadmill under the weight of an Arctic air mass, day three. Dogs, whiskers frosted, reminiscent of unshaven old men. Sky: pink in the east and south; a hint of yellow in the west.

Waning moon, polished but fading. Everywhere else, sunrise blue, pale but promising. Permanent streams: a pair of icy highways for wandering mink. Down the lower streambed yesterday and returned via the upper today. Twenty-four hours among the reeds. Under the moon's silver light, accompanied by shadows, mink left fresh prints on powder, two by two, all five toes distinctive, never leaving the streambed. Over fallen trees and tangled branches, bounding through the snow. Under the road and the snowmobile bridge into a jungle of reeds, over a jumble of rocks, across panes of ice, into the dark shade of the hemlocks. Flexible as a snake, hot blood coursing.

Dark brown fur, the envy of the nineteen sixties. I ran my fingers through my mother's coat a thousand times. Soft, thick, lustrous, earthy brown. Looks better on a mink. Wetlands: mink's freezer chest. For the barred owl, alone in the spruce, the addition of a high-energy competitor, a transitory strand in the weft and warp of the food web. Beyond the western shore, a lonely drum roll, one and done, reclusive pileated. Pond: a plowed rink takes shape. Christmas overtones, the red wooden frame of a hockey goal joins the green bench; otherwise, as Yogi Berra said, in 1961, after Mickey Mantle and Roger Maris hit back-to-back home runs, *It's déjà vu all over again.*

From high on the east-facing shoulder of Robinson Hill, a coyote hurls its voice into the heavy morning air, snug and warm in a coat of gray. The haberdasher Canada Goose offers a head-to-toe coyote snow-suit for over $9,000. Looks better on coyote and serves a real purpose. Hair evolved from reptile scales three hundred million years ago. The first mammal in the fossil record appeared 220 million years ago, fully furred. The tough protein keratin—the stuff of fingernails and feathers—coats each strand of hair. Long, glossy, overlaid guard hairs repel moisture, provide camouflage, and keep soft, downy underfur dry. Shorter and duller, underfur traps body heat close to the skin. For the coyote: built-in Gore-Tex and down, breathable, insulating, stylish . . . comes in shades of dusk.

Raven rows north, propelled by voice, trailed by shadow. An outburst of nuthatches, both species. Sixteen jays convene in aspens, all honking and barking at once, patiently waiting for feeders to fill.

Breakfast on the run: red squirrel digs out three shallow caches of pine nuts. Feeds and then leaves. Gray squirrels, which had waited for the sun to crest the horizon, assemble at the feeders, joined by six jays and three woodpeckers—two hairy and one downy—seven grit-gathering doves, two titmice, and chickadees, too many and too jazzed to accurately count.

It's hard not to pause for chickadees, particularly in the end of January, the coldest morning of the season, when one leans back and sings, instigating three others to join in. At the junction of would-be territories, amid the discharge of thin whistles. Flock in conflict, an early sign of spring. I fumble for binoculars, hands like lobster claws. Chickadees keep singing, four maestros working the score, a dress rehearsal. Like a hatch of mayflies, an ephemeral burst of enthusiasm. Then, stone silence. Amicably, chickadees return to feeding. Peace reigns in the Hollow.

I first heard a chickadee sing on January 11. Now, three weeks later, four. A simple provocation in gelid sunlight, the shapelessness of a new season . . . I listen, sun on my face, chickadees in my heart.

Day 321

01 February 2021

Take fate by the throat.
Ludwig von Beethoven

7:06 a.m. (sunrise one minute earlier than yesterday). -2 degrees, wind NW 1 mph, on the cusp of a nor'easter. Sky: pot-bellied moon in the west, the tarnished remnant of a bright disc. Long clouds, gray-blue, trimmed in pink. In between, the blue light of sunrise. Permanent streams: relics of mink tracks, the evanescent thread of a nomad. Wetlands: archipelagos of sweetgale, brown isles glazed by frost. Tiny crystals outline alder limbs, coat sausage-shaped catkins dangling from the end of twigs like kosher salami. Across the marsh, haunting drumroll of pileated secure in a fortress of pine. Pond: the illusion of invariability. Fools me . . . again.

Tufted titmouse whistles an abridged song, two loud notes, *peter*, *peter*. Less musical, more robust than a chickadee, who sings nearby. Birds seemingly in sync with Gregorian calendar. High in the west, croaking beneath the weight of barometric changes, raven lampoons a sunny morning and anything to do with calendars. He *feels* the pressure of what moves up the East Coast.

Two weeks ago, Linny's friend Ginger called. She wanted Becky and Casey's address. The baby was due in five weeks, and she had a gift to send them. When the sweater arrived, Becky called me, her voice breaking. The hooded-wool sweater, dark blue with intricate bands of reds, whites, and browns, had been more than two decades in the making. Linny began knitting in the late nineteen nineties, a gift for an expectant co-worker. She died before she finished. The woman moved away, storing the uncompleted sweater for twenty-three years. When she heard Casey and Becky were expecting, she shipped the sweater to Ginger, who traded homemade soup to a neighbor to finish the knitting.

Two chickadees whistle, high and sweet. We both know the bright light of the future lies beyond the nor'easter. Adrift in the vagaries of time, I embrace benevolence, the goodness of some people . . . as a long-forgotten circle completes itself; as a grandmother, lovingly and unknowingly, gifts her grandchild.

Day 322

02 February 2021

Groundhog Day

A person who is lucidly aware
of the miracles that surround him,
who has learned to bear up under the
loneliness, has made quite a bit of
progress on the road to wisdom.
M. C. ESCHER

7:04 A.M. (sunrise two minutes earlier than yesterday). 28 degrees, wind NW 7 mph. Sky: shallow and teeming with snowflakes. Eight inches on the ground, a cream-colored dreamland. Visibility is less than a mile. Hemlock branches sag like broken umbrellas. Stunningly quiet (much like the early days of the pandemic). Even the chickadees and jays have nothing to report. Intermittent streams: snow-filled clefts. Permanent streams: visibly and audibly insulated, neither a gurgle nor a splash. Wetlands: an encapsulation in white. Pond: above the east bank, in the path of the wind, red pines blown clean; above the west bank, hemlocks and firs laden with snow.

The first morning bird, a hairy woodpecker, tentatively works a pine limb with soft, well-spaced taps. Where are the crows? The jays? The chickadees? Raven and pileated iced and hidden.

No tracks anywhere but my own.

A lonely panorama, the Hollow embellished in white. By 8:30 A.M., birds arrive, rotating from trees to front-yard feeders. Jays, chickadees, titmice, and nuthatches feed in silence, disciplined by the weather. Jays land in cherry, displacing snow . . . a series of bumps and dents. By 9:45 A.M., birds are elsewhere, a fleeting jubilee. Leaving me to shovel alone.

༄

5:00 P.M. 23 degrees, wind N 10 mph. Sky: lanes of bland light. Wetlands: desolate and scoured, the illusion of remoteness. Trees beyond the wind hold snow.

Fourteen inches of heavy snow, a foot of insulated air space above the ground. Snowshoeing into the reeds, I high-step forward, sink like a mammoth in tar. Earlier in the afternoon, a mink had dimpled and laced the surface, tracks disappearing into self-made tunnels. German shepherds step on my snowshoes. I face-plant. When Jordan would skin up the west saddle of Robinson Hill, the dogs floundering on his skis, he would turn benevolently and shoo them off. The Zen master, his mother's forgiving smile washing across his face. But I am far less tolerant. I scold the dogs, which look at me, trimmed in snow, flakes on lashes, tongues dripping. The language of discipline is lost in translation. Across the marsh, a bumbling trio carves thoroughfares, one step at a time.

Day 325

05 February 2021

Statistics are like bikinis.
What they reveal is suggestive,
but what they conceal is vital.
AARON LEVENSTEIN

7:01 A.M. (sunrise one minute earlier than yesterday). 14 degrees, wind calm 0 mph. Sky: the nearly unlidded eye of dawn hosts five crows and a pastel festival of pink and peach in the south and east, yellow in the west. Overhead, the few blue-gray clouds fringed in rose with a dash of mauve. The color drains, and clouds congeal as I walk. Eventually, horizon to horizon, a heavy lid. Then, snow, an imposition of white. Permanent streams: upper, solar-corroded mink tracks reduced to dimples, direction ambiguous (he's either still in the marsh or has decamped along one of the streams on the western face of Robinson Hill; lower, gift-wrapped in ice and snow, an inarticulate flow. Wetlands: a sleepy white depression, lustrous and birdless. Across the marsh, conifer limbs sag, too stubborn to shed snow. Pond: a clone of yesterday—tracks of children skating, deer walking, me slipping.

To pass the time in the land of ditto, as an anodyne against boredom, I play with my digital thermometer, the one I used on basking rattlesnakes, and take a roster of external temperatures, a doctor in down. Since chickadees are too jazzed for a house call, I examine trees: black cherry, 13.8 degrees; white pine, 17 degrees; barkless white pine, 14.8 degrees; white ash, 16.8 degrees; sugar maple, 15.8 degrees. Then, I expand my informal survey: snow 14.3 degrees, fat dog 34 degrees, thin dog 41 degrees.

Data collection is interrupted by a nuthatch, a white-breasted outburst. I have a lifelong susceptibility to distraction, which is why I face the wall when I write. A moment later, the thermometer pocketed, solitary chickadee whistles slowly and quietly, laying tentative claim to the gnarled pines between the riding ring and road, an audition of sorts. No answer. I whistle much too loudly to be taken seriously by anything other than the dogs. Annoyed, the chickadee stops singing. Switches to *dee, dee, dee.* Dogs, however, enjoy my outburst and look expectantly for treats.

Boisterous and belligerent, blue jay perches on a pine limb. Bare legs in snow, uninsulated. No shivering, no shaking . . . no frostbite. Like my nana's steam radiator on the Upper West Side of Manhattan, the arteries and veins in a bird's legs (and wings) have *countercurrent circulation*. Warm arterial blood leaving the body transfers heat to cold venous blood returning from the legs. Veins and arteries in the upper legs split into smaller vessels and entwine (like so many hibernating snakes). Outgoing blood (arterial) cools. Incoming blood (venous) warms. A continuous transfer of heat all the way to the toes. When blood reenters the jay's body, it has regained 85 percent of the heat loss. Result: bird legs do not freeze.

We have a very rudimentary countercurrent circulation in our arms. Beavers, muskrats, and otters have countercurrent circulation in their tails, snowshoe hare in their ears, wolves in their legs, whales and porpoises in their fins and flukes. All of this meant nothing as I sat wallowing on my nana's radiator on the Upper West Side, eating fancy cookies and watching yellow cabs.

Jay flushes.

Chickadee resumes singing, and I, leaning into the scaffolding of Covid, turn toward an empty house.

Day 327

07 February 2021

Looking up at the stars, I know quite well
That, for all they care, I can go to hell, [. . .]

Were all the stars to disappear or die,
I should learn to look at an empty sky
And feel its total dark sublime
Though this might take me a little time.
W. H. AUDEN

6:58 A.M. (sunrise two minutes earlier than yesterday, twenty-two minutes earlier than the winter solstice). 7 degrees, wind NW 1 mph. Sky: morning muzzled by a flat, dull gray-blue blanket embezzled of color. Permanent streams: upper, openings widen, lengthen, multiply, a mellow gurgle, much louder than yesterday; lower, buried in winter, my feet sinking into a snowbank. I lean into a muffled percolation, my hands cupped to my ears as though amplifying the thin song of a blackburnian warbler, and listen . . . water under snow, delicate and cheerful. Waiting for a clue, dogs sit down. Wetlands: north end, pileated, an adjunct to an empty marsh, cuts loose in the evergreens, drumming reverberating across the reeds—three rounds and done, the mysterious workings of a woodpecker. Alder branches and catkins traced in frost. Pond: blades on ice, the tracks of peewee skaters. Twenty-two years ago, leaning on stacked milk crates, Jordan learned to skate here, gamboling on twin blades, a protégé of the north wind. Who knew I'd endure long winter car rides, cold rinks, and fermented hockey gear airing out by the wood stove until after he graduated college.

Absent for a week, the female pileated apparently abandoned the roadside maple (no fresh woodchips on snow). White-breasted nuthatches vigorously call. Not a peep from red-breasted nuthatches. A hairy woodpecker lays down the morning's meter and grooves on a dead cherry limb. Tentatively, from a nearby alder, chickadee whistles. Others join in. More than a dress rehearsal. Six jays gather driveway grit. No titmice or doves. Two turkeys scratch sunflower seeds under the feeder, a gift from a careless woodpecker.

High and headed east, a raven cruises the sky with fluid, measured strokes. Level flight. Reminds me that my rowing machine idles in the corner of the living room. Crow appears. Smooth flight, also level, but more frequent wingbeats than a raven. Barred owl floats over the road like an oversized, out-of-season moth.

Over the southwest corner of the marsh, a hot-air balloon on a frigid journey suspended above Robinson Hill like a thought bubble. Bald eagle heads southeast toward the Connecticut River, wings like planks, primary flight feathers fingering the breeze. Slowly, rhythmically, barely noticeable strokes . . . the subtlety of power. Oversized bill sunshine yellow. Head and tail immaculately white, body and wings darkest brown. A cream-and-coffee-colored bird.

Caffeinated by the passing eagle, my heart racing on an otherwise glum *Pout-Pout Fish* morning—my outlook pivots. Like Dylan's lyrics and music, no two sunrises ever look or feel quite the same . . . the conspiracy of daybreak.

Day 330

10 February 2021

The sunbeams are welcome now.
They seem like pure electricity—
like friendly and recuperating lightning.
JOHN BURROUGHS

6:54 A.M. (sunrise two minutes earlier than yesterday). 5 degrees, wind E less than 1 mph. Sky: an aerial and time-lapse imitation of plate tectonics, blue-gray cloud continents fracturing, merging, then vanishing into a sea of faint peach that brightens and drains by the moment. With three inches of fresh snow, the world gleams. Permanent streams: upper, closed again and quiet; lower, a silent, trackless, snow-filled cleft. Both are facsimiles of yesterday. Wetlands: as the Earth turns, sunlight spreads slowly down western evergreens and across the marsh, one reed at a time, a slow, luscious descent. From Robinson Hill's shoulder, behind the wall of honey-colored light, pileated issues a manifesto, two well-spaced volleys reverberating against a cold, sunny morning: *I am here. This is mine.* I wait, hoping for the woodpecker to emerge from the woods. No luck. For the moment, only sunlight and a pair of ravens advance above the marsh. Pond: plowed and later visited by a deer. Four ravens on a double date head east, obsidian feathers polished by winter sunlight.

On the southeast side of the marsh, beneath two balsam firs, twigs pepper the surface, each an inch or two long. Product of a red squirrel, snipped by four self-sharpening incisors. Squirrel eats terminal buds and discards twigs. Must have grown tired of a steady diet of pine nuts stored by the gallon in caches under the snow. Squirrel dines *al fresco* on a fir limb, warmed by unblemished sunshine on a still morning, a welcome break from subterranean lunches in dead-end snow tunnels.

Loosened by the sun, raven calling, hollow, bell tones . . . *rock, rock, rock,* the sweetest sound of the morning. Avian linguist. Raven speaks in tongues, uttering at least seventy-nine distinct calls, twenty of known meaning. Some learn calls from mates, others from same-sex neighbors up to ten miles away. So varied the raven's vocal range, the species' repertoire may be *limitless.* Dialects. Accents. Individually recognizable voices. Ravens mimic—other birds, barking dogs, slamming doors, and so forth. A bird with the gift of gab. Announces an absence of action rather than a course of action. *Here's what I won't do* rather than *Here's what I intend to do.*

Two ravens fly north, a nice pair, dwarfed by the sky, wing tip to wing tip, the tandem flight of commitment on the cusp of the mating season, four days before Valentine's Day. Territories are widely spaced. Nesting sites: vertical cliffs and towering trees, both uncommon. The solo bird may join a social club of other unmated birds and patiently wait for a bereaved adult seeking another partner.

Coyote tracks up and down the driveway. Dogs, noses buried in snow, the smell of last night thick and relevant. Along the snowmobile trail, Coyote went in and out of the oaks, the pines, and the maples. A straight, thoughtful path, one foot after another. Wild canid on a solo, searching for something. Dinner? Companionship? A way to irritate the dogs? A midsized, itinerant mammal on the doorstep of humanity, an echo of a long-forgotten Siberian camp, where a curious wolf, light dancing on thick fur, edged closer to a campfire . . . narrowing an interspecies gap. Checking the News of the World on fresh snow.

Chickadees, on standby, remain inconspicuous. Male white-breasted nuthatch, however, breaks loose . . . *wah, wah, wah, wah,* his mating song, over and over from a crown of aspen just above the stonewall. Reminds me of a whispering pileated. The crooner is not alone. Perched below the nuthatch, seven jays, captivated by the simplicity of warmth, face the sun, breasts bright as snow. Nuthatch sings. Jays sunbathe. And I head indoors, to the woodstove, hands of stone, fingers in a knot.

Day 331

11 *February 2021*

It was what I was born for—
to look, to listen,

to lose myself
inside this soft world—
to instruct myself
over and over

in joy,
and acclamation.
MARY OLIVER

6:53 A.M. (sunrise one minute earlier than yesterday). 3 degrees, wind calm 0 mph. Sky: disheveled, gray-pink in the west, nacreous luster in the east, primarily silver-white with a dash of peach; degrades to a windrow of clouds that drift northeast. Permanent streams: upper, ice begins to seal oblong rents; lower, water heard but not seen—like children at my parents' 1950s dinner parties. Wetlands: a landscape defined by birds, everything a visual stagnation. Hidden in the evergreens, pileated releases one salvo, tattooing a resonant limb or trunk. Red-breasted nuthatch vocally energetic, nonstop tooting. (Richie, my longtime birding buddy, reported that red-breasted nuthatches have already reached Florida, wandering up and down cypress and pop ash trunks, peeking at alligators cutting trails through duckweed, their heads flecked with living, green dots.) Overhead, an unaccompanied raven preceded by a croak. Pond: coyote and deer tracks walked around the plowed skating surface, likely not together.

Prospecting for birds, seeking signs of the canting Earth, a new spring arrival, perhaps redwing or cowbird. Or northbound redpolls or nuthatches. I'm not fussy. The quickening of spring. Yes, chickadees and nuthatches have begun to sing sporadically. Hairy and pileated woodpeckers have started to drum, also sporadically. Late yesterday morning, a titmouse cut loose, made a mockery of February . . . and spring became my phantom limb.

What do I have on my plate more critical than witnessing the world turn? I keep prospecting. Clumps of snow pass through a sieve of fir boughs, spilling columns of cold, white smoke striking the paper-thin leaves of beech, which rattle like so many snakes. And I turn to the sound and salute the day, in the company of amber sunlight.

Day 332

12 February 2021

Charles Darwin's birthday

*Science is not a heartless pursuit
of objective information; it is a
creative human activity.*
STEPHEN JAY GOULD

6:52 A.M. (sunrise one minute earlier than yesterday). -2 degrees, wind
NW 5 mph (a musk ox wind out of the Arctic, windchill -12). Sky:
clear and crisp, peach wash yellows slowly and then fades. The crown of
Mount Ascutney is sharp against the southwestern horizon. Permanent
streams: upper, freezing over . . . again; lower, wayfaring mink, after an
absence of a week, returns for an encore performance, off the eastern
rim of the Hollow and down the frozen lane, pale under a sliver moon.
An acolyte of night. Bounding, bounding, wide-open, explosive leaps of
faith across a landscape of hungry owls. In and out of snow tunnels that
lead to black, rushing water. Bitter plunges. Deluxe wetsuit, fur oiled,
thick and luxurious, midnight dark with a white chin. Returned to the
surface, again dripping. Wetlands: welcomed mink. Easy travel through
the marsh, on solid ground beneath an insulating pocket of air and a
foot of snow. Pond: mink left the wetlands, traced the pond's overflow
stream, in and out of the water, through the culvert, and up the bank.
Always spring-loaded bounds. Burrowed into a subnivean tunnel.
Resurfaced. Rushed across the skating rink like a hockey breakaway.
Back into a snow tunnel, pee stains in the foyer. Having been medicated
by boredom, dogs snap to attention, noses in the tunnel. Roof collapsing. Wild dog snorts. I sniff the snow, too . . . a trace of something musky.
Mink . . . maybe.

The stream is the mink's Route 66, a pathway into and out of the
marsh. Tunnels. Paired footprints. Round holes in the snow. Slid down
the bank of the lower stream, a short ride, body as toboggan. If you're
going to live your life alone, a solitary hunter across the frozen ground,
why *not* enjoy the journey? The male only seeks a mate for a short,
intense coupling.

Chickadees whistle in the alders, the pines, the maples, and around the house—plaintive songs, thin and well-spaced. Plumes of breath rise from their beaks like wisps of chimney smoke. White-breasted nuthatch, rapid-fire solo. Reminds me of a house wren, which, somewhere, inches northward. Jays on the wing bark, five of them in loose association. More gang than flock. Head to the feeders, vividly blue in the sunlight.

Crow, huskily cawing, flies north. A flock of red crossbills near the road shares white pine with a single white-winged crossbill. Both species rain calls, a clattering chorus of *gyps* and *tyks*, dry and unmusical. For a moment, crossbills hang on pine cones, tweezing out seeds. Then, decamp. Fly over the marsh and through the wall of evergreens, callings fading behind them. Male hairy woodpecker on a pole-sized, dead pine. An acoustical savant tests three drumming sites, two twice. Makes a selection, a barkless patch just above midtree. Hammers away, head a blur, a percussionist's clock set to spring. Broadcast accompanies me uphill.

Back home, an immature red-tailed hawk in a maple crown stares at the feeders. Chickadees and jays carry on, back and forth for seeds, barely acknowledging the hawk. Conspicuous by their absence, gray squirrels wait somewhere in the shadows. Hawk spots me and relocates, commands an aspen outpost along the edge of the woods. Poise recovered, a dignified brigand, breeze teasing leg feathers. I smile, cold forgotten.

∽

Happy birthday to Charles Darwin. He saw life's single strand woven into millions of distinct patterns, each with a personal history . . . a past, a present, an uncharted future. We may be the only species within the strand that harbors illusory long-term plans . . . flawed, selfish, and out of sync with most other life forms, an unrealized and unrealistic short-lived outlier.

Day 334

14 February 2021

Valentine's Day

*Our life is a faint tracing
on the surface of mystery.*
ANNIE DILLARD

6:49 A.M. (sunrise one minute earlier than yesterday). 19 degrees (a veritable heat wave); wind NW 1 mph. Grayish light, flat and untextured, an absence of warm color, a heavenly malaise unsuitable for Valentine's Day. Permanent streams: no new mink sign or openings or snow, an aching flow dampened by the weight of recent weather. Wetlands: sleepy marsh under a listless sky . . . then, suddenly, bald eagles appear, conjured out of the east. A pair high above the reeds, heading north, lovestruck. Courtship, airborne gymnasts above a lonely marsh. The female, the more significant of the two, rolls over. Flies upside down. Touches the male's talons, the ultimate high five (a high four in this case). And for me, for the moment, transitory bliss. Slow, rhythmic wingbeats, effortless flight, each wing slightly bent at the wrist—both birds cackle, chicken-voiced raptors. Pond: black puck on clear ice in front of red goal.

On the road back home, red crossbills in the pines, their chatter slightly softer than the eagles'. Even though it's twenty-four degrees warmer than yesterday morning, chickadees refrain from singing. Perhaps stymied by cloud cover. Pileated laughs, the insanity of a woodpecker, then nothing—no drumming either by pileated or hairy. February sunshine: lodestone that triggers good thoughts and bird music.

∾

2020, *Year of the Pandemic*: thirty-seven pairs of bald eagles nested in Vermont and fledged sixty-four chicks. A modern-day record. Extirpated as a breeder in the 1940s, eagles returned in 2008. Hopefully here to stay. It's a rare trip down I-91 when I don't see one.

∾

18 February 2017: Addison, Vermont, Route 17, east of the Crown Point Bridge. Birding at fifty miles per hour. A pair of bald eagles and an aerial courtship made driving difficult (if not dangerous). Talons touching, the female upside down. Consummating the romance, eagles landed in the crown of a dead pine. I abruptly pulled over. The male mounted the

female, tails to the side, avian procreation over—an afternoon quickie in the blink of an eye. Birds aloft again. Courting a repeat performance. No time for a cigarette or a glass of water. No sandwich. No nap. No anything. The male dove, wings up, primary splayed like fingers. Talons clenched. Over the female rolled, eyes on the sky. And the eagles flew, brown wings in sync, white tail feathers opening and closing.

⌘

Bald eagles have four sightlines—the *foveae*, a pair of small pits in each retina, points of extreme visual detail, each aimed in a different direction. We have one fovea per eye. Eighty percent of an eagle's fovea is packed with light-sensing rods and color-sensing cones, compared to only 5 percent of ours. Gorging on detail, a bald eagle sees a landscape intensely colored and vividly detailed, four different areas at all times. A world impossible for us to imagine.

I watch the eagles disappear beyond the pines, the wind dissolving their discordant titters . . . a lackluster morning suddenly blooms with possibility.

Day 335

15 February 2021

But my imagination has slipped its berth,
and I can visualize the invisible. And
sense just enough to carry on amid the big mystery,
one marvel after another.
ROBERT MACFARLANE

6:47 A.M. (sunrise two minutes earlier than yesterday). 18 degrees, snow en route, storm due to arrive tonight. Sky: rumpled and glowing with a dash of pink in the east, pastel purple-gray brushed across the south, brightening and dispersing by the moment. A subtle, transitory cloudscape ambushed by the sun. Permanent streams: the joy of recognizing worn-out mink tracks, eroding by the day. Slides, cavities, stream mud on snow, and paired prints edited by the sun. Still legible, still reeking of boundless energy, an *old* manuscript that passed the test of time . . . in this case, a few days. Wetlands: hot-air balloon, a fiery belch behind the evergreens, in and out of view, an inflatable patchwork quilt drifting south. Pileated in the pines, three reverberating riffs. In between, a minute of silence. Then, the patented, maniacal laughter. One run and done. Silence again, except for the balloon. Fir twigs on snow, courtesy of bud-eating red squirrel, an aromatic lunch, a Christmas-scented meal. Pond: ancient deer tracks in the rink; ephemeral fossils flush to the skating surface; smooth, discolored shadows, each wreathed in cream-colored ice, the detritus of an old snowstorm.

Between the marsh and pond, an ermine in the alders. A bundle of energy investigating everything. Short slides. Long bounds. Angel of darkness for a bog lemming. Linguini for an owl.

Red crossbills have been roving in Coyote Hollow pines since mid-October. They've already been here longer than summer's warblers and vireos. But those birds come to breed every year, and I may not see crossbills again for a decade.

Morning music. A hairy woodpecker drums an oak limb, warp speed, Max Roach in a tree. More persistent than the pileated. Over and over. Rapid fire. Barely a pause. Immune to headaches. Six gray squirrels chatter at the feeder. Where's the red-tailed hawk? Above the barn, chickadee whistles in the crown of an oak. Head back, bill skyward. Titmouse whistles a truncated song. Blissfully at ease, I listen for a long while, swaddled in bird gossip, a quintessential joy before the storm.

Day 336

16 February 2021

But you, epicurean raven, may you
be the pole star of the apocalypse,
you stubborn snow trudger,
[. . .] as we reel
headlong into the dwindling unknown.
DORIANNE LAUX

6:46 A.M. (sunrise one minute earlier than yesterday). 18 degrees, wind
N 3 mph. Sky: bruised and busy, visibility reduced, the Hollow hemmed
in, rim to rim. Pixilated precipitation—looks like snow, feels like sleet,
sounds like rain. Tiny frozen balls, more pellet than flake, spraying and
bouncing, oblong waves that rise with each step along the edges of my
boots, then crash like the foamy Atlantic. Snow-peppered beech leaves,
dried to a crisp and thin as thought, sound like so many rain sticks.
Permanent streams: upper, mink headed uphill, cut a hole into crusty
snow, plunged into the dark water, exited a stylish gap in the ice, specks
of stream bottom on snow like pepper on egg whites; lower, bobcat wandered off the eastern flank, walked downstream, *very* faint tracks—four
oblong toe pads, no claw marks, three-lobed heel pad like the interlocked
logo of Ballantine Beer—sinking here and there, well-defined prints
at the bottom of each frozen tube, cross the road. Wetlands: bobcat
entered the alders and cattails and headed southwest across the marsh,
a solitary traveler passing through on the morning side of midnight. Cat
tracks incite dogs, faces stuffed in the snow. Pond: I walk the skating
rink, a plowed figure eight, challenged not to fall. No sign of anything
other than sleek-packed snow, slippery as seaweed.

Dislodged by sleet, spots and streaks of yellow birch seeds decorate
the snow—dark cosmetic on Earth's pale face. Grounded seeds move
when hit by ice pellets, the subtlest of jumps. I stare at the business and
busyness of birch seeds, anxious for the arrival of my first grandchild,
due next month. I want to share the alchemy of flinching seeds in the
shape of turkey feet, to see the world through baby eyes, that unfathomable world of first-time experience . . . very like a miracle.

Surprise under wraps. Birds are hushed and hidden; even chickadees keep to themselves. Suddenly, cheerfully, raven in pine trolls for

company . . . a husky squawk. Perches close to the trunk, shielded from the weather by warp and weave of limbs. A second raven answers. Makes an appointment and flies into the pine. Duets and Talmudic discussions, then abruptly, the second raven leaves, off into the residue of the storm—a dark bird in a hurry on a nasty morning.

Day 338

18 February 2021

Choose joy. Choose it like a child chooses
the shoe to put on the right foot, the crayon
to paint a sky. Choose it at first consciously,
effortfully, pressing against the weight of a world
heavy with reasons for sorrow, restless with need for action.
MARIA POPOVA

6:43 A.M. (sunrise one minute earlier than yesterday). 10 degrees, wind NNW 1 mph. Sky: a featureless gray, edge to edge . . . the word *blah* comes to mind. Permanent streams: synchronously slick and brittle like walking on rigid plastic, flow inaudible. Trackless, mink and bobcat elsewhere. Wetlands: snow dusts the porcelain marsh, deer tracks through the reeds, puncture wounds in crisp, glossy snow. Their weight spread out, coyotes walked on top of the snow, footpad surfers, in and out of the basin. A measured progression. But the dogs and I, hopeless and helpless, slip, slide, flounder, rupture the surface, plunge holes in our wake. Pond: a very ginger stroll on ice, like when I moved the nets to the boards ahead of the Zamboni between periods of Jordan's hockey games.

Above the Hollow: one crow; two hot-air balloons; and droves of garrulous jays, all feeder bound. Pileated drums in the evergreens, a woodland manifesto, six resounding volleys separated by pauses of twenty-five to thirty-three seconds. Then, a stereophonic tunnel of hairy woodpeckers, drumbeats calibrating day length. The sound of resonant limbs accompanies me uphill. Several woodpeckers feed: discordant, arrhythmic clicks like the sounds in my high school typing class . . . hunting and pecking. Tap, tap, tap.

Crows are loud and disagreeable. Two red crossbills fly between pines, calling. No shortage of pines. No lack of cones . . . a feeding station provisioned by the Hollow and the cyclical nature of white pines. Dove asleep in maple, hunched up, looks neckless. In the oratorical world of jays, never a dull moment. Everyone calls at once, a mosh pit of sound. Chickadee flock mills around the front yard, five calling, two singing. Then, a titmouse, *peter-peter*. An unintended interspecies duet.

Black-capped chickadees and tufted titmice are *nuclear* species, forming winter flocks that attract other species: kinglets, nuthatches, and warblers (if any are around). Maybe a creeper or a downy woodpecker. Chickadees and titmice mob perched hawks and owls; their agitated voices almost always attract company, including wayfaring naturalists tuned to trouble.

From the far side of the barn, a second titmouse whistles, a truncated version of spring song. Two *pe-ters* and done. Lone chickadee in maple whistles, almost a whisper. No oomph. No urgency. I pause, listening and watching the morning's slow-motion bloom, a curator marking seasonal transitions like an autumn spark on an August leaf. Of course, being human, I'm hobbled by limited awareness. I cannot see ultraviolet or infrared (or any color beyond the visible spectrum). I cannot hear the ultrasonic conversations of bats and moths or the deepest notes of whales and elephants. Nor the infrasonic mumbles of Earth herself. Changes in barometric pressure. I miss the depth and nuance of what *every* bird and insect has to say. But my imagination does slip its berth, and I visualize the invisible, sensing just enough to carry on amid the big mystery, one marvel after another.

Day 342

22 February 2021

*I have come to believe birds are
the most vivid expression of life. It made me
aware of the world in which we live.*
Roger Tory Peterson

6:37 A.M. (sunrise one minute earlier than yesterday). 10 degrees (a National Weather Service cellphone alert, but it feels colder), wind calm 0 mph. Sky: cloud clogged, blue gray, and spitting snow—tiny flakes, eye-rubbing microstatic, TV static . . . but no television to pound or rabbit-ear antennae to adjust. Permanent streams: upper, mink wandered out of the woods, down the bank, and through the culvert, on assignment in the marsh. Dutifully followed the brook, a line of paired tracks; lower, a silent stagnation, dog-day bland, mum as marmalade. Bobcat crossed the drainage and followed the snowmobile trail north. Wetlands: almost monochromatic, drainage seam snaking through the marsh, a long, white fissure, where the mink patrols under the gibbous moon. Across the marsh, evergreens are dark and dull. Pond: preparing to skate, someone began shoveling the deep, crusted, dense, cement-heavy snow. Then went home.

Tracks in the woods: fisher, first of the winter; shrew troughs; mouse stitching; weasel bounding. A personal and personable advertisement in the snow: fox (red, I think) seeks companionship. A love jaunt. Wanders the road, the woods, the snowmobile trail, the path between the upper and lower pasture, the front yard, and the driveway. An oblique loop, another of life's urgencies.

Morning's tempo sets the pace for the day. From the far corner of the marsh, pileated tattoos dead pine, discloses intentions, a blur of audible activity, approximately fifteen beats per second (much too quick to separate without sophisticated recording equipment), lasting nearly three seconds. Behind me, provoked, a second pileated drums, shorter roll, not as resonant. Perhaps the female. Background vocals from the hemlocks above the southern corner of the marsh, where roving jays honk and scream, a strident *jaaay, jaaay*. Raven flies west, paired croaks, a ten-second pause, and then two croaks again. A formulaic greeting repeated a dozen times as the bird and its voice fade west.

Two hairy woodpeckers, also in tune with late February, work dead limbs. A landscape pulsation. Cadence—raps per second—up to twenty-six, the pause between each beat infinitesimally short. Too short to separate audibly . . . I almost feel the air vibrate—a woodland tuning fork. Drums when the spirit moves, any time of year. Both sexes drum: to define and defend territory (healthier than fighting), often along the borders; as part of courtship and bonding; to solicit sex; for platonic companionship (a helpful technique if Covid keeps me housebound for five more minutes); to communicate over a distance; and . . . for no apparent reason.

The morning unfurls, one note at a time. Chickadee whistles. The sacrosanctity of tuning in. The dogs understand and politely sit at my feet.

Day 344

24 February 2021

I am a man in love with nature. I am
an eco-addict, consuming everything
the outdoors offers in its all-you-can-
sense seasonal buffet.
J. DREW LANHAM

6:33 A.M. (sunrise two minutes earlier than yesterday, fifty-three minutes earlier than the winter solstice). Thirty degrees (warmest dawn since January 16), wind W 3 mph. Sky: bright, clear, and peach infused in the south, gridlocked elsewhere . . . then, twenty minutes later, clouds reassemble into a white, silver-lined flotilla, an eastward drift. Quarter-inch of fresh, wet snow (on top of yesterday's three inches of powder) sticks to everything, even wafer-thin beech leaves, trembling like nervous frosted flakes. Permanent streams: upper, below the snowmobile bridge, three oval openings lengthen and widen; lower, in limbo, a trackless, silent cleft. Wetlands: above the marsh, the sun highlights the leading edge of clouds. Bongo riff of pileated, drumming in the shadows, reverberating the daily dose of courtship across the reeds. Pond: blade marks of an ambitious skater on a brief, friction-filled run.

One crow, a thousand feet above the lower pasture, morning's black gesture flies northwest, aided by the wind's unintentional philanthropy. Others caw from distant points. Chickadees whistle, but not whole-heartedly—softer, disinclined to be repetitive. White-breasted nut-hatches in full voice, short, nasal, single pitch. Does for the pileated what the blue jay does for the red-shouldered hawk—sends a sober version of the woodpecker's louder, more clarion call.

～

I live in the eastern saddle of Robinson Hill. Standing in the lower pasture, I face northwest to the sunbright ledges of the Hill. To the south-southwest, I'm in the sightline of Gile Mountain and the observation tower, a seventy-five-foot edifice capped by a plywood platform, paneled on all sides. The tower rises above the treetops. Perched in the tower on a clear day, I can see sunlight on the metal roof of my house and barn, seven miles away . . . as the redtail flies. To reach the summit, I have to walk half a mile along a woodland trail, under power lines, and up a steep, winding path. The tower tapers, Erector-Set construction with switchback stairs that converge on the platform, whose access is gained through a flimsy trap door. Beside my house, I can see Mount Washington in the northeast, barely visible beyond the summit of Moosilauke. To the southeast, the summits of Mounts Sunapee, Cardigan, and Monadnock. To the south, Mount Ascutney looms large over the Connecticut River Valley. Farther to the southwest, there's Stratton, Killington, and Pico. To the west: Camel's Hump, Hunger Mountain, and Mount Mansfield. And, beyond them, the purple haze of the Adirondacks.

Much closer to the observation tower and directly west, sunlight glances off the South Strafford church steeple; to the south, off a curve of the Connecticut River; and across the river, off Dartmouth's Baker Library bell tower, where Linny and I once watched courting night-hawks. Beyond that, the college's power plant chimney—cumulus plumes spewing—the ultramodern Dartmouth-Hitchcock Medical Center and the entire eastward slant of New Hampshire. Back in the direction of Coyote Hollow, hidden from view, on the flats adjacent to Lake Fairlee, the Post Mills Airport launches colorful hot-air balloons and gliders, which float above the hills like oversized butterflies and hawks, patrons of the wind.

But I climb the tower for immediate panoramas: scudding clouds;

monarch butterflies; warblers and vireos and flycatchers picking their way south, canopy to canopy, caterpillar by caterpillar; blue jays; loons; ravens. Every September, broad-winged hawks ascend from the green woods and mill in the sky, held aloft by columns of hot air that rise off ledges and paved roads. Clouds of hawks circling above the rolling hills. One windless, early September day in 1979, Linny and I counted more than seven hundred broadwings above Gile Mountain. So many hawks passed directly overhead that to count them we lay down on the platform and looked straight up, the hawks spiraling higher and higher or plunging south to the next rising bubble of warm air.

The tower floor is plywood, the sides thigh-high sheet metal. Many years ago, red calligraphy on one panel said *Grateful Dead*, later amended to *Gratefully Dedicated to Earth*. Sunshine bleached both editions. Someone added a few bullet holes.

This morning, standing in the lower pasture, facing Gile Mountain, my home at my back, dogs at my side, I yield to the Paleolithic impulse of memories. The rickety tower helps.

༄

For fifty years, I thought titmice whistled two-syllable *pe-ter, pe-ter*. Today they sound more like cheering in the House of Commons . . . *hear, hear, hear*. In the 1950s and '60s, titmice were not expected along the South Shore of Long Island. With its big estates and towering trees, the North Shore supported titmice, which visited feeders or foraged amid the rubble of maritime woods. As a breeding species, titmice reached Massachusetts in the late 1940s; New Hampshire in 1973; and Vermont in 1976, when I was a graduate student and sanctuary naturalist, living unfettered by the laws of fashion, custom, and logic.

During my lifetime, titmice expanded their range more than three hundred miles north. In the past forty years, they've reached virtually everywhere in Vermont except the northeast corner of the Northeast Kingdom. Never residents of Nantucket, Martha's Vineyard, or Block Island. Apparently, tufted titmice are landlubbers.

Why such success? Titmice benefit from a warming climate, maturing suburban hardwoods, the regrowth of abandoned farmland, and the exponential increase in bird-feeding stations. On Earth, empty spaces soon fill up, continents drift, rivers change course, mountains erode, oceans rise and fall, and species come and go, moving through time and space. Because birds fly and are beautiful, I am thrilled by the magic of their movement, these *ambassadors* of a dynamic planet.

Day 347

27 February 2021

They dined on mince, and slices of quince,
Which they ate with a runcible spoon;
And hand in hand,
on the edge of the sand,
They danced by the light of the moon.
EDWARD LEAR

6:29 A.M. (sunrise one minute earlier than yesterday). 21 degrees, wind WNW 2 mph. Sky: clear at 4:30 A.M., the platinum moon in the west eases through the pines, an atmospheric lightbulb illuminating the gloom. By 6:00 A.M., the sky is gray and snow riddled. Companion of the shadow world, barred owl hollers, embodies the creep of light. Permanent streams: upper, almost open, hosted mink, in and out of dark water, paired prints in slush; lower, shuttered, still. Wetlands: snowflakes from a low ceiling, endless white streaks against dismal green. Holes in clouds emit beams of sunlight; long, dim fingers stroke the marsh. Pileated, sharpened at both ends, flies across the marsh. Chickadee calls in the alders. Pond: cleared ice bumpy from repetitive melting and freezing, not fit for strolling.

Raven, slicing through relentless snow, in and out of sunlight, heads northeast, croaking. White-breasted nuthatches sing, red-breasteds call. Chickadees chase each other, no time for a song. Cohorts in motion, jays become morning background, a real pace change. After a month of disassembling other trees, female pileated visited roadside maple yesterday, fresh wood chips on snow.

Crows engage in raucous discussions. Loud, attention-getting, agitated screams. The Hollow takes notice. Crows above the east side of the pond. One on a pine limb, two on the snow, wings akimbo. All three vocally engaged. Birds on snow in motion, black bobbleheads. There's no sign of food, but activity is nevertheless primordial as breakfast. Two crows on bedsheets of snow, mating.

Crow on limb makes a pest of himself. All three leave. Then, all three return shortly. Two on snow and one in pine, chiding, watching. On the snow, one crow mounts the other, tail to the side. Both scramble, slide, and scream, wings like fans, steadily sweeping. I have no clue if the same birds assumed the same roles—could be a *ménage a trois* ... the result of an unwelcome proxy. Once the birds are through, I examine the calligraphy of mating. Footprints. Feather prints. Beak prints. A late February tryst.

༄

In November 1977, I moved to Vermont after two years in southwestern New Hampshire and nine years split between Indiana, California, Texas, Tennessee, and New Jersey; and boyhood on the South Shore of Long Island, a bike ride from Jones Beach, where clouds of migratory shorebirds gathered on mudflats and every winter owls pitched into twisted pines, last perch before the ocean. I had the winter beach to myself. Sand dunes gave me a link to an imagined landscape far beyond the edge of my reality. One February night on Fire Island, I lay awake in a swale, snug in a mummy bag, lulled by the ocean; the moon and its owls passed overhead ... saw-whets and short-eareds, long, soft wings stroking damp air, headed west down the beach, rocking in flight like oversized moths.

I could not afford to live at Oak Beach, Gilgo, or Point O' Woods, so I moved north to pursue a dream. To find a compatible partner, to make a home, to raise a family, to work for myself, by myself. I wrote and photographed, taught and led tours. I became part of a rural, land-connected community. Coming to east-central Vermont ... unquestionably, one of the two best decisions I ever made. Now, convulsing in the throes of Covid, nearly a year in the company of my dogs, I am humbled but still thankful.

༄

Last night the moon erased the stars. What upright primate has not considered the moon? Moors, Sioux, nomadic herdsmen, all-night truckers. Everyone admires a full moon, bright and round. With that in mind, alone in the front yard, puppet to a virus, I waded into puddled moonlight, heard an owl, and traveled to the edge of childhood. I returned to the beach on Fire Island, swaddled in moonlight, the ocean's phosphorescence pooling around my feet, and those soft, silent wings brushing night. Growing up, my parents had shielded me from death—funerals were not part of my education—but introduced me to the night sky, dimmer over the suburbs than above the beach. Who can dismiss the planet's faithful companion, its gravitational hostage? Together, Earth and moon forged the symbiosis that has shaped and continues to shape life. Time may seem variable, quickening, or dragging on. However, the full moon crosses the night sky every twenty-eight days, the same moon that stirred trilobites and still stirs clams and bloodworms, that guided the Polynesians across an uncharted ocean. A dependable thread from the dawn of time. Under the arcing moon, I sense my place in the family of things; that's the moon's domain, its sanctity . . . navigational aid for art as well as migration. Lunar philanthropy gives me hope.

Day 350

02 March 2021

Walking makes the world
much bigger and thus more interesting.
You have time to observe details.
Edward Abbey

6:23 A.M. (sunrise two minutes earlier than yesterday). 3 degrees (thirty-three degrees colder than yesterday), wind WNW 17 mph (last night: two inches of powdery snow, gusts to 40 mph). Talking to Nancy on the phone last night, I heard the wind roar outside her living room window). Forest scraps litter the snow: needles, twigs, branches, strips of birch bark. Fragile saplings snapped in half. A parade of beech leaves down the road. Sky: bright gray with a hint of lavender. Visibility limited by haze. Permanent streams: upper, small ice shelves over dark water, a primarily open descent; lower, caught in a seasonal limbo, soundproof flow. Wetlands: snow devils curling and swirling across the marsh, pale, dwarf twisters, confidants of the barrens. On the far shore, towering pines and hemlocks were swept clean; shorter trees glazed. Pond: a week of repetitive thawing and freezing leaves the surface textured, a disconcerting stroll like walking on iced bubble wrap.

Except for the bluster of the wind, the day has an altogether quiet beginning. One red-breasted nuthatch toots from thin aspen, high above the stone wall. Chickadee sings in hemlocks, his voice hijacked by the wind—a morsel of sound needing an amplifier. Whistling oomph of a titmouse alone in an apple tree, then hushed. Jays stick to the oaks, kibitz about the wind and rollout vaccines. Four crows cautiously fly into the wind, buffeted and vulnerable—more flight simulation than northbound advancement. Avian isometrics.

A red squirrel in a hurry runs under its curlicue tail, carried like an umbrella. Parliament reconvenes in the black walnut, titmice singing... *hear, hear, hear, hear.* (I give up on *peter, peter, peter.*)

⌒

On mornings like this one, when I returned home from graduate school, reuniting with my childhood bedroom and an overstocked refrigerator, I would head to the West End of Jones Beach, hard against the bay, the inlet, and the angry, white-capped ocean. The air was wet and cold, made colder by the wind. Foam balls rolled down the beach like tumbleweeds and sand blew over the ground like smoke. The crests of waves ripped off breakers and the jetty was slick with spray and algae. Purple sandpipers snipped snails off jetty rocks. Sanderlings patrolled the wet sand; snow buntings, Lapland longspurs, and horned larks kept watch over the dunes and swales. High above the turbulence, gannets plunged for fish like Acapulco cliff divers. Some days, there'd be a snowy owl floating over dunes on long, cambered wings or perched in the open, white as snow. I'd photograph the activity, pressing the shutter with a rosy knuckle, my fingers unresponsive. By midmorning, I'd be standing on the dance floor of the Oak Beach Inn, hands clutched to a cup of clam chowder (Manhattan, of course), absorbing heat directly into stiff fingers. I wasn't sure what I'd do with my life then, so I went to the beach to be soothed.

⌒

Back home in my office, staring at the monitor, hands cupping a mug of coffee . . . I consider the next phase. Where do I turn in a world gone sour? A year into the pandemic, with no end in sight. The evening Linny died, I thought of all the places we'd never go, all the joy we'd never know, the grandchildren she'd never meet. Two decades later, in a house packed with memories, I consider an uncertain future . . . masking in public, the aftermath of insurrection on the Capitol steps, lonely eyebrows over an empty nest.

Outside, the chickadee sings for us both.

Day 352

04 March 2021

. . . the lifespan of a particular
plant or animal appears, not as a drama
complete in itself, but only as a brief
interlude in a panorama of endless change.
ROBINSON JEFFERS

6:20 A.M. (sunrise two minutes earlier than yesterday). 24 degrees, wind NW 6 mph. Sky: unlidded half-moon, bright as polished silver, slightly west of center, alone in blue simplicity. A short wall of lavender-gray clouds hugs the horizon, east to west, on the move, disassociating and enlivening. An atmospheric chameleon, lavender becomes pink, and gray becomes white. Permanent stream: otter followed the lower stream out of the marsh, under the road, and up the valley's eastern wall. Paired prints, much bigger than mink's, show webbing. Long, muscular steerage tail followed feet uphill, cut into snow like dragging a stick. With little to fear of the night, the otter completed an unhurried, unharried ascent. Wetlands: broken clouds sail east, still suggesting pink. The serpentine drainage path of the marsh visibly dents the snow, like the tail drag of Gargantua the Otter. From inside the far shore, pileated drums, light's tempo. Cry of a companionless jay. Pond: coyote and fox tracks.

Full of surprise, a bleak marsh comes to life . . . suddenly. While the dogs sit on the edge of the road, preoccupied with treats, bobcat walks through the alders thirty feet away. Silent feet. Coat of twilight, face like a soiled, fraying softball. Sideburns flare, ears straight up. Searchlight eyes, mustard-colored and slashed by vertical pupils—the original cat's eye marbles. A solitary wildcat keeps his own company. Never looks up. Unintentionally, the bobcat turns the day joyous. I whisper *bobcat*. Not wanting to fracture the moment, I never lift my binoculars; I just watch and breathe. Bobcat walks smoothly and effortlessly through the alders into the cattails and across the narrow south end of the marsh. Never looks back, vanishing in the reeds like a hallucination. I'm ghosted. Drumming pileated jars me out of feline delirium.

Jays gossip. Crows converse. Titmice and chickadees whistle. Hairy woodpeckers drum. And me . . . still lost in a bobcat moment, the morning's embellishment.

Bobcat

Yesterday, I backtracked the otter down the lower stream into the marsh. Otter bounded, slid on toboggan belly, went for a swim, reemerged through the snow, mud on the rim of hole. Into snow tunnels. A toilet filled with scraps of crayfish, claws and carapace.

Nearly twelve months at home, in the company of goshawks, otters, mink, bobcat, solitary sandpipers, crossbills, Connecticut warbler, great horned owl, hatchling milk snake, snapping turtle as big as a sink, courting bald eagles, mating crows. And all day, every day, the delicate companionship of chickadees . . . the fortunate upside during an unfortunate downturn.

Day 353

05 March 2021

The journey is difficult, immense.
We will travel as far as we can, but we cannot
in one lifetime see all that we would like to see or
to learn all that we hunger to know.
LOREN EISELEY

6:18 A.M. (sunrise two minutes earlier than yesterday). 14 degrees, wind WNW 10 mph. Sky: mottled blue and white, half-moon bright behind a screen of gauzy clouds. Permanent streams: upper, thin shelves of ice grow out from the shoreline; lower, visiting weasel followed the streambed off the hill and under the road, then veered into the woods on an endless quest for mice. Old otter tracks, the repository of woodland scraps—primarily bits of bark and pine needles—swept off the snow by last night's wind. Wetlands: Across the marsh, pileated drums in the pines. Pond: pair of coyotes track the surface, two parallel lines, foot by foot, almost single file. Prints dwarf those of fox but are much smaller than my German shepherds', which are humongous, palm sized, and would be mistaken for those of dire wolves if I lived in the Pleistocene.

No bobcat today, just a memory; a mammal of the periphery, an edge walker. I superimpose the bobcat onto every stand of alder, onto the shadows of drooping hemlock boughs, onto the cluster of cattails. In my mind, I place her everywhere but in the white expanse of winter-bent reeds, the realm of wandering black bear or the homebound otter, swollen with pups.

Two eastbound crows locked in conversation a hundred yards apart, hurling voices against the icy wind. Seven chickadees chase each other. Who's in charge? Direction changes repeatedly. Two land on a fir limb. One fluffs out, and the other squeezes feathers tight, letting out insulating air—a submissive posture called *sleek*. Fluffy initiates the chase again. Both chickadees join the other five; now, everyone's chasing.

I read an article this morning that a friend sent me from the *Dartmouth News* about a wooly mammoth rib unearthed in Mount Holly, Vermont, in 1848, during the building of the Burlington and Rutland railroad line. The rib was recently radiocarbon dated at 12,800 years old. A year later, in 1849 a beluga whale fossil surfaced during railroad construction. Very likely, New England's earliest humans knew the wooly mammoth, a supposition until now. Coyote Hollow, my own home ground, was once undulating, rock-studded tundra, and west of the Green Mountains, Lake Champlain was a vast inland sea bridged to the North Atlantic by a tidal Saint Lawrence River.

Imagine an Asian elephant with long, wiry brown fur, conical domes for heads, and curved tusks like snowplows. If you can, you've imagined a wooly mammoth, one of two proboscideans that roamed the Connecticut River Valley after the Ice Age. Mammoths were grazers (like cows). Mastodons were browsers (like deer). The last wooly mammoth died five thousand years ago, on Wrangle Island, in the Bering Sea—a millennium *after* horses and chickens had been domesticated; eight hundred years after Abraham spared Isaac.

What else might have lived in Coyote Hollow? Golden plover? Perhaps. Snow buntings, Lapland longspurs, hoary redpolls, gyrfalcons, and snowy owls, perched on grassy eskers, yellow eyes on barren lands? Twelve thousand years ago, lynx were moving back into New England from glacial refuges farther south. Caribou and wolverines were already in the hills, harbor and gray seals in Lake Champlain. And likely, musk ox grazed the tundra, and Arctic fox followed polar bears over Lake Champlain pack ice. Vermont may have supported Arctic hare, willow and rock ptarmigan, Eskimo curlew . . . who knows? It's fun to speculate.

But of this I'm sure: change, a difficult concept for people, is the only constant Earth has ever known.

Day 354

06 March 2021

The trick is, I find, to tone your wants and tastes
low down enough, and make much of negatives
and of mere light and the skies.
WALT WHITMAN

6:17 A.M. (sunrise one minute earlier than yesterday). 9 degrees, wind WNW 2 mph. Sky: Mount Ascutney juts into a thin façade of pink, engineer-straight from east to west, a fleeting gift from a shy sun. Elsewhere, blue jay colors, mostly shallow white isles in an expansive sea of blue; clouds screen a lean moon, withering and dissolving like night . . . a Polaroid in reverse. Permanent streams: upper, worn otter tracks, fresh weasel tracks, ice withdraws, releasing water music; lower, transformed into a squirrel crossing, footpaths perpendicular to flow. Less water, less freight. Wetlands: long, white-rimmed clouds hanging above a seemingly idle marsh. Curtains of sunlight descend the west-bank evergreens and out across pitted snow. Pileated drums and then laughs; falls eerily silent. Red-breasted nuthatches pick up pileated slack, morning chorus from both sides of the road and across the barren reeds. Pond: laced with fresh coyote tracks, surface firm but squeaky.

Two chickadees, a war of whistles from the invisible edge of a demilitarized zone. One starts, and the other finishes. Barely a pause. Two-note song, an intraspecies catnip. All disputes should be resolved with music. Mine would be straight out of the sixties . . . mostly Dylan, the Byrds, the Beatles, the Loving Spoonful. Joan Baez is a close second to chickadee as my favorite spring soloist.

White-breasted nuthatches sing, a nasal whistle, six to ten soft notes, same pitch, unvaried volume, like a muffled pileated without the derision, the carry, or the entitlement. Ornithologists recognize eleven subspecies of white-breasted nuthatch from the mountains of south-central Mexico north, wherever hardwoods dominate—northeast, southeast, mountain West, up both coasts, and around the Great Lakes to the fringe of the boreal forest. Generally, the farther north and the higher the elevation, the longer the wings. In the East, wing and bill length increase from south to north. But the darkness on the female crown increases southward until virtually black in the tropical hammocks of the Everglades, where nuthatches wander up and down trunks of mahogany and gumbo limbo. Backs are palest in the East, darkest in the Midwest, and medium in the West. Bills are stouter and blunter in the East, tapered and daggerlike in the Midwest and West.

White-breasted nuthatch weighs three-quarters of an ounce, less than a #2 pencil. Subspecies' contact calls vary east to west and north to south, but the song is everywhere similar, just like what I hear now . . . *what, what, what, what, what, what.* A dooryard melody, much closer to home than the pileated, who perches alone on the west side of the marsh, dismantling trees, laughing in the face of sunrise. Recent taxonomy places nuthatches closer to creepers, wrens, and gnatcatchers . . . but farther from chickadees, with whom they associate in winter flocks. Overwhelmed all winter by an irruption of red-breasted nuthatches, white-breasted nuthatches come into their own in early March, singing before the sun and under the crescent moon's horns. Over time, and perhaps with another geographically isolating Ice Age, a few races of white-breasted nuthatches may evolve into new species.

∽

Forty-eight hours out, I still think about the bobcat, locked in my mind's eye, padding across the snow, passing through the alders, a gray ghost on long legs. A noiseless, solitary sojourn. Cat *not* meant to be seen—a shadow hunter, restraint bordering on austerity. Wait, wait, wait, and pounce. Dogs don't share my enthusiasm . . . they sit at the viewing sight, biscuits on their brains, while I wait for the bobcat. Thursday, when the cat jarred the bleakness of early March, time froze substantially, like the marsh itself. My breath crept; my heart raced. I had waited nearly half a century to see a Vermont bobcat. Sadly, twenty years too late to tell Linny, so I told our boys. Very soon, Casey, son on the edge of fatherhood, will understand the joy of storytelling, the pleasure of showing and sharing, and the wonder of seeing the world through virgin eyes. The landscape of learning. Bobcat flipped my switch and turned my eyes youthful. Opened me to thought-free observation and, for a magical moment, infused me with the miraculous, realigning me to the pace of life . . . in the manner of a baby's smile.

Day 356

08 March 2021

The lasting pleasures of contact with the natural world
are not reserved for scientists but available
to anyone who will place himself under the influence
of earth, sea, and sky and their amazing life.

RACHEL CARSON

6:13 A.M. (sunrise two minutes earlier than yesterday). 9 degrees, wind NE 2 mph. Sky: clear, a rumor of peach across the south, thin and transparent as cellophane. Sunlight caresses the summits of Tug Mountain and Gove and Richardson hills, warms Mount Ascutney, forty miles southwest, lavender gray like a cloud fixed to the horizon. Permanent streams: for the moment, an illusion of immutable ice-bound flow; upper, sealing over, again, a see-through lid, otter and weasel tracks eroded, filling with bits of forest scraps; lower, beneath a mantle of rock-solid snow. Wetlands: late with sunlight, early with freeze, an impoundment of cold air, flowing in rivulets down Robinson Hill. Pileated drums in the hemlocks, a resonant ring across the marsh; my fingers too numb to time the pauses. An absence of bobcat . . . but not of memory, which germinates by the alders, fourth day in a row. Pond: surface dense and bumpy, beyond hockey. Hairy woodpecker drums, a speedy, even-tempo reverberation like Meadowlark Lemon dribbling a basketball, more pulse than pound. Crow flies south and calls attention to itself.

DOR: hapless red-breasted nuthatch, first *dead-on-the-road* of the winter, a windshield victim. Bird idles in the cup of my hand. A small bird, tiny tail banded black and white. Yam-colored undertail coverts. White eyebrow set off by black eyeliner, lifelong mascara. The back toe, the *hallux* (the little piggy that went to market toe), longer and stouter than the other three toes, big sickle-shaped toenail, the grappling hook that enables nuthatch to walk headfirst down a tree . . . secret of the avian Spiderman.

Titmice mum, resolute and unswerving, feed in silence. Chickadees surrender to another unmitigated urgency. Rills of warm air and music spill out of tiny beaks, fleeting clouds of exhalation. The politeness of chickadees: first one bird, then the next, song stimulating song, back and forth across the road, an unaccompanied, uninterrupted chorus of soloists . . . not unlike a faculty meeting.

Pileated returned to roadside maple, fresh chips litter the snow. Like any reasonable investment, the reward (carpenter ants) must exceed the expenditure to excavate (energy invested). White-breasted nuthatch singing, calling, feeding, storing, probing, wandering headfirst down bark pathways. Pauses for a moment and then heads back up. Buddha with an upturned bill . . . little agent of the sun.

～

Yesterday afternoon, I could not help myself. I entered the marsh, went directly into the alders, seeking a ghost. Four days behind bobcat, but I'm still overflowingly curious. Cat walked among the alders as though the branches were invisible. I stumbled, broken branches in my wake. Bobcat entered the cattails, crossed where the marsh narrows behind the decrepit beaver dam and followed the west shore north, in the shadow of hemlock and pine . . . where the pileated holds court. Cat preferred shadows, preferred moving. Found a friend, a smaller bobcat, and together they climbed the broken framework of Robinson Hill, into rocky ledges and talus. A crepuscular couple planning for the future.

Across the globe, there are four species of wildcats in the genus *Lynx*: Iberian lynx; Eurasian lynx; Canada lynx; and bobcat (aka red lynx), the most common wildcat in North America. Some 2.5 to 3.5 million roam the United States. Only Delaware, Alaska, and Hawaii are without. Although male bobcats rove up to forty square miles, their defensible territories are less than one hundred acres. Sexes are polygamous, often mating with several partners. For bobcats, the Summer of Love is late winter . . . otherwise, adults are secretive, solitary, nocturnal hunters.

Who would I prefer to track the bobcats with? Charles Darwin? Theodore Roosevelt? John Burroughs? Perhaps Rachel Carson.

Darwin would beguile me with talk of natural selection and the biological meaning of love. Roosevelt had the stamina and determination to track the cats over the Hill and into the next valley; I would cajole him into protecting the glacially inscribed landscape for generations of bobcats and people. Burroughs would have transformed our walk into lyrical prose. Carson would fuse science and art into an irresistible whole, into a *sense of wonder*.

～

There are uncharted paths beyond my doorstep. And every morning in every way, as dark yields to light, I take Coyote Hollow's treble hook and swim downstream, boyishly noshing on daybreak's residual gifts. Walking home, cocooned in the sounds of March, I realize the bobcat—beast of the ten-second glimpse—has entered the realm of personal mythology. I conjure him up, a trophy, a glorified memory, the way I conjure up the golden rattlesnake with the chocolate bands, basking on the stone foundation of a long-gone farmhouse in the woods outside Elmira, New York. Or, nearly fifty years ago, while hitchhiking cross country, an eye-level scarlet tanager perched in a wretched downpour at a Wisconsin scenic pullover. My ride, a coast-to-coast trucker, had never before enjoyed a bird except between slices of toast. Deliciously drenched, we returned to the truck, puddles on the floorboards, talked tanager, and headed west.

Day 360

12 March 2021

Enamored of the parting West—
The peace — the flight — the Amethyst —
Night's possibility!
EMILY DICKINSON

6:06 A.M. (sunrise two minutes earlier than yesterday; one hour and fourteen minutes earlier than the Winter Solstice). 46 degrees (warmest morning since Christmas), wind WNW 13 mph, traffic-voiced and forest-conducting . . . trees creaking in concert. Sky: clear, bright washed in pink, full of hope and magic. Permanent streams: upper, occasional snow and ice bridge, but mostly open, otter and weasel tracks, a solar translation, text and author lost in rendering; lower, mostly closed. Near the marsh, where terrain levels, a twin-tiered flow, meltwater gushing over portions of snow, stream beneath, coming off the hillside, shy flow hidden, snow showing signs of rot, patches soft and transparent like a bruised tomato. Wetlands: stretches of open water in the main channel, everywhere else snowbound. Off the far shore, sunlight slides down hemlocks and pine, turns dull green radiant. Above the reeds, chickadee, a slow, loopy, imperiled flight. Pond: surface mostly cleared and puddled.

Sunlight swarms down Robinson Hill. Oaks and aspen brighten. Pines glow. My homestead, scripted by the sun, defines itself, sparkling in the evanescence of first light . . . new day flares. Standing-seam roof and solar panels gleam; bird feeders, jostled by hungry jays, blink like flashbulbs. Cedar panels brighten. Snowy pastures become intensely white.

Red-winged blackbirds loiter along the rim of the Connecticut River and tributary deltas, waiting for higher-elevation marshes to thaw. At nine hundred feet, Coyote Hollow bides its time.

Sunlight unknots the world. Sap rises. Morning's jubilee: chickadees everywhere singing; titmice holding court in the oaks—*hear, hear, hear, hear*; crows overhead, flying in all directions, buffeted by the wind, barking and cawing, an aerial, three-dimensional parkway, no congestion; jays swarm sunflower feeders and suet, and pick shrimp peels out of the compost; pileated laughs. Both nuthatches calling. White-breasted singing. I share my yard with birds. Unintentionally, they share their lives with me . . . the impassioned pleasures of symbiosis.

Conspicuous by their absence are crossbills. Dove in the driveway picks grit, waits until the last moment, and then bolts and scissors the air, the sweet sound of flight. But owl-voiced doves make noise with throats and wings. The most popular game bird in North America. Of a continental population of approximately 350 million, about twenty million are annually harvested for less than a hotdog's worth of meat. More than the combined total of all other migratory game birds (ducks, geese, woodcock, cranes, and so forth).

Mourning doves have survival strategies: small, flimsy, see-through nests; multiple clutches—two often overlapping; speedy nestling growth; milk produced in crop and regurgitated to nestlings; early fledging, chicks capable of breeding in three months. Delicate nests are constructed (almost) anywhere. Several years ago, a pair of doves raised two chicks on the brick windowsill outside Becky and Casey's living room. I'd crawl to the window, a breakfast voyeur, and watch each chick stuff its head down its mother's or father's throat and sip crop milk . . . imbibing in the crux of doveness.

∾

3:35 P.M. 55 degrees, wind SW 9 mph. On a parcel of the waterlogged front yard, two crows and a robin pick small earthworms out of matted grass. Robin rushes, probes, and tweezes with a sun-gilded bill. I pause by the bedroom window, watching a pedestrian songbird, russet breast and noble posture—chest out, shoulders back, erect as an uppercase *I*, dashing headlong into spring.

☙

Rhapsody above the Hollow, raven inscribes lazy circles in the sun-flushed sky. Wings extended, unbending, gliding into a headwind, dipping, rising, tilting—darkest black against emergent blue. The bird, skirting the morning threshold, accompanies the yellow sun above Robinson Hill. Issues a rolling croak, simplistic and profound, a message of tolerance, imbuing the valley with hope like the amber light. A charitable bird, allows me to assign meaning . . . heralds the miracle of birth; late last night, Isabelle Linny, my granddaughter, arrived in Grand Junction, Colorado. Undoubtedly, the raven knew.

Day 362

14 March 2021

Home for a year

This is a wonderful day.
I have never seen this one before.
MAYA ANGELOU

7:02 A.M. (EDT) (Sunrise two minutes earlier than yesterday EST.) 25 degrees, wind W 4 mph. Sky: bright, light, and cloudless, a quarter inch of fresh snow, perfect for tracking. Clouds coalesce like wisdom, slowly, methodically. Permanent streams: upper, unchanged and churning, ice free; lower, still pinioned by winter, bubbling under frozen meltwater and sagging snow. Mink wandered downstream on a mission of hunger, perfectly paired tracks, five pointy toes, each ending in a claw mark; heel pad thin and asymmetrical, like a crooked *L*. Wetlands: a painterly landscape, a narrow band of fog above the reeds and in front of the snow-dusted evergreens. Clouds trimmed in the pink tones of sunrise hover above everything—aerial mountains in suspension. The main drainage channel snakes through snowbound marsh, black and open; formerly languid and secretive, now swollen and unequivocal. Pond: tractionless and treacherous, made more so by tangled leashes. Dogs and I slip, slide, spill, a trio of gangly cartoon characters. Twelve months of serious comfort eating has an unintended benefit . . . I bounce up, unbroken. Raccoon paid a visit, a plodding gait (by comparison, mink's a five-star ballerina) and coyote, dreaming of spring, searches for company.

Pileated drums, laughs, drums again. Abandons communication. Crows in oaks, screaming, eyes on the compost pile. Brown creeper, song spilling from maples, high, thin, and rich. A run of happy notes, almost inaudible. The bird needs subtitles . . . or I need a hearing aid. I listen but don't see the creeper; which is as hard to find as it is to hear. And its volume is maddeningly turned down.

Fox walked up the driveway, a delicate line of tracks. Maybe a gray fox? Across the front yard and under the fence. A midnight loop. Gray fox, the only native fox in New England, the fox nobody knows and fewer people see. A tree climber. An eater of melons and mice, squirrels, frogs, and snakes, with a taste for carrion. At home in the deciduous East and the desert Southwest, and south into the jungles of northern Columbia. Tracks reappear in a neighbor's yard, camped under the feeder, waiting (perhaps) for mice, waiting for the world to defrost . . . again and again until spring overwhelms the senses.

Crows now in the compost, a breakfast of eggshells and stale bagels. Two roistering jays chase each other through an apple tree, manically zipping from branch to branch, short hops, quick flashes. Around and around, lacing the tree with invisible threads of desire. Everywhere: chickadees, titmice, nuthatches, and small woodpeckers make themselves known. Such a blend of sound, the synthesis of disparate worlds compelled by similar ambitions.

One year ago today, I returned home from Costa Rica, from tapirs and tayras; from five scarlet macaws drinking from a branch cavity, one bird at a time, fifty feet above the ground; from a timberline wren, elfin bird in an elfin forest, wandering amid trees shaped by the will of the wind. From watching Gil's phone light up with trip cancellations, and one of our participant's despair as her son in the Netherlands waited with eight thousand other stranded travelers for a flight home. Little did I know I'd be home for a year, vacationing room to room and across the Hollow? I have become reacquainted with my neighbors . . . resident, transient, nomadic. What have I discovered during a year of observation and thought? The sun rises in the east; sets in the west. Thin ice breaks. And chickadees don't care about pandemics. Observations and insights kneaded into a single gift of the here and now. I've been present, at home, alone . . . seeing with fresh eyes every day, like Isabelle Linny. Calling out to the seasons, rediscovering my world.

Day 364

16 March 2021

Go to the edge of the cliff and jump off.
Build your wings on the way down.
RAY BRADBURY

6:59 A.M. (sunrise two minutes earlier than yesterday; even though time change has wrecked my biorhythms, chickadees don't miss a beat and call to the sun no matter what my kitchen clock says). 5 degrees (fifty-six degrees colder than March 12), wind NW less than 1 mph. Sky: linear clouds, more crowded in the south, pastel streaks—rose, peach, pink—across baby blue, volatile as youth. Permanent streams: upper, ice bound and transparent (again); lower, snow bound and opaque, rock hard and raucous. Wetlands: freezer-chest cold and iron solid (Hannibal could have walked his elephants over the frozen marsh.) Pileated drums north-end hemlocks, the sound reverberating across the marsh, deep, palpable beats, echoes of echoes, the morning's finest and loudest proclamation, *Here Comes the Sun.* Mindful of biscuits in my pocket, dogs wait patiently for me to recover. Grouse explodes from alders, wings whirring and shouting, accomplishes what the dogs cannot. Immediately, I'm back, jarred alert, and chanting, *Who's a good boy?* Pond: green bench and red goal gone, otherwise relentlessly frozen homeostasis.

Road ruts deep, frozen into miniature badlands. Or, perhaps, the caliche canyons above the Salt Fork of the Brazos River, southeast of Lubbock, Texas, where fifty years ago, a pair of great horned owls evicted a pair of cliff-nesting barn owls from their cavity. Horned owls raised two chicks, and I dropped out of graduate school, a longhaired, war-protesting, pot-smoking outcast on the plains of west Texas. 1972 was neither Richard Nixon's nor my most fruitful year.

∾

Except for lengthening days, winter doesn't incrementally progress toward spring. There are fits and starts, and disappointing setbacks. Birds, however, seem unfazed.

Parliament assembled in the maples—*hear, hear, hear*—mitered titmice, regardless of temperature, reaffirm the unstoppable tilt toward spring. Five chickadees tear through a tangle of vines. Hard to tell who's in charge. Positions repeatedly change, chickadees burning around the dooryard—black-capped adrenaline. Keeping warm. Making social adjustments. Crow in compost, dining on my discards . . . linguini, omelet, cornbread. Leans into the second coming of Arctic weather, fortitude in glossy black.

Here, cloistered in the north end of Coyote Hollow, regardless of temperature, I rejoice in the winter sunshine and the business and busyness of neighbors; ten jays, headdresses erect, perch high in the aspens, bathed in a buttery light, pale breasts aglow. I can almost see the pussy willows and hear militant wood frogs clacking in the vernal pools. I anticipate the imminent, inexorable swell and heave toward spring . . . otherwise, I'd be the victim of homebound misery of my own creation.

But birds are coming. Each spring, more than two billion cross the Gulf of Mexico, the *trans-Gulf migrants*: vireos, warblers, flycatchers, hummingbirds, cuckoos, nighthawks, and so forth. Birds that wintered from Mexico and Cuba to Argentina. Pushed by tailwinds, they head north across the Gulf. If the wind changes direction and blows out of the north, they descend on land, everywhere and anywhere and exhausted. The *fallout*. The outer islands of the Gulf Coast are famed for fallouts. We've had them in the Northeast. In May 2006, red phalaropes appeared in Vermont en route to the desolate North. One spent a May morning on Lake Fairlee, swimming in circles and stirring food.

According to the Cornell Laboratory of Ornithology, fallouts are predicted over the Southeast between Saint Patrick's Day and March 19. Simplified explanation: at sunset, calm, southerly winds blow up from the southern Gulf of Mexico; then, the following dawn, northerly winds blow over the Southeast and northern Gulf. It's tough to fly into a headwind. Faster-flying birds (shorebirds and waterfowl and falcons) reach land first and fallout, pitching onto beaches and salt marshes. Later in the day, slower-flying birds arrive. The result: an all-day bird fest, a planetary wonder.

2:48 P.M. 33 degrees, wind SW 3 mph. Red-shouldered hawk above the wetlands, circling. Fallout of one. Voice gores the afternoon. First red-shouldered above the Hollow since October 14. Jay in aspen answers, a rank imitation. The hot, yellow sun urges sap to rise and bent reeds to collapse. Prompts hawk's emotions . . . and the frozen world begins to unlock.

Day 366

18 March 2021

One year of continuous pandemic journaling

Meanwhile the world goes on.
Meanwhile the sun and the clear pebbles of the rain
are moving across the landscapes,
are moving over prairies and deep trees,
[. . .] are heading home again.
MARY OLIVER

6:55 A.M. (sunrise two minutes earlier than yesterday). 34 degrees, wind E 1 mph. Sky: sleepy grade of gray to blue, truancy of color. Mount Ascutney hid behind a curtain of air thick enough to slice. Permanent streams: upper, panels of ice gone, infusion of melted snow. Captivated by the sounds of a louder, more expansive, deeper flow, a jazzy riff, the Dizzy Gillespie of brooks; lower, wide open in the flat woods, entombed under hard snow and ice on both sides of the road, all the way to the marsh. Wetlands: ground and bent reeds emerge under the weight of the sun. Pileated drums, once; red squirrel chatters, nonstop; chickadees calling, varying numbers of *dees*, rapid-fire delivery. A discordant ensemble. Pond: ice untrustworthy.

Late winter 1975, lured by wintering bald eagles, I broke through the ice on the lower Mongaup River outside Forestburg, New York. A hundred yards from shore, the ice gave way, and I was treading water, binoculars in hand, field guide in my back pocket. I attempted a series of muscle-ups, but the ice fractured each time I pushed up. I plowed my way to shore.

∽

For a moment, I imagine the bobcat, searchlight eyes and radar ears, tail docked by the unseen forces of evolution for reasons I cannot fathom . . . an experience worth repeating.

Beneath roadside maple (the pileated-chiseled maple) chips on the snow like ice-house insulation, the tree still alive but opened on both sides, a see-through maple, a window on the Hollow—a tree destined to be undone . . . like winter.

Above the lower stream, a red-eyed vireo nest idles on the snow. Must have fallen last night. Fits in my palm like a worn baseball. Speaks to the dexterity of vireo bills, the warp and weft of the woodland loom. Bark frame, pliant strips of basswood, cup lined with white pine needles. On the outside of the nest decorative birch bark and scraps of a paper wasp nest. A beautiful, fastidious crèche; soft, safe, insulated, and formerly suspended from the fork of a twig. Design honed by millions of years of trial and error—two little birds standing on a twig, weaving. By June, I was bored with their voices. But not in March, the climatically bipolar month of temptation, seduction, and disappointment; I long for vireos and an end to quarantine. Give me freedom and a south wind, a bird wind.

Red-shouldered hawk cries from aspen, a salvo of piercing calls, eyes squirrels scurrying across the front yard, bolts, circles, vanishes into the morning. Chickadee whistles, pure as light. Hairy and downy woodpeckers visit sunflower feeders; spill seeds, which two turkeys scavenge. Doves, gray squirrels, and chipmunks compete with turkeys. A dozen jays compete with everyone.

∽

Victor Shelford (1887-1968) left the University of Illinois in 1946 to found The Ecologist's Union, known today as The Nature Conservancy. In the first half of the twentieth century, the heavyweight biologist integrated animal and plant ecology and terrestrial and aquatic ecology, and developed the *biome* concept together with Frederic E. Clements. A biome is a broad geographic region defined by the similarity of native communities of plants and animals: desert, grassland, tundra, deciduous forest, boreal forest, montane forest, and rainforest (I prefer the name *jungle*, which evokes adventure).

Shelford wrote *The Ecology of North America*, published in 1963 by the University of Illinois Press, five hundred pages of exquisite detail. He divides North America into biomes and then subdivides each biome into respective components, which he discusses at length. Shelford splits the temperate deciduous forest biome into the *northern upland* and *southern lowland*. Coyote Hollow is in the maple-beech-hemlock association of the northern deciduous forest. Within the chapter "Temperate Deciduous Biome (Northern)," Shelford considers life in a hypothetical ten-square-mile circle, circa 1600, based on the academic research of dozens of colleagues.

Here's a distillation of who lives in that hypothetical circle: 750,000 trees, 786,000 saplings, 2,810,000 shrubs, and 230 to 460 million wildflowers. *These plants*, writes Shelford, *usually have their leaves nipped, skeletonized, perforated, deformed, and their sap sucked by a myriad of insects belonging to 10 to 20 species.* During the two months when birds are nesting, nearly twenty-six billion invertebrates, primarily insects and spiders, roam the plants, canopy to roots. Almost four billion are gall-forming insects—gall wasps, gallflies, and plant lice.

The number of mice, primarily white-footed, varies year to year from 160,000 to 320,000, or about one per two trees. About 7,680 pairs of small birds nest in ten square miles of northern hardwoods during leaf-out, approximately one pair per ninety to ninety-five trees. The adult and chicks consume about 386 million insects, almost five hundred insects per nesting pair of birds per day.

Other stats for ten square miles of northern hardwoods:

- Gray squirrel and southern flying squirrel, 10,000 to 20,000 each
- Wild turkey, 200
- Raptors, 2 to 5 per 75,000 trees
- White-tailed deer, 400
- Catamount, 2 to 3
- Wolf, 1 to 3
- Gray fox, 30
- Black bear, 2

Shelford does not list fungi, shrews and moles, bats, red squirrel, mink, otter, short- or long-tailed weasels, fisher, marten, bobcat, lynx, raccoon, moose, hare, cottontail, waterfowl, wading birds, shorebirds, goatsuckers, woodpeckers, swifts, hummingbirds, reptiles, amphibians, fish, or crustaceans. Of course, they were there, too . . . some species (like red-back salamanders) in astrological numbers. Circa 1600, there were no red foxes, opossums, or coyotes in the northern hardwoods. No earthworms, either.

Though diminished since 1600, Coyote Hollow is still awe inspiring, no less than the stars in the sky. And the Hollow stretches to the horizon, just beyond my front door.

SPRING

2021

Day 370

22 March 2021

When spring came, even the false spring,
there were no problems except where to be happiest.
ERNEST HEMINGWAY

6:48 A.M. (sunrise two minutes earlier than yesterday). 23 degrees, wind calm 0 mph. (day three into a seven-day warm spell, sixty degrees or warmer by afternoon, snow and ice in full retreat.) Meltwater gullies along the sides of the road. At that moment, breath condenses and rises like chimney smoke. Sky: on autopilot, clear with a trace of lavender and peach. Crows call at break, sounding agitated as if they woke up on the wrong side of the branch. Permanent streams: impacted by warmth. Upper, infused by snowmelt, a few glimmering specks of ice stuck to a rock and a broken limb, destined to vanish by midmorning; lower, a tunneled flow, revealing more of itself, in and out, and loud. The shape of open water: long, wavy ovals and distorted circles. Clear, refreshing to watch, and wondrous to hear. Wetlands: at least half the snow cover is gone, reeds revealed, bent and busted, crippled by the weight of winter, ends hung with frost. From the hemlocks, pileated relentlessly drums across the bowl of snowless sedges, lots of pauses, lots of repetition. Pond: a corruption of rotten ice, visible soft spots above discharging groundwater. Not to be trusted. Robins call and sing in the pines.

One dog, tangled in leash, jumps and shakes, eventually frees himself. Other dog watches, incredulous. The canine version of *Saturday Night Fever* or *Dirty Dancing*. I'm stunned too.

Pair of creepers courting, their song thin and sweet. Two specks of airborne bark, tree to tree, tail pressed to trunk, a barber-pole journey up cherry and then ash, one creeper after the other. Trailing bird sings . . . the seduction of species-specific songs. Weather evokes thoughts of garter snakes on the stonewall or rattlesnakes on the ledges above Lake Champlain. I wish snakes sang, a single long lung bearing notes of interest, resonating through a thousand-ribbed hall.

Yesterday, I faced the sun in a T-shirt, snug in an Adirondack chair. Red-winged blackbirds, grackles, and juncos under the feeders (FOY). How far off could snakes be, their rocks divinely warm?

To emphasize my point, a robin sings an abridged song in the front yard; then, calls incessantly, commandeering an already blissful morning. Flies into aspen and joins four jays, surrounded by swollen buds. All five birds face the sun, breasts incandescent.

Crows and chickadees are busy before the sun. Red-shouldered hawk screams. Raven croaks. Bird feeder pandemonium. The front yard has become a melting pot, the Ellis Island of Coyote Hollow: two downy woodpeckers; two hairy woodpeckers; two titmice; grackles, purple sheen in the morning light; redwings; eleven juncos; three crows; red-breasted nuthatch; two white-breasted nuthatches; chickadees, too many and too active to count; five jays, noisy, nosy, and naughty. Two chipmunks and a gray squirrel, tail swishing, fattening on the rain of seeds spilling from the feeders.

❧

7:43 P.M. (nautical twilight). 46 degrees, wind NE 6 mph. In the gloaming, two woodcocks perform nuptials above the alders. I listen as light drains from the western sky, from lavender to gray to star studded. Back and forth over the maples, descending into the punky, saturated marsh, where worms loiter on the surface, within easy picking for knitting-needle bills.

Aldo Leopold died in Wisconsin in 1948, helping a neighbor fight a brush fire. A year later, his sparkling essays were curated and published as *A Sand County Almanac*, which has sold over two million copies and remains the only book I've read more than three times. Leopold called the woodcock courtship flight a *sky dance* and concluded that the flight was a *refutation of the theory that the utility of a game bird is to serve as a target, or to pose on a slice of toast*. I cannot see the woodcocks . . . I just listen; my night the richer for it.

❧

The Hollow opens up, and winter is temporarily undone. Spring erupts with a vengeance for a magical day (actually, six). But I've lived in Vermont long enough to know . . . winter will rise again—maybe next week, and perhaps also after that. I'll go outside, stay out, celebrate my version of Passover, a release from the tyranny of the coronavirus, temporarily erasing the darkness of past months, and enjoy . . . the freedom of the present moment.

Day 372

24 March 2021

*It is not the biggest, the brightest or the best
that will survive, but those who adapt the quickest.*
CHARLES DARWIN

7:06 A.M. (sunrise two minutes earlier than yesterday). 28 degrees, wind
NNW less than 1 mph (road puddles glazed). Sky: pink striations across
powder blue; humid, the air thick enough to denature Mount Ascutney,
now a veiled smudge on the southwestern horizon. Permanent streams:
upper, no change, no ice; lower, one tunnel of compact snow, otherwise
open and rushing, full-throated gargle. At the moment, the lower stream
carries much more water and much more freight than the upper . . .
but will occasionally dry up in midsummer, its sources less dependable.
Wetlands: snow mostly gone. Frozen tundra recast into a saturated
sponge. Runoff, delivered by permanent and intermittent streams,
pools in the center of the marsh, an ephemeral pond skimmed in ice.
A transient flock of grackles skirts the eastern shoreline, heading north
(perhaps to compete with jays at the feeders). Pond: ice withdraws from
the shore, inch by inch, elsewhere rotting. Song sparrow (FOY) singing,
a truncated version . . . *Madge, Madge, Madge.* Although there's plenty of
water everywhere, there's no teakettle.

Pileated drumming in the hemlocks, one volley (or so) per minute.
Another, on the eastern apron of Robinson Hill, answers—a percussive
duet—stereophonic drumming. Then, from the hillside, a laugh, a long,
wild *wuk, wuk, wuk, wuk, wuk.* Jungle movie soundtrack.

West along the marsh, where the land flattens, red-shouldered hawk
perches in a crown of pine, one of the tallest trees on the flats. Hurls his
voice against the thick air, four or five screams, clear and squealing—
kee-aw, kee-aw, kee-aw, kee-aw—a vernal zealot. Then, like the pileated,
hawk pauses for a minute. Lets his voice sink in. Gives the blue jays a
chance at interpretation. Hawk, a feathered knot, bolt upright, a dark,
oval silhouette against the gray. Several years ago, red-shoulders mated
on a stout, horizontal oak limb just off the driveway. I stopped the car,
rolled down the window, and watched spring unfold in the oak. Red-
shoulders nest in the main crotch of a large tree halfway up. A basket of
sticks decorated with sprigs of hemlock and pine used again (and again)
unless appropriated by great horned owls.

March 1976, Putney, Vermont. A pair of red-shouldered hawks nested in a giant yellow birch. Twice each week, I paid the hawks a visit. From high in a nearby hemlock, I'd look across a streambed, down into the hawk nest. Tolerant, nest-minding parent looked back, assessing my intentions. Sometimes, I'd bring a friend and we'd sit on a hemlock limb eating sandwiches while mother hawk eviscerated a bullfrog or gray squirrel.

In the limelight: chickadees, titmice, and white-breasted nuthatches during civil twilight, too busy to eat, escort the sun into the sky. Crows join the serenade, offbeat, loud, and infused with annoyance. Mitered heads erect, blue jays in aspen honk, grayer than blue in the dim light. Brown creeper couple sing, then chase each other around a maple, higher and higher. Robins calling and singing.

This morning, *The New York Times* online TimesMachine ran a link to the March 28, 1860, review of Charles Darwin's *On the Origin of Species*. What a treat. What a newspaper. The concluding phrase: *flooding the age with the sunlight of science.*

We all bask in the glow of that sunlight, every chickadee and every crocus, every winter stonefly—one big family of life parading into an unforeseen and unforeseeable (though we can speculate) future. Science lights the stage. People, sadly, have set the tempo.

Jay honks. Two blasts. Another jay answers; also two honks. Both birds carry on, and in the background (now), the hawk screams, four times (again), the conductor, orchestrating a valley in seasonal upheaval. Winter into spring, the linchpin of the year . . . all clocks set to urgency.

Day 377

29 March 2021

Third night of Passover

My garden robin in the Spring
Was rapturous with glee,
And followed me with wistful wing
From pear to apple tree;
His melodies the summer long
He carolled with delight,
As if he could with jewelled song
Find favour in my sight.

ROBERT SERVICE

6:35 A.M. (sunrise two minutes earlier than yesterday). 39 degrees, wind W 12 mph, a triumph of damp, mobile air. Predatory winds prune limbs and topple shallow-rooted birches, now prostrate and scattered, the displaced bones of sunshine. Sky: low ceiling, grayer than blue, thick air spitting snow, round, inbred flakes the gift of shapeless clouds. Below the clouds, two crows head north; above the clouds, a gibbous moon heads west. Intermittent streams: flush. Permanent streams: water on the move; heavy rain begets heavy flow, rising above low spots on the bank, lapping at the edge of the woods. Even the gullies join the chorus. Wetlands: impersonate a pond, main channel swollen, fed by every crease in the marsh. Fully saturated, standing water everywhere. Doing what marshes do . . . holding back floodwaters. No sign of hooded mergansers, which could be anywhere, cruising and diving among the reeds, their world exponentially expanded. But goose music rains . . . a tribute to a season in flux and the imminence of rebirth. Pond: puddled and melting, ice retreating from the shore. Feeder stream opens farther away from the shoreline, water dark as obsidian, and the perfect foil for the translucent glaze, pale as moonlight and synapse-thin.

Monoecious alders: catkins elongate and soften, ready to spill pollen; female flowers, tiny projections, ruddy purple, ready to receive pollen. Dead black cherry, once a favorite of small woodpeckers and bark-searching nuthatches, fallen across the trail.

Jays keep to themselves and forage in silence below the canopy. Juncos trilling. Robins scolding. Creepers whispering. Nuthatches tooting and yanking. Song sparrow at full tilt, clear, hoarse notes, cheery warbles. Chickadees *dee-dee-dee*ing (no songs). Pileated lampoons the vast and quixotic onset of spring. No matter the weather, the red-shouldered hawk hurls vocal darts, piercing the airwaves; a bird of the loudest, if not the most profound, intentions.

More than a hundred robins in the upper pasture (none in the lower), all upright and dignified, stalking. Ground soaked, worms on the surface trying to breathe. Robins waiting, rushing, feeding. Short bursts of activity like sandpipers on a mudflat.

Robins have perfect posture. No slouching. No slumping. Head erect, eyes forward, never contemplate their toes. Casey, a physical therapist, should consider the robin the yardstick for posture-challenged birders (like his father). Robins don't lean like a dove or a junco, eyeing the ground around them. They're sturdy and straight, like a hawk on a limb, the Emily Post of songbirds, studying the pasture beyond their toes. Watching for a worm in the grass . . . then, a burst forward and a short tug of war. A length of protein caught and swallowed, one earthworm after another. Several robins have bulging crops, interior shopping bags crammed with food.

The whole pasture seems in motion. I stand counting. Ninety-seven. One hundred three. One hundred eleven. Too much action for accurate statistics.

Simply put, I'm in a mob of northbound robins who pause for breakfast and will move on to Quebec, Newfoundland, or the edge of Hudson Bay. To the hem of the tundra. North America's most familiar, widely distributed songbird, but *not* the most numerous. At an estimated continental population of only 320 million, robins fall short of dark-eyed juncos, whose population is estimated to be 630 million.

No longer a harbinger of spring, some robins remain all winter, gorging on freeze-dried fruit, mostly winterberries, sumac, and bittersweet. This morning, neighborhood robins call and sing, struggling to be heard over the machinery of the wind. Pasture robins move on by early afternoon, take the express train north beyond the Hollow. Essential migrant flying into Canada, crossing that once permeable border . . . accentuating my confined perspective.

∾

Dirt road reshuffle—ruts and pits, puddles and unconsolidated ridges, landscape attributed to repetitive thawing and freezing and to subsurface flow. And to too-heavy vehicles whose swerving, short-cutting drivers zigzag as if on sodium pentothal. Patiently, I await President Biden's executive order designating Five Corners Road, once and forever *Frost Heaves National Monument.*

Day 380

01 April 2021

5th Day of Passover

April Fool's Day

The less we are able to admit common feelings into our relationship with trees, the more impoverished we become: it must indicate a deforestation of the spirit.
JOHN HAY

6:30 A.M. (sunrise two minutes earlier than yesterday). 37 degrees, wind 11 mph (treachery of the wind, unhampered and free ranging: several more standing-dead paper birches fell last night, released by saturated soil and shallow, rotten roots). Sky: flat light, gray and threatening, sun and crows among the missing. Permanent streams: rain enhanced, unbridled babble drowns out nearby birds. The fluency of running water. Turkey running along lower stream bank—head up, chest out, stiff legged, almost mechanical. Small-headed big bird rushing to the dance party in the lower pasture. Wetlands: sodden and duck filled. Ten on the main channel—three drake wood ducks and a hen, and three pairs of mallards, the males' green heads the only color in an expanse of tan. Everybody is tipping and feeding. Mallards quack, the duck template. Wood ducks scream, soft but piercing, like a hawk with the amplifier turned down. Alder catkins, sausage-shaped flowers, swaying in the wind, purple and lemon-yellow pendants growing longer and softer, some spilling pollen. Pileated silent. Pond: putrefaction of ice; feeder stream open to the far shore, a black swath wedged into thin, gray ice. Winter wren (FOY) sings in the brambles, sweet music out of the gray blah of sunrise. Dogs sit. I listen, almost forgetting the dismal weather, now spitting rain and snow.

On the threshold of spring: bird feeder flattened by a bear (again); peeper peeping (FOY); dog tick on my triceps, imbibing; crocus in the dooryard, blooming. A seductive seasonal wink, a step toward spring, predictably unpredictable, the consistency of change, eternal transitions. The obediently rebellious nature of nature . . . three phoebes (FOY), song harsh and abrupt, like Yiddish or clearing your throat. Dutifully, I open the barn door to them.

Grouse drumming, a full-bodied experience. Pileated, the resident laugher in the hemlocks, finds something amusing and heaves his voice into the morning. A cacophony of robins, singing and scolding. Ravens at the nest. Crows building theirs. Early spring ensemble: chickadees, titmice, both nuthatches, juncos, and song sparrows. Little woodpeckers on sabbatical, absent from front yard suet.

Four big-toothed aspen catkins, not fully developed, idle on the road, victims of the wind. Downy soft, oval, red-speckled pollen chambers. Separate sexes (*dioecious*): male trees, female trees. Fast-growing, shallow-rooted, wood soft. Fortifies the earth for the coming of maple and beech. Grouse eat the buds, beaver the bark. By late April, aspen seeds, airborne, float through the Hollow, stick to everything: dogs, screens, sweaters, unruly hair; gather in the barn and garage . . . dust bunnies of the forest. Useless for firewood, aspen wood does have a sheen, which Donald Culross Peattie compared to olive wood. *Sometimes it happens,* wrote Peattie, *that fancy grains develop—feather crotches, as the veneer salesman calls them—or a small black-mottled figure eagerly sought out.* A decorated crotch, where the trunk and canopy diverge, is rare—maybe two or three per carload. When unrolled from the log, they *appear like sheets of living flame. When finished in 'natural' or slightly brownish tones, paneling of feather-crotch Aspen wood is sought out by department stores as the perfect background for displaying fine female apparel.* I'll search for the *feathered aspen crotch* on my next visit to Victoria's Secret, which hopefully won't happen anytime soon. Most likely, the paneling in department stores and Peattie's excellent book, *The Natural History of Eastern and Central North America,* are heirlooms of the late 1940s.

Around my home, nesting flickers and sapsuckers prefer aspen. Even chickadees excavate nest cavities in punky aspen snags. Several years ago, along the west edge of the marsh, I watched a chickadee ream an eye-level nest hole in an aspen, beak crammed with punky wood, which she dropped some distance from the excavation. The entrance to the cavity was about the size of a quarter.

Blue jay, less concerned about the nature of aspen, perches on a limb, surrounded by swollen catkins, which dangle and shimmy like mute chimes. Leans back, bill slightly open, and displays thespian talents. Echoes a broad-winged hawk—an Amazonian migrant, weeks away—a long, high-pitched whistle, sound washing over me. A well-honed note, commandeering an otherwise dull morning.

Day 381

02 April 2021

7th Day of Passover

It runs through and rearranges me.
I sit at the center of a globe of sound
pointing me toward myself.
RICHARD POWERS

6:28 A.M. (sunrise two minutes earlier than yesterday). 21 degrees, wind NNW 11 mph (*brrrrr*). Sky: overcast, peach light in the east inspires gray bank, everywhere else congested and gloomy. Snow squalls, big flakes stick to everything: my hat, the dogs, rough-barked trees. Birds keep their own council, advertising reduced to a bare minimum, primarily crows and jays, whose strident screams accompany me down the frozen, furrowed road (aka tailpipe reduction and muffler compression zone.) Permanent streams: upper, cold drafts of air trace water downhill and into the marsh. Nearby, a robin rattles in pine, a lonesome, troubling call . . . the sound of disorientation. Lower, I'd linger and listen if it wasn't so cold. Wetlands: driving snow, a screen of white overwhelms a troubled sky. Ice plugs open water, no room for ducks, which loiter somewhere in more dependable current. Out of the horizontal snow, a pileated salvo, one and done. For a moment, I'm invigorated. Dogs, ever respectful, sit and wait beneath headdresses of snow. Pond: yesterday's open water is today's veneer of ice. Mostly snow dusted, a few clear panes too thin to prop a premise.

Two chickadees duel, a battle of whistles from opposite sides of the road. Crow by the compost pile, a knocking call, the banging of sticks, drummer without a drum, awash in the memory of stale bread. In two months, fledglings will join parents at the compost, a crow fest, the knowledge of stale bread passing from generation to generation—the foundation of storytelling.

∾

The Language of Our Time

I remember your idiosyncrasies. How you'd incinerate your toast while preparing everyone else's breakfast; black plumes rising through the seams of the toaster. How you smuggled charred popcorn into the Nugget Theater, which made our row smell like an electrical fire. Someone in the row in front of us told the manager she smelled smoke and the theater was *safely* evacuated. As we milled around the lobby, you realized your popcorn had set all this in motion and we laughed so hard we cried. Everyone got a free ticket.

You drank more water than an elephant, carried more water than a camel, ate more cayenne pepper and hot sauce than any three Mesoamericans, helped more people than Mother Teresa and were as adored by everyone who knew you. In the spring of 1979, I filled out federal employment applications for us both, hoping we'd be chosen by the U.S. Army Corp of Engineers for summer jobs planting grass and shrubs on earthen dams near Denali National Park. I forged your name on the application and we both got jobs. You went to Alaska for the summer and I . . . to the Hanover Sewage Treatment Plant.

During our first winter in Coyote Hollow, you bought Casey a pair of insulated ski gloves for Hanukkah. He left them at Dartmouth Skiway. Six years later, three years after you died, a bank teller from Canaan, New Hampshire, called. Her daughter had acquired a pair of insulated gloves with Casey's name and phone number on the garment tag. Casey had outgrown the gloves, but they fit Jordan perfectly.

You hated to vacuum. You loved to sweep. You stopped eating meat before it was fashionable. Almost every night for dinner, you ate a jumbo salad mounded with no-fat cottage cheese, crowned with fiery pepper flakes. You adored gardening and hosted a seed-ordering party every February. You cried at sad movies. On your last day, we played "What a Wonderful World" for hours, saying goodbye with a cornucopia of love.

I'll tell Izzy the stories. But who'll curate the collection if I forget, the color of memory fading like warblers in autumn?

Day 384

05 April 2021

When you fish for love,
bait with heart, not your brain.
MARK TWAIN

6:23 A.M. (sunrise two minutes earlier than yesterday). 41 degrees, wind NNW 13 mph; a world in motion, the clacking of naked limbs, the swishing of pine boughs; even a few thin, bone-dry beech leaves, once tenacious, let loose, drifting around like scraps of paper, forest confetti in the gutter of the woods. Sky: blue, white, and gray, absent of warm colors. Feels like rain, looks like rain. Permanent streams: upper, musical arrangement enhanced by winter wren, who sings from an overhanging hemlock branch, screened by needles. Little bird, big sonata, buoys glum morning with a cascade of effervescent notes. The rushing water fades into the background, a mere accompaniment to an effusive piccolo; lower, loud, babbling without wren accessories. Wetlands: ice-free and quiet; two geese fly east, raining honks, flapless wings outstretched and curved downward, a tilting glide like paper airplanes. Geese descending, preparing to land nearby. Perhaps one of the three ridgeline ponds? Or the Connecticut River? Pond: opening again, ice on recent water cellophane thin. Second pair of geese, honking and flapping, head south. Stubborn robin, bolt upright, stalks bank, finds nothing—the tip of its yellow bill stained brown from fruitless probes. Dogs ignore robin and focus on shape-changing bubbles along the underbelly of ice. Beneath the blustery sky . . . something for everyone.

Winter wren was recently split into three species, a taxonomic severance. One across boreal Canada and down the Appalachians (retains the name *winter wren*); a second along the West Coast, in giant evergreens, damp and shaded, from the Aleutian Islands almost to Baja (now called *Pacific wren*); a third in the evergreens of Europe and Asia (*Eurasian wren*).

Superlatives do not do the winter wren justice as a songster—a run of loud, sweet notes, up to ten seconds of exuberant warbles and trills. One ornithologist claimed that the winter wren's song has ten times the power of a crowing rooster per unit of weight. Sibley called the song a *remarkable series*, and Donald Kroodsma, birdsong guru from the University of Massachusetts, declared the winter wren the *pinnacle of complexity among songbirds*. Arthur Cleveland Bent, the author of the twenty-one-volume *Life Histories of North American Birds*, published between 1919 and 1968, barely found enough adjectives to describe the winter wren's song: *wonderful . . . charming . . . marvelous . . . startling . . . entrancing . . . copious . . . prolonged . . . penetrating*. Wrote Bent, the winter wren has *a great variety of the sweetest tones, and uttered in a rising and falling of finely undulated melody . . . as if the very atmosphere became resonant . . . gushing melody which seems at once expressive of the wildest joy and the tenderest sadness*. Another ornithologist noted that winter wrens sing as though *trying to burst* [their] *lungs*.

Winter wren is back, the four-inch songbird with the ten-foot song, baiting with his heart—loud enough to be appreciated above a spring freshet and a heavy wind. A tiny bird with a bubbly, outsized voice enriches a dim sunrise. Even diminishes an enthusiastic robin.

Day 386

07 April 2021

People ask me what I do in
winter when there's no baseball.
I'll tell you what I do. I stare out
the window and wait for spring.
Rogers Hornsby

6:19 a.m. (sunrise two minutes earlier than yesterday). 45 degrees, wind
E 1 mph . . . but powers up mid-walk, stirring pine boughs, rattling naked
hardwoods. Sky: crescent moon in the east mingles with dappled windrows of blues and whites, a momentary mackerel-shaped cloud congeals, then reconfigures into frayed puffballs. Overhead, clouds gilded,
silver-white edges. In the west, an atmospheric hematoma, blue gray
and scraping the ridgeline. A dearth of warm color. Permanent streams:
water and sound drawdowns—gentle swirls and soft gurgles accompany
robins, singing and calling. Wetlands: noticeably drier and sans ducks.
The wind picks up, sounds like traffic, and races across the marsh, bent
reeds plastered, a wavy, westerly combover. Woodworking pileated hidden in the hemlocks, lobs drumbeats over the bent reeds, while chickadees and juncos, barely audible to me, deliver songs to more sensitive
ears. Pond: mallard pair bolts. An oval peninsula of hole-punched ice,
otherwise more than three-quarters open. Beneath clear water, pieces of
bleached crayfish exoskeleton. Floating on clear water, a band of pond
scum hugs the southwest shore, mostly alder pollen and dust.

Spent alder catkins dry and easily flaked—fresh catkins soft, pliable,
and yellow. I shake a branch; puffs of yellow pollen flitter away like breath
on a cold morning. Beak hazelnut (*Corylus cornuta*) catkins, a third the
size of alder catkins, conspicuous along the road. Chickadees ate a few
last autumn—a flyby snack or a digestive aid (like kale). Plenty of catkins remain. After diligently searching, I find one female flower open,
tiny, tan-colored, and oval-shaped, a bud with a spray of red confetti
at the end, like the tentacles of a sea anemone. Called *styles*, elongated
extensions of the ovaries wait for pollen—specks of color amid an ocean
of brown.

Brown creeper singing, barely audible, a cascade of delicate notes.
Jays gather in pairs, disruptively voluble, hollering in the aspens. Junco,
tilted south, trills in front yard apple, turns west and trills again, head

slightly back, upper bill immobile, lower bill quivering. Robins sing in pines, maples, and ashes.

In every dooryard, the neighborliest of the eponymous flycatchers, phoebe repeats its name repeatedly and sounds like a chickadee with laryngitis (or, to be anatomically correct *syrinxitis*). Repeats its name over and over. Nonstop and harsh, a grating but welcome voice that somehow avoids inflammation of its vocal cords. One covets the open barn, sits on an oak limb, and faces the western door. From April to October, phoebes perch in the open, tails pumping, fixtures in the yard around the house. What robins are to the lawn, phoebes are to the pasture fence and apple trees: reliable, seasonal acquaintances. Eventually, I'll have three pairs. Their tails mark time, the feathered cadence of the day. The closer I walk toward the phoebe, the more he pumps his tail. Is he balancing or preparing to chase down a moth or winter stonefly?

Recent research suggests that tail-pumping (aka tail-flicking or wagging) has nothing to do with balancing or hunting. It's a sign of nonverbal communication directed at a potential predator. Watching phoebes in the presence of a Cooper's hawk alerted biologists that the more tail flicks, the more significant (or closer) the threat. Phoebe's way of demonstrating: *I see you. I'm fit. Hunt elsewhere.*

The commodity of magic. Morning's small gifts . . . Lilliputian flowers and a strident voice. A conscientious homeowner, I slowly back away from the phoebes. Tail-flicking slows and the crescent moon dissolves into the east . . . the two events, however, may not necessarily be connected.

Day 387

08 April 2021

April . . . hath put a spirit of youth in everything.
WILLIAM SHAKESPEARE

6:17 A.M. (sunrise two minutes earlier than yesterday). 39 degrees, wind N 1 mph (barely a ripple on roadside puddles). Sky: bright pastel colors along the rim; peach in the southwest, lemon in the northeast, elsewhere immaculately clear, crisp, and promising. Shreds of patchy ground fog rise from saturated earth spreading through the marsh and pastures. Moisture does not affect turkey histrionics; two males perform in the lower field, a dynamic, strutting duo. Lovers of lust—an audience of nineteen, primarily oblivious, scratch through matted grasses. Males dance and gobble and play cards with their tails. Wings droop and quiver. Automated dance steps. Permanent streams: upper, less water, softer gurgles, background music for a gathering of songbirds; lower, growing mud bar. Wetlands: rising columns of mist spread horizontally, umbrellas of moisture. Fog, the master landscape illusionist, screens evergreens, lightens reeds, turns a bright sunrise wonderfully barbarous, transforming drumming pileated and ruff grouse into Jungle Grammy nominees. I freeze in place, absorbed by mechanical sound . . . disparate rhythms roll out of the evergreens, drumrolls Max Roach would have appreciated. Pond: no ice, no ducks. Unconsolidated mist vanishes just above the surface. Two green frog tadpoles and a crayfish idle in the shallows. Male hooded merganser (FOY), wings whistling, arrows into view and prepares to land. Then, sees me and abruptly changes trajectory.

Sapsucker (FOY) calling and drumming, a stuttering beat, woodland Morse Code, lots of dots and dashes, pregnant pauses, and then meows like a congested cat. Jagged flocks of geese, back and forth between the Connecticut River and Lake Fairlee, preceded by their voices. Robins perch in bud-swollen maples, hurling songs against the morning. Brown creepers directly overhead, singing. Leaning back to see them, I almost fall over. Scraps of bark chase each other. Males sing high, musical notes, among the first birdsongs to vanish as we age.

Grouse drums in the hardwoods, wings flapping, building crescendo, a blur of motion. A blur of sound. Low as a heartbeat, a vibration felt as much as heard. Grouse music comes from the ground up, creeper music from the top down . . . goose-bump melodies.

Airborne again, a pair of red-shouldered hawks. One flies west into the next valley, driven to distraction by a pesky robin; the other east over the ridge. Their barbed cries fade away. Within minutes, both hawks return, the sky their stage, the sun their set light. Hawks transcribe circuits high above the marsh, gliding and flapping, voices flung into the emptiness.

Three hermit thrushes (FOY) join winter wrens, spinning mist into music, turning my world inside out. Arrived last night after crossing vast and undifferentiated airspaces out of the Southeast, silent confidants of alligators and moccasins stake claim to ledge outcrops and matted forest floor. The original pied pipers. Winter wrens and hermit thrushes compose unintentional duets. Vicariously enriched, I linger on and on and on . . . hooked on grace notes long enough to forget (for a moment) that I have not left home in thirteen months.

The glory days ahead of blackflies, mosquitoes, and ticks. Wood frogs and spring peepers chorused last night. My windows and doors are open. Laundry's on the clothesline. Fresh air and birdsong filter through the house. Turkeys dance in the front yard. Hawks spark the Hollow with sharp, persistent calls, hurling vocal javelins against the sun. An urgency of frogs in woodland pools. All living gifts wakening, returning, procreating.

Spring, the *very* scaffolding of the year . . . what more could I ask for?

Day 392

13 April 2021

We teach them that two and two makes four
and that Paris is the capital of France.
When will we also teach them what they are?
We should say to each of them: Do you know what you are?
You are a marvel. You are unique.
In all the world there is no other child exactly like you.
In the millions of years that have passed
there has never been another child like you . . .
You must cherish one another.
You must work—we all must work—
to make this world worthy of its children.
PABLO CASALS

6:09 A.M. (sunrise two minutes earlier than yesterday). 39 degrees, wind S 1 mph (barely enough to stir the fog). Sky: up there somewhere; for the moment, ground fog, thickest over the Ompompanoosuc River, planes the Hollow's contours and shields treetops. Warps an April morning.

Permanent streams: upper, impinged by drought, a soft gurgle, a pliable babble overwhelmed by birdsong . . . cascading wrens and thrushes, laughing woodpeckers, jaunty chickadees, and a dash of creeper, singing from the trunk of a nearby maple; lower, mud bar grows daily, extending from the bank and hooking into the current, a future source of footprints. Wetlands: far shoreline nearly hidden. Overhead, the emergence of blue sky—the first rays of sunshine gild fracturing clouds with luminous silver—and six honking geese, five in a *V* and one alone, bellies freshened by sunlight, a yellowish radiance. Pond: mist drifts east, gaunt and unsustainable. A pair of hooded mergansers paddle off the opposite shore. The male works fog to his advantage; he raises his hammerhead crest, a white flash, then lowers the crest and disappears like a magic trick. Song sparrows, upright and exposed, enliven the tangles on both banks, sing like there's no tomorrow . . . which may be the case if there are not enough females to go around. The red-shouldered hawk, east of the pond, lances the morning with two drawn-out screams—the envy of every blue jay.

Red maple buds unfurl, a hint of October in the otherwise gaunt woodlands—a subtle inversion of autumn color. Big-toothed and quaking aspen catkins jiggle, gray green in the breeze. Yellow birch catkins, shorter and less robust and yellower than those of either aspen, attract a foraging chickadee, which eats bits of pollen-bearing anthers. A few spent flowers join a robin on the shoulder of the road.

DOR: spring peeper and red eft.

AOR: robin, foraging for exposed earthworms. Four slugs heading west. Eft in transition to newt on its way back to the marsh.

Out of the fog: chickadee whistling seventeen minutes before sunrise; from the hemlocks on the eastern rim of the Hollow, barred owl hoots a minute after sunrise, loud and hollow, double-barreled enthusiasm, hounds the new day. Turkeys gobble and grouse drum. Hermit thrush sweetens the morning, sings two notes simultaneously, an ethereal duet with himself, wringing out the last bit of music—a tapered melody. A wide range of tones, the Aretha Franklin of songbirds.

Robin, also a thrush, high in a white birch, framed by catkins, sings. Although not as sweet as the hermit thrush, robin's song is long and complex, with carols, whistles, pauses, and phrases. Keeps on keeping on, something to contemplate . . . more Leonard Cohen than Aretha. Later this month, scarlet tanagers, those gorgeous pack-a-day songbirds, will drop their gravelly Tom Waits voices out of the oaks. Until then,

Coyote Hollow belongs to hermit thrushes and robins, the sacred and secular.

Haphazard calls of jays everywhere and unsynchronized. Chickadees: if not visiting the feeder, then whistling or being chased by whistler . . . a species-specific unwinding of spring, a repeatable pageant a million years running, playing to a particular audience (as well as a sympathetic observer standing on the edge of a muddy road.) While chickadees were perfecting their two-note love song, one branch of apes was forsaking life in the trees for life on the savannah, fur bristling between their toes.

Under one sugar maple, seven twigs on the ground, swollen buds, infant leaves, and delicate flowers. Nipped by a red squirrel that sits on the branch lapping beads of sap. Rust-colored rodent with a sweet tooth.

∽

I leave for Colorado early tomorrow to meet Isabelle Linny, my itsy-bitsy granddaughter, and to see Casey and Becky for the first time in fourteen months—a hiatus I hope never to duplicate. And when I come home at the end of the month, I'll prepare to leave Coyote Hollow . . . to say goodbye after twenty-four years of joy and heartache. Linny and I had eyed the valley since 1982: the marsh, the inherited sense of isolation, and the proximity to schools and services. We bought the Hollow in 1997, one hundred acres with a long view and a vibrant marsh. To downsize while I'm still ambulatory, to soften the emptiness of a fledged household, and to take advantage of Vermont's escalating real estate market, I sold Coyote Hollow on what I hope is the downslope of the pandemic. Three days on the market. Five offers—several after virtual tours—all more than the asking price.

My life knots across this landscape: my boys grew up here, their mother died here as I stood over our bed wondering if she was still breathing. I've adored my wild neighbors and have taken solace in the seasons, more now than ever before. I've raised chickens, gardened, grown apples, raspberries, and boys. Propagated bittersweet memories.

I've hosted parties, including Jordan's graduation . . . sixty-five sleepover classmates and forty pounds of chicken wings. Who knows how much alcohol?

I fell in and out of love here. And in again.

Every corner of the house has a story, every appliance a tale. Every front yard tree is an ecological parable.

One December, four days after Thanksgiving, we smelled methane in the kitchen. Everyone searched in vain for the source. Eventually, I called the contractor who had renovated the kitchen and installed the gas stove weeks before; he couldn't find the leak. Desperate, I called the propane distributor, who arrived shortly, accompanied by a gas-sensitive wand and an eager trainee with a clipboard and checklist. They stalked around outside the house, examining the propane tank and lines, the elbow joints, all the connector nuts and washers, the basement inlet, and all the indoor pipes. The distributor lectured and explained. The trainee took notes and asked questions. Eventually, they examined the stovetop itself. The magic wand registered gas, but no one could pinpoint the source. The following day, pouring a bowl of cereal, I discovered the gas leak ... cooked giblets idling in a pot of water. I called the contractor and distributor and confessed.

From Jordan's bedroom, lights out, the boys and I would watch summer thunderstorms rolling over the marsh at night. I'd wade knee deep in the muck to record booming bitterns and look for ducks. I've been a steward of the landscape that sustained me for twenty-four years. Although my life has been a rollercoaster of emotion, privilege, and joy, the seasons have been a source of faith, predictably unpredictable, a buttress against loss and a source of fascination. During the pandemic, my valley rediscovered was an unexpected gift.

Now, the time has come to untether, to say goodbye and waltz into the inevitable, unknown future.

༄

Chickadees, cheerful and provocative as ever, my black-capped lifeline throughout an arthritic year ... long may they sing, long may they carry on. And long may I find them endearing.

Day 414

05 May 2021

Cinco de Mayo

Everybody has to be somebody.
You bring yourself wherever you go.
STEPHEN B. RASHKIN

5:35 A.M. (sunrise one minute earlier than yesterday; thirty-four minutes earlier than April 13; two hours and forty-five minutes earlier than on the Winter Solstice). 46 degrees, wind SW 2 mph; rainy morning, soupy ground. Sky: heaven and Earth one, seemingly infinite anastomosis of rising fog and lowering clouds, threads and tubes of moisture rising and falling. Water sound trumps bird sound. Splashing, gurgling, purling toward the marsh. A background chorus of gullies and intermittent streams. Permanent streams: fuller, louder, and surprisingly more transparent than two weeks ago, siphoning the water-logged hillside. Wetlands: visibility and detail are reduced by rain and fog; hints of green amid old reeds, tiered and tired brown, collapsing under the weight of their own infrastructure. The main channel swells and spills across the marsh. Bird silent. Two mallards cut through reflected evergreens, hillside impressions in their wake, a Renoir or Monet knockoff. Peepers peeping and trilling, a protracted breeding season . . . far beyond the last breeding flurry of wood frogs. On deck: pickerel frog, American toad, gray treefrog, green frog, and bullfrog, bloated Buddha calling from the edge of deep water, all mouth and belly propelled by large, edible legs. Pond: dancing raindrops, concentric circles, irises above the bank, and hen merganser that I mistake for a stick (until she flushes). Dogs soaked . . . no interest in duck.

Yellowthroats singing in the reeds, ovenbirds in the woods. Jay masquerades as hawk. Patches of male red maple flowers stain the road dark red, scabs on the ground, roadway measles.

༄

It's good to be home. The airports felt as though many Americans had the same idea I had—not necessarily visiting Casey and Becky in Grand Junction, more like, *Let's go somewhere, anywhere.* In the terminal, American Airlines announced every fifteen minutes that failure to wear a mask above your nose unless eating or drinking may result in a lifetime ban from flying with the airline. And terminals announced federal fines up to $500 for non-face-mask compliance. Everybody in the airport or on the plane seemed either in a good mood or sound asleep.

Some flights were nearly empty; on others, people were packed into rows like sardines in a can. American Airlines served nothing, even on longer flights from Phoenix to Philadelphia and La Guardia to Dallas.

Sad to say goodbye. Vermont: rain and snow and shoutouts to winter. Colorado: warm and bone-dry. Indian paintbrush and claret cup cactus in bloom. One life bird: sagebrush sparrow, running, tail up like a miniature roadrunner, across a dirt road between patches of gray-green sagebrush. The road twisted through a narrow sandstone valley, red walls etched and painted by early Americans. Bighorns. Pumas. Lightning. Stylized people. Circles and lines . . . a lasting tribute to the tenacity and endurance of human expression.

Beyond the bassinet: at seven weeks, Isabelle may have yet to fully appreciate the petroglyphs and pictographs (or the hurried sparrow). I kept her bird list, *Birds Seen While Sleeping or Nursing*, which included an imperious loggerhead shrike, nattily feathered; vesper sparrow; black-headed grosbeak; Gambel's quail; black-billed magpie; house finch; Say's phoebe; cardinal, red as a poinsettia; and white-crowned sparrows, traveling minstrels headed north. And, while watching the day draw to a close, two desert bighorns on a ledge, ewe and lamb.

ᕲᕰ

Back home: last night, turkeys and owls, an evening duet, seemed to answer each other.

Broadcast in the rain. Two geese, low, rain rolling off their wings, head north. Ovenbird and broad-winged hawk, one monotonous, the other piercing. Blue-headed vireos, branch to branch, sluggish as molasses. Red-eyed vireos either have not arrived in the Hollow or have taken a vow of silence. Chipping and white-throated sparrows in the front yard. Pileated and red-shouldered hawks yoked to nests, both conspicuous by their vocal absence.

What a difference a year makes: last year, May 5 was drier and greener, spring progressed more quickly—bitterns called in the marsh, tanagers in the pines. Rose-breasted grosbeaks visited the sunflower feeder, black and white warblers the trunks of maples. Everywhere winter wrens sang their hearts out. Spring is the DNA of the new year. This year is wetter and colder—birds remain bunched in southern woodlands waiting for an opportunity to move north.

Sitting in front of the computer on a rainy morning, wet and chilled, I think of Becky and Casey, and of Isabelle's infectious smiles, her new-found horizons expanding . . . may they never stop.

Day 416

07 May 2021

Growing, ripening, aging, dying—
the passing of time is predestined, inevitable.
SIMONE DE BEAUVOIR

5:33 A.M. (sunrise one minute earlier than yesterday). 30 (bleak) degrees (unfortunately, I already packed my mittens and ski cap), wind S 1 mph. Sky: nearly flawless, several suggestions of clouds along the southern rim, tender twists of mauve, all that remains of daybreak; a far cry from yesterday's Technicolor rainbow and the pair of geese that crossed in front, flushed with lemon light. Permanent streams: upper, calming down; lower, two phoebes perch over the water, tails flicking, their nest either on the underside of the snowmobile bridge or in the opening of the cement culvert under the road, the mouth of a twenty-first-century cave. Wetlands: frost glazed and green along the main channel; pools reflect hemlocks and pine, a Saint Patrick's Day green. Hidden in the old, broken reeds, peepers broadcast from unseen bowls of water. Across the marsh, barred owl caterwauls behind a screen of evergreens. Pond: rolling mist, a loss of heat.

Hints of color, an inversion of autumn. Moldering (male) flowers of red maple on the road transformed into red-brown scabs, floral measles. Infant leaves: aspen sage-green; red maple red green; sugar maple lime green, black cherry Kelly green; all the rest of the woods a run of olive and mint and jade . . . the birth of another year. Beech leaves unwind, long and soft. Ebony buds of white ash linger, dark as ravens, round as marbles . . . leaves open late, drop early.

In 1948, Donald Culross Peattie, in *A Natural History of Tree of Eastern and Central North America*, wrote,

Every American boy knows a great deal about White Ash. He knows the color of its yellowish sapwood and the pale brown grain of the annual growth layers in it. He knows the weight of White Ash not in terms of pounds per cubic foot but in the more immediate and unforgettable sensation of having lifted and swung a piece of it, of standard size. He even knows the precise resonance and pitch, the ringing tock of it when struck. For it is of White Ash and White Ash only, that good baseball bats are made.

No longer. Last night, I watched the Yankees play the Houston Astros. I lost count of the number of maple and hickory bats that shattered, barrels sailing across the infield. Ash is not too brittle, and the wood is flexible and pliable, but not too soft. Ideal for a baseball bat. Evening grosbeaks love the tan seeds that dangle like ornaments from the winter trees and create spots of vegetative mist in a hardwood forest. Unfortunately, the invasive emerald ash borer loves ash heartwood, and throughout its range white ash is threatened. The twenty-first century's version of the chestnut blight and Dutch elm disease. And, increasingly and sadly, splintered maple and hickory baseball bats and airborne kindling have become commonplace in our national pastime.

❧

For the love of the game, a baseball memory: summer of 2008, Jordan, twelve, was just out of sixth grade, a middle infielder and pitcher with an exaggerated leg kick—a la El Duque, the steady Yankee starting pitcher who had defected from Cuba. Jordan played for an unaffiliated youth team I coached, the Twin State Peregrines, a band of eleven- and twelve-year-olds, all members of the Connecticut Valley Little League all-star team. In August, I chaperoned the Peregrines on a Good Will Baseball Tour of Cuba. After two years and four tries, the U.S. Treasury Department's Office of Foreign Assets Control (OFAC) granted me permission to travel with the boys and five other coaches. (Not having a *real* job and being the son of a Jewish mother, I had the time and persistence to keep reapplying.) For the Peregrines, going to Cuba was as remote as going to the moon—several had never been on a plane; one had never been to Boston.

A South Florida congressman publicly opposed the trip. A Vermont senator publicly supported it. President George W. Bush, who once owned the Texas Rangers, apparently didn't care. In deference to American foreign policy and Cuban American blowback, however, Little League International refused to sanction the trip. The media were on board. *Sports Illustrated, National Public Radio, The Boston Globe, The Miami Herald,* and *The Washington Post* covered our preparations. CNN, MSNBC, BBC, *The Guardian,* and *The Boston Globe* covered the games, some of which we won. Fidel Castro's younger brother traveled with us and organized a statehouse dinner at the Hotel Nacional de Cuba, where we were joined by Cuban and American diplomats. Players learned the art of giving an interview.

The boys played hard in oppressive heat and humidity, listened to a *very* long sermon in a chapel without air conditioning, and ate mangos in the outfield during games—one ball field had three fruit-bearing trees in left center; whenever a baseball landed among the trees, it was ruled an automatic *mango double.* The boys traded baseball cards and gave donated equipment to opposing team members. No Peregrine spoke Spanish; no Cuban ballplayer spoke English. A translator helped broker in-game disputes. Everyone swung aluminum or titanium bats. Wooden baseball bats in Cuba were cut and milled in Ontario, mostly maple and hickory. Ash bats were rare.

After most games, the opposing Cuban coach gave a speech thanking us for coming and helping to normalize the relationship between two countries separated by less than a hundred miles of ocean—but also by an ideological gulf that seems to go on forever. (A point of geographic proximity: Key West is closer to Havana than my writing desk is to Boston.) During their speeches, Cuban coaches often mentioned George Washington and Abraham Lincoln, which told me two things: 1) Cubans knew more about our history than we did about theirs; and 2) Cubans honored our founding principles. Principles we've gone to war to uphold . . . yet for reasons beyond my comprehension were discarded during the last presidential election—and particularly on January 6.

The Peregrines, being adolescents, were oblivious to national politics . . . but *not* to unique Caribbean birds. The left fielder saw a bee hummingbird, the smallest bird in the world; everyone saw green woodpeckers, bananaquits, clouds of black vultures, and red-legged thrushes rushing around gardens and ball fields, upright and well postured like front lawn robins.

On the side of a government building in downtown Havana, an enormous metal sculpture, a minimalist profile of Che Guevara . . . the suggestion of beret, nose, beard, and unlidded eye open to the plaza. Jordan mistook sparse Che for Bob Marley, neither of whom had much to do with baseball bats.

Ovenbirds arrived overnight, ahead of most other neotropical migrants. In the absence of red-eyed vireos . . . ovenbirds pick up the slack. Did these ovenbirds avoid an over-Gulf flight and spend the winter in Florida, foraging among coral snakes and ground skinks?

Parula whispers in the pines. House wren cuts loose in the thickets. Flickers laughing in the aspens, not the derisive laugh of pileateds, much higher and faster. As red as a poinsettia, the neighborhood cardinal is ostensibly here to stay. Perched in sapling ash, leans back and whistles— long, downward slurs—one of the few birds I converse with (I think we dialogue; I'm not sure what the cardinal thinks). My dogs, in unconcealed bewilderment, sit on the driveway, tongues lolling between blunt teeth, patiently awaiting a helpful signal as they watch the day open up and me lost in memory.

Day 419

10 May 2021

Let me have wisdom, Beauty, wisdom and passion,
Bread to the soul, rain when the summers parch.
Give me but these, and though the darkness close
Even the night will blossom as the rose.
JOHN MASEFIELD

5:29 A.M. (sunrise one minute earlier than yesterday). 46 degrees, wind S less than 1 mph. Sky: the day's somnolent beginning. No breach in the cloud ceiling, gray and misting, raindrops cling to every twig, bud, and infant leaf. Permanent streams: clear as gin, a concise flow, background vocals for male turkey gobbling and strutting in a woodland clearing; lower, just above the bank, a pair of silent catbirds (FOY) forage in moldering leaves. Wetlands: three geese in the main thread flanked by thin blades of green, white breasts bright, the pledge of the struggling sun. Pond: sprinkles dimple the surface, shallow, concentric circles expanding into oblivion.

Shadbush in flower, narrow white petals limp like wet paper. Purple trillium in bloom. Wan seed heads of coltsfoot look like bleached daises. Five morels rise from the char below the driveway, beneath a gnarled pine, where I burned autumn leaves and needles. Something to look forward to . . . mushrooms and eggs for breakfast.

Sapsucker drills around a maple branch, faint tapping, a ring of shallow, oozing holes. Future food for hungry warblers and hummingbirds.

Without the sun as impresario, birdsong reduced to cardinal's slurred whistle; titmouse; chickadee; the slow and measured notes of blue-headed vireo (soon to be overwhelmed by motormouth red-eyed vireos); and ovenbirds—many, many ovenbirds. A solitary, improvising catbird, the Charlie Parker among songbirds, no note repeated in succession. One yellowthroat sings in gnarled honeysuckle, head back, bill quivering, lemon-yellow breast, black Covid mask. I don't recall yellowthroats and ovenbirds arriving in the Hollow before black and white warblers and myrtle warblers.

Late or not, cool or warm . . . spring remains a triumph of green, soft and emergent green, multitinted green, a lifeline in a tattered world. Mourn or celebrate the roller coaster ride, the imperious demands of a rapidly evolving planet. In *The Sea Around Us* (1952), Rachel Carson devoted four pages to climate change. Few listened. Few saw the associated cost of melting glaciers and rising oceans, the northward march of ticks and tropical diseases, and income disparity. Homelessness. It's not the largest, the strongest, or the smartest that survive; it's the most adaptable. Marooned by Covid, that's all some of us talk about now . . . a liminal landscape, magical and frightening. Yellowthroat tilts his head back and pours out a song, the shocking beauty of an unremarkable song . . . he takes what the Earth gives him. Win or lose.

Day 422

13 May 2021

Alternatively, anyone who favors intelligent design
in lieu of evolution might pause to wonder
why God devoted so much of His intelligence
to designing malarial parasites.
DAVID QUAMMEN

5:25 A.M. (sunrise one minute earlier than yesterday). 37 degrees (feels like winter, sounds like spring), wind calm 0 mph. Sky: mostly clear, the south horizon rinsed in rose. Permanent streams: both volume and volume diminishing. Wetlands: flying in from the north, three loud geese bathed in warm light, bright against the sky. Pitch into the marsh, wings bowed and feet lowered like landing gear. Land with a splash, heads periscoping above the new growth. Off to the south, scarlet tanager (FOY) sings in the pines, measured and harsh. Yellowthroats, heads tilted back, cut loose through the alders and cattails. No sign of catbirds. Pond: mist drifting west; turkey gobbling in the clearing on the hillside above seems late to the party. Red-eyed vireo (FOY) singing in the red pines south of the feeder stream, over and over and over. Even the flight up from the jungles of Amazonia wasn't enough to dull his quest. *Brace yourselves*, I tell the dogs. *He's with us for a while . . . and there's a lot more of them on the way.*

Aristocratic remove: on a cold morning pileated and flicker call, a wild duet, proclamations so loud and incessant that even my skin notices, the woodpeckers themselves hidden. Red-shouldered hawk, preceded by a scream, flies across the marsh, head down, searching for a wayward vole or chilled sparrow. Bitterns are back, and hummingbirds, rose-breasted grosbeaks, chipping sparrows, and black and white warblers whispering in the duff. Ravens and crows conspicuous by their absence, jays by their silence. Ovenbirds. Blue-headed vireos. Purple finches. Phoebe and robin feeding chicks, one inside the barn, the other in a shrubby cedar. No bats behind the barn door.

In the disheveled pines along the road, rapid-fire delivery of house wren. With each stanza, the lower half of the slightly decurved bayonet bill and short, stiff tail bounce in cadence, quivering body parts. Chums for company, the audio version of Tinder. A second wren appears.

Watches and listens and then inspects a vintage hairy woodpecker hole, in and out. Emerges, a bill full of debris, a spring-cleaning. Then, two wrens share a pine snag, one singing, the other listening, evaluating— king and queen of the thicket. Perhaps an eventual mixing of genomes, the scaffolding of evolution. The palette of natural selection.

Day 427

18 May 2021

There's a slow, slow train
comin' up around the bend.
Bob Dylan

5:21 A.M. (sunrise one minute earlier than yesterday). 46 degrees (cool enough to hold black flies at bay but not mosquitoes), wind N less than 1 mph. Sky: textured, shades of blue and gray; in the west vaguely colorized, a lavender wash. Permanent streams: upper, limpid and quiet; lower, slower flow, mumbles like a disembodied bittern, a hollow-sounding tribute. Wetlands: green growth traces both sides of the main channel; everywhere else (at the moment), a green wash amid older, timeworn reeds, broken by the weight of winter. Marsh slowly coming of age. Swamp sparrow (FOY) trilling in the alders. Red-shouldered hawk, yesterday's provocateur, is today mute. Pond: apple petals afloat, floral canoes, spring's finest flotilla. Catbird in the tangles meows and then riffs through sunrise. Hen merganser on the shoreline spit, the second morning in past four days. Bolt upright like a murre on a crag. We look at each other, her yellow eyes burning holes in the morning. Then, she leaps into the air . . . no taxiing across the water, no stirring of the apple petals, which drift, fade, sink with the burden of the season.

Yellow birch catkins litter the road like so many pale-green caterpillars. Aspen seedpods are more conspicuous than leaves, dangling, a dull, pale green. Young beech leaves two toned and delicate, neon green with copper edging, a transient, vernal treasure. Cherry, apple, crabapple petals drift on the tides of the season . . . on the tree, the air, the ground. Ostrich and cinnamon ferns unfurling, trillium flowers fading. Roadside dandelions setting seed.

AOR: hermit thrush, three robins, two tiny efts, a bright toxic orange.

The gloaming: owl pulled down the curtain. Daybreak: titmouse cranks it up.

In limited release: veeries and Nashville warblers arrived in the Hollow last night (both FOY). The impatience of flickers: rapid-fire delivery, rapid drumming, rushing headlong into the morning. Hermit thrushes singing (I can't get enough of hermit thrushes). Blue-headed vireos own the airwaves and still outnumber red-eyed vireos. Where are the red-eyes?

Spring migration 2021 more tiptoe than a road race. When picking Jordan up from Kenyon College the second weekend in May 2016, I visited Magee Marsh on the rim of Lake Erie, between Oberlin and Toledo, and saw twenty-one species of warblers, including more bay-breasted and Cape May warblers than I had seen collectively in my entire life. Second weekend in May 2019, same place for the same reason, I had twenty species, including resident prothonotary and hooded warblers. A friend who recently visited Magee Marsh emailed me last night; she had seen *two* species of warblers. Neotropical migrants taking their time, buffeted by northwest winds and cold snaps.

May 18, 2020: nine species of warblers in Coyote Hollow. May 18, 2021: five (yellowthroat, chestnut-sided, Nashville, ovenbird, black-throated green).

Like baby smiles, no two springs are identical. 2021: broad-winged hawks on time; olive-sided and alder flycatchers still missing. I saw a woodcock yesterday, a plump patron of the alders, wandering through the tangles. Bill down, probing for soft, animated edibles. Eyes up, scanning, hoping not to become something else's soft, animated edible.

Even when the season appears disjointed, I cannot go wrong wandering outside . . . there's always something going on, something to take my mind off packing and eventually leaving home.

Day 429

20 May 2021

Morality is simply the attitude we adopt
towards people whom we personally dislike.
OSCAR WILDE

5:18 A.M. (sunrise one minute earlier than yesterday). 48 degrees (mosquitoes slow but determined), wind WNW less than 1 mph. Sky: a short-lived, romantic atmosphere, a soft, fragile blue-white; clouds washed in rose and peach, margins indistinct . . . a moment of pastel bliss that quickly grades into morning. Permanent streams: moving water second fiddle to birdsong, an uninterrupted outpouring of sweet music and discordant notes. Upper, to my left, yellowthroat in brambles, five notes over and over; to my right, house wren in gnarly pines, wound tight and effusive, a vocal artillerist. I pirouette in the road from one bird to another, leashes encircling my legs. Wetlands: a band of emaciated ground fog suspended above the marsh; bittern in the reeds, camouflaged—streaked like tired cattails—beige and fawn and tan, yellow eyes and bill a lethal combination. Peeper stalker, a compulsive treefrog's worst nightmare. Catbird in the alders, mallard in the main channel, green head gleaming. Pond: apple petals, a recent source of intense beauty, collect along the south shore, sink into muck, another of the year's striations . . . a gift for a future paleobotanist.

DOR: peeper, spread-eagle.

AOR: robin (always robin), hermit thrush. White-lined sphinx moth on fresh raccoon scat imbibing moisture (and who knows what else). Dogs startle moth. Moth bolts. The thinner shepherd snaps unsuccessfully. Moth returns to dung, pointed wings up, tongue unfurling like a New Year's Eve party favor, dowses scat for unimaginable treasures. The original water witch.

High in the soft sky, three crows head east. Grouse drums. Turkeys gobble. Chickadees and titmice whistle. Around the pond, white-throated sparrows sing a clipped version of *Ol' Sam Peabody, Peabody*. Those closer to home release the unabridged version (three or more *Peabodys*). Least flycatcher (FOY) in the thickets along the upper stream; sings a short, snappy, and unmusical *CHEbek, CHEbek* . . . more like an insect than a bird. Warblers: black-throated green, chestnut-sided, yellowthroat, ovenbird, Nashville, redstart, and parula. High in a black cherry, red-eyed vireo, a four-inch songbird with a penchant for repetition, unchains his melody, kick-starts summer. Gray treefrogs in the aspens calling. Suddenly, the Hollow is green and warm, the ground dry, as May slides emphatically toward June.

Rosalie Edge, a woman with a lot of money, patience, and determination, energized friends in Manhattan to buy a chunk of the Kittatinny Mountains in eastern Pennsylvania, an S curve known as Hawk Mountain. The Kittatinny, the last Appalachian ridgeline before the flat Atlantic coastal plain, is a lodestone for migrating hawks (and many other species of southbound birds). Tens of thousands of hawks, eagles, osprey, falcons, and vultures pass Hawk Mountain every fall, birds from as far away as the Barren Grounds. Men had gathered at Hawk Mountain to ambush hawks, a dark tradition with a loyal following. The goal: to eliminate birds deemed morally reprehensible. To stop the slaughter, Rosalie Edge bought the mountain. Through the years, in part thanks to her insight, we've made peace with raptors. Now, we go to Hawk Mountain (and elsewhere) to watch hawks pass by, paying our respects to a dramatic and gorgeous force of nature.

When will we give blue jays, crows, shrikes, and house wrens their proper due? We judge these birds by a moral code best applied only to humans. House wrens punch holes in bluebird eggs and take over the nest cavity. Crows and jays grocery shop in robin and oriole nests. But birds don't kill for fun . . . they kill to survive.

House wren on a limb, singing, dagger bill aquiver. A small bird with a big appetite. Disposable energy. Needs a cavity. Needs a home for five or six brown-speckled, dime-sized eggs. House wrens, tree swallows, and bluebirds coexisted in North America for a million years before humans left Africa. Wrens are not grim miscreants or godless demons; they are not vengeful, disrespectful, or blasphemous. House wrens sing and steal with verve, enthusiasm, and an absence of morality . . . that's a human concept.

Day 431

22 May 2021

Memory,
native to this valley, will spread over it
like a grove, and memory will grow
into legend, legend into song, song
into sacrament.

WENDELL BERRY

5:16 A.M. (sunrise one minute earlier than yesterday). 63 degrees (spring masquerading as summer), wind N less than 1 mph. Awash in the pale light of the moon, owl calling at dawn; titmouse calling at midnight. Sky: clouds almost indistinguishable, traces of blue-white, a drapery of haze; ground fog, thin and sprawling; Mount Ascutney masked. Intermittent streams: puddled. Permanent streams: rapid drawdown on the toe of a drought. Wetlands: mallard quaking in the mist; around the edges of the marsh, catbirds, swamp sparrows, and yellowthroats; in the interior, peepers peep and bittern tails off after an all-nighter. Pond: covered by a veneer of woodland trash—pollen, petals, leaf fragments; like a graceful finger doodling on a dusty table, the breeze inscribes the surface ... curlicues, spirals, flourishes of morphing art. Surface scrimshawed.

DOR: gray squirrel.

AOR: two ravens eating gray squirrel.

A triumphant world of living green: only the ashes are bald, the black-beaded twigs waiting their turn. Striped maple flowers, strings of tiny bells, one above the other, dangle like forest chimes. Yoke-yellow, golden Alexander blooms along the edge of the road. Foamflower—white, lacy, snowflake-like flowers—on thin stems adjacent to a moss-covered stonewall.

Then, as if conjured out of the duff, four morels, big as pine cones, appear next to the foamflowers. Honeycombed and hollow, a mushroom hunter's gold standard. Reflexively, I pick them, mushrooms spilling out of my palm. Breakfast? Dinner? Soup? A Holarctic treat found across the Northern Hemisphere (also in Patagonia). Many species. Taxonomy in dispute, if not disrepair—three species, fifteen species, twenty species. Fake news: an online account claims morels evolved fifty thousand YBP (years before present) from yeast cells, analogous to claiming amoebas begot hummingbirds during the last Ice Age.

Morels followed dinosaurs out of the Jurassic. Unlike most dinosaurs, however, they survived the asteroid strike sixty-five million years ago. Mushrooms fed early humans wandering out of Africa; they provided the first immigrants in the New World, circa 15,000 YBP, a delicious alternative to mammoth pudding, and a treat for every other person that crossed the Atlantic and Pacific after that. Like the location of a timber rattlesnake den or a brook trout pool, mushroom hunters keep mum about morel geography. I look for more on the way home. Find none.

Marvels of athletic accomplishment: ruby-throated hummingbird crosses the Gulf of Mexico nonstop; red-eyed vireo sings nonstop, dawn to dusk, a woodland broken record.

Veery spins tunes out of mist. Flicker loud, an imperious outburst. Pileated silent. Sapsuckers chase each other, an agitation of woodpeckers. Great-crested flycatchers holler. Scarlet tanager, elegance erased, hidden in the oaks, its song a throat-clearing version of the robin's, avian phlegm removal. Yiddish birdsong. Is there a more vibrant red anywhere?

Marsh magnetism: female American toad east of the lower pasture, swollen with eggs, takes an overland path to the breeding pools; treefrogs, trilling in the aspens, take an arboreal route.

On the verge of another day, amid mosquitoes and blackflies, lemony sunlight veiled by haze filters across the Hollow, the transcendency of sunrise. Secular insects and sacred sun . . . dawn effloresces into morning. And I bear witness.

Day 433

24 May 2021

37 days left in Coyote Hollow

If you're brave enough to say goodbye,
life will reward you with a new hello.
PAULO COEHLO

5:15 A.M. (sunrise one minute earlier than yesterday). 39 bracing degrees (mosquitoes quarantined by cold, stiff inside tiny hangers), wind S 2 mph. Sky: delicate rose and blue, a few wispy clouds; ground fog above the East Branch of the Ompompanoosuc River—landscape illusionist transforms hills into islands, the mundane into the magnificent, a glimpse of primal America (or, at least, my vision of early America . . . a green, unmodern world, clean air, clean water, and an absence of combustion engines); beyond my sightline, loon agrees, wild notes spilling out of the pastel sky. Permanent streams: barely audible, water levels dropping by the day. Wetlands: greening reeds across the marsh; dewy spiderwebs on sweetgale isles, white strands on dark brown, ephemeral décor. A colorful hot-air balloon floats over the marsh, in and out of view. Pond: a cauldron of unrepressed mist. In sparsely leafed ash, a chestnut-sided warbler sings his heart out. I stand awed. Dogs sit, puzzled.

DOR: southern flying squirrel, seriously pancaked.

AOR: robins and three turkeys, a gobbler and his harem out for a stroll.

Lilacs, purple and white, flower along the barn driveway. Rich, redolent flowers, a transformative aroma that once lured me and a friend into a remote Arizona dooryard, where we buried our faces in the smell of New England. Aspen seeds, cream-colored dust motes, and white pine pollen, talc-like and golden, drift and settle as pond scum. Japanese honeysuckle and pin cherry in bloom.

From the wooded ledge, the song of a hermit thrush rolls out of the shadows in concert with a pair of dueling veeries, one of which flies over the road, a warm chestnut-red bird. Calls a loud, nasal, piercing . . . *veer.* And then another. Two honks like an impatient motorist. Warbler roster: black and white; black-throated green; chestnut-sided (my new favorite); Nashville; black-throated blue; blackburnian; yellowthroat; ovenbird, the most numerous, the most emphatic, the most persistent, at the moment in close competition with red-eyed vireos for control of the airwaves.

౿

I've struggled with change my whole life. When I was young, whenever Nana returned to Los Angeles after staying with us for six weeks, my mother might have been happy to send her off, but I'd be devastated and cry myself to sleep. I still trade in nostalgia, particularly dates and places and anniversaries, but also feathers, rocks, rattlesnake ribs, skulls, fossils, and owl pellets that may sit unopened for years. When I picked up my autorefill prescription yesterday, I fondled the container, my last refill in the Hollow, rolling it around my hand as though attempting to intuit the meaning of time and nature of life.

After twenty-four years, I have forgotten how difficult it is to move. I'm older, and books and furniture are heavier. Apparently, I never threw much away. After forty years of disuse, I still have my mother's cups and saucers, more suitable for dollhouse refills than a twenty-first-century kitchen. I have outdated college textbooks, term papers, and high school yearbooks, where my hair is long and sun streaked. I found a functionless college roach clip, an elementary school sculpture of a Neanderthal, New York Yankee Yearbooks from midchildhood, my parents' Super 8 home movies, almost every piece of artwork Casey and Jordan ever produced, Linny's journals and pressed plants, condolence cards crammed into two ornate wooden boxes, and my baby album with its scallop-edged black and white photographs. One is a picture of Mrs. Anderson, a severe-looking Swedish matron dressed in a sterile white, hair in a bun tucked under a white pillbox hat. She's feeding a sad newborn his bottle—no indication that seventy-two years later, that unhappy baby would sit in a front yard Adirondack chair in rural Vermont, having joyfully gathered wild mushrooms and listened to warblers, with birds at his beckon, legs crossed, hands gloved, remote from the tyranny of moving . . . If I were any more distracted I'd leave for Costa Rica.

Day 436

27 May 2021

34 days left in Coyote Hollow

Isn't it enough to see that a garden is beautiful
without having to believe that there are fairies at the bottom of it too?
DOUGLAS ADAMS

5:13 A.M. (sunrise same time as yesterday). 61 degrees, wind W 4 mph; looks like summer, feels like summer, sounds like late April. Where are the red-eyed vireos? Sky: big moon in the west, a sliver short of full, the same color as the ground fog, which rises out of marshes, lakes, ponds, seeps and springs, wet meadows, rivers, and streams. Below the moon, a hint of lavender. Permanent streams: last night's cold front triggered a series of thunderstorms, resetting the valley's hypothalamus—Coyote Hollow flirted with ninety degrees yesterday afternoon—adding ground fog . . . but very little water. Wetlands: an arch of mist above the green leaves, far canopy screened by haze. Gray treefrog trilling. Heard but not seen, red-shouldered hawk impales the morning with a single squeal—long, high, and compelling. Pond: still surface with rising mist. Pileated laughs louder than a flicker and with fewer notes, a disturbing laugh, the voice of the unbalanced. Then drums, a powerful riff—tree becoming a tuning fork. A good morning transforms into a better morning.

DOR: wood frog.

AOR: June beetle on its back, legs sculling air. I perform a *mitzvah*. Flip it over. Beetle wanders off on six legs, a chorus line of one.

Starflower (*Trientalis borealis*) blooming, an array of nine sharp white petals and a whorl of long, thin leaves. Plant hugs the ground, clusters brighten pinewoods. Starflower, a perennial, grows in poor, acidic soil around the world's crown. As a boy, I met starflower in the swales of Jones Beach and Fire Island, flanked by sand dunes, growing alongside sphagnum moss and cranberries, shaded by pitch pines and serenaded by gulls, terns, and whippoorwills. Whenever I see starflower, I'm reminded of the ocean, the freedom of summer . . . long walks on the beach and cheering for the Yankees from the bleachers.

It takes work to look for mushrooms and birds simultaneously. I find one morel, a straight-up pine cone of a mushroom, and hear two Nashville warblers, a small accomplishment that propels me into the day.

Where are all the red-eyed vireos? (Never thought I'd say that.) Every spring is different. Water levels are high some years, frog choruses deafening. In other years, water levels are low, choruses politely quiet. One spring, a moose. Another, a golden eagle. But this spring (so far), a silence of vireos. During May 2020 pandemic birding, I'd walk through a tunnel of red-eyed vireo songs, woodland elevator music, small overlapping territories, one after the other. A gradation of vireos—the most abundant songbird in the Hollow—the most abundant songbird in eastern North America. But this year, for the moment, the valley belongs to ovenbirds, emphatically screaming out of mosquito-infested shadows.

～

Yesterday, I read an article in *Proceedings of the National Academy of Sciences* titled "Global abundance estimates for 9,700 bird species." That's out of approximately 10,500 species currently recognized. The authors believe there are fifty billion birds on Earth, six birds for every human, an estimate quantified from *eBird*, an online citizen science database. To check for accuracy, *eBird* data was cross-referenced with more rigorous scientific data from *Partners in Flight* and *Birdlife International.*

The authors noted that nearly twelve hundred species, about 12 percent, have populations of less than five thousand (among the struggling: great spotted kiwi at 377 individuals; Javan hawk-eagle at 630). Nowhere do they mention the California condor, whose wild population barely crests three hundred.

The authors' list of the ten most abundant species in the world is what amazes me the most. The top two, house sparrow at 1.6 billion and European starling at 1.3 billion, are no surprise. However, numbers three and four, ring-billed gull at 1.2 billion and barn swallow at 1.1 billion, are. Number six, alder flycatcher (896 million); number eight, horned lark (771 million); and number ten, savannah sparrow (598 million), are also surprising. Colonial pelagic birds—glaucous gull, black-legged kittiwake, and sooty tern—round out the top ten. Missing from the list are rock dove, dark-eyed junco, and red-billed quelea, a sub-Saharan weaver whose population has been estimated by other biologists to be a billion and a half.

I'm unsure what to make of the list. At its most productive, Coyote Hollow hosts six pairs of alder flycatchers. Where are the other 895,999,988? Are they jammed into the Canadian muskeg? One flycatcher for every couple of black spruce? Competition with its boreal neighbors and close relatives, yellow-billed and olive-sided flycatchers, must be severe.

A billion barn swallows, coursing over the fields of Earth! That would be a sight . . . birds of the wind, graceful and free.

༄

A broad-winged hawk whistles. I rush outside. A blue jay flies away . . . duped again.

Day 441

01 June 2021

29 days left in Coyote Hollow

If a man loves life, and feels the sacredness and mystery of life
then he knows that life is full of strange and subtle
and even conflicting imperatives. And a wise man learns to recognize
the imperatives as they arise—or nearly so—and to obey.

D. H. Lawrence

5:10 A.M. (sunrise same time as yesterday). 45 degrees, wind calm 0 mph, June impersonating April. Sky: latent sunlight, a world swaddled in fog, visibility barely one hundred yards; serrated treetops softened, ridges erased. Mist masquerading as rain condenses on leaves . . . drip, drip, drip. Sounds like a shower, feels like a shower. Pants wet. Dogs soaked. Birds in woods singing regardless—amped-up titmice sling notes, voices slicing through the fog like a sharp ax through soft wood. *Hear, hear, hear.* Over and over. Permanent streams: after nearly a day of rain, upper refreshed, but the volume less than expected; lower, the mudbank is still prominent but smaller. Wetlands: far-shore evergreens soft, amorphous, grayish white, a rolling wave frozen in place. Lone peeper peeping from somewhere in the vast misty green. Nearby, an alder flycatcher calls from the top of a dead and broken alder, gray bird on a gray branch. Voice as challenged as its perch . . . *freeBee, freeBee, freeBee.* Today's marsh give-away. Alder flycatcher perches upright like phoebe but smaller, grayer, and without a tail flick. Pond: rising mist joins fog. Painted turtle at the surface, periscoping, a cautious disc that sinks when it spots me. Chestnut-sided warbler singing from thickets along the eastern shore (Last year, he sang from the west side of the pond. My side.)

AOR: robins eating numb earthworms and dead June bugs, hit-and-run victims.

Catbird, a foggy morning bonus. Cab Calloway, with rufous under-tail coverts and a complex song—high, low, soft, loud, rambling warbles and screeches, phrases both guttural and sweet, full of variation. I look from alder flycatcher to catbird, back and forth. Both lean back, lift their heads skyward, and sing, their lower bills quivering with each note. But comparing the quality of a catbird's song to that of an alder flycatcher would be like comparing a jazz aria to a lifeguard whistle.

White ash in various stages of leafing out. Black cherry and mountain maple flowering. Also in bloom: false Solomon's seal and Jack-in-the-pulpit. In undergraduate botany, I called Jack-in-the-pulpit *Jack-in-the-pupik*, Yiddish for *bellybutton*. Wordplay, a gift from my mother, who had converted the Los Angeles Dodgers' Black catcher, Johnny Roseboro, into *Johnny Rosenberg* whenever Sandy Koufax, the other half of her imaginary all-Jewish battery, pitched.

Five flycatchers sing emphatic, simple songs, collectively balming a cool, wet morning. Least flycatcher. Alder Flycatcher. Great crested flycatcher. Phoebe. Eastern wood pewee, spinning a high, clear, mournful whistle. Known as *suboscines*, flycatchers are a related group of more than a thousand species of primitive songbirds with less-than-stellar voices. Many produce their species-specific song without an example. In other words, there's no learning. Music is innate, like breathing. Male phoebes, for instance, raised in isolation (or deafened), require no auditory feedback to produce their raspy, simple, and signature *feebee, feebee, feebee*.

On the other hand, hermit thrushes produce the most ethereal song in the Hollow, and catbirds, with the most varied song, are punctilious learners—listening, practicing, and modifying. If either emerged from a lifetime of isolation singing fully developed songs, it would be as startling for an ornithologist as if a human child reared in isolation emerged from confinement singing "My Back Pages."

Day 443

03 June 2021

27 days left in Coyote Hollow

*Cultivate the habit of being grateful
for every good thing that comes to you,
and to give thanks continuously.*
RALPH WALDO EMERSON

5:09 A.M. (sunrise same time as yesterday; three hours and eleven minutes earlier than on the Winter Solstice). 57 degrees, wind SE 3 mph. Sky: bland and doughy; drizzle passing through the sieve of branches, leaves drip, and ground fog crawls into narrow valleys . . . crisscrossing like dispersing snakes. Fog overturns the familiar and ignites the imagination. Permanent streams: upper, water level recedes (again), a nearly speechless descent into the marsh; lower, the tongue-shaped peninsula of silt and mud growing (again). Wetlands: mist softens colors and textures, blunts intractable evergreens—the world through atmospheric gauze. Tiny, lacy sheet webs, rich with dew, stretch from twig to twig, reed to reed, the wicked snares of spiders—a welcome ally in the biting insect wars. Pond: female merganser bolts.

DOR: two-year-old garter snake.

AOR: robins (of course), juncos, and two red efts, both neon orange.

Least flycatchers and chestnut-sided warblers rule airwaves above the upper stream; red-eyed vireos and black-throated blue warblers above the lower. Voice of the veery, everywhere and gorgeous.

Turtle on a hook. Yesterday afternoon, Jordan came home for a visit, and we walked the dogs to the pond, listened to warblers, swatted mosquitoes, smashed blackflies, and reviewed packing protocols.

You deal with your stuff; I deal with mine.

Midway on the pond's west shore, where the outflow pipe directs water under the road and across the marsh, a foot-long iron spike had been hammered into the bank. Tied to the tip, two blue nylon cords. One idled in the brown water, and the other moved subtly. Microripples spread along the surface like breath on water. I reeled the cords in. One end tapered into a monofilament fishing line and a naked hook; the other expanded into an unhappy female snapping turtle the size of a bathroom sink. Jordan ran home for a pair of shears, a machete, or a cleaver. Something sharp and significant . . . something big enough to keep our fingers away from the business end of wedge-faced antiquity.

Five hundred mosquito bites later, my arms looked like a relief map of the Appalachian Mountains. Jordan returned with the red-handled salad scissors—one size up from fingernail clippers—more suitable for lettuce than an irascible snapping turtle. Our pod of dogs and people exuded excitement. Jordan controlled the dogs. I pulled the turtle up; her snap-trap jaws were agape. Her wide, pink mouth looked soft, almost velvety. Her beady eyes were black and shiny. Half a dozen leeches dangled from sutures between her scutes like deflated balloons, annelid ornamentations. Mosquitoes bit me; leeches bit turtle . . . bloodletting on both ends of the blue nylon line. Halfway up the bank, the fishhook popped out of the turtle's mouth. Hissing, she slid back into the pond and sunk into safety, a cloud of muck in her wake.

Rescue, a *mitzvah*. Pea-brained turtle the color of mud, an expressionless, irritable, subsurface beast, never rendered an opinion. Long may she live, feasting on the Hollow's discards, a slow-motion sanitary engineer. Crossing between marsh and pond, repetition, decade after decade.

I take solace in repetition, too, sunrise walks, my long-term response to Covid. Isolated at home every day, month after month, and into the second year with no end. In four weeks, I'll leave Coyote Hollow, likely overwhelmed by change and the loss of the familiar, caught on the fishhook of my past. Who will I be when I leave the Hollow? Turtle, as a Buddhist teacher . . . let go, yet continue, accept loss (and they do pile up as time goes on), lean on change and contradiction, life's unavoidable commodities. I have defined myself, in part, by where I live . . . but now I must leave, fortified by memories as the borderline fades between past and future.

Day 446

06 June 2021

24 days left in Coyote Hollow

> *Grief will come to you.*
> *Grip and cling all you want,*
> *It makes no difference. //*
> *Catastrophe? It's just waiting to happen.*
> *Loss? You can be certain of it. //*
> *Flow and swirl of the world.*
> *Carried along as if by a dark current. //*
> *All you can do is keep swimming;*
> *All you can do is keep singing.*
> GREGORY ORR

5:08 A.M. (sunrise same time, third day in a row; fifteen hours, nineteen minutes of light). 64 degrees, wind N 1 mph. Sky: splendid mix of textures and shapes—an aerial six-pack; shades of blue, mostly pastel, a hint of mauve advancing across the east. Without fog, but *not* without mosquitoes, which convene on the dogs' snouts and my sandaled feet. Permanent streams: the volume of water dropping; the volume of birdsong rising—least flycatcher and house wren along the upper; black-throated blue warbler and red-eyed vireo along the lower. Wetlands: green tones, reeds hide open water. On the wing: hooded merganser hen skimming the treetops, duck with a plan, pitching over the alders, wings bowed, rocking and tilting—a fast flapless descent—the warble of flight calls attention to itself. Lands on the pond with a splash and skips on the surface like a shell. Pond: merganser, off the far shore, feathered helmet opening and closing, calling—more bark than quack. Dives once. Twice. Three times. Each surface is a bull's eye within the heart of unfurling ripples. Bobs up like a bathtub toy, once with a tiny crayfish in her bill. No sign of ducklings. Snapping turtle idles against the steep mudbank, head just below the surface. The third morning in a row. Sees me and turns around, scooting along the bottom . . . a descent into salvation, clouds of deeply disturbed silt spread in her wake. Whirligig beetles embroider the surface, aquatic penmanship and fleeting script. Sunrise serenade: hermit thrush shoehorns voice into the morning, supplanting turtle, beetles, and duck. Boy with a new toy, overwhelmed by brilliance.

DOR: garter snake and peeper, small and delicate.

AOR: robins foraging, primarily on grit-encrusted earthworms and broken June bugs.

Five red-eyed vireos, making up for a slow start. One off the end of the driveway, dawn's broken record, leads me down the road and back again, barely pausing. Female cardinal singing along the upper stream—short, choppy whistles and flares. Pileated drum rolls. Agitated grouse bursts out of roadside weeds, wings fluttering, tail fanned, a noteworthy performance. Dogs are interested but restrained.

Two veeries chase each other across the road, brown on the verge of orange. One pauses on a branch and sings, music spiraling out of damp woods. An article published in *Scientific American* suggests that veeries sense a busy Atlantic hurricane season months in advance and prematurely stop re-nesting attempts and head for Brazil on the red-eye. As a hurricane predictor, the abandonment of second (or third) nesting attempts was more accurate than leading meteorological computer models, wrote the paper's author. Although his sample size was small, the Delaware biologist studied a population of veeries for two decades.

We live in a mysterious world, more mysterious than we can possibly imagine.

As buttery light slides down Robinson Hill, I leave the angelic-voiced veeries for an angelic-voiced wood thrush. I'm lured by songbirds, enthralled by their music, Earth music . . . a salve against the task of bubble-wrapping my life. In between sunrise thrushes and an early-evening gin and tonic, the discarding of the flotsam and jetsam of my life. Then, packing, boxing, lugging, scrubbing, vacuuming, sweeping, dusting, disinfecting. And, of course, complaining . . . summoned from the roots of my being. Anything to hold grief at bay.

Birdsong, a lifeline, flung at reality.

Day 449

09 June 2021

Three weeks left in Coyote Hollow

Wilderness is an antidote
to the war within ourselves.
TERRY TEMPEST WILLIAMS

5:07 A.M. (sunrise same time, third day in a row). 70 degrees, wind SE 1 mph. Sky: air thick and soupy—foggy, muggy, sticky, drippy. Rolling thunder, lightning-tempered low-hanging clouds. Permanent streams: last night's downpour fed the atmosphere but not the tributaries; the susurrus of the upper stream is drowned out by energetic vireos; the lower stream's mudbank is as prominent as yesterday. Wetlands: the world stops at the far edge of the marsh, shoreline shrouded in mist, a mere suggestion of trees; green frog joins a chorus of gray treefrogs and peepers, piping and twanging. Strafed by mosquitoes, blackflies, deerflies, and no-see-ums, I'm challenged to stand still. Spilling and shedding blood in Coyote Hollow, an involuntary donor to the *Woodland Red Cross* and reluctant enrollee in the neighborhood food web, the benefit of my contributions not immediately apparent. Pond: insects follow me down the road, a noisy crowd of disparate wings and proboscises. My walk a mobile hemorrhage. Hidden in a patch of blue flag irises, bullfrog belches. Whirligig beetles dashing around and around and around, ephemeral drafts of surface calligraphy. I'd happily watch them longer, but I would be exsanguinated.

DOR: red eft, an orange dot on a brown road.

AOR: female junco, bill crammed with dog fur. German shepherds donate to another nesting season; last year, they contributed to the welfare of chickadees. Farther down the road, a pair of juncos in distress, rapid-fire chips and clicks. Their distraction performance drives us from a hidden nest.

Pileated emerges from an auditory slump, drumming and screaming. Flicker, hushed and hidden within the woodland umbra, a shadow within a shadow. Red-shouldered hawk out of obscurity, barbed voice hurled across the valley, flies circuits in the fog.

June 2021 versus June 2020: more black-throated blue than black-throated green warblers. Ovenbirds quieter, settling inside domed nests under grassy roofs, having left the airwaves to chestnut-sided warblers, yellowthroats, red-eyed vireos, and veeries.

∽

11:27 A.M. 85 degrees, wind N 6 mph, fog dissipating. Inside the house, my thirst for peace of mind slackens amid the dismantled furniture, stacked boxes, and naked walls. Outside, the dogs are barking. I open the front door, expecting UPS or FedEx. Neither. Nor a car nor a hot-air balloon floating languorously over Robinson Hill. Just the slow ebb of a humid morning and dogs ballistic. Beyond the garden, in a front yard lollipop oak, a black bear hugs the tree trunk, tenuously and tentatively like a kid midway up a streetlight, Popeye forearms rippling, claws long enough to open mail savaging the bark. Treed by overexcited German shepherds. Expansive, expressionless dogface, set with black beady eyes, topped by nubbin ears. Dark nose, flat and large, reads layers of the world humans no longer understand . . . the forgotten language of quadrupeds.

Black bear backs down the oak, its weight supported by claws. Although bears walk like us, flat footed and sometimes upright, this one runs like Seabiscuit across the front lawn. In a dash, Usain Bolt, the graceful Jamaican Olympian, reached twenty-eight mph. A robust black bear, a lumbering bundle of muscle and fat, covers forty-four feet a second, hitting speeds of thirty to thirty-five mph. Legendary NFL fullback the late Jim Brown ran the forty-yard dash in 4.5 seconds, a black bear

Black Bear

in less than three. When I was a boy, a camp counselor told me, *If a bear chases you, run downhill, stop, and turn either left or right*—supposedly, the bear couldn't stop and change direction. Nonsense. Black bears are quick and agile . . . the leaner, the faster. The bear's gone in a moment, crashing through the pole-sized pines west of the garden.

Whistling and grinning, I recall leather-bound Fess Parker. Whatever became of my coonskin cap and Davy Crockett bubblegum cards and lunchbox? Consigned to the dustbin of youth. Heeding my past . . . amid a great sense of disorder, I wonder, how many slotted spoons and ceramic pitchers do I really need?

Day 452

12 June 2021

18 days left in Coyote Hollow

*. . . rearrange the
rules to suit yourself.*
TRUMAN CAPOTE

5:06 A.M. (sunrise same time as yesterday). 52 (ideal) degrees, perfect for sleeping on a mattress on the floor in a conflicted and discombobulated bedroom, wind W 1 mph. Sky: overcast, flat shadowless light. Intermittent streams: a necklace of disconnected puddles, the perfect repository for mosquito eggs. Permanent streams: more pulse than flow, water levels dropping and drought tightening. From inside a nearby alder, male yellowthroat chips nonstop, black beak an extension of the black mask, vivid against the yellow throat. The forehead band is more gray than white. Chips in a cold morning, beak barely open. Yellowthroat follows me down the road, alder to alder, calling. Reluctant to leave. Perhaps there's a nest wedged into the crotch of a twig. A second bird answers, a female. Now, both yellowthroats chipping, dry, sharp notes, a repeated duet that fades and stops as I pass out of their territory. Pond: female merganser flies over the pond, quacking, muffled croaks like a mallard with a sinus infection. Turns around and flies back. Circles the pond twice, then lands next to two other female mergansers. When I climb the bank, an atmosphere of crisis prevails. All three ducks flee west, squawks in tow.

Cool air holds deerflies and blackflies at bay. Not mosquitoes. Mobile and persistent, they commandeer my walk, darting around my head like kamikaze pilots. Swallows and swifts elsewhere. Bats on life support. Where can I find a "Rent-A-Dragonfly" service?—maybe three or four?

9 June: 5:07 A.M. 52 degrees, wind N less than 1 mph. The moon passes before the sun, a partial solar eclipse. I can't see the eastern sky and its half-hidden sun, but light in the woods ebbs, dawn idles, shadowless and eerie. Both sunshine and birds are subdued, the songscape held hostage by the eclipse. A few sing, mostly veeries and titmice, a quieter world, less driven by impulse and territorial imperative that on any other June morning would rock the woodlands and the marsh and leave me exalted. Homeward bound, I hear thrashing and snapping along the edge of the lower stream, as though an ATV plowed through the alders. Dogs, leashes taut, face the sound. Less than a hundred feet away, a shadow congeals into a black bear, frozen midstep, midnight dark, head as big as a football, a shadow within shadows. Then, an inaudible pandemonium, breath frozen in place like the hands of a rundown clock. We stare at each other, the bear and I. Then, bear pivots, hurtling through the alders and across the marsh. Dogs relax, leashes slacken, and I head home to boxes piled high with a lifetime of detritus.

On the pasture fence two chipping sparrows; on the garden fence two brown thrashers (FOY). Birds condense time, turning minutes into seconds, enough to inspire even the most philistine of road walkers. I surrender, again, moored to the sparrows and thrashers. Thoughts leach away. Deadlines dissolve. For the moment, the here and now calls. Packing can wait.

Day 455

Behold my friends, the spring is come;
the Earth has gladly received the embraces of the sun,
and we shall soon see the results of their love.
SITTING BULL

5:06 A.M. (sunrise same time, fifth day in a row). 61 degrees, wind N
1 mph. Sky: unadorned, a taut sheet of hoary clouds. Modestly misty.
A cable of fog above the East Branch of the Ompompanoosuc, shredding and fraying. Permanent streams: disappointing flows (I expected
more water after yesterday's rain). Wetlands: from emerald to army, fifty
shades of green. Frogs silenced, miserly as Ebenezer Scrooge. Covid-era
cattails sport last year's seedheads, brown clubs on hollow stalks. Pond:
only the aquatic penmanship of whirligig beetles and water striders and
an oxygen-starved trout (Fish and Game release) disturb the surface.
Yesterday's quartet of mergansers elsewhere. From mud to magic: blue
flag iris, flower fountains spewing above sword-shaped leaves.

On a slight bank, just off the road, thirty square feet of delicate
maidenhair ferns like overlapping, green, luminous hands. False
Solomon's seal and maple-leafed viburnum blooming. Striped and
mountain maple in seed. Every red oak seedling, of which there are
many, echoes its recent history, a tribute to a glut of acorns and the
neglect of squirrels and blue jays.

Wandering through overarching birdsong: red-eyed vireos; yellowthroats; ovenbirds; black-throated blue and black-throated green
warblers; black and white warbler; chestnut-sided warblers; scarlet tanagers; veeries, virtuosi of predawn light; white-throated sparrows; cardinal; rose-breasted grosbeak; alder and great crested flycatchers; phoebes;
catbirds; lonely blue jay; chickadees; white-breasted nuthatches; titmice;
far-off crow, rolling caw like distant thunder. Pewees, sad songs out of
deep shadows; mourning doves, sad songs on the driveway. Pileated and
flicker drumming. Hairy woodpecker calling. Chipping sparrow gathering dog hair on the front lawn, one strand at a time.

The sweet spot of the morning: red-shouldered hawk, one valley to
the west, hurls its voice lancelike, an indelible impression . . . the world of

wonder prevails (again) amid the drudgery and perseverance of packing. I'll leave behind so many pieces of myself, the heartbreak of loss, the joy of birth. For twenty-four years, I have been part of the landscape, every bit as much as the hawk and the tanager. Next spring they sing without me. Amid bittersweet memories is joy . . . I'll be eighteen miles closer to Colorado and my granddaughter.

Day 457

17 June 2021

Casey's 34th birthday

13 days left in Coyote Hollow

The clock is ticking
. . . the red tulip of the fox's mouth;
the up swing, the downpour, the frayed sleeve of the first snow—

so the gods shake us from our sleep.
MARY OLIVER

5:06 A.M. (sunrise same time, seventh day in a row). 43 (I-can-see-my-breath) degrees, wind calm 0 mph. Sky: underbelly rinsed pink by unseen sun, cloudless. Permanent streams: upper, an anemic flow; lower, more than half the main channel a stone pathway. Wetlands: see-through fog hanging above the marsh, frogs silent, but not pileated, who drums behind the malnourished curtain. Pond: rolling mist with an energetic chestnut-sided warbler, high in a cherry, a quiver (or is it a shiver?) accompanying each note, the jittery melody of an intimate of the Neotropics.

Oxeye daisies and red clover bloom along the road's edge, hemmed in freshly fallen needles, courtesy of white pine, arranged by the wind. Three waxwings gorge on juneberries. Crow flies through the woods, subtly twisting and turning to avoid limbs. Chipping sparrow sings from pasture fence, tail like a metronome, a measured cadence that bounces with every note, a whole-body mechanical trill. Phoebe clutch out of the nest, out of the barn, assembled on the pasture fence, already tail-flicking.

Big eyes gather dim light—minstrels of daybreak and dusk. Veery wakes me up and hermit thrush puts me to bed. Songs in harmonic series, simple ratios of vibrations. Known to thrushes. Known to whales. Known to nightingales. Known to wrens. Available to whom else? Harmony, the hallmark of human music, biological—not cultural, follows mathematical and physical principles, earthly sequences, appreciated and employed by other species—hermit thrush the unquestionable virtuoso, its song lush and lovely, rousing shadows.

Flicker, laughing up the sun, knows nothing about packing, owns nothing, just the feathers on his back, leaves when the spirit moves him.

⌒

Late yesterday morning, after a hefty basswood fell across the road, taking down the power lines and forcing me to turn my car around and drive back, I found a painted turtle midroad, below the bank of the pond. The turtle was black and shiny and as big as my hand, an egg-swollen mother—stiff bulges on the inside of her upper hind legs. I picked her up and made three big wishes—for world peace, the end of starvation for elephants and red knots and humans, and an appreciation of the planet we live on. And one little wish, unlikely to be granted or achieved . . . a painless, unemotional move from the outback of *Desolation Row*.

⌒

Her body ravaged by cancer, her laugh remained angelic. The turtle had become Linny's totem, a symbol of slow-paced living and longevity. Our home had become a repository for turtle kitsch and knickknacks: turtle nightstand; ceramic turtle whistle, so piercing that Yogi, the border collie, heard it from the edge of the marsh and came home; turtle jewelry; turtle figurines; turtle carvings in bone and wood; turtle necklace; and an impractical bowl with a tiny porcelain turtle on the bottom that snagged cereal spoons.

On the blue edge of life: I still have the damn bowl, now chipped, and it still snags spoons . . . and memories nearly every morning.

SUMMER

2021

Day 462

22 June 2021

2 days after the Summer Solstice

8 days left in Coyote Hollow

And the seasons, they go round and round
And the painted ponies go up and down
We're captive on the carousel of time
We can't return, we can only look
Behind from where we came
And go round and round and round
In the circle game.

JONI MITCHELL

5:07 A.M. (sunrise same time, third day in a row; one minute later than June 19). 66 (humid) degrees, wind SSW 2 mph. Yesterday evening's well-spaced thunderstorms lit the Hollow, watered the woods and marsh, freaked out the dogs, and accented a red-shouldered hawk that circled beneath the blockade of bruised and angered clouds. I walked into the husk of Jordan's room and watched the storm hurl crooked harpoons into the marsh, my breath and memory echoing off empty walls. Sky: saturated air, rising fog meets low clouds, woods dull grayish-yellow light and dripping; forest debris strewn across the road, the lawn, the driveway, and the roofs of shingled houses. Permanent streams: surf's up (for the moment), a temporary fix that noisily tumbles west. Storm-enlivened catbirds sing from thickets along both streams—emperors of the alders, ministers of the willows—a chorus of joyous improvisation. Wetlands: encapsulated haze. Veeries animate the mist in descending spirals, self-serving duets. Pileated cuts lose, penetrating drum rolls through the fog like ambitious thought. Pond: water level oddly unchanged, striders and whirligigs amid shoals of pine needles. Painted turtle upright in the water, head periscoping. Sinks as I pass. Famished mist rises to knee level, dissipates . . . then gone.

DOR: southern flying squirrel on the driveway, cutest rodent on Earth. The heavy irony of death: round head, big expressive eyes, small ears, an oar for a tail, and parachute flaps on each side of the body between the front and hind legs.

AOR: pair of juvenile crows scavenge eastbound earthworms, lugging sleeves of grit. Fearless birds move slowly downhill, eat and hop, always watching me. Eventually, one flies onto an overhanging limb and the other disperses into the fog.

In front of me, ancient aspen drops a limb. Dogs freeze, but in a neighboring aspen, a black-throated warbler, unfazed, carries on singing while the forest reconfigures. Big-toothed aspen: gray bark, deeply fissured into broad flat ridges. Shallow rooted and short-lived, its wood weak. Tree leans, branches rising in supplication as though begging for longevity. For several years, I've waited for the tree to fall, for the roots to let go after a torrential downpour, *Yet this tree, of no great fame*, wrote Donald Culross Peattie (1948), *only moderately beautiful, and plebeian in its uses, has its secrets.* Herewith are my five big-toothed aspen secrets: 1) triangular leaves burn flame-yellow-orange in late October, after the rest of the hillside has cooled; 2) ruffed grouse and evening grosbeaks eat the buds; 3) woodpeckers nest in the soft wood (even chickadees can excavate a cavity); 4) wood rots quickly, nursing slower-growing, more durable hardwoods; 5) when the wind blows, the leaves speak in tongues—I hear the ocean, the sound of my boyhood . . . the rampant flow of time.

Late August 2015, Gambier, Ohio. Jordan's college orientation, my disorientation. Inside the Kenyon College Bookstore, I found the perfect memento to bring home to Vermont: a plum-purple travel mug that said *Kenyon Dad*. On the sidewalk outside the store, Jordan noticed I walked out with the wrong mug—mine read *Kenyon Mom*. Later in the afternoon, after the parent seminar, the academic dean asked me about Jordan. I told her my daughter was an incoming freshman. Too flustered to correct myself, I left the lecture hall in a daze, said goodbye to Jordan, and began the heavy-hearted seven-hundred-mile ride home, my first cope with an empty nest. Five years later, Covid would be the next.

Catbirds wake me at first light, everywhere and vocal, the jazz riff of the Hollow. There are many more this year than last. Phoebe chicks on the pasture fences, tail-flicking and tolerant. Yellow, black, and white, an evening grosbeak stops at the birdfeeder, empty for a week now. Checks for sunflower seeds in the hollow plastic tube . . . a prisoner of its own history visiting a once-dependable food source. Phantom feeding station, like phantom limb, triggers visceral memory.

Besides oxygen uptake, the grosbeak and I have something else in common. At night I go to read in a chair . . . no longer there.

Day 468

28 June 2021

2 days left in Coyote Hollow

Now more than ever you can be
generous toward each day
that comes, young, to disappear
forever, and yet remain
unaging in the mind.
Every day you have less reason
not to give yourself away.
WENDELL BERRY

5:09 A.M. (sunrise same time, second day in a row; two minutes later than Tues, June 22). 72 degrees, wind SSW 3 mph. Sky: the moon, midvalley, a bulge of more than half, oversees the rose pink of dawn. Scattered clouds grade to mauve, then brighten into overexposed white that thickens like meringue. Intermittent streams: clefts in mud. Permanent streams: upper, an aqueous version of a blackburnian warbler song—high, thin, cheery—but desperately diminished flow; lower, puddled and silent, almost vacant. Wetlands: in the throes of drought; a shallow isle of fog, midmarsh. Red-shouldered hawk, also midmarsh, perched at the top of a snag, veiled in mist, surrounded by green, thirsty reeds, bludgeons the morning—hurls voice against the rising sun. Coyote songs flow down Robinson Hill, invigorating break. (Hawk and wild dogs—no boxes to schlep—have time to sing.) Pond: brushstrokes of haze; striders and whirligigs skate through a mosaic of pine needles. A child's neon balloon, midpond, an island of unwelcome color, floats on the surface, deflated, as out of place as a video game on a camping trip.

AOR: along the mouth of the driveway, two worn and homeless kitchen chairs; a crow on a mission wanders past the chairs, considers them, and then continues uphill and out of sight. Midroad, grit-picking robins, two. Aimless robins, three. One veery, dull pumpkin-colored, big eyes black and moist, flushes, then sings.

⌒

Two days from departure, two days left in the home where my boys fledged and Linny died, where I nursed the long scar. Dogs, cats, hamsters, chickens, and chinchillas, loved in their time, lie in unmarked graves. Memories like waves undulate, rolling in at every turn. Veery, harmonizing with itself in a moment of bliss, a one-bird duet, sends notes cascading to lighten the dark and soothe a distracted mind. I pause, listen, and draw up a half-hearted smile. Obedient, if oblivious, dogs sit, snapping flies, tongues lolling, waiting, unknowingly, for their lives to be uprooted.

⌒

Midmorning, 22 June, the most prominent roadside tree fell, a grandfather white pine, thick, crooked, and imposing. Upper limbs, great sieves of green needles that filtered sunlight. Lower limbs weathered and busted like swords of surrender. A deep, oblong cavity in the lower trunk, soaked by a thousand rainstorms. Dark brown heartwood, punky and absorbent, rotted and spread until living sapwood gave out behind the bark, and, unceremoniously, the tree fell. A week later, the air still smells of broken pine.

When the pine fell, it took other trees with it, ripping a half-moon crater in the surrounding canopy, lighting hundreds of square feet of earth. Scarred maples and aspens stand in disorder along the edge of the opening, sheets of bark stripped or peeling as if rubbed by an enormous buck.

⌒

Young crow cawing. Gravel-voiced tanager, high in aspen, keeps company with ten thousand whispering leaves. Three young nuthatches, in partial down, walk up an oak trunk. Pileated flies by, wings flashing. In the front yard, evening grosbeaks and blue jays compete for ripening cherries. Two bats behind the barn door.

My tenure in Coyote Hollow concludes on June 30, the baton handed to another family, whose children will sit upstairs in Jordan's room and watch storms cross the valley and the ladder of stars rise into the sky. Cloistered at home for the past fifteen months, I have reacquainted myself with the seasons, ordering my mind by watching and writing, satisfying my curiosity, centering my thoughts. Recently, for a few magical moments every morning, the Hollow has allowed me to forget I was leaving one home to create another. I've never lived anywhere longer than here and never loved anywhere more. Plumbing the depth of memory and the fickleness of time, I joyously jettisoned useless belongings. Yet I am undone by moving. Finally, as I face the next zip code, perhaps the last act, the seams of well-being frayed but secure . . . I'll press on coloring my life outside the lines.

∾

1:17 P.M. 92 degrees, wind W 8 mph. Coyote midroad, gray and shaggy, fur in tufts like a neglected dog, runs south down the Hollow, crosswise to the wind, beneath a flotilla of clouds. Weathervane fur. Mammalogists call them *Canis latrans*, Latin for *talking dog*. We call them *coyote*, from Mexican Spanish, the most vocal wild North American mammal: barks, woofs, growls, yips, howls, and sings in a chorus, the woodland choir. Coyotes (like people) vary their social structure according to their needs . . . packs, pairs, solitary. Packs are extended families: alpha male and female, betas and omegas—two-year-olds from last year. Alphas breed. Everyone else helps: babysitting, playing, teaching, protecting.

The very beast that lent the Hollow its name. What more could I ask for as I brace myself on the eve of departure? A lone coyote like me— sometimes social, sometimes solitary—facing our uncertain future.

Day 493

23 July 2021

Hurricane Hill

To every thing there is a season,
and a time to every purpose under heaven:
A time to be born, and a time to die;
a time to plant, a time to reap that which is planted;
a time to kill, and a time to heal;
a time to break down, and a time to build up;
a time to weep, and a time to laugh;
a time to mourn, and a time to dance.

BOOK OF ECCLESIASTES

5:29 A.M. (sunrise one minute later than yesterday; twenty minutes later than June 28, when I teetered on the precipice of relocation). 54 degrees, wind E 2 mph. Sky: sun rising red hot above the south rim of Smarts Mountain, twenty-three crow miles to the northeast. Then, turning pink, yellow, white—turning the eastern horizon rich with possibility. An ephemeral brushstroke: rose and pink electrify the east horizon. Farther north, Mount Moosilauke, the southern edge of New Hampshire's White Mountains, twenty miles beyond Smarts Mountain, capped by serrated clouds the same shade of blue-gray as the mountain, the color of weathered granite lit by the sun. Mist peels off the White River, merging with mist peeling off the Connecticut, a cotton-thick echo of flow. The two rivers cast moisture like snakes shedding skins, visibly, viably, vibrantly transforming a walk into momentary triumph. Above the fog, across the White River, dark cows wander a florescent hillside pasture. All around me, dewy webs glisten, spider bling. I hear the highway whine, the empty whistle of a train, the language of a raven.

Hermit thrush, its shadow psalm rising out of the hemlocks, reminds me of the pine barrens of Long Island, the slopes of the Green Mountains, and the shadowed creases of Robinson Hill, a devotion to daybreak. Red-eyed vireos committed to tedium. A sapling rises out of a knotted grapevine, hosting three tolerant cedar waxwings, which attend the grapes. Some fruit ripe, some green, a wild vineyard along the brushy edge of a meadow. And, then, in succession, each species replacing the one before it, three bluebirds, two chipping sparrows, a catbird, and a phoebe, tail pumping rhythmically. One of the bluebirds returns—bill up, head back—and swallows a small, green grape.

Tanager in the open, summer bright and full of song. Needs a lozenge. Athletic catbird grips a Jerusalem artichoke along the edge of a paved driveway, one foot above the other, a sideways perch below a perfection of yellow flowers. Blackbird traffic—more than thirty, low overhead, an amalgamation of flapping sounds. I turn, expecting a car. A juvenile eastern bluebird, perched on an electric line, basks in sunshine. Morning prevails.

Rain puddles dot the road. A slug tries to beat the sun to the other side. Water purls toward the White River in shallow wrinkles below overarching ferns. Two juvenile woodpeckers, downy and sapsucker, share a gray birch that bends toward the ground. Probe holes, one after the other, a diligent investigation. Woodpeckers look like toddlers and act like toddlers. Bump into each other, visibly careless, seemingly forgiving.

I hear chickadees and titmice and jays. See mourning doves, and a male cardinal flying across the yard every afternoon, from maple to oak, a flash of red in an ocean of green. But thus far, all four species have avoided the feeders that hang from shepherd hooks off the deck. The first bird to visit my avian food bank, a juvenile ruby-throated hummingbird, almost immediately after the sugar water went up. Now, four or five belligerent hummingbirds zip around the deck, perch on the railing and rocking chairs, or chase each other, jousting bills like lances . . . poking, prodding, jabbing.

First bird to the sunflower feeder: a male American goldfinch. Second: a dark-eyed junco, which displaces the goldfinch. Third: a chipping sparrow, the most submissive of the three. For the moment, the feeders are theirs.

❧

My neighbor has two beehives, a statue of the Buddha, a line of colorful prayer flags, a forty-six-mile view to the northeast, and an indigo bunting singing in the crown of a pasture maple . . . a leafless limb with electric color. *Passerina cyanea*, a fitting epithet, jungle blue, bright like a morpho butterfly. Although unambiguously gorgeous, blue feathers of bunting (and of bluebird and blue jay) are a conspiracy of light—structural color, not the work of pigment. Feathers scatter blue light, absorb all other wavelengths. Indigo bunting, bill up, spilling paired phrases, loud and prominent, a chromatic imposter . . . presumed color that rivets my attention.

On my deck, eleven hundred feet above sea level, gazing down the slope of Hurricane Hill, northeast through a green portal into a new neighborhood. Up the road, the Hartford Town Forest and Hurricane Wildlife Refuge, more than five hundred acres of woodlands, streams, vernal pools, and three fallow reservoirs. Same world, same perspective, different angle from Coyote Hollow. On the forest floor, sun-dabbled shadows like a fawn's coat. A sweep of hemlock boughs. Broad-winged hawk clutches a terminal branch, rocks in the breeze, an avatar of trans-location—Vermont to Brazil, and back again (hopefully)—a biannual performance staged beneath a legion of clouds, above the scaffolding of the hemisphere. Makes my move from Thetford Center to White River Junction seem insignificant . . . but emotions run heavier than feathers.

Eighteen miles south of Coyote Hollow. A new geographic pan-orama, a new verse in the poetry of a watershed. A profoundly blue de-parture and homecoming laced with sadness and tension. My last night in the Hollow, my voice bouncing around an empty house amid the largesse of memory, I slept on the floor of the glassed-in sunroom, on a dog bed and a pile of blankets. Bluebirds and buntings continue to make me feel at ease here on the Hill. In time, I found my missing toothbrush and measuring cups. The dog food bowls reappeared in a clothes hamper beneath a pile of towels and a parka. Books will be sorted out in time . . . But like an amputee, I feel my phantom limb. I can close my eyes and sense Robinson Hill and the grand marsh, its green field of hip-high reeds bent by the wind. The hawk and bittern call across my dreams. I still have the urge to fill feeders that hang else-where . . . and when the owl calls at night, I open my eyes to the dark, geographically dislocated.

Day 501

31 July 2021

Longevity milestone

One month on Hurricane Hill

Attention without feeling,
[. . .] is only a report.
MARY OLIVER

5:38 A.M. (sunrise one minute later than yesterday). 48 degrees, wind WNW 4 mph (wild geese come to mind). Sky: a relocation of nighttime raindrops, leaves shaking and dripping; the sun conducts from behind a bank of clouds; overhead, the half-moon loses its midnight luster, tarnishing, fading, vanishing. Across the north, peach brushstrokes grading to lavender; east of Smarts Mountain, clouds like molten iron, underbellies rimmed in sunlight . . . on fire. North, beyond Moosilauke, a bruised blue gray. South and west, clear and bright. Not a trace of fog nor a hint of Manitoba wildfires. Two flocks of blackbirds skim the treetops, flying northwest, a glimpse of autumn.

In a roadside tangle, the dark forest looming, strips of meadow flowers: mullein, stalks of small, yellow flowers above rosettes of diaper-soft leaves; black-eyed Susan; Queen Anne's lace; last of the oxeye daisies; morning glory; vetch. Honeybees gather pollen, monarch butterflies nectar.

Virginia creeper, unspeakable color, one line of red leaves in an ocean of green.

AOR: red fox, in no particular hurry, trots up a neighbor's driveway (noses to the ground, dogs interpret what they didn't see); deer tracks and bear scat. Chipping sparrow eating ragweed seeds. An adventurous slug.

Fuzzy-headed bluebird on a fence post, second clutch out of a nest box. Phoebe, on the next post, tail idling. Brown creeper spirals up the trunk of a large maple, its thin, decurved bill taking the pulse of the tree . . . probe, probe, probe. Then wanders under a long, curled strip of bark. Emerges. Flushes, driven by a rowdy trio of white-breasted nuthatches. Background vocals: red-eyed vireos (of course) and indigo buntings.

Two house wren fledglings pester a parent, chasing and begging . . . the incessant demands of youth.

The hem of Kings Highway belongs to waxwings and goldfinches, nesting in the thickets. The former eat berries and insects, the latter seeds. Male hummingbird perched in a gray birch, gorget dull as dusk, waits for the sun. Bunting in birch eating seeds. Yellowthroat in a lilac— familiar song from a different shrub. In Coyote Hollow, yellowthroats convened in alders along the edge of the marsh; here, on Hurricane Hill, they populate the verge of a dooryard, companionable as chickadees. Catbird kvetching. Crow hollering. Blue jay mimics a red-shouldered hawk, a barb on the wind.

In an ungrazed paddock, a duo in blue . . . bunting and bluebird.

༄

Poison ivy grows along the edge of my property in a sunny strip between woods and the road. Trailing along the ground and snaking up tree trunks, a slow-motion slither. Knee-high shrubs. All my life, I've lived with the curse of poison ivy. *Urushiol*, the oily resin in the leaves, roots, and berries, which triggers the infamous blistery rash, sticks to clothes, dog fur, shoes, and baseballs. And, like the Tenth Plague on the House of Egypt, it travels in the smoke of the burning bush.

Every spring and summer during boyhood, the itchy rash graced my arms and legs, face, back, chest, stomach, and sometimes unmentionable places. (A cousin once used poison ivy as toilet paper.) I could not keep out of the sand dunes and bird-busy swales of Jones Beach. Drinking in the dunes didn't help, either. Once, with a severe case, I missed school for two days. I attended senior prom welted with blisters. Calamine lotion, like war paint, streaked my face and limbs pink every summer, as critical to my well-being as ice cream.

Botanists call ivy berries *fruit flags*—tiny, white, toxic knots hard as stone that beckon robins, catbirds, flickers, waxwings, hermit thrushes, myrtle warblers, bluebirds, thrashers, and phoebes. Maybe tree swallows. The bright color of the ripening fruit lures these birds toward a food supply critical for a migrating fruit eater that doesn't know its way around the neighborhood.

I declare war on poison ivy, a homemade, environmentally tolerable war. I dissolve a cup of table salt in a gallon of warm white vinegar. A couple of squirts of dish soap emulsify the concoction (a Long Island friend adds over-the-counter arthritis medicine). Then, happily, I spray. Some leaves yellow in hours and die in days. Then, I strip the thin, shallow roots out of the soil (gloved, of course). It's an all-out war.

I walk around pods of rattlesnakes. Pluck ticks. Slap mosquitoes. Have endured Covid restrictions for seventeen months. But for poison ivy, I have a single, unwavering strategy: annihilation (which is always a losing battle).

∾

Hurricane Hill, my new home, is a promising landscape. Like an auspicious first date, she's filled with possibility. As I struggle to maintain balance, the Hill, untempered and untethered, indefatigably fresh as the dawn, delivers buntings and bluebirds. I saw my first indigo bunting in an Indiana hedgerow, my first eastern bluebird on a Jones Beach sand dune, the bulk of Long Island hanging heavily across the Bay. Mornings on Hurricane Hill are another edition of a timeless story. I just have to remember to pay attention and not dwell in the tower of thought. Transition accomplished (sort of), I'm a limited edition within an ensemble of characters, an older player on new terrain just trying, like Curtis Mayfield, to keep on keepin' on.

Day 505

04 August 2021

35th day on Hurricane Hill

The basic fact of human existence is not
that it is a tragedy, but that it is a bore.
It is not so much a war as an endless
standing in line. The objection to it is
not that it is predominantly painful,
but that it is lacking in sense.
H. L. MENCKEN

5:42 A.M. (sunrise one minute later than yesterday). 52 degrees, wind E 1 mph, more September than August. Sky: pink gossamer and the tarnishing of midnight silver. As the sun exerts itself, the moon's horns fade directly behind a mist screen. Enchanted reiteration, mountains and hills rise island-like out of a sea of ground fog—Moose, Smarts, Cube, Moosilauke, and beyond. Echo of a post-Ice Age landscape when debris dammed the newly minted Connecticut River, flooded adjacent valleys, converting a cold, turbulent meltwater river into a deep, dendritic trout-filled lake . . . one element of the episodic narrative called *physiography*, a story without an end. An unseen, noisy stream drains a spongy hillside and churns through a tunnel of green (whether intermittent or permanent, I have no idea—time will tell . . .).

Between walking the dogs and spraying poison ivy, I slowly meet the neighbors, all of whom lead quiet lives on the north slope of Hurricane Hill. Threads that bind us include (but are not limited to) fog, long view of life and landscape, slow-paced comings and goings on a dead-end road, and proximity to a pharmacy. My beehive neighbor feeds the same birds and recalcitrant bear I feed. Another neighbor, husband and wife optometrists, agreed to let me set up a kestrel nest box in their unmowed meadow, a haven for voles, shrews, and grasshoppers.

Bird parade: female blackburnian warbler, pastel-orange head and throat, white tail feathers flashing, forages in a roadside oak. Phoebe, on a neighbor's deer fence, its tail a metronome, tracks the cadence of the morning. Pewee in the open, on a maple, a low, melancholy whistle, one long, slurred eponymous note uphill, then down (phoebe look-alike, without guttural voice and nervous tail). Red-eyed vireos, everywhere and boisterous, free-for-all singing. Overhead crow. Cardinal in juniper, calling. House finch, female on the road, gathering grit. Chipping sparrow on gray birch strips seeds. Goldfinches, undulating in flight, marionettes on strings, up and down above a sea of goldenrod. Yellow above, yellow below, glazed in lemon sunlight.

On the highest branch of a midmeadow maple, male indigo bunting sings, leans back, nonstop salutations to a new day, sunrise accented with iridescent blue. I stop to look. Dogs have other plans. Noses to the ground, they strain and pull, leashes taut, knocking my binoculars cockeyed and bouncing. Bunting, in and out of view . . . like watching a bird from a boat. Voice rises into the morning. Enough to make me forget (for the moment) that I spent two months downsizing, discarding, uprooting, fretting (a lot of fretting), unpacking, searching (still) for pie plates, stirring spoons, and two small oil paintings, trying to remember a new phone number, notifying everyone of an address change (magazines were challenging), scheduling contractors, shopping for household items, arranging and rearranging old furniture, ordering new furniture.

All the while waiting patiently for geography's connective tissue to fasten me to Hurricane Hill and make me feel at home again.

Day 512

11 August 2021

42nd day on Hurricane Hill

*...almost nothing important that ever happens to you
happens because you engineer it.*
DAVID FOSTER WALLACE

5:50 A.M. (sunrise one minute later than yesterday). 72 degrees, wind S 5 mph, a humid, haze-softened world as though looking through tissue. Dog Days. An unsociably pale sun lacks dominance. Wrinkled landscape defined by river fog, unraveling like spun sugar. The north ridge along the White River and Moose Mountain, in Hanover, New Hampshire, along the east side of the Connecticut River, blue-gray undulations above a fog-leveled landscape. Beyond them, distant hills are overshadowed by haze. Low clouds scud north, high clouds are stable. Below an archway of withering ferns, an intermittent stream descends into a series of silent puddles.

Roadside grace: Jerusalem artichokes, yolk yellow, a hundred durable flowers, brilliant as a goldfinch, a thousand edible tubers, leaves like sandpaper; jewelweed; Queen Anne's lace; last of the oxeye daisies, petals tarnished.

August brushed by autumn, a musical pageant: grasshoppers in the meadow, cicadas in the woods. Evening cameos: crickets and katydids, tuning up for primetime performance. Each morning for the past week, a flock of roving blackbirds, primarily grackles, have skimmed the treetops. This morning, the swirl of wings, the sound of shredding paper over a meadow bright with goldenrod. Juvenile bluebirds on a power line. Phoebe on a limb, tail in motion.

Cardinal emerges from a thicket, broadcasts the richest red this side of a chrysanthemum. Blue jay. Crow. Two mourning doves. Hairy woodpecker wanders a dead birch, dowsing and probing. Nashville warbler on a maple branch, olive-green back, washed-out yellow breast, bright white eye-ring, momentarily motionless, faces east toward the long, gentle decent down Hurricane Hill, beyond the field of flowers and bent grasses, beyond the rollercoaster flight of goldfinches and power-line bluebird, beyond the thickets—the cheerful sparrows and brooding catbirds—into the realm of fog, still fraying and luminous.

Goldfinch, the original vegan, dines on seeds, seeds alone, avoiding insects and spiders. Stretches summer . . . a late nester. Spider silk secures the nest to meadow shrubs. Forages in unmowed meadows, pastures, and on my sunflower feeders, in the company of house finches, chickadees, white- and red-breasted nuthatches, titmice, chipping sparrows, mourning doves, juncos, cardinals, around the deck from hummingbirds.

Goldfinch yellow, the ultimate yellow, is more brilliant than Jerusalem artichoke. In the company of lemon and butter. Each breast and back feather is two toned. Yellow anterior, cream-white posterior. Overlapping feather tips reflect yellow light. The light that penetrates the white portion of the feathers bounces back. Creates a photographer's dream of synchronized front- and backlighting . . . seen from the deck, against the green woods, goldfinches like aberrant specks of sunlight. Audubon painted thistles with his goldfinches, which leap from the page, as they do from my backyard, with incandescent brilliance. A shy but persistent songbird, goldfinches flush with the slightest provocation but, lured by hunger, return. Forgiveness is the essence of hope.

❧

Late yesterday afternoon, a black-throated green warbler landed on my refinished picnic table. I looked at the bird, close enough to extend a hand, and watched it stroll across black Rust-Oleum, an incongruous but gorgeous sight. Not as plump as goldfinch nor as ambitious as a hummingbird, the dart-faced drone that maneuvers above the deck.

Another addition to the catalog of serendipity, the seed of wonder that leaves one slack-jawed and stunned: summer 1997, Denali National Park, a wolverine, conjured out of Alaskan spruce, crossed in front of Casey and me; and on a whale-watching trip, thirty miles beyond the Isles of Shoals, an exhausted Wilson's warbler landed on my knee.

❧

Last night, two bats (species unknown) seined for insects above the deck and meadow, silhouettes below a pale, thin moon. Back and forth, around and around, dipping and turning. Pivoting on wingtips, spinning compasses, an unencumbered flight. Slow enough to follow, fast enough to appreciate. For a moment, I stood free from the grief of an unhinged climate, free from the misery of the *delta* and *lambda* variants, free from the anguish of having moved, lost in the amnesty of the moment . . . lashed to bats on the rim of endlessly empty space. *Survivors of the white-nosed holocaust. Another sign of hope. I could not take my eyes off the bats.*

Day 524

23 August 2021

54th day on Hurricane Hill

I pray to the birds. I pray to the birds
because I believe they will carry the messages
of my heart upward. I pray to them because I believe
in their existence, the way their songs begin and end
each—the invocations and benedictions of Earth.
I pray to the birds because they remind me of what I love
rather than what I fear. And at the end of my prayers,
they teach me how to listen.

TERRY TEMPEST WILLIAMS

6:03 A.M. (sunrise, one minute later than yesterday). 66 degrees, wind SSW 3 mph, humid. Moisture condenses on dogs, which sit in the road, facing north, heads erect. Sky: low-textured ceiling, an unspackled crack or two, otherwise thick, gray, not overambitious. Somber and somnolent woodlands, the darkest shade of green. Hurricane Henri, churning up the East Coast, has veered out to sea, significantly reducing the chance of a wind waif in Vermont, a Caribbean bird or two swept north in the cyclonic headwinds: sooty tern; bridal tern; brown booby; white-tailed tropicbird, elegant as a snowflake.

Crickets murmur, an undercurrent of dawn, a preamble to September. I feel Earth tilting—the gray dampness, the cheerful voice of goldfinches, catering to chicks recently fledged, voices rising and falling in flight . . . *per-chick-o-ree, per-chick-o-ree.* Yellow specks below concrete clouds, commuting in every direction. Blue jay harvests green acorns. White-breasted nuthatches. Chickadees. A lone cardinal, whistle faltering. High over the Hill, a throat-clearing raven, avian Yiddish.

Other birds fatten for departure: the warbler; the wren; the vireo, snacking on tiny green caterpillars high in an oak; the kvetching catbird, an agitated proclamation.

Long excursion: broad-winged hawk in the firmament, a haze-slicing whistle, one pitch, two notes, the first shorter than the second. Hawk, somewhere overhead, unseen, heads to Amazonia. Short excursion: pewee on a maple limb chases a moth.

∾

Finding Solace in a Broken World   385

Yesterday, staining the deck railing in advance of the hurricane, I looked up and glimpsed a bald eagle, high over the hemlocks and pines, heading north beyond the delta of the White River, sunlight flashing off its white head and tail. The afternoon anointed, a momentary sacrament . . . just enough to keep me staining for a couple more hours.

∿

As much as I yearn to travel to outlying landscapes, if I'm stuck at home (again), I'll remain a patron of sunrise and hone my senses to a new home ground. I'll try to accept the dimensions of my life. Give thanks for the companionable chickadee, the lemon-colored finch, the occasional eagle, head and tail white as fresh snow. I'll try to embrace the obstacles aging presents . . . I'll rock on the deck, recently stained blue gray, waiting, as autumn, multidimensional like a dragonfly's eye, recasts Hurricane Hill into the Land of Oz.

Day 526

25 August 2021

56th day on Hurricane Hill

Linny's 70th birthday

The archaeology of grief is not ordered.
It is more like Earth under a spade,
turning up things you had forgotten.
Surprising things come to light:
not simple memories, but states of mind,
emotions, older ways of seeing the world.
HELEN MACDONALD

6:04 A.M. (sunrise one minute later than yesterday). 66 degrees and humid, wind N 3 mph. Sky: waning three-quarter-moon low in the west, dulled by the catalytic nature of daybreak and river fog. Inside a rising cloud, eye-level visibility is less than two hundred yards.

Doe bounds across a meadow, tail up. Suddenly curious, dogs gather themselves to full height, leashes tighten, then relax as the deer disappears like the moon into an amalgam of mist and diffused sunlight. Sheet webs glisten in the grass like bright doilies, and a long sagging spider line runs across the road from oak to birch. Garrotes an unsuspecting pedestrian . . . me. I imagine the spider floating on the directionless zip line of its own construct, riding the night currents unencumbered, free of curious vireos and warblers, which gather at dawn to comb through woods, silent and hungry.

All around, late August balances on a pinhead, teeters toward autumn. Inside the woods, chickadees whistle and call. Outside goldfinches stammer, undulating over the goldenrod. Blue jays honk. Hummingbirds pollinate jewelweed, blurred wings whisking the mist. Taking no chances, indigo buntings, conspicuous by their absence, appear to have left ahead of Hurricane Henri. The silence of warblers. From inside the lilacs, cardinal whistles and catbird purrs.

A stand of big-toothed aspens, leaves swirling like an undisciplined mind, hosts a mixed flock of southbound songbirds. Warblers on parade: black-throated green and black-throated blue work the underbelly of leaves, one after the other; redstarts chase moths; a trio of Tennessee warblers, the color of fog, flit from limb to limb; and yellowthroat, bright as a goldfinch, prunes light green caterpillars from dark green leaves. Pewee idles on a branch, taking it all in. Yellow-throated vireo poses on a branch; then, like an overly medicated warbler, leisurely searches for caterpillars . . . a poster bird for not eating on the run. Vireo, a nonchalant songbird in a contorted world, faces a long flight back to the mountains of northwestern South America.

Linny would have turned seventy today, her thick, wavy mountain of hair likely having turned white. She'd be surprised I left Coyote Hollow. But she would have understood why. She was good that way. She always listened . . . considered. Rarely, did she pass judgment. I left two handfuls of her behind . . . one in the garden and the other in the marsh. Eight years after she died, the boys and I scattered the rest of their mother in Alpine Gardens of Mountain Washington, among the rocky fields of moss campion and Lapland rosebay. Casey built a cairn of white quartz on a gray boulder emblazoned with orange lichen. We stood for a while and looked up into the sunny, summer sky, clouds like boats scudding by. I thought of Linny and the passage of time. Of things she loved:

cottage cheese and nutritional yeast; hot sauce and cayenne pepper; burnt toast . . . and beer. Friendship. Teaching children about the nature of their home. The year before she died, she returned to the classroom and taught elementary school science and math. One last opportunity to help children learn.

Once I was twenty years old. Now, I'm seventy-two. Seems like yesterday I drank beer in the weeds and smoked pot in parking lots. I have never understood the nature of time, other than you can't get it back. There are no do-overs. Casey and Jordan became men. I left Thetford, not as free as the vireo that flies south with nothing but the feathers on his back. More like autumn leaves . . . one final burst of color, then stripped by the wind.

Life plays no favorites; as time passes, losses pile up—species disappear, loved ones die. There is, of course, the iron thread of continuity. Some species become other species; some radiate into many species. If you were here now, you'd see the joy for life rising in your boys and in your granddaughter, who laughs like you and eats like me, both irrepressibly. You'd see me leaning into the future. Was there ever another choice?

～

Honey-colored sunlight pours through a hole in the fog. Stiff-necked, I head down the road . . . back *home*.

Epilogue

Hurricane Hill, White River Junction, Vermont
01 January 2023

Well, my friends are gone and my hair is grey
I ache in the places where I used to play
And I'm crazy for love but I'm not coming on.
I'm just paying my rent every day in the Tower of Song.
LEONARD COHEN

I've lived on Hurricane Hill for eighteen months now and have watched the seasons come and go from the deck above my backyard, which looks down a gentle, tapered meadow pinched by hardwoods and evergreens. Since I left Coyote Hollow, I'm down one dog, up one boy (graduate school). I still attend the reveille of the rising sun and pay tribute to the new day, trying to balance myself on the tractionless path between dislocation and discovery.

To the east, the horizon spills away, hill after hill, like a pod of whales surfacing in the mist. Miles of hills. The north horizon, closer, shorter, is a mosaic of green-pastured dairy farms and dense forests, a ridgeline that undulates above the eastbound White River. Beyond, sky and sky alone. Trees trim the view west and south. Owls live among the trees, their hollow voices resonating through the hall of darkness. On cool October mornings, when river fog hangs below the summit of Hurricane Hill, dense and frayed like spun sugar, turning the distant pods of hills into an archipelago, crows disperse from their night roost for a day afield, emerging out of the creampuff, twenty or more, noisy, hurried, black wings stirring damp air. Garbled crow-speak trailing across the valley.

In late summer, meadows along the road paved yellow with goldenrod and Jerusalem artichoke. Here, bees keep busy. My neighbors' hives up the road produced amber honey, all the richer because I live on the

Hill where pollen is spun into gold. I have lowered my expectations about annihilating poison ivy . . . not a truce, precisely. I still attempt to control where ivy grows, but it is a near-hopeless endeavor, like teaching a dog to play chess. Although the characters and the view changed when I left Coyote Hollow, the basic plot remains the same . . . the cadence of Earth, the shifting seasons, life churning, burning, evolving. There's always something happening on Hurricane Hill—indigo buntings and eastern bluebirds on the power line above a summer meadow, a lone hawk with an apple-colored tail. Time may appear to shift gears, seasons may appear disjointed, and the sheer force of world events may gnaw at me . . . but chickadees still draw me close.

Periodically, I'm visited by black bears (some things don't change). As Jordan and I washed dinner dishes one evening last spring, a bear walked across the deck, stood on its hind legs, leaned over the railing, and shoveled in sunflower seeds. When we slid the kitchen door open, he strolled off the deck, crossed the lawn, lay down and took a catnap on the edge of the woods. Several minutes later, refreshed, he stood on his hind legs and marked a hemlock with grappling claws, then rubbed his back against the tree, up and down like a furry piston. From Colorado, Casey and Becky watched on FaceTime, while, in the spirit of the British Broadcasting Corporation, Jordan and I parodied David Attenborough, the bear fifty feet away, easygoing and cooperative.

༄

I found everything I thought I had lost when I moved: slotted spoon, spatula, mixing bowl, two small oil paintings, lawn mower (don't ask), and microspikes. Several friends have died since I landed on Hurricane Hill: death by tumor, snakebite, falling out of a hot-air balloon, stroke, long Covid, and the exhaustion of having lived too long, having seen too much. Sadly, my losses pile up with age . . . but, thankfully, so does birth. Izzy's almost two, and a brother or a sister will join her in several months. She toddles up to her mother, pats her broad midsection, and announces, *Baby, come out.*

Is the baby going to be a boy or a girl? Becky asks.
Boy.
What shall we name him?
Channeling Johnny Cash, Izzy boldly answers, *Girl.*
But what if the baby's a girl? What shall we name her?
Boy.

The same cast of Coyote Hollow characters assemble at my Thanksgiving table on Hurricane Hill, and I still open the oven twenty times during roasting to peek at the turkey. By the fourth night of Hanukkah 2022, I ran out of candles; found only one yarmulke. Like Jews of old, Jordan and I were forced to improvise . . . wooden matches and a potholder replaced the more standard affair.

I live ten miles closer to Nancy. See her more frequently. The ride to Pomfret over a backcountry dirt road is gorgeous—rolling hills and valleys speckled with dairy farms, pocket ponds, and marshes hemmed by dark, sullen evergreens. A fisher bounded through my high beams one night, and an owl perched in the open by the road, staring into a frog-congested cattail pond, round-faced and hungry. Arriving on her doorstep remains the highlight of most days.

Moving eighteen miles farther south has not freed me from the visitations of an unbuckled climate. On a rainy December 6, a gray treefrog hopped in front of my car, the first December amphibian I have ever seen in Vermont—only the fourth record of a December treefrog in the state, all in the past seven years. Ten days later, after two feet of wet snow and heavy wind, a pair of pileateds stopped by the deck. Out of a lifetime of feeding birds, I had *never* entertained a pileated. The male swung on the suet cage, crest on fire. Back and forth, pecking. The female struggled for sunflower seeds . . . too big to perch on the feeder's dowels; too small to lean out from the deck railing. (Pileated, a bird built to walk up tree trunks, destined to be vertical—two toes in front, two toes in back— looks awful horizontal in the same way a snake looks awful unspooling on frictionless glass.) Eventually, she got a seed or two, leaned too far from the railing, and fell into flight. I wondered whether chickadees thought her abrupt departure as amusing as I did.

Ten days after the heavy snowfall, three days before Christmas, rain fell for thirty consecutive hours, melting much of the snow. The temperature rose to fifty-one degrees, wind gusted over fifty mph, trees on Hurricane Hill swayed in succession like the wave passing around Yankee Stadium. Overnight, temperatures plummeted to minus-two, ice everywhere . . . you could have played hockey on the driveway.

As a concession to Covid, I haven't gone to a movie theater in three years, but Nancy and I have dined out, at first outdoors and then indoors, tables well spaced. My time in airports has been trimmed to essentials, four trips to Colorado, and I haven't driven farther south than Long Island, farther east than the rocky coast of Rhode Island. But I plan to return to Costa Rica soon, to jungle and jungle rivers. To wash away the memory of confinement.

My new house continues to evolve into a home: carpeting removed and replaced with composite flooring and rugs. New bedroom, guest room, and office windows. I bought contemporary furniture: a chair, a loveseat, a sofa, and a bed big enough to hold infield practice on. I assembled counter and dining room chairs, a bookcase, and a night table. With friends, I painted the downstairs and the deck, planted ornamental shrubs, built two raised beds, a raspberry fence, a compost bin, and a dog pen, and set a screen door, which fell off last week when the temperature hit minus two. I bought an estate-sale, one-piece kitchen table, pecan and gorgeous. As a concession to aging and to Izzy, I had a banister built. At eighteen months and counting, however, the mudroom advances in increments, baby steps—the Great Wall of China rose more quickly.

In March 2022, I had Shadowfax euthanized. It's never easy to put a dog down, especially a faithful buddy who had accompanied me twice daily, sunrise and sunset, for eight-and-a-half years. That final morning, the red sun climbed above Moose Mountain, gilding the river fog pink as a light-bodied rosé all the way north to Thetford. We walked alone, the crippled dog and me. There were birds that morning—I'm sure—but I wasn't in the mood to watch them.

November 2021, Jordan returned home from Boston for graduate school, a would-be physician's associate. He's completing a two-year residency downstairs, the Apple TV at his disposal. I'm his guinea pig for medical exams, which are frequent and varied. He begins each exam with a reassuring proclamation: *Patient has a large, irregularly shaped nose but otherwise appears normal.* After spring-term finals 2022, Jordan went to a ballgame at Fenway Park and returned with Covid. We ate our meals together, sort of, me on the deck, Jordan on the lawn below, the month of June passing between us.

Jordan wasn't my first brush with the coronavirus. In October 2021, I had a notorious visit to Colorado. Four days in, one by one, Becky, Casey, and then Izzy lapsed into Covid. I vacationed in the in-law suite, tarried in the high desert each morning, shopped and cooked. We ate meals well spaced outside, under the umbrella of a yellowing ash. Thus far, I have avoided Covid. (Nancy thinks I'm too congested for a viral beachhead.)

This past April (2022), I returned to Colorado. One morning, after breakfast, Becky and I hiked Monument Canyon Trail, a footpath into Colorado National Monument that unspools along the side of a high desert hill, several miles of loose, fractured sandstone the color of driftwood. Flowers embellished the otherwise open, bland hillside: lipstick-red Indian paintbrush; snow-white desert primrose; locoweed, purple white and familiar. Izzy, a year old and in her mother's backpack, was along for the ride. Several miles in, a herd of desert bighorn sheep, twenty ewes, six or seven subadult males, and thirteen lambs bounced downhill and across the trail, dust and rocks clattering in their wake. The sheep stopped below us on a lush (for the high desert) plain of juniper and pinion, Mormon tea, and green grass brought to the surface by recent rain. Several pairs of the males squared off . . . rose on hind legs, pitched forward, and headbutted like guards on the line of scrimmage, sharp cracks riding the airwaves. While the ewes grazed, several lambs nursed. And Izzy, lounging in the freedom of infancy, watched, eyes wide . . . charmed by her dust-gray cohorts, fragile and cute and hungry. A union of innocence, baby recognizes babies . . . interspecies familiarity.

I do my best to remain charmed by portals into the rough edges of Earth, where I simply watch like Izzy watched the bighorns. Those edges humans cannot control . . . I am bound to forces that rule the currents, the waves and the weather and the night sky. Synagogue and I parted ways long ago. I'm a secular Jew bouncing from joy to loss . . . and back again, cushioned by hope. The cold light of the stars and moon still warm my heart and make me pause and wonder. May it always be so . . . may I always return to the child, piggybacked on Izzy's passport into the everyday world of the miraculous.

I need more time to do all I want to do, to see all I want to see. My emotional scaffolding sags when I'm reminded that some goals may never be realized. Then, I get stuck in a feedback loop, an album skipping on the turntable upstairs while I'm downstairs groveling, immobile . . . a Groundhog of the heart. Something eventually breaks the spell, tosses me a lifeline, and induces a smile. Conjures hope, triggers imagination. Sunlight slanted through a sieve of pine needles. The cry of a hawk. A fish-shaped cloud disintegrating in a blue sky. The rhythm of the wind across a meadow. A pileated pecking at a frozen apple.

Chickadee

The Promise of Sunrise

and dirt roads. Relentless wind whipped and broke teeth from the comb of trees. Bone-numbing cold. I looked for relief, to rotate back toward the bliss of sunrise. One morning, walking in a stupor, halfway up Hurricane Hill, four or five chickadees sang, one after the other. I watched and listened under the thick wool hat Linny knitted for my fiftieth birthday. Chickadees flitted in all directions like rogue electrons, pausing for a moment, notes and breaths rising into the morning. Why sing the day after Christmas, the temperature thirteen degrees, the low December sun three months from the equinox? Holiday cheer? Whatever their reason, the untrimmable birds accomplished something for me. I paused, my soundtrack silenced, reset the lens of contemplation. We dwell in a land of everyday miracles, where an aspen turns into an October rainbow, and the contents of an egg no bigger than my pinkie nail flies across the Gulf of Mexico . . . and back again.

Imagination restored, Tenaya and I continue down the road, the gray birds singing, the red sun ascending.

Acknowledgments

Day 888 on Hurricane Hill

06 January 2024

Ordinary experience, from waking second to second, is in fact
highly synthetic . . . and made up of a complexity of strands,
past memories and present perceptions, times and places,
private and public history, hopelessly beyond science's power to analyze.
JOHN FOWLES

7:23 A.M. (sunrise, same time, seventh day in a row). 24 degrees and humid (like winter on Jones Beach), wind ESE 5 mph. Feels like rain. Looks like rain. Sky: waning crescent moon hidden by a taut curtain of gray. Rime decorates leaves and stems. Ice sleeves creek-side rocks. A snowless, frozen landscape as hard to fathom as a quadratic equation. Brittle leaves broadcast every footstep . . .

Inside the Hartford Town Forest, wandering the WB Brown Trail: chattering red crossbills, flashes of rose . . . itinerant northern birds sweeping through cone-laden pines, crown to crown, tweezing pine nuts with twisted bills, spilling voices and transparent scraps of winged seeds. Sibilant siskins and whispering kinglets, flickering wings, almost hovering. High on an aspen snag, less than a hundred feet off the trail, back to me, a pileated drums . . . hatchet-faced hammering, a seemingly out of sync territorial proclamation suspended in the gelid air. I hold my breath and listen, captivated by the moment. Then, a chickadee whistles. Another scolds me. A third whistles, sweetness on the edge of a blunt sunrise. Winter moving in two directions at once . . . and I along for the ride, promising myself to never stop walking and to remain haunted by the possibilities of dawn.

Two hours later, Casey calls. From the backseat, while passing through cattle country on the way to daycare, Izzy shouts with the unbridled enthusiasm of a chickadee . . . *Popi I saw a golden eagle!*

༄

Just before dawn, for thirteen months, I wandered through Coyote Hollow rediscovering my home ground, my place within the walled-in, saturated valley. Watching, listening, taking note as the seasons pulled themselves apart, by turns a witness and a scribe. On 1 July 2021, I sold my home, and moved to Hurricane Hill in White River Junction, and began to unravel the mysteries of my new geography.

On 18 March 2020, I began posting daily dispatches from Coyote Hollow on two listservs, UV-BIRDERS and VTBIRD, both email discussion groups, the former out of Dartmouth College, the latter out of the University of Vermont. Two months later, at the urging of friends, I also published the missives on Substack, an independent online newsletter, under the title *Homeboy at Home During the Coronavirus.* Every morning: one walk, three rewrites, activities that cost me nothing but time. I was home alone, a Covid refugee, and my time made better by readers' comments, which kept me writing, rewarding observation and nostalgia. Ah, such a compulsive and pleasurable cycle.

By early September 2021, I felt I had a raw book, a hewn stone that required further shaping—chiseling, sanding, eventually buffing. No one kept me on task more than Stephen Rashkin. Stephen read every entry, and together we discussed what I had, what I needed . . . and what needed to be cut. I read aloud to Stephen over the phone and in person from opposite ends of a brown Colorado sofa. Together, we walked through Coyote Hollow and gazed across the summer marsh and reminisced. Eternally optimistic and endlessly encouraging, he forever challenged me to unthread my life. A psychologist by profession, and a friend by choice since I was seventeen, Stephen remains my brother from another mother. The debt runs deep. Thank you.

I am honored to have Dede Cummings as my publisher and book designer. From the onset, she understood what I was trying to accomplish. As did Marian Cawley, who edited the final draft, adding uniformity and clarity. Marian nourished embryonic thoughts, encouraging me to dig deeper to explain myself. I love Jeanette Fournier's art (in retrospect, I wish we featured more). Kudos, Dede, Marian, and Jeanette. Thanks to the team at GWP, especially copyeditor Justin Bigos, and editorial assistants Leah Mowry, Gwen Peavey Hunter, and Haley Hutchinson.

Thank you, too, to Rob Gurwit, who ran a link to my Substack site every other week in *Daybreak*, his carefully curated weekday newsletter. And to Susan Apel, who taught me how to post on Substack, leading me out of my cave into the Information Age.

Earlier versions of several entries appeared in the summer 2021 issue of *Northern Woodlands*. Thank you editors, Cheryl Daigle and Elise Tillinghast. *Vermont Almanac: Stories From & For The Land* selected several "days" for inclusion in Volumes I and II. Thank you, Dave Mance III and Patrick White, editors.

Rob Gurwit and Lee Michaelides commented on both the prologue and epilogue, and Susan Tiholiz on many of the earliest versions of the daily entries. Joan Waltermire, Ginny Barlow, Tom Sherry, and Chris Rimmer fielded numerous questions. Thank you, thank you.

Thank you, as well, to Tuesday morning's breakfast club—loud, funny, and politically confused (if not incorrect). Charlie Berger, John Tiholiz, John Douglas, Ford von Reyn, Steve Atwood, Lee Michaelides, Jeffery Hamelman, Richard Stucker, and Michael Shoob, diverted me again and again (whether on Zoom or in person) from the compulsive urge to edit.

One byproduct of publishing on Substack was reaching a wider audience, frequently dialoguing online with like-minded strangers. As our virtual community grew, the communication became increasingly meaningful. Covid was nothing if not isolating. And, living alone in the country, I thrived on electronic correspondence, which meant more to me than you might imagine. Thank you everyone who took the time to write. I am indebted to all your comments, suggestions, and stories, and to none more than Julia Strimer, who wrote me nearly every day from her home in Michigan. Old friends and colleagues also emerged from the wireless wilderness. Thank you for appearing in my inbox, for sticking with me: Dave Anderson, Mitchell Thomashow, Stew Miller, the late Mike Yankovich, Harry Greene, Tom Junod, Dan Keyler, Ian Baldwin, Susan Brison, Brian Bielema, Jean McIver, Bob Fritsch, Betty Smith, Bill Hoffman, Erin Donahue, Penny McConnell, Marty Frank, Deecie Denison, Tom Slayton, the late Terry Osborne, Elise Tillinghast, the late Frank Asch, Jan Asch, Joann Puskarchik, Jim Kenyon, Doug Fraser, and Steve Swinburne.

Nothing in my ragged life prepared me for dating in my seventies... let alone for falling in love. Day in and day out, Nancy Griffin suffered the rehash of my walks. She was and remains my language guru, dedicated to shortening my sentences.

Shadowfax and Tenaya gave me reason to walk. Good naturedly, they tolerated long pauses, sitting patiently at my feet, enthusiastically accompanying me regardless of weather. Their senses extended my own. Although no one would confuse either German shepherd for Rin Tin Tin . . . their loyalty guided me through Covid-19.

I am grateful that Jordan and Casey often and patiently listened to me read, frequently over the phone, commented on Jeanette's illustrations and the Coyote Hollow map . . . as well as my porous memory. My ultimate debt is to them and to William. They grew up on the untamed shoulder of Robinson Hill . . . not exactly the children of wolves just the wild boys who fed off the corrugated landscape . . . and for 526 days I tried to follow their example.